THE BRITISH ISLES
0
100 Miles
0
200 km
M3 motorways
A3 main through routes
National parks
airports
Mainland
Orkney Islands
Lewis
Outer Hebrides
Skye
Inner Hebrides
Mull
Islay
Wick
Moray Firth
Elgin
Inverness
Drumnadrochit
A82
Loch Ness
Peterhead
Aberdeen
A9
Fort William
Ben Nevis
Grampian Mountains
Scotland
North Sea
Dundee
Perth
St. Andrews
Firth of Forth
Glasgow
M8
Edinburgh
A1
Firth of Clyde
Ayr
A77
Southern Uplands
A74
Tweed
Northumberland National Park
Gretna Green
A75
Stranraer
Newcastle
Carlisle
Hadrian's Wall
Solway Firth
Londonderry
Northern Ireland
Enniskillen
Belfast
Sligo
Lake District National Park
Isle of Man
Yorkshire Dales National Park
Lancashire
Middlesbrough
Blackpool
Blackburn
Bradford
Irish Sea
M62
Hull
Galway
Dublin
Manchester
Leeds
IRELAND
Isle of Anglesey
Liverpool
Kirkby
M1
Grimsby
Holyhead
Llanfair P.G.
Speke
Sheffield
Snowdon
Chester
M6
Peak District NP
Derbyshire
England
A5
Stoke-on-Trent
Limerick
Snowdonia National Park
Mountains
Shrewsbury
Nottingham
Derby
Norfolk
Norwich
Leicester
Great Yarmouth
Waterford
Rosslare
Wales
Peterborough
Aberystwyth
Birmingham
Coventry
Warwick
A1
A11
Cork
Pembrokeshire Coast National Park
St. George's Channel
Fishguard
Cambrian
M5
Northampton
Worcester
Stratford-upon-Avon
Cambridge
A12
M11
Ipswich
Braintree
Brecon Beacons National Park
Luton
Hatfield
Harwich
Gloucester
Colchester
Pembroke
M4
M50
Oxford
Essex
London
Swansea
Newport
Swindon
Thames
M40
Wembley
M25
Southend on Sea
Cardiff
Bristol
Bath
Greenwich
Bristol Channel
Exmoor NP
Westbury
Windsor
M2
Stonehenge
M3
Canterbury
M20
Dover
Devon
M5
A303
Salisbury
Ashford
Southampton
Sussex
Tunnel
Calais
A30
Exeter
Brighton
Hastings
Eastbourne
Bournemouth
Portsmouth
Dartmoor National Park
Isle of Wight
Paris
Cornwall
Plymouth
Strait of Dover
Penzance
Falmouth/Penryn
English Channel
Land's End
Scilly Is.
Lizard Point

Learning English

Swift 2

Lehrwerk für Englisch als 2. Fremdsprache

von

Stephanie Ashford
Noreen O'Donovan
Helmut Reisener

Ernst Klett Verlag
Stuttgart Düsseldorf Leipzig

Learning English Swift 2

für Englisch als 2. Fremdsprache

von
Stephanie Ashford, Villingen-Schwenningen; Noreen O'Donovan, Pforzheim;
Dr. Helmut Reisener, Lüneburg sowie Wolfgang Funk, Bamberg

Beratende Mitarbeit
Wolfgang Funk, Bamberg; Axel Plitsch, Wülfrath; Klaus-Peter Thieser, Dillingen/Saar;
Traute Werner, Heidelberg

Visuelle Gestaltung
Christian Dekelver, Weinstadt (Layout + Grafik); Elsie Lennox, London (Zeichnungen)

Kassetten und CDs

SB Begleitkassette zum Schülerbuch für zu Hause und für den Unterricht mit Texten, Liedern, Ausspracheübungen (Klettnummer 547028)
Begleit-CD zum Schülerbuch mit gleichem Inhalt (Klettnummer 547068)

HV Kassette mit den Hörtexten für den Unterricht (Klettnummer 547029)
CD mit gleichem Inhalt (Klettnummer 547069)

Lernsoftware
Zu diesem Band gibt es ein Vokabel- und ein Grammatikprogramm. Diese Programme bieten abwechslungsreiche Übungsformen, Leistungs- und Lernzielkontrollen und ein Lexikon mit dem Wortschatz des Lehrwerks.

1. Auflage 1 11 10 9 8 7 | 10 09 08 07 06

Alle Drucke dieser Auflage können im Unterricht nebeneinander benutzt werden, sie sind untereinander unverändert. Die letzte Zahl bezeichnet das Jahr des Druckes.

Internetadresse: http://www.klett.de

Redaktion: Redaktionsdienst ETS, Stuart Amor, Stuttgart;
Lektorat Projekte, Gaby Bauer-Negenborn, Starnberg

Verlagsredakteur: Andrew Hutchins
Herstellung: Eckhard Schultze

Umschlaggestaltung: Christian Dekelver, Weinstadt
Reproduktion: maurer media + more, Tübingen
Druck: Druckerei Appl, Wemding
ISBN 3-12-547020-X

9 783125 470200

Vorwort

Hallo und herzlich willkommen bei *Swift 2!*

Wir ‚heben ab' zur zweiten Runde mit **Swift**.

Dieser 2. Band enthält nur noch acht *Units*. Sie sind genauso gegliedert wie in **Swift 1**: *Check-in, Check-out*, dazwischen drei *Steps* und zwei *Tracks*. Was darin alles passiert und geleistet wird, weißt du ja bereits aus Band 1.

Im Bereich der grammatischen Strukturen kommen in **Swift 2** natürlich neue Pensen hinzu, aber sie sind gut zu schaffen, wenn du immer wieder in den *Grammar*-Anhang hineinschaust. Auch die Vokabelseiten im Anschluss an die *Units* solltest du sorgfältig durcharbeiten. Damit dir das Einprägen leichter fällt und möglichst wenig vergessen wird, gibt es auf diesen Seiten jede Menge Lernhilfen. Bitte wieder beachten, dass der neue Wortschatz aus *Track* 2 auf den Vokabelseiten mit einem hochgestellten $^{+}$ gekennzeichnet ist. Dasselbe gilt für die Übungen außerhalb der *Track* 2 Seiten und die Grammatikpunkte im Anhang.

Im Anschluss an die acht *Units* findest du ab Seite 138 in *Extra* interessante Originaltexte als Zusatzlektüre. Sie sind thematisch auf die *Units* abgestimmt. Den Abschluss bildet ein Projekt. Auf *Extra* folgt das Kapitel *Translation* mit Übungen zur Übersetzung deutscher Texte ins Englische. Auf Seite 161 beginnt die *Grammar* und am Ende von **Swift** findest du das *Dictionary*, das übrigens nicht nur alle Wörter aus **Swift 2** enthält, sondern auch den kompletten Wortschatz von **Swift 1**. Du hast auf diese Weise dein **Swift**-Wörterbuch immer zur Hand.

So, nun weißt du bereits alles Wesentliche. Zur raschen Orientierung hier noch einmal die Symbole, die dir in **Swift** begegnen werden. Dann kann es wirklich losgehen.
Viel Spaß!

SB — Alle Texte, Lieder, Gedichte und Ausspracheübungen, die auf der Begleitkassette / -CD zum Schülerbuch (SB) aufgezeichnet sind, erkennst du an diesem Zeichen.

HV — Übungen mit diesem Symbol verweisen auf die Kassette / CD zum Hörverstehen (HV). Die Hörtexte sind nicht im Schülerbuch abgedruckt.

G 1 — In den Übungen, die mit diesem Symbol gekennzeichnet sind, wird neue Grammatik eingeführt. Du findest die Erklärungen unter dem entsprechenden Punkt im Grammatikanhang.

Dieses Piktogramm verweist auf schriftliche Übungen. Lege dir einen Ordner (*folder*) an, in den du alle deine schriftlichen Arbeiten und Textprodukte aus **Swift** einheftest.

WP — Dieses Piktogramm kennzeichnet alle Wortschatzübungen. *WP* steht für *word power.*

YOU — In Übungen, die mit diesem Symbol versehen sind, kannst du über dich und deine persönlichen Erfahrungen sprechen.

R — Neu in **Swift 2** ist dieses Symbol. *R* steht für *revision.* Du findest dieses Piktogramm bei Übungen, in denen bereits bekannte grammatische Pensen wiederholt werden.

Inhalt

Unit 8 Emergency

⟨Extra⟩

UNIT 1

LET'S GO TO THE

1 Notting Hill Carnival

It's the last weekend in August …
It's hot in London …
The holidays are nearly over …
School hasn't started again yet …
So where can we go to have one last bit of fun?

Notting Hill is in West London. Like Islington, it is an interesting part of London, all the year round. But for one weekend in August it becomes more than interesting – it becomes the centre of London! Everybody wants to be there.

On the Sunday and Monday of the long weekend, crowds fill the streets. Activities start at 12 noon. The main event is a big parade with lots of colourful floats, bands and Caribbean music. It finishes officially at 7 pm. Of course, the unofficial activities go on much longer!

NOTTING HILL CARNIVAL!

1 Listening comprehension: Weekend plans

a) *Listen to the dialogue to find out –*
1. Who is speaking to who on the phone?
2. What other person is there?

b) *Now, before you listen again, get pencil and paper and prepare to make lists:*
1. What Londoners are going to go to the Carnival?
2. What people have come to London for the Carnival?
3. What people are not going to the Carnival?

Going		Not Going
Londoners	Others	

c) *Listen again and find out why some people aren't going to the Carnival.*

d) *Now find out when and where the speakers want to meet. Use the map on the next page – it helps you to understand what they are saying.*

1

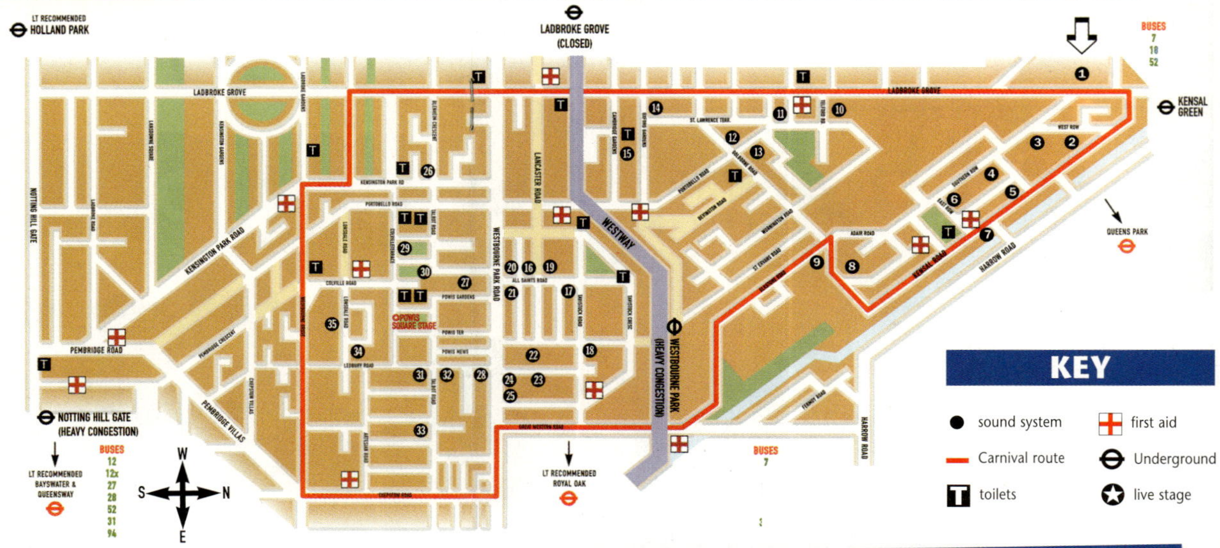

2 Plan your day

Use the information on this page to make a plan for your day at the Notting Hill Carnival. Decide these points:

- When do you want to go?
- How do you want to go there?
- Where would you like to meet your friends?
- What are you going to take with you? (Have you got all the things on the right, or can you get / buy / borrow them? What else do you need?)
- Where would you like to watch the parade?

Now write out your plan.

3 Role play

Now form pairs or small groups – as if you are going to the Carnival together – and make one plan: when you go, where you meet, who carries what, etc. Some ideas:

Let's go at 3 pm.

Oh, that's much too late! Let's …

OK. But where can we meet?

What about …?

No, I think we should …

And bring …

Well, …

Oh, I haven't got …

…

What you need at the Carnival

1 One Day Travelcard

Don't set off without it. It's the one time of the year when £3.50 is not too much to pay to travel on the sad and dirty London Underground.

2 Trainers

Forget fashion – comfort is more important. Your friends may not want to know you, but isn't it better that you can still walk after 12 hours? (Anyway, who's looking at your feet?)

3 Mobile phone

It is an Official Rule of the Carnival that you lose your friends a minute after arrival. This is the only way to find them again.

4 Money

You need lots of it at the Carnival e.g. to buy food, drink, plastic whistles on red, gold and green string …

5 Deodorant

Hours of dancing and walking can make you less than nice to know. Please think of the people around you! (Where is that smell coming from? Could it be …?)

6 Camera (cheap)

Of course you can get great photos at the Carnival, but it is not a good idea to bring your expensive camera. You don't want to lose it, do you?

7 Sunglasses

In sun, rain or snow, a pair of dark glasses can make a model of coolness out of even the worst style-free geek (or tourist). Wear them on your head, or on a string down your back. (On your nose only at night.)

Adapted from the article by Jamie de Cruz in *Touch – The 1998 Guide to the Notting Hill Carnival*

A weekend in London

<u>Friday, August 28th</u>
I packed my bag this morning and after lunch I walked to the station – without Milly! – and tried to read while I waited for the train. Then I travelled to London, and arrived at Tessa's house at about 6 pm. It's great to be back in the city! Tessa and I talked for hours in her room!

<u>Saturday, August 29th</u>
We walked around Islington to see all the old places – the school, our favourite café, Dad's old shop ... I even looked in the window of our old house! I cried because of all the different things inside, but Tessa just laughed at me! Later we watched TV for a while and listened to some music. Then Tessa showed me her holiday photos.

<u>Sunday, August 30th</u>
Today I woke up very early, I was so excited! Carnival day!! I put on my coolest gear. But when Tessa saw my shoes, she said they were silly, so I changed them. We both wore our old trainers. I packed my shoulder bag, but put most of my money in Tessa's special bag for under her sweatshirt. (Better to be safe than sorry, she said!) Kevin came at 11, and we set off. Tessa nearly forgot her mobile phone, but went back for it. We walked to the Underground station where we bought our One Day Travelcards. Jimmy and Maike were waiting for us at Queensway, but we didn't see them at first because of the crowd – until Jimmy shouted. That's when things started to go wrong.

G 1-3

1 Finding the rules

a) *Look at Liz's diary for Friday and Saturday. Make a list of the verbs in the past tense.*

to pack	–	packed [t]
to walk	–	
to try	–	tried [d]
to wait	–	waited [ɪd]
...		...

These forms are regular.
Can you find the rule?
How do you make regular past forms?
Are they the same for different persons?

b) *Now look at her diary for Sunday. Make a list of her verbs in the past tense.* Some forms don't follow your rule – they are irregular. *Can you guess what verbs they are from?*

Example: "woke" is from "to wake"

There is no rule. Learn them by heart, and put new ones on a list.

HV

2 Listening comprehension: A crazy afternoon

G 1-3

a) *First look at the list below. These are the new past tense forms from the dialogue. Then say:*

– Which ones are regular, and which irregular?
– What verbs do they come from?
(If you are not sure, guess!)

b) *Now listen to the rest of Liz's story as she told it to her brother Liam on the phone. Look at the picture below.*

More past tense forms

was / were	had	found
met	pushed	got
gave	told	answered
could	stayed	decided
asked	knew	took

c) *Now read the following sentences. Say which of them are right, and which are wrong.*

Start: Number 1 is wrong. Liam didn't … … .

1. Liam phoned Liz to find out about the Carnival.
2. Everything went well in the end.
3. Liz met Tessa and Kevin at Queensway station.
4. Maike gave her train tickets to Tessa.
5. Maike walked fast through the crowd.
6. Liz could see Kevin in the crowd all the time.
7. Tessa was with Liz all the time.
8. Tessa called Jimmy on her mobile phone.
9. Maike found someone with a mobile phone.
10. The people pushed Maike up on their float.
11. Maike tried to jump off the float.
12. They put flowers in Liz's hair.
13. Jimmy took photos of Liz and Maike.
14. Maike missed her train.

Then correct the wrong sentences.

SAVE

They were	They weren't …
They could	They couldn't …
But most verbs are like this:	
They walked	They didn't walk …
They met	They didn't meet …

3 But how did it all start?

The Notting Hill Carnival wasn't always as big as it is now. It started in a very small way in the year 1965. A teacher at a London school had the idea for a festival to bring the different people of Notting Hill together. This teacher – Mrs Rhaune Laslett-O'Brien – is now very old, and is in a wheelchair. But she still lives in London, and sometimes reporters come to interview her. *Work in groups for a) and b).*

a) *Imagine you want to interview Mrs Laslett-O'Brien. Prepare your questions about the first Notting Hill Parade. For example:*

Who gave you the idea …?
Who helped you …?
What groups took part in …?
How many people …?
…
Were you … ?
Did you think … ?
Did you expect … ?
…
Did other people … ?
…
When did you … ?
Why did you … ?
How did you … ?
…
Where did the parade start?
Where did it … ?
…

b) *Imagine you are Mrs Laslett-O'Brien. Prepare what you want to tell the 'reporters'.*

c) *Now act your interviews.*

This is an old article from 1965. It was in the 'West London Observer'. You don't need to understand every word, but it may help you to prepare your 'interview'.

Children dressed as characters from Dickens at the London Free School fair

LOTS OF FUN AT THE NOTTING HILL PARADE

A parade organized by the London Free School filled the streets of Notting Hill with music and laughter on Sunday afternoon. It was so successful that they now want to make it an annual event.

Said Mrs Rhaune Laslett, the organizer: "We set out to liven up the community, and we certainly did that." She added: "There are many different nationalities living in Notting Hill, and they all joined in with the singing and dancing in the streets."

Four bands, including the London Irish Girl Pipers, a West Indian marching band, and an Afro-Cuban band, took part in the parade. It started in Acklam Road, went through Ladbroke Road, Holland Park Avenue, Notting Hill Gate and Westbourne Grove, and returned via Great Western Road.

The parade was part of the London Free School's summer fair. After the parade, an international song-and-dance night was 'a complete sell-out'.

Mrs Laslett told the *West London Observer*: "We didn't expect so many people at the parade or the dance night."

From *Touch – The 1998 Guide to the Notting Hill Carnival*

G 5

4 The day after

<u>Monday, August 31st</u>

When I woke up this morning, the sun was shining brightly through red curtains. I didn't know where I was! Then I heard Tessa's voice: "Get up, Liz! We're all having our breakfast – don't you want any?" When I came into the kitchen, the whole family were sitting around the table. (It was a bank holiday, remember?) While I was finishing my cornflakes, Jake switched on the TV. The programme was coming live from Notting Hill – the Carnival was still going on, of course. "Want to come with us today?" he asked. "No, thanks!" Tessa and I said together.

While I was having fun in London, Liam was sailing with his friends. He left Friday morning before me, and still wasn't back when I reached home this evening. Must be tireder than me!

I go ... – I am going ...
I went ... – I was going ...

The past progressive ('I was going') is easy to form. *But when do you use it?*

a) *Find the past progressive forms in Liz's report about the day after the Carnival.*

b) *Then say what the first three of these actions have to do with:*

wake up   come into   switch on

c) *What about the other actions? What do they have to do with each other?*

G 5

5 What was going on?

Look at the pictures and say what was happening when something else happened. Use the past progressive and the simple past.

Example: Liam was sailing (on the sea) when Liz left for London.

1

Another city afternoon

1 Before you read

Here are the names of some of the characters in the story: Julia Winter, Nathan Browne, Mrs Henrey.
What can you already say – or guess – about them from their names? What do you not yet know? As you go through the story, look for new bits of information about them.

London isn't always an exciting place – as this story shows!

The air was hot. It came in through the open windows with the sunshine of another city afternoon. The children were tired, and Mrs Henrey couldn't stand them in the classroom any more. Class 8 were going to the park for the last hour, to play rounders.

Only two of the twenty-four children didn't want to go, and one of those two was Nathan Browne. A small black boy, he looked at the world through thick glasses, and hated most of what he saw. Nathan had no friends. He stood up.

"Please, Mrs Henrey, can I stay behind?"

"No, Nathan, you can't," Mrs Henrey answered. "We're all going."

Nathan sat down. He made a face at the teacher's back. Julia Winter saw the face and called out, "Mrs Henrey, Nathan made a face at you!"

Mrs Henrey didn't want to know about the face. "Don't tell tales, Julia. That's not nice."

Julia's thin face went red, and she tossed back her sandy hair. She could never understand grown-ups, she decided. They wanted you to be good, but when you showed them how good you were, then they didn't like it.

Julia didn't want to go to the park any more than Nathan did, but thought it was better to say nothing about it now. Julia was an only child, and she had no idea how to make friends. When she came to school first, at the age of five, she took all the other children's crayons, hit them, and whined all day. So the others turned against her. Now Julia didn't hit people or take their pencils any more. But they still didn't like her.

"Line up with your partners," Mrs Henrey told the class. This was what Julia was afraid of. Because no one ever wanted to walk with her.

Nathan was afraid of it too. He didn't really want a friend, he thought to himself. If that lot didn't want him, he didn't want them, so there! But he didn't like it much when he was without a partner.

Mrs Henrey counted the pairs of children. Julia was looking at a comic, as if she didn't care.

"Put that rubbish away, Julia! Are you the last? Oh, no, there's Nathan. Nathan, Julia can be your partner. Well, come and stand next to her. Come along, we haven't all day. She isn't going to bite you!"

Nathan gave one angry look at Mrs Henrey, and another at Julia. He came and stood a few steps behind his partner.

"Stand with her!" said Mrs Henrey, and Nathan moved forward a step. "Rat-bag!" he hissed at Julia.

Julia moved away, and turned her back. "Must I walk with him, Mrs Henrey? Can't I walk with you? Can't I be your partner?"

"No, Julia, you can't walk with me. Nathan is your partner. Denise and Sharon, Sanjay and Paul, you go and get the rounders things. Meet us at the gate. Now come along, the rest of you."

Outside, the sun was shining on the hard playground.

"It's too hot for rounders," someone said.

"It's cooler in the park," said Mrs Henrey.

The crocodile moved slowly up the road. Nathan fell behind, away from Julia. A tabby cat on a garden wall miaowed at him, and he stopped to stroke it. He liked cats. Cats were much nicer than people. The cat rubbed its head against his hand. Then it jumped off the wall and rubbed

against his feet. This made Nathan happy, just for a moment. Then Mrs Henrey's sharp voice cut through his enjoyment, and told him to keep up with his partner. The class was waiting for him. Nathan moved forward. The class moved on again. Nathan stepped on Julia's foot.

"Ow!" said Julia – her foot really hurt.

"Not so much noise, Julia!" called Mrs Henrey from the front.

"Nathan kicked me!" Julia whined.

"I never ... ," said Nathan, and stepped on Julia's foot again. "He kicked me again!" Julia cried.

"Walk straight, Nathan," called Mrs Henrey.

Nathan tried to kick Julia a third time, but missed. Then, he saw the chance of even more fun. Paul and Sanjay were the goodie-goodies. Mrs Henrey's pets. Nathan gave them a hard kick each, from behind.

"Stop it, Nathan!"

"It wasn't me. It was Julia."

"It was you," said Sanjay. "I saw you."

"Less noise back there," called Mrs Henrey.

Nathan went to kick Sanjay again, but Paul was too quick for him, and hit Nathan on the side of his head. Then Nathan really went at Paul, like a little animal. Lovely to be so angry!

"Stop it!" shouted Mrs Henrey. "Stop it, both of you. Paul, I'm surprised at you."

"Nathan started it," said Julia.

"I didn't ask you," said Mrs Henrey angrily. She was feeling very hot. She began to think it wasn't such a good idea to go to the park.

"Nathan, come and walk with me at the front. Any more trouble from anyone, and we're going back to the classroom to do ... er, ... spelling!"

Nathan grinned. There was nothing he liked better than spelling. He was good at it. It was one of his best lessons. His other best lessons were reading and writing stories. He was thinking how he could do something really awful, so that they could go back to the school to do spelling. But he missed his chance, and they arrived at the park. Nice and green, yes, but awful for Nathan because of the awful game of rounders, where balls came at him out of nowhere. Even with his glasses he couldn't see things like balls very well. No one played rounders worse than Nathan. Except Julia, of course.

"Sharon and Paul are captains, and choose teams," said Mrs Henrey.

"My foot hurts," said Julia. "I can't run on it."

"Run on the other one," said Mrs Henrey. She wasn't feeling friendly.

There was no way out for Julia. Or for Nathan.

Adapted from *The Runaways* by Ruth Thomas, 1997

2 What did they do wrong?

a) *Say what these people did wrong in the story:* Julia – Nathan – Paul – Mrs Henrey. *(Use the past tense of the verbs on the right.)*

b) *Try to explain why it was wrong.*

c) *The people in the story aren't very nice. But do you like any of them? Try to explain why (not).*

make a face at ...	kick ...
tell tales (on ...)	tell a lie
hit ...	go for ...
take ...	say ...
call ... a bad name	tell ... to ...
step on ...	be unfriendly

3 What the author wants

Whether you like the characters in a story or don't like them depends on what you know about them.

a) *Go through the story again, and find the places where the author lets you know what a character is thinking. Write down the names and the line numbers.*

b) *Look at exercise 2 c) again. Can you now explain a bit better?*

4 Make up a story!

'Another city afternoon' is just the beginning of a longer story. *Can you imagine how it goes on? The cover picture of Nathan and Julia and the title can give you some ideas. Write a little scene to go with it. Useful phrases:*

find money	get a present of ...
steal ...	run away (to ...)

1 Where did they come from?

Londoners come from all over Britain – and from all over the world! There are a lot of immigrant families in the city.

For a school project, Tessa collected information about the history of her friends' families. She wanted to know where they (or their parents or their grandparents) lived before they came to London, when they came, why they came, etc.

Read the beginning of her report below, and then use her notes to finish it. It is easy to guess the right words. She uses these verbs:

be born, grow up, come, go, arrive, want, travel, move, leave, marry, be, get, open, find

You can work in groups for the different families!

If you go back far enough, we're all immigrants!

<u>Us (Cliftons)</u>: about half English, half Scottish (but Dad's grandmother from Wales) – Dad b. London, but gr. up Cardiff – family m. back → London 1963 (father g. new job) – Mum b. Edinburgh, Scotland, c. → London 1972 (to study art history) – Mum / Dad m. 1980 – all of us b. / gr.up in London

<u>Modi family</u>: half English, half Indian – Aunt Hilary same as Dad – Uncle Hassan b. London, but both parents from India: his father c. → Britain 1959, w. to find work, but op. shop in Liverpool; his mother c. 1956, to marry his father – Uncle H. c. → London to study, m. Aunt Hilary 1976 – cousin Tara and all other children b. and gr. up in London

<u>Smiths</u>: all children / parents / 3 grand-parents b. / gr.up in London – but one grandparent German – (grandfather l. Germany 1935 because of Hitler)

<u>Wilsons</u>: children and parents b. / gr. up London, but grandparents from West Indies: father's parents tr. from Jamaica → London, 1948 / 50 – mother's parents arr. 1956 from Trinidad – all f. work fast

<u>Mannings</u>: both parents Irish – Kevin b. in west of Ireland (Dingle) – family c. → London when he w. young (father f. better job in computers)

<u>Bradens</u>: Liz / Liam b. / gr. up London, but not their parents: mother b. Cornwall, m. here 1980 for job with big newspaper; father b. N. Ireland, l. Belfast 1976 because of 'troubles' – family w. → Cornwall last year – NOT LONDONERS ANY MORE!!!

Report: London families

We Cliftons are about half English and half Scottish, but one great-grandmother (my father's grandmother) was from Wales. My father was born in London, but grew up in Cardiff, Wales. The family moved back to London in 1963 because the father got a new job. My mother was born in Edinburgh, Scotland, but came to London to study …

2 Cartoon fun

a) *Can you say what's funny about this cartoon? (Think about what the man says: Is it different in some way from what people usually say?)*

b) *What does the cartoon tell you about the people of London and Britain?*

"If there's one thing I can't stand, it's the characteristic smell of British cooking!"

3 In the year 1973 …

Look at Tessa's notes again, and find out what was happening in all the families in that year. Example:

In the year 1973, Tessa's parents were living in … . Her mother …

live

study

work

1 A singer and a song

The people from the Caribbean brought their music with them to Britain. You know reggae – that kind of Caribbean music started in the 1970s. But before that, there were other Caribbean musicians. Like 'Lord Kitchener' (not his real name, of course!). He came to Britain with the first big group of immigrants from the West Indies, on the famous ship, *The Windrush*, in 1948. They came to Britain to look for work – but also to see what they called 'the mother country'.

a) *Read why 'Lord Kitchener' wrote his song, and put in the missing verbs in the past tense.*

"But when the boat (have) ... about four days to land in England, I (get) ... this kind of wonderful feeling that I'm going to land on the mother country. And I (write) ... that song *London is the place for me.* The feeling, how can I describe it? It (be) ... just a wonderful feeling. Imagine how I (feel) ... – here's where I want to be, London. So I (sing) ... :

London is the place for me, London, that lovely city.
You can go to France or America, India, Asia or Africa,
But you must come back to London city.
I said, London is the place for me, London, that lovely city."

b) *Listen to the way he sang his song on the ship, just after he arrived in London.*

2 On Tuesday everything went wrong ...

Some days, nothing goes right. a) *Look at the pictures, and say what went wrong for Kevin on the Tuesday after the Notting Hill Carnival. You can start like this:*

On Tuesday morning, he didn't wake up until half past eight. He ...

not wake up until ...

miss

be late for

forget

be sick

lose

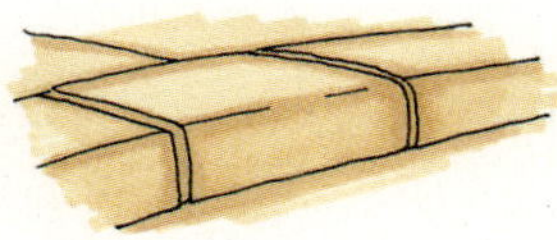

not see

fall

break

not find

drop

not sleep

b) *Now work in pairs. One asks questions about Kevin's bad day, and the other gives (short) answers.*

Example: Did Kevin wake up at 8 o'clock? – No, he didn't. ... Did he catch / miss the bus? – ... Was he ...?

1 A good idea or a bad idea for the Carnival?

Are these suggestions good or bad? Start: I think ...ing ... ... is a / good / bad idea, because ...

1. "Bring a lot of money."
2. "Wear a really cool costume."
3. "Wear fashionable shoes."
4. "Wear your old trainers."
5. "Take the Underground to Notting Hill Gate."
6. "Bring a camera."
7. "Bring your best, most expensive camera."
8. "Carry a mobile phone."

2 "Round up the usual suspects!"

R

G 6

The title is a famous line from the film 'Casablanca'. (It means that the police don't care if they get the right person, or not!)

a) *First read about these 'suspects'.*

b) *Make two or three sentences about each of these people. Use gerunds, and start like this:*
... is good at ... .
He / She likes ... .
He / She doesn't like ... .

c) *Imagine you are one of them, and you were at this year's Carnival. Write a little story about what you did there. Be sure to say what you liked / didn't like this year.*
Example:
... ... I really liked meeting so many German tourists. ...
... ... I didn't like picking up all those dirty bottles. ...

Adapted from *Touch – The 1998 Guide*

THE USUAL SUSPECTS

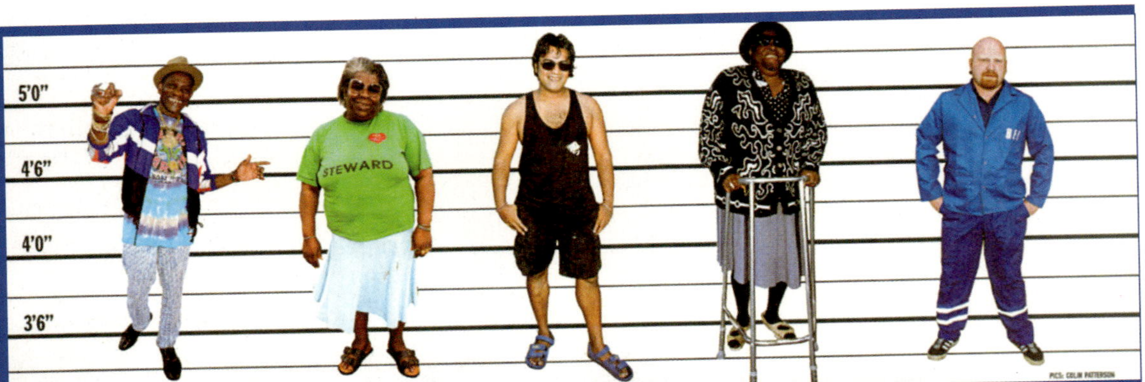

The costume designer	The food-stall holder	The float organizer	The resident	The road sweeper
Name Rocky Byron	**Name** Mrs Heslop	**Name** Richard Ali	**Name** Evelyn Thomas	**Name** John
Part in Carnival Designing and making up to 250 costumes every year for the Real Steel Band and their friends	**Part in Carnival** Cooking some of the best snapper fish this side of Jamaica	**Part in Carnival** Getting the neces-sary money, selling T-shirts, wiring up the sound system	**Part in Carnival** Enjoying it (she has lived in the Notting Hill area for a long time)	**Part in Carnival** Cleaning up after the Carnival crowds for the past eight years
+ Seeing his beautiful costumes on people in the street	**+** People liking her food. "This year lots of people from America wanted to take my fish back with them!"	**+** Getting a buzz out of the whole thing when things go right	**+** Letting herself go once a year. "It doesn't hurt – I'm up in my flat for most of the year!"	**+** Finding interesting things – and some money when he's lucky! Last year he found chairs, and a barbecue ...
– Working around the clock as the big day gets nearer; the British weather	**–** Nothing! She enjoys every minute of it!	**–** Being under stress all the time; not getting enough money; all the ups and downs	**–** Hearing people say she's too old for all this. "Rubbish!" says Evelyn	**–** ... but also a dead man! Talking to the police wasn't nice

WP

1 What are they to you?

What are the right words for …

1. … your mother and father's other child (girl)?
2. … your mother and father's other child (boy)?
3. … your father's sister?
4. … your mother's sister?
5. … your mother's brother?
6. … your father's brother's children?
7. … your mother or father?
8. … your mother's mother and father?
9. … your father's mother?
10. … your mother's father?
11. … your mother's father's mother?
12. … your father's mother's father?

HV

2 Listening comprehension: The story of Dick Whittington

This is the beginning of a famous old story. It is only a story. But there really was a Sir Richard Whittington, and he became Lord Mayor of London three times (in 1397, 1406, and 1419).

a) *Put in the right verbs in the past simple or progressive.*

Dick Whittington … a poor boy. His parents … dead, and nobody … after him. Dick … … what to do. The people in Dick's village often … about a far-away city called London. "You can find gold and silver in the streets there," they … Dick. So one day, Dick … to go there himself. He … a little bag, … it over his shoulder, and … off with his only friend – his cat.	be be look not know talk tell decide pack put set
It … a long way to walk, and he … on the road for three days. But at last he … . There … crowds of people, and beautiful, big buildings – but he … … any gold or silver in the streets! Tired and hungry, Dick … down outside the door of a big house. He … when the owner of the house, a rich man called Mr Fitzwarren, … him and … him a job in the kitchen. Rats and mice … around there, but Dick's cat soon … an end to that problem! He … happy there at first.	be be arrive be not find lie sleep see give run put be

b) *Now listen to the rest of the story to find out what went wrong, and why it was all right in the end. Correct these sentences:*

1. Mr Fitzwarren was also the captain of a ship.
2. Dick ran away to sea and left his cat behind.
3. Dick heard voices in the wind. They were saying: "Go home, Dick!"
4. Dick found work in a far-away country and became rich there.

3 Questions about the *Windrush*

The *Windrush* is a famous ship. It landed in London in June 1948. A passenger from that ship now knows a lot about the facts. A reporter (Mrs Braden) is interviewing him. *You can read his answers. What are Mrs Braden's questions?*

1. … – No, they weren't. There were quite a lot of black people in Britain before that.
2. … – Well, we were the first big group of immigrants from the West Indies.
3. … – There were about 500 passengers on the ship, mostly men from Jamaica, like me.
4. … – It sailed from Jamaica on May 24th, and then picked up more passengers in other parts of the West Indies.
5. … – I left Jamaica because there was no work there, and there was a lot of work in England then.
6. … – Yes, I did. I was lucky, and found a good job in a restaurant on my first day in England.
7. … – No, I didn't. I later became a bus driver, and stayed in that job until I was 60.

Vocabulary

Auch in **Swift 2** findest du nach jeder *Unit* eine Liste mit den neuen Vokabeln. Hier zur Erinnerung noch einmal die verwendeten Symbole und Abkürzungen:

Symbole

⟨ ⟩	=	fakultativer Wortschatz
+	=	*Track* 2-Wortschatz
*	=	unregelmäßiges Verb (siehe Seite 228)
[']	=	Hauptbetonung
[ˌ]	=	Nebenbetonung
[‿]	=	enge Verbindung zweier Wörter
~	=	Auslassung des zu erklärenden Wortes

Abkürzungen

BE	=	*British English*
AE	=	*American English*
so.	=	*someone* = jmd(m/n) / jemand(em/en)
sth.	=	*something* = etw / etwas
sing.	=	Singular
pl.	=	Plural
coll.	=	*colloquial* = umgangssprachlich

CHECK-IN

	Notting Hill [ˌnɒtɪŋ'hɪl]	*Stadtteil im Westen Londons*
	all the year round [raʊnd]	das ganze Jahr über
	crowd [kraʊd]	(Menschen-)Menge
	noon [nuːn]	Mittag
	event [ɪ'vent]	Ereignis
	colourful ['kʌləfl]	farbenprächtig, farbenfroh
	float [fləʊt]	Festzugswagen, Umzugswagen
	Caribbean [ˌkærɪ'biːən]	karibisch, Karibik
1	to **prepare** [prɪ'peə]	vorbereiten
	speaker ['spiːkə]	Sprecher(in)
2	**One Day Travelcard** ['trævlkɑːd]	Tageskarte, Netzkarte *(London)*
	to **set off** [ˌset‿'ɒf]	losziehen, (eine Reise) antreten
	important [ɪm'pɔːtnt]	wichtig
	whistle ['wɪsl]	(Triller-)Pfeife
	smell [smel]	Geruch, Duft
	sunglasses ['sʌnglɑːsɪz]	Sonnenbrille
	sun [sʌn]	Sonne
	rain [reɪn]	Regen
	geek [giːk]	Langweiler(in), Spießer(in)
	coolness ['kuːlnəs]	*hier:* Lässigkeit
	down [daʊn]	herunter, nieder; nach unten
	back [bæk]	Rücken

all the year round = all twelve months of the year

A crowd is a large number of people.

Let's set off at noon.

Reggae is music from the Caribbean.

STEP A

	while [waɪl]	während
	because of [bɪ'kɒz‿əv]	wegen
	better to be safe than sorry	lieber auf Nummer sicher gehen
	to **be excited** [ɪk'saɪtɪd]	aufgeregt sein
	when [wen]	als
	Queensway ['kwiːnzweɪ]	*U-Bahn-Station in London*
	at first [ət 'fɜːst]	zunächst
	to **go wrong** [ˌgəʊ 'rɒŋ]	schief gehen
1	to **learn by heart** [ˌlɜːn baɪ 'hɑːt]	auswendig lernen
2	**first** [fɜːst]	zuerst
	as [æz]	wie
	all the time ['ɔːl ðə 'taɪm]	die ganze Zeit
	to **take a photo** [ˌteɪk‿ə 'fəʊtəʊ]	ein Foto machen
3	**wheelchair** ['wiːltʃeə]	Rollstuhl
	fair [feə]	Fest, Jahrmarkt

You carry a rucksack on your back.

Please wait a while!

She was very excited about the Carnival in Notting Hill.

laughter ['lɑ:ftə]	Gelächter, Lachen
successful [sək'sesfl]	erfolgreich
organizer ['ɔ:gənaɪzə]	Organisator(in)
to **set out to do sth.** [ˌset‿'aʊt]	etw fest vorhaben
to **liven up** [ˌlaɪvn‿'ʌp]	beleben, aufmuntern
community [kə'mju:nəti]	Gemeinschaft, Gemeinde
certainly ['sɜ:tnli]	gewiss, sicherlich
to **join in (with)** [ˌdʒɔɪn‿'ɪn]	teilnehmen (an)
dancing ['dɑ:nsɪŋ]	Tanzen
to **include** [ɪn'klu:d]	einschließen, einbeziehen
marching band ['mɑ:tʃɪŋ ˌbænd]	Marschkapelle
to **return** [rɪ'tɜ:n]	zurückkehren
sell-out ['selaʊt]	Ausverkauf
to **expect** [ɪk'spekt]	erwarten
4 to **shine*** [ʃaɪn]	scheinen
brightly ['braɪtli]	hell, leuchtend
curtain ['kɜ:tn]	Vorhang
to **get up** [get‿'ʌp]	aufstehen *(vom Bett)*
(bank) holiday [ˌbæŋk 'hɒlədeɪ]	öffentlicher Feiertag
to **switch on** [ˌswɪtʃ‿'ɒn]	einschalten
to **have to do with** [ˌhæv tə 'du:]	mit etw zu tun haben
each other [ˌi:tʃ‿'ʌðə]	einander

colour	⇔	colourful
to laugh	⇔	laughter
cool	⇔	coolness
to organize	⇔	organizer
life, to live	⇔	to liven up

franz communauté *lat* communitas
engl community

Come and join in the dancing!

franz certainement *lat* certe
engl certainly

The sun shines brightly.

The last Monday in August is always a bank holiday in GB.

STEP B

air [eə]	Luft
I can't stand (it) [ˌkɑ:nt 'stænd]	ich halte (es) nicht aus, ich ertrage (es) nicht
rounders ['raʊndəz]	Schlagball
to **stand up** [stænd‿'ʌp]	aufstehen *(vom Stuhl)*
to **sit down** [sɪt 'daʊn]	sich setzen
to **make a face** [feɪs]	ein Gesicht ziehen
to **tell tales** [ˌtel 'teɪlz]	petzen, klatschen
to **toss** [tɒs]	werfen
sandy ['sændi]	rötlich, rotblond *(Haarfarbe)*
an **only child** [ˌəʊnli 'tʃaɪld]	Einzelkind
crayon ['kreɪɒn]	Farbstift
to **whine** [waɪn]	jammern, wimmern
to **line up** [ˌlaɪn‿'ʌp]	(sich) aufstellen
to **count** [kaʊnt]	zählen
to **care (about)** [keə]	sich Sorgen machen (um)
she didn't care [keə]	es war ihr egal
Come along ['kʌm‿əˌlɒŋ]	Komm schon!
to **bite*** [baɪt]	beißen
rat-bag ['rætbæg]	Miststück
to **hiss** [hɪs]	zischen, fauchen
gate [geɪt]	Tor
playground ['pleɪgraʊnd]	(Schul-)Hof
crocodile ['krɒkədaɪl]	Krokodil, *hier:* Menschenschlange
tabby ['tæbi]	getigert; getigerte Katze
to **stroke** [strəʊk]	streicheln
sharp [ʃɑ:p]	scharf, hart
to **cut*** [kʌt]	schneiden
enjoyment [ɪn'dʒɔɪmənt]	Freude, Spaß
to **keep up (with so.)** [ˌki:p‿'ʌp]	Schritt halten (mit jmdm)
to **step on so.'s foot** [step]	jmdm auf den Fuß treten
noise [nɔɪz]	Geräusch, Lärm
(at) **the front** [frʌnt]	vorne

Public holidays and bank holidays

Easter Monday
May Day (1st May)
Spring Bank Holiday
(last Monday in May)
Summer Bank Holiday
(last Monday in August)
Boxing Day (26th December)
(If 25th or 26th are at the weekend, the weekend that follows is a holiday.)

In Scotland, 2nd January is a public holiday. (If 1st or 2nd January falls on a Sunday, 3rd January is a bank holiday.)

In Ireland, St Patrick's Day (17th March) is a bank holiday too.

→
STEP ON NO PETS (a palindrome)
←

1

	to **miss** [mɪs]	nicht treffen, verfehlen
	goodie-goodie ['gʊdiˌgʊdi]	Streber(in), Brave(r)
	pet [pet]	Haustier, *hier:* Liebling
	to **go at so.** ['gəʊ ˌət]	auf jmdn losgehen
	to **be surprised (at)** [sə'praɪzd]	überrascht sein (über)
	to **feel*** [fi:l]	fühlen
	spelling ['spelɪŋ]	Rechtschreibung
	to **grin** [grɪn]	grinsen
	to **arrive** [ə'raɪv]	ankommen
	worse [wɜ:s]	schlechter
	except [ɪk'sept]	außer
3	to **depend (on)** [dɪ'pend]	abhängen (von)
4	**cover** ['kʌvə]	(Buch-)Umschlag
	to **run away** [ˌrʌn‿ə'weɪ]	weglaufen

Don't step on a pet's foot!
It may hiss and then bite.

Mind the spelling
expect *(erwarten)* – except *(außer)*

English spelling is difficult!

arrival ⇔ to arrive
noisy ⇔ noise

STEP C

1	**all over** ['ɔ:l‿əʊvə]	überall (in)
	beginning [bɪ'gɪnɪg]	Anfang, Beginn
	grandparent ['grænˌpeərnt]	Großelternteil
	to **grow up** [grəʊ‿'ʌp]	aufwachsen
	grandmother ['grænˌmʌðə]	Großmutter
	grandfather ['grændˌfɑ:ðə]	Großvater
	Jamaica [dʒə'meɪkə]	*karibischer Inselstaat*
	Trinidad ['trɪnɪdæd]	*Inseln der Kleinen Antillen*
	not ... any more [ˌnɒt ... ˌeni 'mɔ:]	(überhaupt) nicht mehr
	great-grandmother [ˌgreɪt'grænˌmʌðə]	Urgroßmutter
2	**cooking** ['kʊkɪŋ]	Küche, Essen, Kochkünste

Your great-grandmother is your grandma's or your grandpa's mother.

I don't play rounders any more.

My great-grandfather's cooking is always wonderful.

awful
beautiful
wonderful
successful
...

TRACK 1

1	**Lord Kitchener** [ˌlɔ:d 'kɪtʃɪnə]	*Künstlername eines Sängers aus der Karibik*
	the West Indies [ˌwest 'ɪndiz]	Westindien *(Inseln in der Karibik)*
	The Windrush ['wɪndrʌʃ]	*Name eines Schiffes*
	wonderful ['wʌndəfl]	wunderbar, wundervoll
	Asia ['eɪʃə]	Asien
	Africa ['æfrɪkə]	Afrika
2	to **be late (for)** [leɪt]	zu spät kommen (für), spät dran sein
	to **catch*** [kætʃ]	fangen; (einen Bus) erreichen

A man catches a fish.
A cat catches a mouse.
...

to hold	–	holder
to sweep	–	sweeper
to drive	–	driver
to sing	–	?
...		

TRACK 2

1	+**fashionable** ['fæʃnəbl]	modisch, schick
2	⟨to **round up the usual suspects**⟩ [ˌraʊnd‿'ʌp ðə 'ju:ʒl 'sʌspekts]	die üblichen Verdächtigen festnehmen
	⟨**line**⟩ [laɪn]	*hier:* Zitat
	⟨**holder**⟩ ['həʊldə]	Inhaber(in), Pächter(in)
	⟨**snapper fish**⟩ ['snæpə ˌfɪʃ]	*tropische Fischart*
	⟨to **wire up**⟩ [ˌwaɪə‿'ʌp]	eine Leitung (ver)legen
	⟨to **get a buzz out of sth.**⟩ [bʌz]	Spaß haben bei etw
	⟨**sweeper**⟩ ['swi:pə]	Straßenkehrer(in)
	+to **pick up** [pɪk‿'ʌp]	aufheben, -lesen
	+to **be lucky** ['lʌki]	Glück haben
	+**barbecue** ['bɑ:bɪkju:]	Grill *(im Freien)*

What does a holder hold?
What does a sweeper sweep?
What does a driver drive?
What does a ...?

You're lucky – you're having a barbecue on Saturday.

BAR-B-Q

CHECK-OUT

2	**Dick Whittington** [ˌdɪk ˈwɪtɪŋtn]	*Bürgermeister von London (1358?–1423)*	
	to **become*** [bɪˈkʌm]	werden	
	mayor [meə]	Bürgermeister(in)	
	put an end to sth. [ˌpʌt‿ən‿ˈend]	einer Sache ein Ende setzen	
3	**mostly** [ˈməʊstli]	meistens, hauptsächlich	
	to **be lucky** [ˈlʌki]	Glück haben	

COGNATE WORDS

author [ˈɔːθə]	Autor(in)
to **begin*** [bɪˈgɪn]	beginnen, anfangen
carnival [ˈkɑːnɪvl]	Karneval
chance [tʃɑːns]	Gelegenheit, Chance
characteristic [ˌkærəktəˈrɪstɪk]	charakteristisch, kennzeichnend
comfort [ˈkʌmfət]	Bequemlichkeit, Komfort
cool [kuːl]	kühl; locker, lässig
cornflakes [ˈkɔːnfleɪks]	Cornflakes
deodorant [diˈəʊdrnt]	Deodorant
+**designer** [dɪˈzaɪnə]	Designer
drink [drɪŋk]	Getränk
feeling [ˈfiːlɪŋ]	Gefühl
immigrant [ˈɪmɪgrənt]	Einwanderer / Einwanderin
to **kick** [kɪk]	treten, (mit dem Fuß) stoßen
kick [kɪk]	(Fuß-)Tritt, Stoß
to **miaow** [ˌmiːˈaʊ]	miauen
mouse, *pl.* **mice** [maʊs, maɪs]	Maus, Mäuse
parade [pəˈreɪd]	Parade, Aufmarsch
passenger [ˈpæsndʒə]	Reisende(r), Passagier
programme [ˈprəʊgræm]	Sendung
rat [ræt]	Ratte
+**resident** [ˈrezɪdnt]	Bewohner(in), Einwohner(in)
singing [ˈsɪŋɪŋ]	Singen
to **steal*** [stiːl]	stehlen
+**stress** [stres]	Stress, Anspannung
to **study** [ˈstʌdi]	studieren
sunshine [ˈsʌnʃaɪn]	Sonnenschein
trouble [ˈtrʌbl]	Ärger, Schwierigkeiten
via [vaɪə]	über

The suffixes *-er, -an* and *-ish*

When you want to say where people come from or what language they speak you give them different suffixes. Three of them are:

-er	-an	-ish
London – Londoner	America – American	Cornwall – Cornish

What about languages or things or people from: Australia, Dublin, Italy, Ireland, India, Scotland, Britain, …?

The prefix *un-*

'*un-*' is one of the negative prefixes and means 'not'. It can go with a lot of English adjectives or participles. *Make a list. How many examples can you find? Be careful: in dictionaries or word lists you won't always find 'unhappy'. You must go to 'happy'.*

+	–
happy	unhappy
used	unused
natural	…

UNIT 2

2

Music and the movies

In the early days of film-making there were only silent movies. The films had no sound track. A piano player would play some music to go with the scenes on the screen to 'underline' the feelings and emotions. But then came the sound track and with it the film music. Today there is even an Oscar award for the best film music.

1 Film music

a) *Look at the scenes on the right. Then listen to the recording and say which piece of music goes with which picture. (There isn't a sound track for every scene!)*

Example: The first film music goes with picture B.

b) *What kind of music (instruments) would you choose for the other scenes?*

c) Sometimes the music of a film becomes more popular than the film itself. Whitney Houston's songs in the film 'Bodyguard' were a big hit. There is an example on page 32 and on the recording. *Can you think of any other examples of famous film music?*

2 An interview

Interview your friends about films. Think of about ten interesting questions. Here are some ideas:

Have you seen the film ... ?
Have you ever seen a ... film?
Who were the actors?
What was the music like?
Did they nominate it for an Oscar?

accordion didgeridoo bagpipes harmonica trumpet

3 Talking about film music

In a western film ...
In a thriller ...
In a love story ...
In a silent movie of the early days ...
In a comedy ...
In a road movie ...

If the setting is in Spain / Paris / New York / Ireland / Scotland / Australia / Jamaica / New Orleans / ...

... I'd choose ...
... people expect ...
... I'd like ...
... they usually have ...
... people like ...
... they always use ...

... soft rock.
... techno.
... hip hop.
... jazz.
... blues.
... reggae.
... country and western music.
... Irish folk.
... rock'n'roll.
... classical music.
... piano music.
... guitar music.
... music with drums / banjo and harmonica / accordion / bagpipes / didgeridoos / trumpet / violin and cello / ...

Film-makers have always been interested in Shakespeare's plays. This scene is from the latest film version of 'Romeo and Juliet' with Leonardo di Caprio.
It is set in Los Angeles. There is some more information about William Shakespeare on the next page.

All the world's a stage

Romeo and Juliet

The New Globe Theatre in London (opened 1997)

Let's get this straight: Shakespeare didn't write his plays for pupils to read at school or for teachers to use. Shakespeare wanted people to have fun! He became popular because he knew what they liked and he wrote what they wanted. But the people were also interested in the actors. The star actors were like the pop stars of today. Theatre companies usually had about eight men and a few boys to play the women's parts.
The theatres in Shakespeare's time were large open-air circles of seats with a stage at one side. But the seats were only for the rich people. There were no seats in front of the stage, so the audience often had a hard time. They had to stand for two, three or even four hours to see a play. And if they grew bored, they would just talk among themselves or throw food on the stage or boo at the actors.
Of course, as a great entertainer Shakespeare used music. His plays are full of songs. Unfortunately the original music has been lost, and we're left with reconstructions. (There are some examples on the recording.) Anyway, if you think of an open-air concert in our time, you get an idea of what was going on in the theatres in Shakespeare's time 400 years ago.
For almost 400 years experts have discussed how to perform Shakespeare's plays. The New Globe Theatre has been open for a number of years now, and since then it has performed a lot of Shakespeare's plays exactly as in his days.

R 1 Everything ready?

a) Before the all-night open-air concert starts, people have been busy and have done lots of jobs. *Look at the picture at the bottom of page 26 and match the parts of the sentences.*

Workers	have	positioned their fire engines.
Electricians		put up their stalls for food and drink.
The bands and stars		set up the stage.
The Red Cross people		done their sound checks.
Other workers		installed all the electric equipment.
Other people		brought in waste containers and bottle banks.
Firemen		put up signs.
The authorities		set up a first aid station.

b) *What else have people done? Think of things like:* to inform people, to sell tickets, to write reports, to interview people.

2 Right or wrong?

a) *Go back to the text about Shakespeare and put the wrong sentences right.*

1. The audiences were also interested in the actors.
2. All the actors were women.
3. The rich people had to stand for hours.
4. Sometimes the people grew bored.
5. Shakespeare used music in his plays.
6. We're left with the original music.

b) *Now check the sentences about the open-air concert and put the wrong ones right.*

1. The bands are going to do their sound checks.
2. The Red Cross people have set up the stage.
3. The firemen sell snacks and drinks.
4. Electricians have put up the signs.
5. The authorities have brought in containers and bottle banks.

R 3 When Grandma was young

A boy wants to know what the media were like in the 60s. *Use the pictures to act little dialogues between the boy and his grandmother.*

Example: What about CDs in the 60s, Grandma?
There weren't any CDs then. We bought records for our record players.

buy

watch

use

go (to)

play

learn (with)

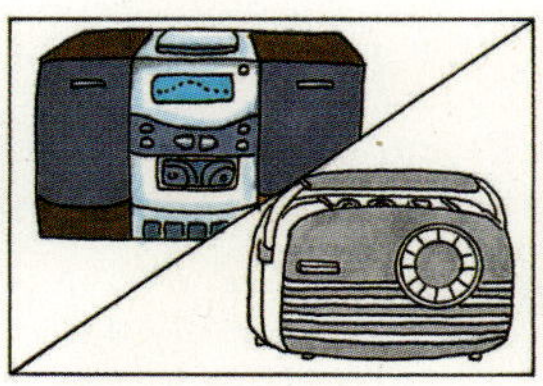

listen (to)

enjoy

4 +Do you enjoy listening to film music?

Make sentences. Example: Today my grandma enjoys listening to film music.

Today 60 years ago	my grandma young people not everyone elderly people my grandpa lots of people some people	like / likes / liked enjoy / enjoys / enjoyed can't / couldn't stand hate / hates / hated is (are) / was (were) good at	VERBing	... to discos. ... to film music. ... silent movies. ... to the theatre. ... to bagpipes. ... Shakespeare's plays.

5 Entertainment talk

G 9/10

Work with a partner and take turns. Ask and answer lots of questions about the theatre, plays, films, music, people in show business and so on. Here are some ideas:

Have you ...

1. ... been to a theatre in the last few months?
2. ... seen a silent movie in the last few years?
3. ... heard of William Shakespeare?
4. ... ever been on stage?
5. ... ever been to an open-air concert?
6. ... seen the latest Star Trek film yet?
7. ... ever been to a musical?
8. ... ever met an actor or an actress?

Example: 1. Have you been to a theatre in the last few months?
No, I haven't been to a theatre **since** I was ten.
Or: No, I haven't been to a theatre **for** two years.
Or: Yes, I have. I went to see 'Romeo and Juliet' two weeks **ago**.

SAVE

present perfect

Use 'since' for a fixed time:
... since my last birthday.
... since Christmas.
... since February.

Use 'for' to say how long it has been:
... for three months.
... for six hours.
... for four weeks.

present perfect	**simple past**
just over *just done it* *just finished* ⇓ since – for ever – never	*all over now* ⇓ ... ago adverbs of past time

6 Small talk

G 9/10

Use the right verb forms to complete these sentences.

These are the new scenes for our school play. Our teacher (write) them in the summer holidays.

I (hear) a lot about Shakespeare, but I (never see) his plays.

I'd like to be on stage again. I (act) in a play for two years.

Two weeks ago we (see) a musical.

They (show) four western films on TV since Sunday.

Last summer we (go) to a film museum.

In the early days lots of European film-makers (go) to California.

I know a lot about pop stars but I (never meet) one.

Night at The Oscars

Emily Moore finds out how the Oscar awards began and what they mean for films and their stars.

Every year in March the biggest movie event of the year, the Oscar ceremony, takes place in Hollywood, in the United States. Over a billion people in more than 100 countries watch it on television.

When were the first films?
The two brothers Auguste and Louis Lumière showed the first cinema film in Paris in 1895. Their ten short films were silent and in black and white. People have been interested in picture shows for a very long time. Shadow puppet plays were known in places such as Java, China and India as far back as 3,000 years ago.

Why has Hollywood become so important?
From 1910 on, many European film-makers went to California and set up the film industry in a small town called Hollywood near Los Angeles. Film-makers needed a lot of sunshine, space and a varied landscape – California was the perfect location.

What are 'The Oscars'?
It is the awards ceremony that The Academy of Motion Pictures Arts and Sciences holds to reward outstanding achievements in film. It all started in the year 1927 when people in the Hollywood movie business set up The Academy. The first ceremony was in 1928. There are now many categories: Best Actor / Actress, Best Picture, Costume, Documentary, Make-Up, Music, Sound, Visual Effects, and so on. The Academy can nominate the same film for any number of awards – for example, it nominated the film 'Titanic' for 14.

How do you get an Oscar?
Over 5,000 members of The Academy, people in the movie business, nominate and vote for the winners. But no one knows who the winners are until they open the envelopes on stage (with lots of famous people in the audience).

What does getting an Oscar mean?
One thing it does mean is money. A nominated film can increase its takings at cinemas by £25 million, and a film that wins can double that!

Does everyone love Oscars?
No. The director Woody Allen has never attended the Oscar ceremony – even though they nominated him for an Oscar over a dozen times. He said: "I have no regard for that kind of ceremony. When you see who wins those things or doesn't, you also see how meaningless this Oscar business is."
Some of the most talented people in film history who never received an Oscar were Charlie Chaplin, Alfred Hitchcock, Greta Garbo, and Cary Grant.
And did you know? The Oscar record-holder is the American film 'Ben Hur'. It won 11 Oscars in 1959.

An Oscar is a statuette just 34 cm tall. It weighs nearly 4 kg.

How did Oscars get their name?
The official name for the statuettes is The Academy Award of Merit. 'Oscar' is a nickname. When Margaret Herrick, the librarian for The Academy, noticed the statue looked just like her Uncle Oscar, the nickname stuck!

Adapted from *Guardian Education*, 4/6/1996

1 What we know now

a) *Complete these sentences.*

1. The first short cinema films were …
2. Hollywood was a perfect place for the European film-makers because …
3. In 1927 people in the movie business …
4. The Oscar record-holder is the film 'Ben Hur' because …

b) *Match the parts of the sentences.*

1. People have been interested in picture shows
2. From 1910 on, many European film-makers
3. The awards ceremony started
4. No one knows who the winners are
5. A film that wins an Oscar

- until they open the envelopes on stage.
- for a very long time.
- can double its takings at cinemas.
- went to California.
- when people set up the Academy in 1927.

2 A film mind map

a) *Complete this mind map. Make a big poster for your classroom.*
b) *Make another mind map about 'the theatre' or 'open-air concerts'.*

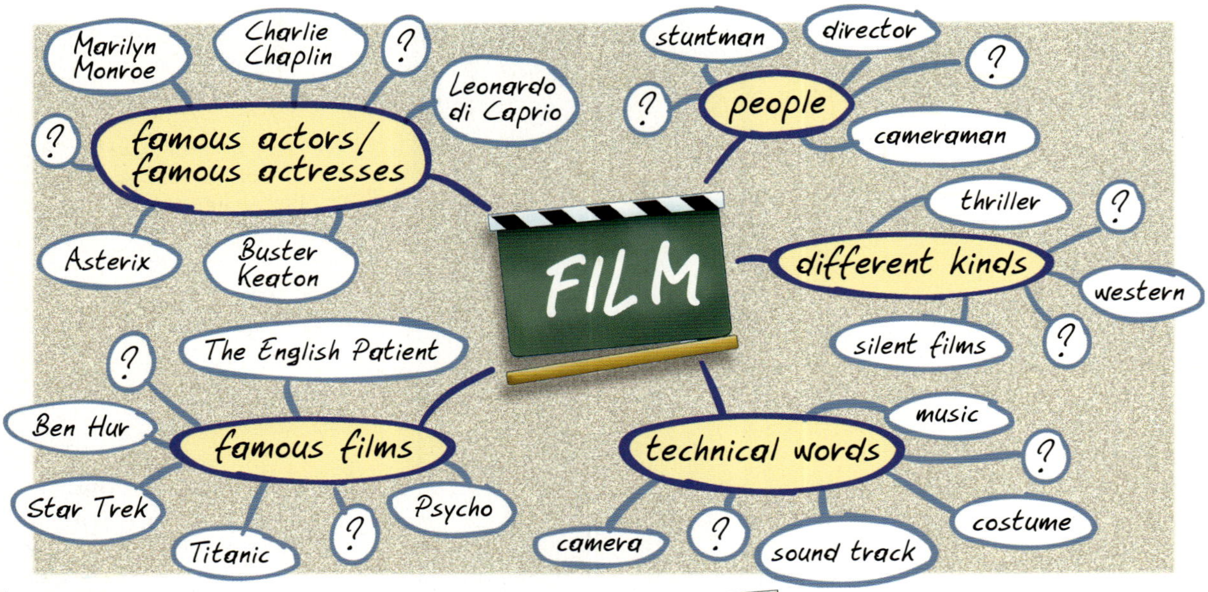

G 11

3 Question tags

a) *Put in the right question tags.*

1. Charlie Chaplin was an actor in silent films, …
2. Stuntmen do the stunts, …
3. There is no famous song in 'Psycho', …
4. 'Ben Hur' got 14 Oscars, …
5. Silent movies didn't have a sound track, …
6. Asterix and Obelix were good friends, …
7. Alfred Hitchcock wasn't American, …

… is there? … was he? … weren't they? … wasn't he? … don't they? … didn't it? … did they?

b) *Look at the article on page 29 again and work out a dialogue about the Oscars. Use question tags.*

SAVE

question tags

+	–
It's a lovely day,	isn't it?
They live in Stuttgart,	don't they?
You can come,	can't you?
I'm your best friend,	aren't I?
He was late,	wasn't he?
–	**+**
You aren't 16 yet,	are you?
I'm not in this group,	am I?
It doesn't help you,	does it?
He hasn't seen it,	has he?
They didn't enjoy it,	did they?

When you say something with a question tag, you hope the other person agrees. Your voice goes down at the end of the tag.

YOU

4 Your nominations

a) *Write down your 'nomination(s)' for your favourite movie(s). Think of:* best picture – best actor / actress – best supporting actor / actress – best director – best song – best visual effects – best music – best make-up – …

b) *Compare your nominations with the others in your class. Make a list starting with the best.*

1 Sound groups

LEARNING TO LEARN

a) *Add as many words as you can to go with the different sound groups.*

b) *Try to make some more sound groups with these sounds:*

[ɪ] [aɪ] [eɪ]

[ɑː] [ʌ] [ʊ]

[əʊ] [eə] [ʊə]

[ɜː]: turn, learn, work, ?, her, girl

[uː]: school, two, you, ?, blue, shoe

[ɔː]: August, storm, awful, four, walk, warm

[iː]: beach, three, people, ?, piece, he

[e]: weather, bed, again, friend, guest, says

[i]: volleyball, money, lady, anyone, assembly, many

2 Got it all wrong

a) *Imagine you are producing western films. Your cameraman is just getting ready for an important scene. You stop him and shout:*

"Stop! The ... is wrong!"

"There were no ... in the early days!"

"They didn't have any ... at that time!"

"Stupid! Have you ever ... of a western with ... ?"

b) *Look at the picture on the right. What else would be wrong in a western film?*

3 Whose are they?

R

G 12

Example: Picture No. 1 shows Michael Jackson's jacket.

Michael Jackson	shoes
Charlie Chaplin	teeth
King Kong	hand
Mr Bean	play
Shakespeare	jacket
Mr Spock	sword
Obelix	ears
Dracula	face
King Arthur	trousers

G 12

4 What can you hear?

Put your head on your arms, relax and close your eyes. You are watching a film now. Say what you can hear.

Example: In a film set in a city I can hear the voices of children.

In a	film set in a city western film horror film film set on a farm …	I can hear	the voices the sound the noise	of	children women men sheep horses a banjo buses …

5 ⟨Song: I'm every woman⟩ by Whitney Houston

Intro[1]
Whatever you want,
Whatever you need,
Anything you want done, baby,
I'll do it naturally
'Cause I'm every woman
It's all in me.
It's all in me, yeah!

Chorus[2] *1*
I'm every woman,
It's all in me.
Anything you want done, baby,
I'll do it naturally.

Chorus 2
I'm every woman,
It's all in me.
I can read your thoughts[3] right now,
Every one from A to Z.

Verse[4] *1*
I can cast a spell[5],
Of secrets[6] you can tell,
Mix[7] a special brew[8],
Put fire inside of you.
Anytime you feel danger or fear[9],
Then instantly[10]
I will appear[11] 'cause …

(Chorus 1)

Verse 2
I can sense[12] your needs[13]
Like rain unto[14] the seeds[15]
I can make a rhyme[16]
Of confusion[17] in your mind.
And when it comes back to
some good old-fashioned[18] love,
I've got it, I've got it, I've got it,
got it, baby, 'cause …

(Chorus 1)
(Chorus 2)

Bridge
I ain't[19] braggin'[20] 'cause I am the one
You just ask me, oh, it shall[21] be done.
And don't bother to compare[22],
I've got it.

Ad lib[23]
I'm every woman …

[1]['ɪntrəʊ] *Einleitung* [2]['kɔ:rəs] *Refrain* [3][θɔ:t] *Gedanke* [4][vɜ:s] *Strophe* [5][ˌkɑ:st‿ə 'spel] *(jmdn) verhexen* [6]['si:krət] *Geheimnis* [7][mɪks] *mischen* [8][bru:] *Gebräu* [9][fɪə] *Angst* [10]['ɪnstəntli] *unmittelbar, sofort* [11][ə'pɪə] *auftauchen* [12][sens] *spüren* [13][ni:d] *Bedürfnis* [14]['ʌntu:] *auf* [15][si:d] *Samen* [16][raɪm] *Reim* [17][kən'fju:ʒn] *Verwirrung* [18][ˌəʊld'fæʃnd] *altmodisch* [19][aɪ 'eɪnt] = I am not [20][bræg] *angeben* [21][ɪt 'ʃæl] *es wird* [22][kəm'peə] *vergleichen* [23][ˌæd 'lɪb] *nach Belieben*

Did you know? The National Academy of Recording Arts and Sciences gives Grammy Awards each year for the best in popular music. The best record in 1994: Whitney Houston, *I will always love you.* The best album in 1994: Whitney Houston, *The Bodyguard.* The best in 2004? …

To find the lyrics of Whitney Houston's songs, go to Whitney Houston's homepage in the Internet.

1 A parcel for the Troublemakers

a) The Troublemakers would like to go on a picnic at the weekend. "But we can't just sit around all the time when we're out in the country. Have you got any ideas, children?" "Yes, I know what," said Henry. "I'm going to …" And Mary said: … *Look at the pictures. What are the Troublemakers going to do out in the country? And what about Megan?*

b) "And I'm going to take Uncle Ron's letter with me," said Mr Troublemaker. "I must write to him." At ten o'clock they were ready. Mrs Troublemaker wanted to be sure that they had everything with them, so she asked some questions:

Have	we you	checked brought down forgotten got packed	anything? my camera? your magazines? our food? the car? our coats? Megan's food?

c) *Put in the verbs in the simple past.*

The Troublemakers … out into the country. At about twelve o'clock they … a lovely field, so they … there. The Troublemakers … hungry and thirsty. They … all their things out of the car and … to eat and drink. Megan … happy too. She … to run after some sheep, but Mary … her. Later in the afternoon the weather … bad. There … dark clouds and then, suddenly, a thunderstorm. So they … up the most important things and … back home.

to drive (2x)	to find
to stop	to be (3x)
to get (2x)	to begin
to start	to call
to pick	

d) Two days later Mrs Troublemaker [wɒz] at home with their  when she [hɜ:d] the 

. She [went] to the  . "A parcel for you," said the postman. Mrs Troublemaker [tʊk] it into the kitchen and ['əʊpənd] it. What a shock! In the parcel there [wɜ:] two empty  and Mary's  and a box with wet  . And also Uncle Ron's  with their address on the envelope. And there [wɒz] another  to the Troublemakers.

Sunday evening

Dear Mr and Mrs Troublemaker,

I hope that you had a nice time in my field. Do you always leave so many things behind you? I have collected them all and I am sending them to you. Now you can put them in the right place.
My fields are not for people. They are for my sheep. Your rubbish is not good for them. Perhaps you can remember that. And remember that my sheep are afraid of dogs.
Yours sincerely,
John Graham
John Graham (Farmer)

YOU e) *What can you, must you and mustn't you do in the country?*

The hitchhiker

Urban legends are unusual stories – perhaps they happened, maybe they didn't. They are very popular all over the United States and Canada. The story on the right is told as a poem. It takes place somewhere in North Carolina.

At 12.04
On a cold dark night
My headlights[1] stabbed[2] the rain;
A girl stood sadly[3] thumbing a ride[4]
With a look of fear[5] and pain[6].

She was white, she was silent, she was eerie[7]
Her body[8] shook[9] with cold
Her eyes stared[10] unmoving[11] and
I gave her my jacket to hold[12].

We reached her house in the pouring[13] rain
Where she turned and whispered[14],
"Thanks again."
"Keep the coat," I softly[15] said,
"I'll get it back tomorrow."
"Thanks," she smiled and lifted[16] her head
But her eyes were filled with sorrow[17].

Next day at her house
Empty[18] and bare[19]
A mysterious[20] old lady
Gave me a scare[21]
Whispering
"There's no girl here, not any more
She died last year at 12.04.
It was a cold rainy night
On the night that she died.
She was hitching a ride[22] with a boy at her side.
And now every night she continues[23] to roam[24]
Searching[25] for him and a way to get home."

My jacket turned up
On a white headstone[26]
And I stared at the photo
Of the girl so alone[27].
I knew it was her
With her dark dark eyes
And I thought I could hear
Her soft soft sighs[28].

And now every night
At 12.04
I drive in the rain as I did before
And pick up the girl so sad and alone
And hope that tonight we can both get home.

1 What they do

a) *What can you say about the narrator? Start like this:* He or she is the driver of the car. The driver saw a girl thumbing a ride. He or she stopped the car and ... Then ... After that ...

b) *Now describe what happened to the girl:* She was thumbing a ride. She got into the car. There she ... Then ...

c) *Write out the lines which hint that the girl is a ghostly figure.*

2 Some more questions

1. What do you think the driver feels when he or she sees the photo of the hitchhiker on the headstone?
2. How does the last line change the whole story?
3. Write down the rhyming words in pairs.
4. What effect does the use of direct speech have on the poem?

[1]['hedlaɪt] *Scheinwerfer* [2][stæb] *(ein)stechen* [3]['sædli] *traurig* [4][ˌθʌm‿ə 'raɪd] *per Anhalter fahren* [5][fɪə] *Angst* [6][peɪn] *Kummer* [7]['ɪəri] *gespenstig* [8]['bɒdi] *Körper* [9][ʃeɪk] *schütteln* [10][steə] *starren* [11][ʌn'mu:vɪŋ] *regungslos* [12][həʊld] *halten* [13][pɔ:] *gießen, schütten* [14]['wɪspə] *flüstern* [15]['sɒftli] *sanft* [16][lɪft] *(an)heben* [17]['sɒrəʊ] *Kummer* [18]['emti] *leer* [19][beə] *kahl* [20][mɪ'stɪəriəs] *mysteriös, geheimnisvoll* [21][skeə] *Schreck, Angst* [22][ˌhɪtʃ‿ə 'raɪd] *per Anhalter fahren* [23][kən'tɪnju:] *weitermachen* [24][rəʊm] *herumwandern* [25][sɜ:tʃ] *suchen* [26]['hedstəʊn] *Grabstein* [27][ə'ləʊn] *allein* [28][saɪ] *Seufzer*

1 How long has it been?

Example: When did you last see a thriller?
I haven't seen a thriller for three weeks. *Or:* I haven't seen a thriller since August.

see a thriller — buy a video — receive a reward — ? — play tennis
go to the cinema — dance in a disco — ? — watch a video clip
? — perform a play on stage — hear some film music — ?

2 Have you ever ... ?

a) *Match the questions and answers.*

1. Have you ever played a didgeridoo?
2. Has your brother finished the video game?
3. Have you been to the new cinema centre?
4. Have your friends brought back my CDs?
5. Has your father watched our video?
6. Has the teacher checked your homework?

a) Yes, he watched it yesterday evening.
b) Oh, sorry! They've forgotten them.
c) Yes, I played one two years ago.
d) Yes, she checked it yesterday.
e) No, he hasn't finished it yet.
f) Yes, we went there last week.

b) *Now make the same questions with question tags. Start:* You've played a didgeridoo, ...

WP

3 More words

How many more words can you add to these groups?

1. thriller, science fiction, western, ...
2. The Beatles, The Rolling Stones, Whitney Houston, ...
3. Charlie Chaplin, Marilyn Monroe, Leonardo di Caprio, ...
4. soft rock, reggae, blues, ...
5. director, actor, singer, ...
6. keyboard, cello, guitar, ...

4 There's no business like show business

Put in 'of' or people's names.

1. Romeo and Juliet is the title ... a play.
2. They perform ... plays at the Globe Theatre.
3. 400 years ago boys had to play the ... parts.
4. The star actors in ... time were like the pop stars ... today.
5. In our time the Oscar ceremony is the biggest movie event ... the year.
6. Mr Bean films are ... favourites.
7. But not everyone likes ... kind of humour.

G 13

5 Word pairs

Find the singular and plural pairs and write them down.

life	child	price	comedy
stage	scarf	boy	actress
woman	sheep	man	play
cameraman	glass	knife	milk
foot	hobby	watch	roof

men	roofs	lives	children
milk	hobbies	watches	stages
cameramen	actresses	comedies	knives
prices	feet	hobbies	sheep
scarves	glasses	women	plays

2

CHECK-IN

	silent ['saɪlənt]	still, stumm
	would play [ˌwʊd/wəd 'pleɪ]	spielte gewöhnlich
	screen [skri:n]	Leinwand
	Oscar ['ɒskə]	*amerikanischer Filmpreis*
	award [ə'wɔ:d]	Preis, Auszeichnung
1	**itself** [ɪt'self]	(es) selbst, sich
	Whitney Houston [ˌwɪtni 'hju:stn]	*amerikanische Sängerin*
2	**didgeridoo** [ˌdɪdʒri'du:]	Didgeridoo *(australisches Blasinstrument)*
	harmonica [hɑ:'mɒnɪkə]	Mundharmonika
	bagpipes ['bægpaɪps]	Dudelsack
3	**setting** ['setɪŋ]	Schauplatz, Umgebung
	Spain [speɪn]	Spanien
	Paris ['pærɪs]	*Hauptstadt von Frankreich*
	New Orleans [ˌnju: 'ɔ:liənz]	*Hafenstadt in Louisiana, USA*
	William Shakespeare [ˌwɪljəm 'ʃeɪkspɪə]	*berühmter englischer Dichter (1564-1616)*
	Leonardo di Caprio [ˌli:ə'nɑ:dəʊ dɪ 'kæpriəʊ]	*amerikanischer Schauspieler*
	to **be set in** ['set‿ɪn]	in ... spielen
	Los Angeles [lɒs‿'ændʒɪli:z]	*Hafenstadt in Kalifornien, USA*

STEP A

	part [pa:t]	*hier:* Rolle
	large [lɑ:dʒ]	groß, weitläufig
	circle ['sɜ:kl]	Kreis
	seat [si:t]	Sitz(platz)
	rich [rɪtʃ]	reich
	audience ['ɔ:diəns]	Publikum, Zuhörer
	to **get bored** [bɔ:d]	sich langweilen
	to **get** [get]	werden
	themselves [ðəm'selvz]	sich, (sie) selbst
	unfortunately [ʌn'fɔ:tʃnətli]	unglücklicherweise, leider
	idea [aɪ'dɪə]	*hier:* Eindruck, Vorstellung
	to **go on** [gəʊ‿'ʌn]	vorgehen
	ago [ə'gəʊ]	vor *(zeitlich)*
	for [fɔ:]	seit
	almost ['ɔ:lməʊst]	fast, beinahe
	to **perform** [pə'fɔ:m]	aufführen, vorführen
	New Globe Theatre [ˌnju: 'gləʊb 'θɪətə]	*Shakespeare-Theater in London (eröffnet 1997)*
1	**worker** ['wɜ:kə]	Arbeiter(in)
	Red Cross [ˌred 'krɒs]	(das) Rote Kreuz
	fireman ['faɪəmən]	Feuerwehrmann
	authority [ɔ:'θɒrəti]	*hier:* Amt, Behörde
	fire engine ['faɪə‿ˌendʒɪn]	Feuerwehrauto
	equipment [ɪ'kwɪpmənt]	Ausrüstung, Ausstattung
	bottle bank ['bɒtl ˌbæŋk]	Altglascontainer
	sign [saɪn]	Schild, Zeichen
	first aid [ˌfɜ:st‿'eɪd]	Erste Hilfe
3	**record player** ['rekɔ:d ˌpleɪə]	(Schall-)Plattenspieler
5	to **enjoy** [ɪn'dʒɔɪ]	genießen, mögen
	month [mʌntθ]	Monat

franz silencieux *lat* silens
engl silent

The Oscar, the Emmy and the Grammy are awards.

The famous actors in a film are often more important than the film itself.

The didgeridoo is to Australia as the bagpipes are to ...?

Didgeridoos, harmonicas and bagpipes are musical instruments.

to set ⟷ setting

franz cercle *lat* circes
engl circle

franz audience *lat* audiens
engl audience

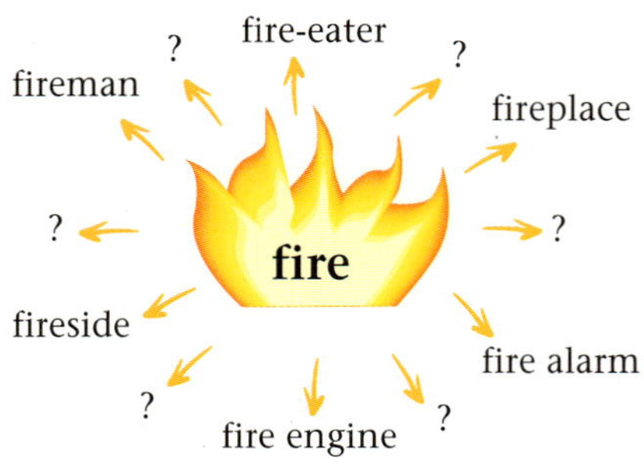

– Where is the nearest bottle bank?
– I don't know. Ask the authorities.

You play records on your record player, and you play CDs on your CD player.

actress ['æktrəs]	Schauspielerin	The euro is European money.
European [ˌjʊərə'pi:ən]	europäisch	
California [ˌkælɪ'fɔ:niə]	*amerikanischer Bundesstaat*	California is called 'the sunshine state'.

STEP B

to **take place** [ˌteɪk 'pleɪs]	stattfinden	In the evening the shadows become longer and longer.
Hollywood ['hɒliwʊd]	*Stadtteil von Los Angeles*	
television ['telɪvɪʒn]	Fernsehen	
shadow ['ʃædəʊ]	Schatten	
puppet ['pʌpɪt]	(Hand-)Puppe, Marionette	Hollywood is the favourite location for motion pictures.
Java ['dʒɑ:və]	*Insel in Indonesien*	
China ['tʃaɪnə]	China	
from ... on [frəm ... 'ɒn]	ab ... *(zeitl.)*	
to **be called** [kɔ:ld]	genannt werden; heißen	
space [speɪs]	Raum	The Oscar rewards outstanding achievements.
varied ['veərɪd]	verschieden(artig), unterschiedlich	
location [ləʊ'keɪʃn]	Standort, (Dreh-)Ort	They voted for the supporting actress.
motion picture ['məʊʃn ˌpɪktʃə]	Film (*wörtl.:* Bewegungsbild)	
art [ɑ:t]	Kunst	
science ['saɪənts]	Wissenschaft	Did you attend that performance?
to **reward** [rɪ'wɔ:d]	belohnen, auszeichnen	
outstanding [ˌaʊt'stændɪŋ]	hervorragend, überragend	
achievement [ə'tʃi:vmənt]	Leistung, Errungenschaft	
visual effects [ˌvɪʒuəl ɪ'fekts]	(optische) Tricks	They need a dozen actresses for this play.
to **vote** [vəʊt]	wählen	
envelope ['envələʊp]	(Brief-)Umschlag	
to **increase** [ɪn'kri:s]	(an)steigen, zunehmen	
takings *pl.* ['teɪkɪŋz]	Einnahmen	
to **double** ['dʌbl]	(sich) verdoppeln	
to **attend** [ə'tend]	beiwohnen, besuchen	*franz* mérite *lat* meritum *engl* merit
though [ðəʊ]	obwohl, obgleich	
dozen ['dʌzn]	Dutzend	
regard [rɪ'gɑ:d]	(Hoch-)Achtung, Wertschätzung	
meaningless ['mi:nɪŋləs]	sinnlos, bedeutungslos	I'm Jonathan, but they call me Jack – that's my nickname.
to **receive** [rɪ'si:v]	erhalten, empfangen	
merit ['merɪt]	Verdienst, Leistung	
nickname ['nɪkneɪm]	Spitzname	
librarian [laɪ'breəriən]	Bibliothekar(in)	
to **notice** ['nəʊtɪs]	bemerken, wahrnehmen	
4 **supporting actor** [səˌpɔ:tɪŋ‿'æktə]	Schauspieler in einer Nebenrolle	

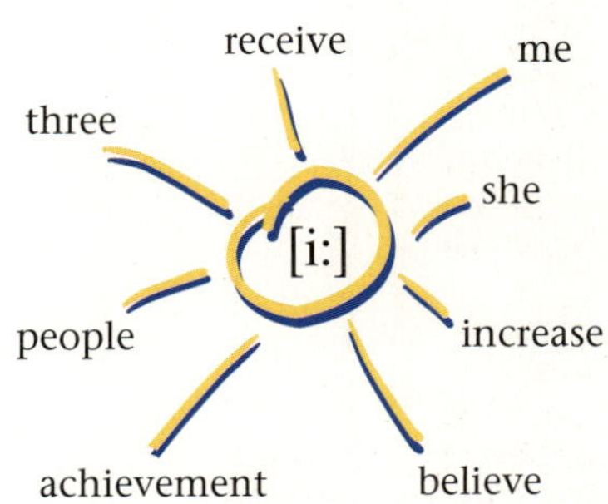

STEP C

2 **stupid** ['stju:pɪd]	Dummkopf, Blödmann	
3 **tooth**, *pl.* **teeth** [tu:θ, ti:θ]	Zahn, Zähne	
ear [ɪə]	Ohr	
sword [sɔ:d]	Schwert	
4 **eye** [aɪ]	Auge	
⟨5⟩ **Grammy** ['græmi]	*amerikanischer Musikpreis*	*franz* stupide *lat* stupidus *engl* stupid
lyrics *pl.* ['lɪrɪks]	(Lied-)Text	

2

2

TRACK 1

1	in **the country** ['kʌntri]	auf dem Lande
	parcel ['pɑ:sl]	Paket, Päckchen
	to **be thirsty** ['θɜ:sti]	Durst haben
	cloud [klaʊd]	Wolke
	thunderstorm ['θʌndəˌstɔ:m]	Gewitter
	empty ['emti]	leer
	to **leave (behind)** [ˌli:v bɪ'haɪnd]	zurück, -hinterlassen
	Yours sincerely, [ˌjɔ:z sɪn'sɪəli]	Mit freundlichen Grüßen *(Briefschluss)*

weather words

wind, windy, sun, sunny, rain, rainy, cloud, cloudy, fog, foggy, thunderstorm, storm, …

TRACK 2

	+**hitchhiker** ['hɪtʃhaɪkə]	Anhalter(in), Tramper(in)
	+**urban** ['ɜ:bn]	städtisch
	+**unusual** [ʌn'ju:ʒl]	ungewöhnlich
	+**Canada** ['kænədə]	Kanada
	+**North Carolina** [ˌnɔ:θ kærə'laɪnə]	*amerikanischer Bundesstaat*
1	+**narrator** [nə'reɪtə]	Erzähler(in)
	+**to thumb a ride** [ˌθʌm‿ə 'raɪd]	per Anhalter fahren, trampen
	+to **hint** [hɪnt]	andeuten, anspielen (auf)
2	+**headstone** ['hedstəʊn]	Grabstein

jobs with -or / -er

narrator	teacher
mayor	driver
author	farmer
actor	smuggler
…	…

COGNATE WORDS

academy [ə'kædəmi]	Akademie
accordion [ə'kɔ:diən]	Akkordeon
⟨**album**⟩ ['ælbəm]	Album
banjo ['bændʒəʊ]	Banjo
billion ['bɪliən]	Billion, Milliarde *(AE)*
blues [blu:z]	Blues *(Musikrichtung)*
bodyguard ['bɒdigɑ:d]	Leibwache
to **boo** [bu:]	auspfeifen, -buhen
business ['bɪznɪs]	Geschäft
cameraman ['kæmrəmæn]	Kameramann
category ['kætəgri]	Kategorie, Klasse
ceremony ['serɪməni]	Zeremonie, Feierlichkeit
comedy ['kɒmədi]	Komödie
company ['kʌmpəni]	Gesellschaft, Firma
container [kən'teɪnə]	Behälter, Container
director [dɪ'rektə]	Regisseur(in)
documentary [ˌdɒkjə'mentri]	Dokumentarfilm
drama ['drɑ:mə]	Drama
electrician [ˌelɪk'trɪʃn]	Elektriker(in)
emotion [ɪ'məʊʃn]	Gefühl, Emotion
entertainer [ˌentə'teɪnə]	Unterhaltungskünstler(in)
expert ['ekspɜ:t]	Experte / Expertin
farmer ['fɑ:mə]	Landwirt(in), Bauer / Bäuerin
+**figure** ['fɪgə]	Gestalt, Figur
film-maker ['fɪlmˌmeɪkə]	Filmemacher(in)
hip hop ['hɪpˌhɒp]	Hip-hop *(Musikrichtung)*
hit [hɪt]	Hit, Schlager
horror ['hɒrə]	Entsetzen, Horror
humour ['hju:mə]	Humor
industry ['ɪndəstri]	Industrie
to **inform** [ɪn'fɔ:m]	informieren, benachrichtigen
to **install** [ɪn'stɔ:l]	installieren, einbauen
make-up ['meɪkʌp]	Makeup, Maske
media ['mi:diə]	Medien

⟨**national**⟩ ['næʃnl]	staatlich, national
to **nominate** [ˌnɒmɪneɪt]	nominieren, ernennen
nomination [ˌnɒmɪ'neɪʃn]	Nominierung, Ernennung
open-air [ˌəʊpn'eə]	im Freien, Freiluft-
original [ə'rɪdʒnl]	original, ursprünglich
patient ['peɪʃnt]	Patient(in)
piano [pi'ænəʊ]	Klavier
to **position** [pə'zɪʃn]	aufstellen, in Position bringen
postman ['pəʊstmən]	Briefträger(in), Postbote / -botin
reconstruction [ˌri:kən'strʌkʃn]	Wiederherstellung, Rekonstruktion
record-holder ['rekɔ:d ˌhəʊldə]	Rekordhalter(in)
+to **rhyme** [raɪm]	(sich) reimen
rock'n'roll [ˌrɒkn'rəʊl]	Rock 'n' Roll *(Musikrichtung)*
soft rock ['sɒft ˌrɒk]	Softrock *(Musikrichtung)*
star [stɑ:]	Star
statuette [ˌstætju'et]	Statuette
stunt [stʌnt]	Kunststück
stuntman ['stʌntmən]	Stuntman, Double
talented ['tæləntɪd]	begabt, talentiert
talk show ['tɔ:k ˌʃəʊ]	Talkshow, Gesprächsrunde
technical ['teknɪkl]	technisch
techno ['teknəʊ]	Techno *(Musikrichtung)*
the 60s ['sɪkstiz]	die Sechziger (Jahre)
thriller ['θrɪlə]	Thriller, spannender Film
trumpet ['trʌmpɪt]	Trompete
version ['vɜ:ʃn]	Version
video clip ['vɪdiəʊ ˌklɪp]	Videoclip
violin [ˌvaɪə'lɪn]	Geige, Violine
western ['westən]	Western
winner ['wɪnə]	Gewinner(in)

Stress and grammar

You should know these words. They are nouns. The stress is on the first syllable. Read them out aloud.

– •	• –
record	to record
subject	to subject
protest	to protest
transport	to transport
present	to present
project	to project

You don't know (but can learn) these words. They are verbs. The stress is on the second syllable. Read them out aloud too.

Tricky pairs: [s] or [z] ?

The words written in phonetics mean different things. It is important that they sound different too. *Read the sentences out aloud. Then copy them into your exercise book.*

Example: She thinks a lot of things.

1. She [θɪŋks] a lot of [θɪŋz].
2. He [pleɪz] music at his [pleɪs].
3. What's the [praɪs] if you want to win a [praɪz]?
4. There's one more [saɪt] on this [saɪd] of the river.
5. In Germany you must [raɪd] your bike on the [raɪt].
6. He [rəʊt] the word 'children' on the [rəʊd].
7. We [bɔ:t] lots of things, but then we were [bɔ:d].
8. They wanted to [hɪt] him and so he [hɪd] behind a car.

UNIT 3

Discover Britain

3

Devon & Cornwall - enriching, enchanting and so very different.

Devon and Cornwall, part of a mystic Celtic peninsula, are steeped in myth and legend and offer miles of rugged coastline, wild expanses of open countryside, and over one million years of heritage. Explore our romantic heritage coast and hundreds of sandy beaches, bays and secret smuggler's coves and experience the unique autumnal colours of the National Parks of Dartmoor and Exmoor. Wander through miles of lush, rolling green countryside, stopping in one of the many medieval market towns and historic cathedral cities for a refreshing pint of traditionally brewed cider and some speciality shopping for antiques, crafts and local produce. Discover historic houses and castles, magnificent cathedrals, ancient fishing villages and spectacular subtropical gardens,or see Tintagel, birthplace of the legendary King Arthur.

1 The 'Celtic fringe'

a) *Look at the brochures on the left, and find out what parts of Britain they are about.*

b) *Check the map: Are these areas part of England, or do they have borders with England?*

c) *Look up what the word 'fringe' means. Then say if you think it is a good word for these parts of Britain.*

d) Some parts of these areas are poor, and there are not many big cities. So the people there want more tourists – all the year round. *Look at the brochures again. How do they make these places look and sound interesting for tourists?*

e) You don't need to understand all the words. In fact, some are not English! *Find them (but don't try to say them – the rules are different from English!). What languages do you think they are?*

2 How to get there

The Cliftons in London know a lot of people in these parts of Britain. Tessa's mother is from Scotland (see Unit 1, Step C), her best friend has just moved to Cornwall, etc. *Imagine how they travel when they want to visit them. You can find out about the main roads, motorways, and airports on the map at the front of your book.*
And on the right you can see where the fast trains go. (There are other, slower trains, but the Cliftons don't want to use them.) Work in groups, and talk about the best way to visit:

1. a grandmother near Loch Ness (north end), and an uncle in Aberdeen,
2. two aunts in Wales, one in Cardiff and one in Swansea,
3. another uncle in Dublin (Ireland isn't part of Britain, but it's Celtic too!),
4. Liz and Liam in Penryn, Cornwall.

train	car	bus	(not) as ... as ...
plane	ferry	taxi	the only way
fast	slow	safe	safer/... than ...
expensive		cheap	the fastest/... way

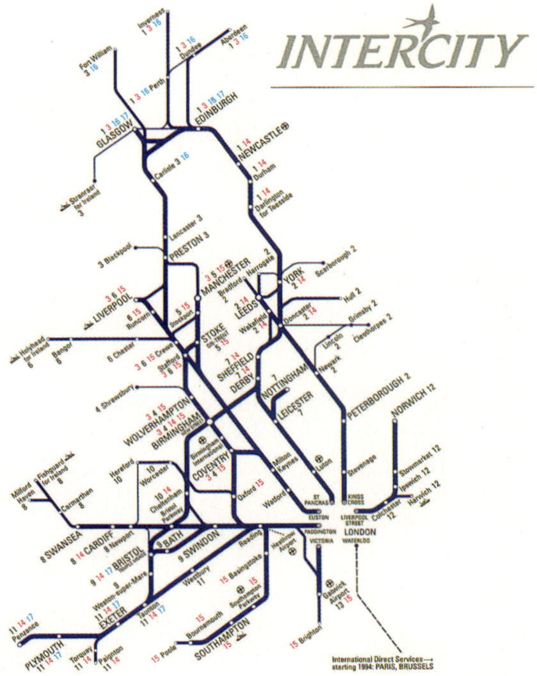

3 More interesting places

The Cliftons would also like to visit these places some time. Maybe they can go there on one of their journeys to their many aunts, uncles, friends, etc.? *Find out where these famous places are on the map, and then work out a possible route for each of them.*

History lessons

Liz: You know what, Liam? We're Celts – real Celts! You see, Mum is Cornish, and Dad's from Ireland, so we must be ...

Liam: Do you really believe that? I think that's stupid nonsense. The Celts lived a long time ago. Anyway, you usually say you're a Londoner. It's your usual answer when anyone calls you a country girl!

Liz: Now you're talking stupidly.

Liam: No, I'm not!

Liz: Yes, you are! It's a really stupid thing to say. I haven't said that for a long time. Not since ...

Liam: Not since that new History teacher came? That awful Mr Evans! Is it possible ... ?

Liz: He's not awful – I think he's awfully nice!

Liam: Yeah, and suddenly you're interested in Celtic history! Well, now we can easily explain the sudden change!

Liz: Oh, you're awful! Mr Evans is a good teacher. He teaches very well, and explains things clearly.

Liam: He speaks too fast.

Liz: So what if he is a fast speaker! That's possibly because he's so interested in his subject. Anyway, what I said first is right: We *are* Celtic – even you've got a Celtic name. 'Liam' is Gaelic for 'William'.

Liam: Hah! Why don't you listen to your Mr Evans? Even he says the Celts were Celtic-speaking people! We don't speak Celtic!

Liz: Kernow bys vykan!

Liam: Huh? Can't you speak clearly?

Liz: That *was* clear – it's Cornish! It means 'Cornwall for ever!' Don't forget I went to Ms Trelawne's Cornish classes last summer! It's a lovely language, and it's easy – for us Celts, I mean!

G 14

1 What are adverbs for?

Adjectives give you more information about something or somebody:

real Celts — her usual answer

Adverbs give you a different kind of information.

a) *Look at the adverbs with -ly in this dialogue (there are eight). What words in the sentences do they give you more information about?*

b) Not all words with -ly are adverbs. There is one adjective with -ly in the dialogue. *Can you find it? How can you tell it is not an adverb?*

c) A few adverbs are irregular – you form them irregularly. *Find the adverbs of 'good' and 'fast' in the dialogue, and add them to your* SAVE *list. And these: hard, late, early – they are adjectives* <u>*and*</u> *adverbs!*

SAVE

adjective	*adverb*
real	really
usual	usually
stupid	stupidly
easy	easily
possible	possibly
...	...

G 14

2 How they do it

A lot of adverbs say how you do something.

a) *Read the dialogue again and say:*
- how Mr Evans speaks,
- how he teaches,
- how he explains things.

b) *Work in pairs, and talk about your own teachers (quietly, they may hear you!).*

c) *Work in pairs. Use these words (and any other useful ones in your* SAVE *list) to talk about yourself. How well or* badly *do you do these things?*

sing swim
paint ride run
play tennis
write stories
learn languages

slow / slowly
quick / quickly
careful / carefully
loud / loudly
strong / strongly
happy / happily

Example:
Are you a good singer?
Yes, I can sing quite well. /
No, I sing badly (but loudly).

3 Mr Evans on the Celts

G 14

Put in the adjectives – or their adverb forms.

"We don't know ... (exact) when the first Celts arrived in Britain, but it was an ... (early) arrival, ... (possible) before 1000 BC. They ... (quick) spread over the British Isles. They lived and travelled in ... (small) tribes, but we can divide the tribes into two ... (big) groups: the British Celts and the Gaelic Celts. The British Celts, or Britons, came ... (direct) into the country from the continent of Europe. The Gaelic Celts arrived ... (separate) via a ... (different) route – first into Ireland, and from there into Scotland. Cornish, Welsh and Breton all come from the language of the British Celts, and that is why a Cornish speaker can ... (easy) understand the other two languages. All the Celts were Iron Age people, and they ... (real) how to work with metal. They made ... (beautiful) things with gold and silver, and decorated them ... (beautiful) with colourful stones.

The women wore ... (loose) dresses, and the men wore trousers. Both wore their cloaks ... (loose) over their shoulders, held together with their ... (lovely) gold jewellery. The Celts were also ... (good) farmers, and lived in ... (small) villages with ... (round) houses. And so they lived ... (happy) – until the Romans came in 54 BC. The Romans were just too ... (strong) for them, and ... (easy) destroyed the power of the ... (local) chieftains and Druids. Most Britons then tried to live ... (peaceful) with their Roman rulers. But not Boudicca, the ... (famous) leader of one British tribe."

4 Listening comprehension: Mr Evans again

HV

G 14

"There are some examples of Celtic stone art – in fact they possibly made these stone figures much earlier. But they worked best and most interestingly in metal."

Listen to what Mr Evans said next, to answer these questions:

1. What did Liam ask Mr Evans to do?
2. What did Mr Evans ask Liam to do?
3. Who works the hardest in Mr Evans' class?
4. Why didn't the Celtic King Arthur fight against the Romans?

SAVE

Compare adverbs with added -ly like this:	*But watch these – they have the same comparatives and superlatives as the adjectives:*
slowly more slowly most slowly	well – better – best badly – worse – worst early – earlier – earliest *Also:* fast, hard, late

5 Celts and Romans

G 14

Complete what Liz and Liam are saying, with the right adverb forms. Most – but not all – are comparatives/superlatives.

1. "The Romans fought ... (clever) than the stupid Britons!"
2. "But nobody fought ... (proud) or ... (brave) than Queen Boudicca!"
3. "The Romans built roads ... (good) than anyone else at the time."
4. "Yes, building roads was what the Romans did ... (good) of all. But they didn't work metal as ... (beautiful) as the Celts did. And they didn't tell stories or make music as ... (good) as the Celts!"
5. "You can't ... (possible) know that. But even if they lived ... (happy), they were less civilized before the Romans came."
6. "Well, the Romans never controlled the area north of Hadrian's Wall. So are you saying that Scotland isn't ... (real) civilized?"

1 Before you read

SB

This poem was originally part of the script of a Post Office film. The film tells how a special night train brings the post (the mail) from London to Aberdeen in Scotland, and to all the towns and cities on the way. The famous author spoke his poem for the film.
Before you read, listen to him, but do not try to understand it at first. He reads part of it very fast, like a rap.

2 Understanding the poem

a) *Divide into four different groups. Each group looks for the words and phrases about one thing:*

1. the train and how it moves,
2. what is on the train,
3. senders of letters,
4. places and landscape on the way.

b) *Then get together and tell the other groups what you found.*

c) *Now read the whole poem together.*

3 The good, the bad, and the ugly

G 15

This title of an old film shows that adjectives can become nouns. The poet does this a lot in his poem.

a) *Find as many examples as you can, and say what these forms actually mean.*

Example: the rich (l. 3) = the rich people

b) *Now use some of those forms from the poem to complete these sentences:*

1. ... ... should give more money to ... ...
2. I love looking at ... ... of the sky and ... ... of the clouds.
3. I like it when it's hot, but I hate ... ... in the winter.

What do the words mean in these sentences?

[1]['bi:tək] [2]['greɪdiənt] *Steigung* [3]['kɒtngrɑ:s] *Wollgras* [4]['mɔ:lənd] *Heidemoor(land)* [5]['bəʊldə] *Felsen* [6]['blæŋk͵feɪst] *ausdruckslos; hier: fensterlos, ohne Fenster* [7][͵tɜ:n 'kɔ:s] *Richtung (ver)ändern* [8]['freʃn] *auffrischen* [9][rɪ͵si:tɪd 'bɪl] *quittierte Rechnung* [10][ɪn'spekt ͵nju: 'stɒk] *neue Ware prüfen* [11]['tɪmɪd] *schüchtern* [12][͵sɜ:kəm'stænʃl] *durch die Umstände bedingt* [13]['snæps tə ɪn'lɑ:dʒ] *Schnappschüsse zum Vergrößern*

Night mail

by W. H. Auden

I This is the Night Mail crossing the border,
Bringing the cheque and the postal order,

Letters for the rich, letters for the poor,
The shop at the corner, and the girl next door.

Pulling up Beattock[1], a steady climb:
The gradient's[2] against her, but she's on time.

Past cotton grass[3] and moorland[4] boulder[5],
Shovelling white steam over her shoulder,

Snorting noisily as she passes
Silent miles of wind-bent grasses.

Birds turn their heads as she approaches,
Stare from the bushes at her blank-faced[6] coaches.

Sheepdogs cannot turn her course[7];
They slumber on with paws across.

In the farm she passes no one wakes,
But a jug in a bedroom gently shakes.

II Dawn freshens[8]. Her climb is done.
Down towards Glasgow she descends. (...)
All Scotland waits for her:
In the dark glens, beside the pale green sea lochs,
Men long for news.

III Letters of thanks, letters from banks,
Letters of joy from girl and boy,
Receipted bills[9] and invitations
To inspect new stock[10] or visit relations,
And applications for situations,
And timid[11] lovers' declarations,
And gossip, gossip from all the nations,
News circumstantial[12], news financial,
Letters with holiday snaps to enlarge[13] in,
Letters with faces scrawled in the margin[14],
Letters from uncles, cousins and aunts,
Letters to Scotland from the South of France,
Letters of condolence[15] to Highlands and Lowlands,
Notes from overseas to Hebrides –
Written on paper of every hue[16],
The pink, the violet, the white and the blue,
The chatty[17], the catty[18], the boring, the adoring[19],
The cold and official and the heart's outpouring[20],
Clever, stupid, short and long,
The typed and the printed and the spelt all wrong.

IV Thousands are still asleep,
Dreaming of terrifying monsters
Or a friendly tea beside the band in Cranston's or Crawford's[21]:
Asleep in working Glasgow, asleep in well-set[22] Edinburgh
They continue their dreams;
But shall wake soon and long for letters,
And none will hear the postman's knock
Without a quickening[23] of the heart.
For who can bear to feel himself forgotten?

4 Rhyme and reason

The poem is in four sections.

a) *What is different about each section? Think about:*
- the content (what the section is about),
- the form (rhyme, rhythm, repetition, sounds).

b) *Listen again to the way the poet speaks his poem. Does he speak all sections the same – or differently? Try to think of adverbs to describe the way he speaks each section.*

c) **Rhyme:** *Look again at the section with the most rhymes. Are they all very good rhymes, or are some of them not very exact? Do you specially like any of the rhymes? Why?*

d) **Rhythm:** *Which part of the poem has the best rhythm? Read the lines out loud to find out.*

e) **Repetition:** *Find the lines where the poet repeats a lot of words. Why does he do this? Does he repeat sounds too?*

f) *Have you got a favourite line or lines? Compare them in groups, and try to explain why.*

5 Changes

a) The film and the poem are from the year 1936. How long ago is that? *Think of your own family – who was living at the time? What was happening in the world?*

b) Trains still bring the mail from London to Scotland – and from Scotland to London – and to and from many other places, of course. But some things have changed. *Work in pairs, and write some sentences: What has changed? What was different then? What is different today? In what way?*

steam	diesel	electric	road
transport	planes	airmail	faster
more / less important (than) ...		e-mail	credit cards

⟨c)⟩ *Write a short little poem of your own about e-mail. You can start:*

These are the e-mails buzzing through cyberspace ...

14[ˌskrɔːld‿ɪn ðə ˈmɑːdʒɪn] *an den Rand hingekritzelt* 15[kənˈdəʊləns] *Beileidsbekundung, Kondolenz* 16[hjuː] *Farbton* 17[ˈtʃæti] *geschwätzig, redselig* 18[ˈkæti] *boshaft* 19[əˈdɔː] *bewundern, verehren* 20[ˈaʊtˌpɔːrɪŋ] *Gefühlserguss* 21[ˈkrænstənz / ˈkrɔːfədz] *Namen von bekannten Cafés* 22[ˌwelˈset] *wohl situiert* 23[ˈkwɪknɪŋ] *Beschleunigung*

3

G 16

1 A job interview

Wanted: Tourist guides for the summer season
Are you interested in history and culture? Do you love nature? If your answer is yes, and you are not afraid of hard work and a long day, then the work of a tourist guide on bus tours along Hadrian's Wall could be the thing for you. The job is ideal for students of Roman History. But even if you've forgotten all you learnt at school, there is hope for you: All our guides get a short course in the history of Hadrian's Wall. You also learn about the landscape around it – many visitors want to tour the whole area by bus.
Tel. (0434) 605225 or simply come for an interview to the school in Corbridge village, 2-4 pm, Mon, May 5th.

No article with:
- *general terms, e.g.* history, culture, nature, ...,
- *'institutions', e.g.* school, church, bed, work, ...,
- *means of transport, e.g.* (by) bus, train, ...,
- *general plurals, e.g.* students, tourists, ...

But: the history of the Wall, the bus is late, the school / the church (building), the work of a ..., the students at our school, etc.

Anna from Newcastle upon Tyne has seen this ad, and would like to get the job. a) *Complete the interview with definite articles if they are necessary:*

Interviewer: Well, Anna, I hope you found your way to ... school easily. The ad wasn't too clear, I'm afraid.
Anna: Oh, yes. I came by ... bus, and the driver of ... bus said it was near ... church.
Interviewer: Good. Now tell me why you would like to do ... work of a tourist guide.
Anna: Well, I'm very interested in ... history, especially ... Roman History. I learned all about Hadrian's Wall at ... school, and would like to tell ... tourists all about it.
Interviewer: I see. But ... work can be hard, and I hope you can manage ... early hours. ... German tourist groups sometimes like to start as early as 7 am!
Anna (laughs): Well, I do like to stay in ... bed late, but I often get up early to go birdwatching.
Interviewer: So you are interested in ... nature?
Anna: Oh yes, but I'm afraid I don't know much about ... landscape around here. You see, I'm new to ... area.
Interviewer: That's all right. We give a course on ... geography of ... area as well as on its history.
Anna: So does that mean I get ... job?

b) *Discuss in pairs: Do you think Anna got the job? Why?*

c) *You want the job yourself. Apply by letter.*

2 Role play: Tourists and guides

You are now the guide for one of these two places. So read the basic facts about it. For the other, you play tourist!

Hadrian's Wall: The Romans built it in 122-8 AD, under Emperor Hadrian, to keep out the Celts of the north; 73 miles (117 km) long, 4.5 m high, 3 m thick; Celts broke through in 139 and 367 AD; land between Wall and Scottish border now a National Park.

Roman Baths, Bath: The Romans arrived in 43 AD, and called the natural springs 'Aquae Sulis' after a Celtic goddess; built a town and roads to it; today you can visit their swimming pool, sauna, etc.

Good morning/afternoon. Let me welcome you to ... . This tour is in English, so please tell me now if this is a problem for you.

Er, we're from ...

Well, there are tours in ... . Would you like ...?

Yes, please. What time ...?

Oh, no. I think we can manage.

The next one is at ... .

Thank you.

Oh, we can't wait that long. Let's stay with this tour.

Very well. Would you like me to speak slowly, and more clearly?

That would be nice. / ...

So let me begin. We are now in / at ... . This is ... .

When did ...? / Who ...? / Why ...? / Did ...? / Was ...? / Is ...?

Er, that was ... / I think ... / I'm not sure, but ...

And when / where / why / how long / what kind ...?

You can imagine the rest!

3 ⟨A Gaelic song: Tìr a' Mhurain⟩

by Calum and Rory MacDonald (words and music)

The title of this song means 'Land of marram grass'. That kind of grass grows best near the sea. You can see a lot of it on the coast of Scotland and on the Scottish islands. The boys in the group 'Runrig' all grew up on the Scottish islands, so 'marram grass' means home to them. They sing this song in Gaelic, their native language, but there is an English translation with the CD. *Listen and enjoy it.*

Chorus: Trobhad is coisidh rium Ri taobh a' chuain, Is seallaidh mi dhuit Tìr a' mhurain.	*Chorus:* Come and walk with me By the side of the bay, And let me show you The land of marram grass.
Fàilte gu mo dhàn, Sìol is meas nam bàrd, An fomhair bha feitheamh orm Bho an là a bha mi òg.	Welcome to my song, To the seed[1] and the fruit of the bards[2] To the harvest[3] that has waited for me Since the days when I was young.
Fàilte go mo thìr, Eilean geal an iar, An t-àit a chi gach tuigse is fìrinn Glaiste 'na mo chridhe.	Welcome to my landscape, To the bright[4] island of the west, The place where its meaning and truth[5] Is locked away[6] in my heart.
Fàilte gu mo chainnt, Is i dh' ionsaich mi 'nam phàisde: Canan uasal mòr nan Gaidheal Mar bhratac dhom gach là.	Welcome to my language, I learned it as a child: The great language of the Gaels[7] Is like a flag[8] to me every day.
Is ged a dh' fheuch iad ri cur as dhuinn, Chi mo theaghlach cnoc nan linn; Is ged tha ar canan leoint le strì, 'S an tìr seo bidh i beo.	And although they tried to destroy us, My children will see the hills of generations. Although our language is hurt from the fight, In this land, it will live on.

1[si:d] *Samen, Saat* 2[bɑ:d] = Celtic musician, *Barde* 3['hɑ:vɪst] *Ernte* 4[braɪt] *hell, schön* 5[tru:θ] *Wahrheit* 6[ˌlɒkt‿ə'weɪ] *eingeschlossen* 7[geɪl] = Gaelic Celt 8[flæg] *Fahne*

4 ⟨What is it like?⟩

Donnie Monroe
vocals

Rory Macdonald
bass, vocals

Malcolm Jones
drums

Iain Bayne
drums

Peter Wishart
guitar, accordion

Calum Macdonald
keyboards

a) Have you listened to the Gaelic song? *If not, listen to a little bit. Then try to describe the language. You can choose some adjectives from the list on the right to say what it sounds like to you. Work in pairs.*

You can start:

The language sounds ... to me.
It also sounds ... .
I (don't) think it is ...
German / English / ... .
And it seems ... to learn.
What do you think?

be / seem / sound / look / taste / smell / feel + adjective (not adverb!) – *when they say what something or someone may be like*

easy / hard to learn
strange
nice
beautiful
ugly
awful
(not) clear

(a bit) like ...
the same as ...
(very) different from ...

English / German / ...

b) You don't know the members of the band 'Runrig'. But if you look carefully at their photos, you can try to guess what they are like. *Make sentences about them with 'seem' and 'look'. Example:*

I think ... looks nice / angry / proud / clever / stupid / ...
And he sings / plays his instrument nicely / angrily / ... too. /
But he doesn't sing ... ...

3

5 The new bridge

The Isle of Skye (find it on your map!) is no longer a real island!

a) *Read this letter to a newspaper, to find out why some people are not too happy about it.*

b) *Imagine you live on the island, and are happy about the new bridge. Write a letter in answer to it.*

c) *Write another letter against the new bridge. Make it a horror story about a trip to the island by car. Use the phrases on the right, and put the verbs in the past tense (past progressive for the verbs with *).*

Dear Sir / Madam,
I have visited the beautiful Isle of Skye frequently over the last ten years, and have always enjoyed the peace and quiet, the feeling of being in a different world with a completely different culture from the rest of modern Britain. But not any more! When I was there last July, the traffic jams were simply terrible. Why did you ever build that awful new bridge?

Elizabeth Blake, London

drive* along ... / have to stop suddenly
lots of cars / stand* on the road
still five miles to bridge
sun shine* on roof of car / get* very hot
finally reach bridge / hour later
drive* slowly over bridge / ferry pass under us

6 Reading tips

LEARNING TO LEARN

You have just read a long poem with a lot of new words in it. But you had a teacher to help you. What do you do if you have to read something new on your own? There are certainly some new words in it, and you probably haven't learned all the grammatical forms. So what do you do? Give up? No way! You probably can understand more than you think. The first rule is: DON'T PANIC! Then you should ask yourself these questions:

1. *What kind of a text is it?* (Story, poem, advertisement, newspaper article, magazine article, part of a book, ...)

2. *What's it about?* (Maybe the title will tell you, or a picture will give you a hint, or the first line.)

3. *What do you want from it?* (Maybe you only want to get some special information from it.)

Try them out on the text on the right.
To help you with question 1: It's part of a page from one of the tourist brochures on page 40. But maybe a quick look at the text will tell you *which* brochure – as well as answering question 2. And what about question 3? Maybe you simply want to find out what a certain person has to do with a certain country?

– *Even if you do want to understand a lot – always* **skim** *first. Move your eyes quickly down the text, and try to get the main idea. What is it here?*

– *Now you can read more closely, but don't try to understand every word.*

– *How many words can you guess from the context, or because they are like other (German / English / ...) words?*

Myths and Legends

Wales is a land of legend. Of fire-breathing dragons, powerful magicians, and terrible giants. But what of the greatest figure of the early middle ages – King Arthur? Did he really exist? Or is his story just a myth that lives on because it's so romantic? The answer lies in Wales. Many documents show that Arthur was in fact a 6th-century Welsh leader. He lived in the time after the Romans left Britain. But he could not live in peace. He had to fight against a new horde of invaders: the Saxons. And what about Merlin? Well, there are many Welsh stories about this Druid and wise man. The name of the town of Carmarthen (Caerfyrddin) really means 'Merlin's Castle'.

1 All about Nessie

Surely you've heard of Nessie, the monster of Loch Ness? If you hope to see her, the best place to stay is the village of Drumnadrochit. (The name is from the Gaelic, and means 'top of the bridge'.) More people say they've seen her there than anywhere else! And there's lots to do in the village.

a) *Look at the picture, and imagine you went to Drumnadrochit last year. Make up a story about what you did there.*

b) *Some people think Nessie is real – others don't. What are their arguments? Make complete sentences with the words on the right. Be careful with the adjective/adverb forms, and with the tenses of the verbs.*

c) *Which of them are arguments for, and which are against a real Nessie?*

d) *Now say what you think about Nessie. Talk in groups.*

2 A small village in Wales

Some Welsh place-names are very long. If you travel by train from London to Dublin, you pass a railway station with the longest name in Britain. The local people just say 'Llanfair P.G.'. But not everybody knows that …

a) *Look at the cartoon. Then write out the story of what happened, as the man would tell it. For example, you could start:*
"I was driving from London to catch the late-night ferry to Ireland, when somewhere in North Wales …" (You needn't spell all of the name!)

⟨b)⟩ *Just for fun – try to read the full name out loud. Here are some of the rules for Welsh:*

ll – [hl] or [θl]	w – [ʊ] or [u:]
ch – as in German	y – [ɪ] or [i:]

"… and finally 'H' as in 'Horse'. I'm just outside the railway station."

All about Stonehenge

1 What are the facts?

Stonehenge is Britain's biggest and most famous stone circle. We don't know much about its Stone Age builders, except that they lived before 2000 BC. We don't know why they built it, except that it probably had something to do with astronomy, especially with the movements of the sun and moon. When the Celts came, their Druids might have used the circle for their ceremonies, but this is not certain. *Try to find out more facts and opinions about Stonehenge. You can use books, encyclopedias, or the Internet.*

2 Save Stonehenge!

Today it is a great tourist attraction – and that is where the problems start. It is easy to get there by road – Stonehenge is exactly where the A344 crosses the A303. There is a big car park and visitor centre near the stones. But because some people have damaged the stones, there is now a fence around them, so that you can't get really near them.

a) *Read what these three people say.*

Darina May

"The Stones are very important to me and my friends. We try to continue the religion of the Druids, and want to meet at the stones for festivals every solstice and equinox. We call ourselves World Peace Builders. But it hasn't been easy since English Heritage put up that awful fence. My boyfriend got arrested when he climbed over the fence last summer solstice – he only wanted to play his trumpet inside the circle and pray for peace on the most important day of the year!"

Helen Curry

"We at English Heritage are doing our best to save Stonehenge. We know that fence is not pretty, but we can't let all those thousands of visitors near the stones! Our present plan is to close the present car park and visitor centre, and build a much bigger centre about a mile away. Some people will be happy to just watch the video shows there. Others can go by special bus to the stones – or on foot, if they wish, and walk freely among the stones. Then the fence can come down. We also want to close the A344 and put the A303 in a tunnel, to make the landscape the way it was."

John Howard

"Stonehenge is going to be a £164 million Disney-land if English Heritage, the group responsible for the monument, get what they want! They are planning a visitor centre with a virtual reality tour, shops, restaurants, a monorail to the stones and parking for 3,000 cars. They hope to get financial support for the project from businesses, and attract 1.8 million visitors a year. I think it's crazy!"

b) *Work in groups, and write a dialogue for these three people.* Or:

c) *Decide whose side you are on, and discuss the topic.*

d) *Can you think of any controversies like this in your own country?*

WP

1 One word, two ways to use it

You can use each of these words in two different ways,
– for example as a noun and as an adjective,
– or as an adjective and as an adverb,
– or as an adjective and as a noun.

Roman Welsh Cornish
rich poor fast early better

Make sentences with each, to show the two different meanings. Start:
'Roman' can be a noun or an adjective ...

2 An interesting exhibition

Here is part of an article from a travel magazine. *Put in the correct adjective or adverb forms. Be careful: some of them are comparatives or superlatives!*

If you are travelling in north Wales, or – to be more ... (exact) – along the northern half of the Welsh coast – be ... (sure) to visit the ... (little) town of Machynlleth. That's where you can now find the ... (wonderful) 'Celtica' exhibition. It is in a ... (careful) restored old house, now full of ... (interesting) things. In one room there are ... (wonderful) ... (clear) photos of ... (Celtic) sites and monuments from all over Wales. In another, you can use the ... (late) and ... (good) information technology to find out all about ... (Welsh) history. You can buy ... (beautiful) replicas of Celtic silver jewellery – ... (good) ones than I have seen anywhere else. If you are travelling with children, you can ... (safe) leave them in Celtica's 'Tír na nÓg' – 'the land of ... (young) people'. If the name sounds ... (strange), it's because it is from a ... (famous) ... (Irish) legend. But Celtica is more than a ... (simple) exhibition – its ... (virtual) reality tour is a ... (real) experience. They do it very ... (good), much ... (good) than I can ... (possible) describe here. Celtica is ... (real) one of the ... (interesting) tourist attractions in this part of Wales. It is open until 6 pm every day, but it is ... (good) to come much ... (early) than that. Not only because of the ... (long) queues at the door – but because you may ... (possible) miss the ... (main) event. The ... (last) tour starts at ... (exact) 4.40 pm – and don't let anyone tell you the Welsh always start ... (late) than they advertise. It is ... (simple) not ... (true). And one more tip: The cakes in their café taste ... (great)!

HV

3 Listening comprehension: The virtual reality tour

a) *Listen to the beginning of the tour, and say:*
– what the people on the tour are going to hear;
– what they are going to learn about;
– what they can enjoy.

b) The speaker uses most of the words on the right in two different ways. *Listen again to find them, and write them down.*

c) The speaker does not use one of these words. *Find it, and make a sentence-pair of your own with it.*

time
music
culture
legend
story
history

4 Around Britain quiz

1. Name two big cities in Scotland.
2. Name two big cities in Wales.
3. What is the Celtic language of Scotland?
4. What two other languages are closely related to Welsh?
5. What did the Romans build near the Scottish border?
6. How did the city of Bath get its name?
7. What is England's most famous stone circle?
8. What is the word for a British autobahn?
9. What is the word for a Scottish lake?
10. When is an island not an island?

Two points for each correct answer. 16–20: very good; 10–15: well, OK; under 10: try again!

3

CHECK-IN

	to **discover** [dɪ'skʌvə]	entdecken
1	**Celtic** ['keltɪk]	keltisch, Keltisch
	fringe [frɪndʒ]	Franse, *hier:* Rand-
	to **be about** [ə'baʊt]	sich handeln um
	border ['bɔ:də]	Grenze
	poor [pɔ:]	arm
	language ['læŋgwɪdʒ]	Sprache
2	**main** [meɪn]	Haupt-
	slow [sləʊ]	langsam
	Loch Ness [ˌlɒk / ˌlɒx 'nes]	*See in Schottland*
	Aberdeen [ˌæbə'di:n]	*Stadt in Schottland*
	ferry ['feri]	Fähre
3	**journey** ['dʒɜ:ni]	Reise
	Hadrian's Wall [ˌheɪdriənz 'wɔ:l]	Hadrianswall
	Stonehenge [ˌstəʊn'hendʒ]	Denkmal aus der Stein-/ Bronzezeit
	Bath [bɑ:θ]	*Kurort in Südwestengland*

opposites

rich	–	poor
slow	–	fast
regular	–	irregular
good	–	bad
usual	–	unusual
…	–	…

Tourists go to see Loch Ness and Stonehenge all the year round.

Hadrian's Wall was once the border between England and Scotland.

We don't know *who* built Stonehenge, but we know *how* it was built.

STEP A

	Celt [kelt]	Kelte / Keltin
	Londoner ['lʌndənə]	Londoner(in)
	usual ['ju:ʒl]	gewöhnlich, üblich
	to be interested (in) ['ɪntrəstɪd‿ɪn]	interessiert sein (an), sich interessieren (für)
	sudden ['sʌdn]	plötzlich, unerwartet
	change [tʃeɪndʒ]	Wandel, Umschwung
	to **teach*** [ti:tʃ]	unterrichten, lehren
	well [wel]	gut
	Gaelic ['geɪlɪk]	gälisch, Gälisch
1	**irregular** [ɪ'regjələ]	unregelmäßig
2	**strong** [strɒŋ]	stark
3	**BC (= Before Christ)** [ˌbi:'si:]	vor Christus
	to **spread* (over)** [spred]	sich ausdehnen, sich verbreiten (über)
	tribe [traɪb]	Stamm
	Briton ['brɪtn]	Brite/Britin
	Europe ['jʊərəp]	Europa
	Breton ['bretn]	bretonisch; Bretone
	Iron Age ['aɪən‿eɪdʒ]	Eisenzeit
	loose [lu:s]	lose, locker
	cloak [kləʊk]	Umhang, (weiter) Mantel
	to **hold*** [həʊld]	halten
	jewellery *(BE)* ['dʒu:əlri]	Juwelen, Schmuck
	Roman ['rəʊmən]	Römer(in)
	chieftain ['tʃi:ftn]	Häuptling, Anführer(in)
	peaceful ['pi:sfl]	friedlich
	ruler ['ru:lə]	Herrscher(in)
	Boudicca ['bu:dɪkə]	*berühmte Keltenführerin*
	leader ['li:də]	Anführer(in)
4	**to ask so. to do sth.** [ɑ:sk]	jmdn. bitten, etw. zu tun

Gaelic is a Celtic language.

That rain was very sudden, but now the sun is out again.

You speak English very well.

"The Germans live in Germany.
The Romans live in Rome.
The Irish live in Ireland.
But the Britons live at home."
Anon

The Iron Age came after the Stone Age.

Be careful! Your scarf is loose. Don't lose it!

There were many peaceful tribes in Europe.

Boudicca was a chieftain of the Britons at the time of the Romans.

She was a good leader.

5	**proud** [praʊd]	stolz
	brave [breɪv]	tapfer, mutig
	to **build*** [bɪld]	(er)bauen

Asterix and Obelix are proud and brave, but not peaceful when they meet Romans.

STEP B

1	**originally** [əˈrɪdʒnli]	ursprünglich, anfänglich
2	to **look for** [ˈlʊk fɔː]	suchen
3	**actually** [ˈæktʃuəli]	tatsächlich, wirklich
	sky [skaɪ]	Himmel
I	to **cross** [krɒs]	überqueren
	postal order [ˈpəʊstl‿ɔːdə]	Postanweisung
	next door [ˌnekst ˈdɔː]	nebenan
	steady [ˈstedi]	ständig, ununterbrochen
	climb [klaɪm]	Steigung, Aufstieg
	on time [ɒn ˈtaɪm]	pünktlich
	past [pɑːst]	vorbei (an)
	to **shovel** [ˈʃʌvl]	schaufeln, schippen
	steam [stiːm]	Dampf
	to **snort** [snɔːt]	schnauben
	to **pass** [pɑːs]	vorbeifahren, -kommen
	to **bend*** [bend]	biegen, beugen, knicken
	to **approach** [əˈprəʊtʃ]	sich (an)nähern (an)
	to **stare** [steə]	starren
	coach [kəʊtʃ]	(Eisenbahn-)Wagen
	to **slumber** [ˈslʌmbə]	schlummern, schlafen
	paw [pɔː]	Pfote
	jug [dʒʌg]	Krug, Kanne
	gently [ˈdʒentli]	sanft, mild
	to **shake** [ʃeɪk]	schütteln
II	**dawn** [dɔːn]	Dämmerung, Tagesanbruch
	Glasgow [ˈglɑːzgəʊ]	*Großstadt in Schottland*
	to **descend** [dɪˈsend]	absteigen, hinunterfahren
	beside [bɪˈsaɪd]	neben
	glen [glen]	(enges) Tal
	pale [peɪl]	bleich, blass
	loch [lɒk/lɒx]	See *(schottisch)*
III	**joy** [dʒɔɪ]	Freude, Vergnügen
	invitation [ˌɪnvɪˈteɪʃn]	Einladung
	relation [rɪˈleɪʃn]	Beziehung; Verwandte(r)
	application [ˌæplɪˈkeɪʃn]	Bewerbungsschreiben
	declaration [ˌdekləˈreɪʃn]	Erklärung
	gossip [ˈgɒsɪp]	Klatsch, Tratsch
	Highlands [ˈhaɪləndz]	Hochland
	Lowlands [ˈləʊləndz]	Tiefland
	note [nəʊt]	Notiz, (kurzer) Brief, Mitteilung
	overseas [ˌəʊvəˈsiːz]	in/im Übersee
	Hebrides [ˈhebrɪdiːz]	*schottische Inselgruppe*
	heart [hɑːt]	Herz
IV	to **be asleep** [əˈsliːp]	schlafen
	to **dream** [driːm]	träumen
	terrifying [ˈterəfaɪɪŋ]	erschreckend, grauenvoll
	to **continue** [kənˈtɪnjuː]	fortfahren, weitermachen, fortsetzen

I live in New York, but I came from Bath originally.

Be careful when you cross the road.

The weather was bad and our ferry wasn't on time.

There are steam trains, electric trains and diesel trains.

The train approached the station.

The people in the coach stared out of the window.

There is a jug of water on the table.

He was still asleep, so she shook him gently.

franz descendre *lat* descendere
engl to descend

franz invitation *lat* invitatio
engl invitation

Your father is not a relation of your mother, but both your father and your mother are your relations.

The dream was really bad, it was terrifying.

to slumber = to be asleep
to continue = to go on

	dream [driːm]	Traum
	shall *(old)* [ʃæl]	*hier:* werde(n)
	to **long (for)** [ˌlɒŋ‿ˈfɔː]	sich sehnen (nach)
	none [nʌn]	keine(r/s)
	knock [nɒk]	Klopfen, Pochen
	to **bear*** [beə]	ertragen, aushalten
4	**rhyme** [raɪm]	Reim
	reason [ˈriːzn]	Grund, Ursache
	section [ˈsekʃn]	Absatz, Abschnitt
	content [ˈkɒntent]	Inhalt
	repetition [ˌrepɪˈtɪʃn]	Wiederholung
	out loud [ˌaʊt ˈlaʊd]	laut (vorlesen, sprechen)
5	**how long ago?** [ˌhaʊ lɒŋ‿əˈgəʊ]	wie lange her?
	to **buzz** [bʌz]	surren, schwirren

3

STEP C

1	**Newcastle upon Tyne** [ˌnjuːkɑːsl‿əpɒn ˈtaɪn]	*Industriestadt in Nordostengland*
	driver [ˈdraɪvə]	Fahrer(in)
	guide [gaɪd]	Fremdenführer(in)
	especially [ɪˈspeʃli]	besonders, vor allem
	to **manage** [ˈmænɪdʒ]	bewältigen, schaffen
	birdwatching [ˈbɜːdˌwɒtʃɪŋ]	Vögel beobachten
	as well as [əz ˈwel‿əz]	sowie, sowohl als auch
	visitor [ˈvɪzɪtə]	Besucher(in)
	Corbridge [ˈkɔːbrɪdʒ]	*Dorf in Nordostengland*
	term [tɜːm]	Ausdruck, Terminus
	means [miːnz]	Mittel
2	to **welcome** [ˈwelkəm]	begrüßen, willkommen heißen
	AD (= Anno Domini) [ˌeɪˈdiː]	nach Christus
	emperor [ˈemprə]	Kaiser
	Hadrian [ˈheɪdriən]	*römischer Kaiser (76-138)*
	deep [diːp]	tief
	spring [sprɪŋ]	Frühling
	goddess [ˈgɒdes]	Göttin
⟨3⟩	**marram grass** [ˈmærəm ˌgrɑːs]	Marramgras
	Runrig [ˈrʌnrɪg]	*Name einer Musikgruppe*
	home [həʊm]	Heimat, Zuhause
	native [ˈneɪtɪv]	Heimat-, Mutter-
	translation [trænzˈleɪʃn]	Übersetzung
⟨4⟩	to **be (/sound/look/ ... like** [laɪk]	sein/sich anhören/ aussehen wie
	to **taste** [teɪst]	schmecken
	to **smell** [smel]	riechen
	vocals [ˈvəʊklz]	Gesang
5	**Isle of Skye** [ˌaɪl‿əv ˈskaɪ]	*größte Insel der Hebriden*
	island [ˈaɪlənd]	Insel
	frequent [ˈfriːkwənt]	häufig
	peace [piːs]	Frieden
	quiet [ˈkwaɪət]	Stille, Ruhe

	traffic jam [ˈtræfɪk ˌdʒæm]	Verkehrsstau
	finally [ˈfaɪnli]	schließlich, endlich
6	**on one's own** [ˌɒn wʌnz‿ˈəʊn]	allein, ohne Hilfe
	certain [ˈsɜːtn]	bestimmt, gewiss
	probably [ˈprɒbəbli]	wahrscheinlich
	hint [hɪnt]	Hinweis, Andeutung
	to **skim** [skɪm]	flüchtig lesen, überfliegen
	close [kləʊs]	*hier:* genau

TRACK 1

1	**Nessie** [ˈnesi]	*Ungeheuer von Loch Ness*
	Drumnadrochit [ˌdrɒmnəˈdrɒxɪt]	*Ort in Schottland*
	storyteller [ˈstɔːriˌtelə]	Geschichtenerzähler(in)
	St Columba [ˌsnt kəˈlʌmbə]	*Missionar aus Irland (521-597)*
2	**Llanfair P.G.** [ˈhlænfeə ˌpiːˈdʒiː]	*Ort in Nordwales*
	just [dʒʌst]	nur, bloß

TRACK 2

1	+**builder** [ˈbɪldə]	Erbauer(in), Begründer(in)
	+**movement** [ˈmuːvmənt]	Bewegung
	+**might** [maɪt]	könnte(n), dürfte(n)
	+**opinion** [əˈpɪnjən]	Meinung, Ansicht
2	+**fence** [fens]	Zaun
	⟨**solstice**⟩ [ˈsɒlstɪs]	Sonnenwende
	⟨**equinox**⟩ [ˈiːkwɪnɒks]	Tagundnachtgleiche
	+**ourselves** [ˌaʊəˈselvz]	wir (selbst)
	+**heritage** [ˈherɪtɪdʒ]	Erbe
	+to **get arrested** [ˌget‿əˈrestɪd]	verhaftet werden
	+to **pray** [preɪ]	beten
	+**pretty** [ˈprɪti]	hübsch, nett
	+to **let*** [let]	lassen
	+**on foot** [ɒn ˈfʊt]	zu Fuß
	+to **wish** [wɪʃ]	wünschen
	+**monorail** [ˈmɒnəreɪl]	Einschienenbahn
	+**support** [səˈpɔːt]	Unterstützung
	+to **attract** [əˈtrækt]	anziehen, anlocken
	+**controversy** [kənˈtrɒvəsi]	Streitfrage, Kontroverse

CHECK-OUT

1	**meaning** [ˈmiːnɪŋ]	Bedeutung, Sinn
2	**half** [hɑːf]	Hälfte

Machynlleth [mə'kʌnhleθ]	*Ort in Wales*
Celtica ['keltɪkə]	*Name einer Ausstellung*
to **restore** [rɪ'stɔ:]	wiederherstellen, restaurieren
site [saɪt]	Gelände, Platz
latest ['leɪtɪst]	neuste(r/s)
replica ['replɪkə]	Nachbildung
Irish ['aɪərɪʃ]	irisch, Irisch
queue [kju:]	(Menschen-) Schlange
to **advertise** ['ædvətaɪz]	ankündigen, werben
cake [keɪk]	Kuchen
4 to **name** [neɪm]	nennen
to **be related (to)** [rɪ'leɪtɪd]	mit etw zusammen hängen, mit jmdm verwandt sein
lake [leɪk]	See

COGNATE WORDS

airmail ['eəmeɪl]	Luftpost
argument ['ɑ:gjəmənt]	Argument; Streit, Auseinandersetzung
bush [bʊʃ]	Busch
cheque [tʃek]	Scheck
civilized ['sɪvlaɪzd]	zivilisiert
complete [kəm'pli:t]	vollständig, komplett
continent ['kɒntɪnənt]	Festland, Kontinent
to **control** [kən'trəʊl]	beherrschen, überwachen
course [kɔ:s]	Kurs(us), Lehrgang
credit card ['kredɪt ˌkɑ:d]	Kreditkarte
culture ['kʌltʃə]	Kultur
cyberspace ['saɪbəˌspeɪs]	Cyberspace
to **decorate** ['dekəreɪt]	dekorieren, verzieren
diesel ['di:zl]	Dieselöl, -motor
dinosaur ['daɪnəsɔ:]	Dinosaurier
Druid ['dru:ɪd]	Druide
+**encyclopedia** [ɪnˌsaɪklə'pi:diə]	Nachschlagewerk, Enzyklopädie
+**exact** [ɪg'zækt]	genau, exakt
figure ['fɪgə]	Figur, Gestalt
financial [faɪ'nænʃl]	finanziell, Finanz-
general ['dʒenrl]	allgemein, generell
geography [dʒi'ɒgrəfi]	Erdkunde, Geografie
gold [gəʊld]	Gold
grass [grɑ:s]	Gras
history ['hɪstri]	Geschichte
institution [ˌɪnstɪ'tju:ʃn]	Institution, Einrichtung
interviewer ['ɪntəvju:ə]	Interviewer(in)
lover ['lʌvə]	Liebhaber(in), Geliebte(r)
mail [meɪl]	Post
metal ['metl]	Metall
monster ['mɒnstə]	Ungeheuer, Monster
+**monument** ['mɒnjəmənt]	Baudenkmal, Monument
nation ['neɪʃn]	Nation, Volk
national ['næʃnl]	staatlich, national
national park [ˌnæʃnl 'pɑ:k]	Nationalpark
nature ['neɪtʃə]	Natur
nonsense ['nɒnsəns]	Unsinn, Quatsch
to **panic** ['pænɪk]	in Panik geraten
paper ['peɪpə]	Papier
pink [pɪŋk]	rosa
poet ['pəʊɪt]	Dichter(in), Poet(in)
post [pəʊst]	Post
post office ['pəʊstˌɒfɪs]	Postamt
power ['paʊə]	Kraft, Stärke, Macht
+**present** ['preznt]	gegenwärtig, momentan
rap [ræp]	Rap *(Musikrichtung)*
reality [ri'æləti]	Wirklichkeit, Realität
+**religion** [rɪ'lɪdʒn]	Religion
rest [rest]	Rest
rhyme [raɪm]	Reim
rhythm ['rɪðm]	Rhythmus
round [raʊnd]	rund
sender ['sendə]	Absender(in)
situation [ˌsɪtju'eɪʃn]	Situation, *hier:* Arbeitsstelle
student ['stju:dnt]	Student(in)
tour [tʊə]	Reise, Tour
to **type** [taɪp]	tippen, mit der Maschine schreiben
violet ['vaɪəlet]	violett
virtual ['vɜ:tʃuəl]	virtuell
+**virtual reality** [ˌvɜ:tʃuəl ri'æləti]	virtuelle Realität

UNIT 4

English in the world

1 Who speaks English?

a) *Can you say what countries the pictures on the left are from? If you find it difficult, there are some clues on this page!*

b) *Look at the map of the world at the back of your book, and try to find these countries. Are they all coloured pink? Or is one of them a country where English is not usually spoken?*

c) *Talk about the situation in your own country: What English signs would you normally see on the street? Why are they in English?*

d) *Divide into groups for the four of these countries where English is an official language. Each group finds out the facts about all the languages they speak there, and how important English is in that country. Compare your results and talk about other countries that are like these.*

SB

2 Homeless (a song – with listening tips)

LEARNING TO LEARN

This song is only partly in English – the rest is in Zulu, a South African language. It happened like this. The American singer Paul Simon heard some recordings of South African music, and asked to work together with the musicians.

For this song, he sent a demo tape to Joseph Shabalala, the lead singer of the vocal group 'Ladysmith Black Mambazo'. It had one line of a song on it: "Moonlight sleeping on a midnight lake." He asked them to add something to it, and change it any way they wanted. In fact, they translated it into Zulu and added an extra verse in English. When they met in the recording studio in London, they improvised some more.

– Nobody ever understands everything!
The bits you don't understand aren't usually in Zulu – but they sometimes sound like it! Often they are not important. (If they are important, you can usually ask someone to repeat them. If it's a recording, you can play it again and again.)

– Try to get the gist first.
For a song, listen to the whole thing, just to enjoy the sound. Then ask yourself what words you picked up and remembered. These are usually the important words that the singers repeat. What were they in this song?

– Then try to understand a bit better.
For this song, pick out the bits that are in English. How many English verses are there? Is there an English chorus? How many times do they sing it? Are there some English words in the Zulu verses?

– Activities.
For example, you could sing along with the bits you understand. A good place to start would be the "Somebody say ..." section. (Surely you understood that!) Then maybe some of the repeated English lines. And if you want to try the Zulu – why not?

(For the words of the song, see p. 196)

Tara's project

Tara Modi has been working on a project for the last two weeks. She has been spending a lot of time in the library and collecting information on the Internet. Her mother thinks she hasn't been sleeping properly since she started on it! Tara hasn't quite finished yet. But she has already collected a lot of information about the way the English language began. She is now working on two posters for the classroom ...

Where's Tara?

She's been in her room since four o'clock, working on that project of hers!

Can't one of you guys help me? I've been looking everywhere for my list of French words!

G 18

1 What have they been doing?

a) *Fill in the verbs in the right tense.*

1. Dr Modi ... (work) in his office all day. He must be very tired!
2. Tara's brother Rizwan ... (practise) a new dance in his room. Tara wishes he would stop!
3. Her mother ... (try) to get Tony Clifton on the phone since three o'clock, but the phone is busy.
4. Since Friday, Tessa ... (help) her with pictures for the project. She ... (already / find) some good ones.

b) *And what have you been doing all day today? Talk in pairs or groups.*

SAVE

present perfect
She has collected ... – RESULT
She has been here (since) ... – STATE TO NOW

present perfect progressive
She has been collecting ... – ACTIVITY TO NOW

4

The story of English

The early **Britons** did not speak English! The language which they spoke was Celtic. It was probably a bit like the language that you can hear today in the West.

Two people who did not speak English!

The **Romans** were the people who built the first roads and towns in Britain. But all that they left of their language were the names of those towns. They didn't change the language of the people that they met.

The people that invaded the country after the Romans left were called **Angles and Saxons**. The language which came into Britain with them was a kind of English.

Him pā ellenrōf andswarode,
wlanc Wedera lēod, word æfter spræc
heard under helme: 'We synt Hiʒelāces
bēodʒenēatas; Bēowulf is mīn nama.

Old English – from a story about a man who kills a terrible monster. Can you understand it?

The **Vikings** are most famous for the beautiful boats which they sailed in. And for their terrible attacks on the coast.
We often forget the many Viking words that came into English when they settled here.

G 19

2 Who – which – that

a) *Look at the first of Tara's posters and find all the relative clauses. Then try to work out the rule: When do you use 'who' and when do you use 'which'? And what about 'that'?*

b) *Now use relative clauses to define people or things. Make a quiz for a partner.*

What do you call	someone the people the thing an animal ...	who which that	you can travel over water in? barks? fought against King Arthur? speaks English? ...

SAVE

No commas with defining relative clauses!

G 19

3 Talking to Tara

Some of her friends have seen the first of Tara's posters and they have some questions for her.

a) *Look at what they ask. The relative clauses they use are a bit different from those on Tara's poster. They are contact clauses. In what way are they different?*

b) It is not possible to make contact clauses with the other relative clauses on the poster. *What is special about those clauses? (Think about the function of the pronouns 'who/which/that'.)*

c) Here are some more things Tara explained. *Put in relative pronouns – but only if necessary.*

1. Yes, that's the statue of Boudicca ... stands near Westminster Bridge in London.
2. King Arthur was a real person ... fought against the Saxons.
3. The Romans, the Angles and Saxons were people ... the Britons fought against at different times.
4. The Saxons were the people ... they hated most. They were the ones ... drove them out of England.
5. Yes, the boats ... the Vikings came in were really like the one in the comic.

d) *What were the questions they asked Tara?*

'The language you can hear in the West' – do you mean Welsh, Tara? That's the language my aunt in Swansea speaks!

Oh, yes. I forgot it was hers!

Who were 'the people the Romans met', Tara?

The Britons, of course – the British Celts, people like Boudicca.

I saw one of the boats the Vikings sailed in. It was in a museum in Newcastle.

4

This is part of the famous Bayeux Tapestry. It is a kind of 'comic strip' that tells a story – the story of how the **Normans** came to Britain. *This figure is the Norman king whose army defeated Harold, the Saxon King, in 1066, and who then became King of England. He is called William the Conqueror. The Normans were really 'north-men' (or Vikings) who settled in France and whose language became a kind of French. A lot of 'English' words are really theirs.

Most of English came from the Angles and Saxons, but here are some words that came from –

the Vikings
get, take, die, call, skirt, leg, egg, knife, happy, low, wrong

the Normans

other languages
glen, loch, whisky (Scotland)
sofa, alcohol (North Africa)
bungalow, verandah (India)
didgeridoo (Australia)
chocolate (Mexico)

G 20

4 Whose language?

a) *Find the new kind of relative clause that Tara uses for the Normans:*

1. This figure is the Norman king ... (His army defeated Harold.)
2. They were really 'north-men' ... (Their language was now French.)

b) *Now use this kind of clause to add important information:*

1. The Celts of Scotland were the people ... (Their language gave us ...)
2. India was the country ... (Its treasures first attracted Europeans.)
3. Native Americans and Australian aborigines were some of the many people ... (Their countries became British.)
4. English is the language ... (Its popularity is growing fastest.)

c) The words on Tara's 'Norman' list are from these French words:

couleur cousin cité leçon village

What are they in English?

G 21

5 Why do they need English?

People whose own language is not English often need to learn it – for a number of different reasons. a) *First make a list of people who need to know some English.*

people who ... / want to ... / do business in ... / take part in ...
organize ... / work for ... / perform ... / act in ...
people whose job it is to ... / whose job takes them to ...

pilots
sailors
waiters
scientists
long-distance truck drivers
business people (who ...)
sportsmen and -women (who ...)
travel agents (who ...)
reporters (who ...)
...

b) *Then talk in pairs about why certain people need English.*

Start: My mum is a pilot, so she ...

4

G 22

6 The Modis in India

The Modi family from London are on holiday in India. Now they are in a restaurant in South India, where they don't understand the local language. Dr Modi can speak one Indian language, but not theirs. So he has to use English.

They asked for:
- masala dosa[1] with vegetables (Tara Modi)
- lamb vindaloo[2] (Rizwan)
- chicken korma[3] (their mother)
- fish curry (their father)

But the waiter forgot who asked for what.

[1][məˈsɑːlə ˈdɒsə] *südindischer Pfannkuchen*
[2][ˌvɪndəˈluː] *sehr scharfes Fleischgericht*
[3][ˈkɔːmə] *mildes Fleischgericht*

SAVE

my map	–	mine	our plane	–	ours
your idea	–	yours	your tickets	–	yours
his car	–	his	their table	–	theirs
her bags	–	hers	*Also:* a friend of hers,		
Tara's book	–	Tara's	that idea of Tara's		

a) *Complete the dialogue between him and Dr Modi with the right possessive pronouns.*

Waiter: The chicken korma is for you, sir?
Dr Modi: No, ... is the fish curry. The chicken korma is ..., isn't it, Hilary? Yes, it's ... .
Waiter: And the girl wanted lamb, I think.
Dr Modi: No, wrong again! The masala dosa is ... . Here it is, Tara – a real South Indian dosa!
Waiter: And does the boy get the lamb vindaloo or the chicken curry?
Dr Modi: The lamb vindaloo is ... . I don't think any of us asked for a chicken curry, did they? No, it isn't ... . I think it must be for the table over there. Yes, I'm sure it's ... .
Waiter: I'm so sorry! Today is not my day!

b) *Complete what Tara and her cousin said. You will also need the 'double genitive' (of his, etc.):*

Imran: These postcards ... ... – do you want me to post them? I'm going to the post office.
Tara: Oh, they are not ..., that's my dad's writing. But please post them, and take these three ... ... too. I wrote them yesterday and forgot about them. And these two ... . But don't tell Rizwan I've been carrying them around so long!
Imran: These Cliftons – are they good friends ... ... ? There are two postcards to that family.
Tara: Oh, they're more than that. They're relatives ... . Tony Clifton is Mum's brother.

Eddie the inventor

The writer Farrukh Dhondy[1] now lives in London, but he grew up in India. Gujarati[2] is the language of Farrukh's people, the Parsees[3]. But a different language is spoken in Poona[4], where he went to school. So English was very useful to him down on the 'Chowk'[5] or market square of Poona ...

The Chowk was the heart of our neighbourhood, two hundred yards down the street from where I lived. Our side of the Chowk was the city side, and the other, towards Main Street, was the 'camp' side – so called because the British built it for the soldiers and administrators. The Chowk and our neighbourhood were between the narrow streets of the city and the spacious squares of the camp with its barracks and bungalows.

The Chowk was the place for the traders and bookies. It was the hangout of all the men in the neighbourhood. The rich stopped their cars there to pick up snacks, drugs, flowers, or to visit one of the doctors who had offices around the Chowk. The poor hung out there because there was nothing better to do.

The two cafés were the hangouts of the older schoolboys and the businessmen who ran the bakeries and the bicycle shops. On the Chowk they called me *nalha*[6], small one. At first I only went to the cafés when my aunts sent me there for something. Then regularly on the way to school my friends and I would drop in to pick up some chewing gum or sweets.

One regular customer was Sol Kolmi[7]. His business was illegal gambling. He was the Chowk's main bookie. When he wasn't sitting at a table in one of the cafés, he was sitting on the pavement, collecting pieces of paper which people gave him, with the names of horses or the numbers of the cotton figures game on them.

The cotton figures game was a clever invention. It was a simple game. What one had to do was, before seven o'clock each weekday evening, guess the numbers after the decimal point in the price of cotton on the New York market.

The boys at the street corners in Poona were very interested in the New York cotton market. It was legal to be interested in the figures, but illegal to bet on them. In one day, the opening price would be 37.85, and the closing price 38.22. It was the '85' and the '22' that you betted on. If you got one right, you won at nine to one. If you got both right, you got over 80 to one. In the end, the bookies got rich.

Kolmi took bets from anyone – from the rich, the poor, the beggars and policemen, but not from the young. If I or my friends wanted to bet, we had to do it in the name of someone else.

The first time I ever placed a bet with Kolmi was for Eddie the Inventor. I made friends with Eddie the day he repaired my broken glasses in his workshop off Dastur Meher[8] Road. It was the strangest place. There was an old table with lots of old electronic equipment. It seemed there were headphones everywhere, and copies of *Popular Mechanics* and *Popular Electronics* thrown all round the room.

He was building the best system of radio communications outside America, he said. He never let us touch the 'Big Boy', his serious work, but taught us, over the weeks, how to put together a simple radio set.

The Big Boy grew from day to day. When it started working, Eddie couldn't control his excitement. He put the headphones over my ears and turned the knobs.

"What's coming through?"

"All sorts of beeps and buzzing and the sound of the sea," I said.

"It all means things, signals, *nalha*, signals. I'll be rich. This is it."

The next day, Eddie asked me to do something for him. He pulled a five rupee note out of his pocket. "Take this money and go to the Chowk and put all the money with Sol Kolmi on '69'. Don't tell anyone who gave you the money. They don't take cotton figure bets from me. Tell them it's your grandfather's."

At the café, everyone was reading the morning papers. All that week, they were full of the first Russian space adventure. The words 'sputnik' and 'Gagarin' were part of the talk at school, at home, in the streets. Kolmi was in an argument about it. I went up to him, and said I had a bet.

"What's this, what's this? You know the rules. We don't take money from children."

"It's for my grandfather," I said. He didn't believe me at first. Everyone on the Chowk knew that my grandfather didn't gamble.

"He said take the bet, but don't make it public."

"Are you sure your grandfather gave you this?"

---

[1][fæˌru:k ˈdɒndi] [2][ˌgʊdʒəˈrɑ:ti] [3][ˈpɑ:si] [4][ˈpu:nə] [5][tʃaʊk] [6][ˈnælhə] [7][ˌsɒl ˈkəʊlmi] [8][ˈdæstu:r ˈmɜ:her]

"Where would I get five rupees?" Kolmi took the money. "All right," he said. "All right, we'll see."

The number didn't win. I went back to Eddie and told him. He didn't look too disappointed.

"First time unlucky. I'll break the code, *nalha*. Those Russians can't fool me. I'll be rich, wait and see." I didn't know what he was talking about, and didn't ask.

A few days later he asked me to place another bet for him. Again he lost.

The third time he won. Kolmi counted out 400 rupees. I stuffed the money in the pockets of my shorts, and went back to Eddie.

"You've won."

"Tomorrow again," he said. "I've broken the code."

Ten more times Eddie sent me out in the evening to place bets for him. He won only once more.

In the evening, my grandfather always took a walk. In his long Parsee jacket and carrying a walking stick, he'd walk down to Main Street and sit with friends from his generation and talk about the old times, the good old days of British rule. Then back by way of the Chowk.

It was on one of these walks that Kolmi spoke to him. I heard about it later from my friend Dinsy.

"He called your grandfather a liar in front of fifty people!"

My heart sank into my canvas shoes. How could I go home now? I didn't know what he would do to me. Maybe I should run away?

The lights of our verandah were on when I got back. My grandfather was there. I looked over his shoulder to my aunts. Beside them stood my sister, looking as scared as I felt.

"So you've become a gambling man?" he said.

"No, sir," I said in Gujarati.

Then he sent my aunts and sister away. He was interested. He wanted to know where the money came from. "Eddie," I said.

"When have you been going to see Eddie?"

"Just a few times. He shows us electronics." I was telling my grandfather about Eddie's great discoveries. "Sputnik has been giving out signals. The Russians have been telling the New York cotton figures to the whole world! When the code is completely clear, Eddie will be rich!"

There was a sound from the verandah. We saw Dinsy and two other boys running away.

"I've been protecting that friend of yours too long," my grandfather said. "Do you know who he is? They threw him out of the army because he fell asleep when important signals were coming through in the war."

For a week I didn't go to the Chowk or to see Eddie. At school, Dinsy told me what happened. One of the boys from the verandah told Kolmi about Sputnik, and that night he and some other bookies smashed Eddie's workshop. They broke all his equipment, including Big Boy.

I saw Eddie three weeks later, on his bike. He called to me. He didn't look sorry or sad.

"I am a scientist and an inventor," he said. "These little things don't stop me. You know why we didn't win every day? Big Boy wasn't strong enough. I've been catching Poona Military Airport signals. But the next stop is Sputnik!"

Adapted from *Poona Company* (1980) by Farrukh Dhondy

1 Characters

a) *Make a list of all the characters. Then pick out the four most important, and decide which of these adjectives go best with each:*

proud	silly	clever	businesslike	young
crazy	sad	illegal	optimistic	strict
good	bad	friendly	excited	stupid
old	interested in ...		afraid of ...	angry

b) *Choose one character each, and get together in groups to talk about that one character. Have you all got the same adjectives? If not, why not?*

c) *In the group, write a little 'character sketch'.*

2 Right or wrong?

a) *Correct what is wrong.*

1. Kolmi took bets from everyone.
2. Eddie won all his bets.
3. The men destroyed Big Boy.

b) *Make more right/wrong sentences like these and test each other.*

3 Time and place

a) *When does this story take place?*

b) *Look for the details that tell you something about India – its history, what life is like there.*

1 Listening comprehension: Voices

On the recordings, you can hear the voices of six people from (partly) English-speaking countries. Their names are George, Eileen, Carmen, Abby, Bruce and Rukhshana.

a) *You don't need to understand everything. Just find out which pictures belong to which names and voices.*

A
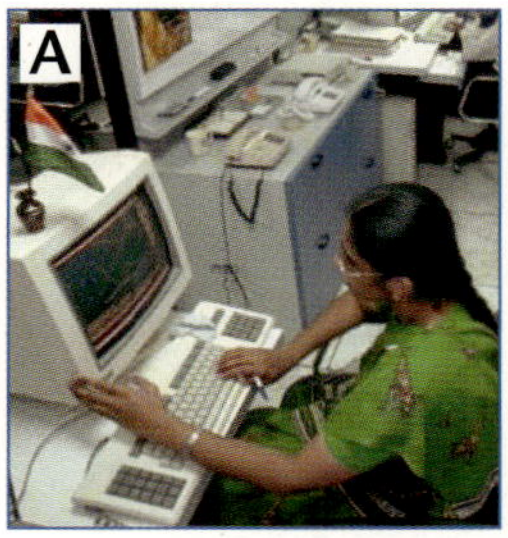
B
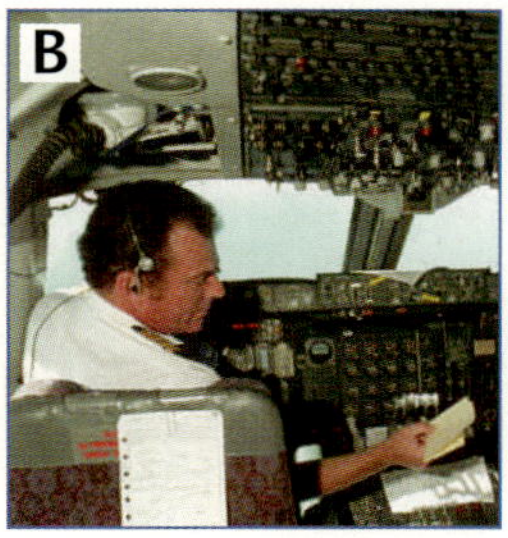
C

D

E

F

b) The speakers have very different accents. *Which voices did you find most difficult to understand? Which were easy to understand?*

c) *Which of these people live in countries you have already talked about? Form groups to find out about the other countries.*

2 Room service

Sometimes international communication can be difficult, even with English as a world language.

a) *Read what happened when a hotel guest rang Room Service one morning, somewhere in Asia:*

– Morny. Rune-sore-bees.
– Oh, sorry. I thought I dialled room service.
– Rye, Rune-sore-bees. Djewish to odor sunteen?
– Uh ... yes. I'd like some bacon and eggs.
– Ow July den?
– What?
– Aches. Ow July den? Pry, boy, pooch ...?
– Oh, the eggs! How do I like them? Sorry. Scrambled, please.
– Ow July dee baycome? Crease?
– Crisp will be fine.
– Hokay. An Santos?
– What?
– Santos. July Santos?
– Uh. I don't know ... I don't think so.
– No. Judo one toes?
– Look, I feel really bad about this, but I don't know what 'judo one toes' means. I'm sorry.
– Toes! Toes! Why djew Don Juan toes? Ow bow cenglish mopping we bother?
– English muffin! I've got it! You were saying toast! Fine. An English muffin will be fine.
– We bother?
– No. Just put the bother on the side.
– Wad?
– I'm sorry. I meant butter. Butter on the side.
– Copy?
– I feel terrible about this, but ...
– Copy. Copy, tea, mil-
– Coffee! Yes, coffee please. And that's all.
– One minnie. Ass rune torino fee, strangle aches, crease baycome, tossy cenglish mopping we bother honey sigh, and copy. Rye?
– Whatever you say.
– Hokay. Tendjewberry mud.
– You're welcome.

From *Far-East Economic Review*

b) *Now try to work out what the person at Room Service was really saying. Write out his/her words in the kind of English the guest would understand.*

c) *What English sounds did he/she have most trouble with? Are they different from the sounds a German speaker would have problems with?*

4

1 How long?

How long have these people been doing these things? Use 'since' or 'for'.

Peter – play

(three hours)

men – work

(started last Tuesday)

cat – play

(found it an hour ago)

Jennie – wait

(arrived at 7:30 pm)

2 Just for fun

a) *Where do you think this story is happening?*
b) *Tell the story – or act it out in pairs.*
The people use English, of course!

From
The New Yorker Album
1925–1950

WP 3 Make an army mind map

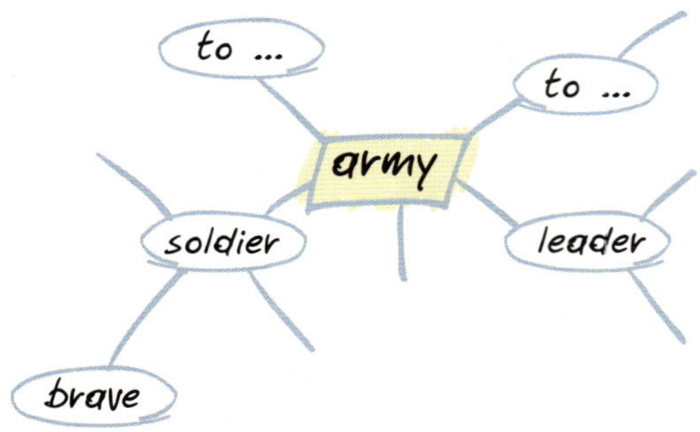

4 Defining things

Imagine somebody doesn't know what these words mean. Explain them with defining relative clauses.

actress	comedy	parcel
audience	cover	passenger
author	ferry	pet
bagpipes	grass	rat
cameraman	mouse	thriller

a person who / that ... an animal that ...
a thing that people ...
a group of people ... someone ...
something you can ...
a woman ... a kind of ... that ...

From Plymouth to Plymouth

Plymouth is a town on the south coast of England, a bit east of Cornwall. (*Look at the map.*) Liam took the top photo when he went there on a sailing trip. One of his American Internet friends wanted it for a high school history project. (*Remember B. J. in Florida?*) Soon after that, Liam got a copy of his friend's project ...

1 Test yourselves!

How quickly can you learn new facts? And how well can you remember them? Read these two pages from B. J.'s project. Then turn the page and try to answer the questions.

They came on the Mayflower

Lots of American towns have taken their names from places in Europe, usually after the places the first settlers came from. The most important of these is Plymouth, Massachusetts. If you go there today, you can see a replica of the famous ship 'Mayflower'. It is a gift from the people of England. People come from all over the USA to see it because it is so important for American history. They are often surprised because it looks so small. It is hard to imagine how about a hundred people bravely sailed across the Atlantic in it from England – yes, from Plymouth, on the south coast (see top photo).
This was in September 1620. We call these people 'Pilgrims' because for them it was a religious journey. They were Puritans. They wanted to start a new life where they could freely practise their religion. And speak their own English language. (This wasn't so easy in the Netherlands, where some of them had lived for a while.) Actually, two ships set off. But the other one, the 'Speedwell', had to turn back because it was taking in water. Its passengers joined those who were already on the 'Mayflower'. In November, they landed in what we now call 'New England'. The Pilgrims found themselves in wild country. The weather was very bad that first winter, and they didn't have enough food. Many of the Pilgrims died. It looked as if the 'Plymouth Colony' was at an end.

The first Thanksgiving

But there were native people there, and they knew how to live in that kind of country. The Pilgrims asked them for help. In the spring, the 'Indians' (as they called them) showed them how to grow the right kind of food corn, for example. That year they had a very good harvest. To say 'thanks' to God, they had a big 'Thanksgiving' feast (see old picture, with their friends, the Indians at the table). Today Thanksgiving is a very important holiday in the USA. Families come together for a big dinner with turkey, corn, and other American foods. And they remember that the Pilgrims came all the way from England to start a new life in a new country.

2 How much have you learned?

a) *Test yourselves: Write down your answers to all these questions before you turn back to check.*

1. In what part of England is the English Plymouth?
2. In which American state is the other Plymouth?
3. In which Plymouth is the replica of the Mayflower?
4. B.J. lives in the southernmost state. Which one is that?
5. What was the name of the other ship that set off with them?
6. What happened to a) that other ship, b) its passengers?
7. For what reason did the Pilgrims leave their country?
8. What was the Pilgrims' religion?
9. What language did they speak?
10. What other country had some of them tried living in?
11. In what year did the Pilgrims travel?
12. What ocean did they cross?
13. In what month did they a) leave England, b) arrive?
14. What was their name for the colony they started?
15. What problems did the colony have in the first winter?
16. What did they call the native people they met there?
17. With which of their problems did the natives help them?
18. What kind of food did they learn to grow?
19. What American holiday has to do with the Pilgrims?
20. What colour is the shirt of the native American on the right?

G 24/25

b) *Check each other's answers. Give two points for each correct answer. You can give one point for an answer that is half right. Add up the results.*

Score

38–40: Excellent!	20–25: OK.
32–36: Very good!	14–18: Could do better!
26–30: Good.	Under 14: Oh dear!!

G 23

c) *Look at the general rule for the question words 'which' and 'what'.*

Which part ...? The north, or the south?

SAVE

What ...? – *from an open number*
Which ...? – *from an exact number*

But: It depends on what the speaker is thinking of!

Now look at the quiz questions and explain the question word. In which of them could you use the other word – if you are thinking of something special?

3 Make your own quiz

Divide into groups. Each group makes a quiz with ten questions for the other groups. Each quiz should be about one of the stories or other texts in this book. Use all the question words – but be careful with 'which' and 'what'!

Some examples for 'Eddie the Inventor':
– ... was the name of the market square?
– On ... side of the square did Farrukh live?
– ... was Sol Kolmi's business?
Go on!

4 B.J.'s message

Hi Liam!
I sent that project of mine by snail-mail. Did it arrive yet? I can't remember if I sent a postcard with it. Did you enjoy the sailing trip? OK, it's a silly question! I always enjoy myself when I'm on a boat, and I'm sure you enjoy yourself just as much. I simply can't imagine NOT having fun at sea! But no more sailing for me for some time: I fell off the rigging last week and hurt myself quite badly. I can't move for two weeks!
Yours, B.J.

a) *Read B.J.'s message to find the reflexive pronouns. Can you also find some verbs which are not reflexive, though they are in German?*

SAVE

Some verbs can be reflexive:
He enjoyed the trip. – He enjoyed himself.
It hurt her. – She hurt herself.
Also: ourselves / yourselves / themselves

b) *Complete Liam's answer with reflexives – but only if they are necessary – and translate it into German.*

Sorry to hear you hurt ... . I can't imagine ... not being able to move ... for two weeks! Thanks for the project, it was very interesting. We really enjoyed ... this summer. We didn't go away anywhere, but I can't remember ... a better summer! Regards, Liam

WP 1 What is the word for ...?

a) *Give the right nouns for ...*

1. a man who does business.
2. a person who buys something from a business.
3. all the things you need for a job.
4. a person whose job it is to take bets.
5. a group of people that fight for a country.
6. a person whose job it is to fight for a country.
7. a house with only one floor.
8. a part of a house where you can sit outside.
9. the part of a street that you walk on.
10. what T-shirts are usually made of.
11. a thing on a door or an old radio that you turn.
12. what you can use to listen to music quietly.

b) *Give the verbs that mean ...*

1. to make something that is really new.
2. to put your hand on something.
3. to put money on a horse that you want to win.
4. to go down (under water, for example).
5. to go into a country in a big crowd.
6. to make your home in a new place.
7. to say exactly what a word means.

c) *Give the adjectives that mean ...*

1. not funny.
2. belonging to soldiers, armies, etc.
3. thinking only good things will happen.

2 Rizwan's postcard

3 +Tara's postcard

4

The rainy season has just begun in India, so some of the Modis' postcards have got wet. *Write out clearly what Rizwan and/or Tara wrote.*

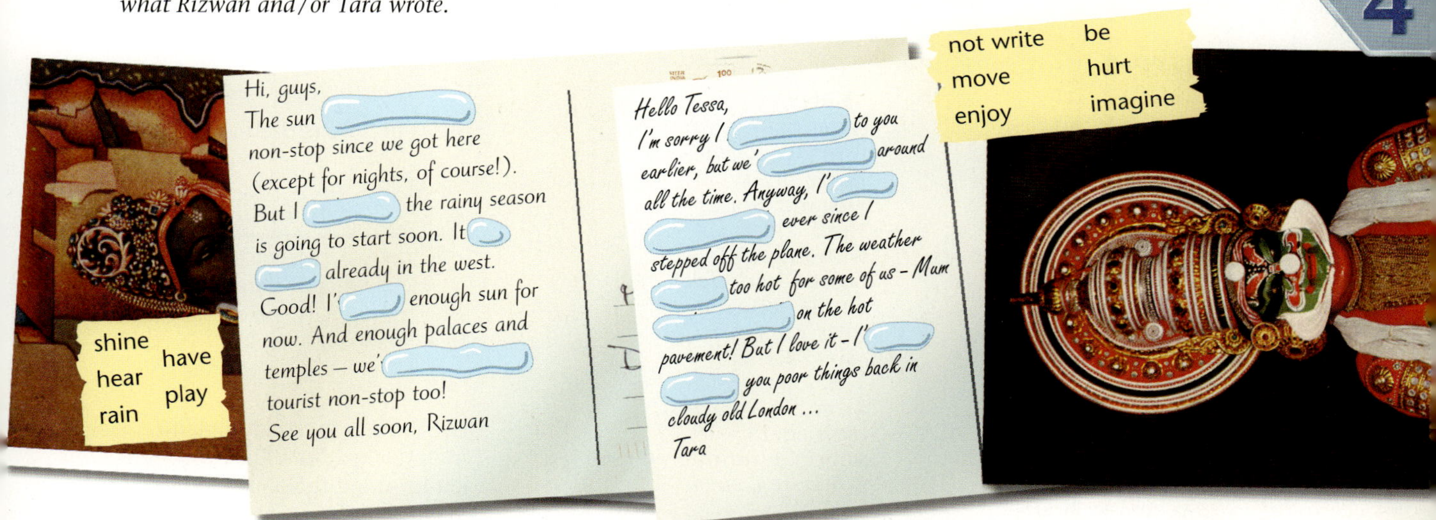

Rizwan's missing verbs are in the present perfect or the present perfect progressive.

+*Tara's missing verbs are also in the present perfect or the present perfect progressive – and two of them need a reflexive pronoun.*

HV 4 Listening comprehension: Australians

Complete these sentences with defining relative clauses. But first listen to the radio talk for the facts that you need.

1. The Aborigines were the first people ...
2. They were nomads – that is, people ...
3. The stories ... were all about a magic world ...
4. The Dutch were the first Europeans ...
5. James Cook was the man ...
6. For the British, Australia was the ideal place to dump the people ...
7. The immigrants ... did better than those early settlers.
8. Many got rich from the gold ... or as sheep farmers.
9. They drove any Aborigines ... off their farms.
10. Many white Australians are now getting interested in the culture ...

CHECK-IN

1	**clue** [klu:]	Anhaltspunkt, Hinweis
	at the back [ət ðə 'bæk]	hinten
	is **spoken** ['spəʊkn]	wird gesprochen
2	**homeless** ['həʊmləs]	heimatlos, obdachlos
	partly ['pɑ:tli]	teilweise, zum Teil
	Zulu ['zu:lu]	*afrikanische Sprache*
	African ['æfrɪkən]	afrikanisch, Afrikanisch
	Paul Simon [ˌpɔ:l 'saɪmən]	*amerikanischer Popmusiker*
	Joseph Shabalala [ˌdʒəʊzɪf ˈʃɑ:bəlɑ:lə]	*afrikanischer Sänger*
	vocal group ['vəʊkl ˌgru:p]	Musikgruppe mit Gesang
	Ladysmith Black Mambazo ['leɪdismɪθ ˌblæk məm'bɑ:zəʊ]	*afrikanische Musikgruppe*
	line [laɪn]	Zeile
	moonlight ['mu:nlaɪt]	Mondlicht
	midnight ['mɪdnaɪt]	Mitternacht
	in fact [ɪn 'fækt]	tatsächlich
	verse [vɜ:s]	Strophe, Vers
	gist [dʒɪst]	Kernpunkt, (das) Wesentliche
	chorus ['kɔ:rəs]	Refrain; Chor

4

STEP A

A	**properly** ['prɒpli]	ordentlich, pünktlich
	hers [hɜ:z]	ihre(r/s), der/die/das ihre
	guy [gaɪ]	Junge, Kerl
	state [steɪt]	Zustand, Status
1	**dance** [dɑ:ns]	Tanz
	to **wish** [wɪʃ]	wünschen
	to **be busy** ['bɪzi]	besetzt sein (*Telefon*)
	to **invade** [ɪn'veɪd]	einmarschieren
	Angles [ˌæŋglz]	(die) Angeln
	Saxons ['sæksnz]	(die) Sachsen
	Viking ['vaɪkɪŋ]	Wikinger(in)
	attack [ə'tæk]	Angriff
	to **settle** ['setl]	(be)siedeln
2	to **define** [dɪ'faɪn]	näher bestimmen, definieren
3	**Westminster Bridge** [ˌwestmɪnstə 'brɪdʒ]	*Brücke in London*
	to **drive so. out** [ˌdraɪv‿'aʊt]	jmdn verjagen, hinausjagen
B	**Bayeux Tapestry** [baɪˌjɜ: 'tæpɪstri]	*berühmter Teppich in Bayeux*
	Norman ['nɔ:mən]	Normanne/Normannin
	army ['ɑ:mi]	Armee, Heer
	to **defeat** [dɪ'fi:t]	besiegen, schlagen
	Harold ['hærəld]	*König von England (1022?–1066)*
	William the Conqueror [ˌwɪljəm ðə 'kɒŋkrə]	*König von England (1027?–1087)*
	really ['rɪəli]	in Wirklichkeit, eigentlich
	whose [hu:z]	deren, dessen
	theirs [ðeəz]	ihre(r/s), der/die/das ihre
	leg [leg]	Bein
4	**treasure** ['treʒə]	Schatz
	to **attract** [ə'trækt]	anziehen, anlocken

'Streets of London' is a song about homeless people.

Look at the map of the world at the end of your book: English is spoken in lots of African countries.

Moonlight is the light from the 'sunny side' of the moon.

That guy is just too busy to learn a new dance.

Her is to hers as their is to theirs.

verb / noun	
to / a → dance	wish, attack, defeat, bet, place, post, …

The Vikings invaded England and attacked the villages. They settled along the North Sea coast.

The Bayeux Tapestry tells the story of the Norman attack.

William the Conqueror defeated the English with a strong army.

'Treasure Island' is a very famous book.

	Native American [ˌneɪtɪv‿ə'merɪkən]	amerikanische(r) Ureinwohner(in)
	Australian aborigine [ɒs'treɪliən ˌæbə'rɪdʒni]	australische(r) Ureinwohner(in)
5	to **need to** [ni:d]	müssen
	long-distance truck driver [ˌlɒŋ'dɪstns 'trʌk ˌdraɪvə]	Fernfahrer(in)
	sailor ['seɪlə]	Matrose, Seemann
	waiter ['weɪtə]	Kellner
	travel agent ['trævl‿ˌeɪdʒnt]	Reisebüroangestellte(r)
6	**vegetable** ['vedʒətəbl]	Gemüse
	lamb [læm]	Lamm(fleisch)
	chicken ['tʃɪkɪʒ]	Huhn, Hähnchen
	to **post** [pəʊst]	abschicken, zur Post geben

STEP B

inventor [ɪn'ventə]	Erfinder(in)
writer ['raɪtə]	Schriftsteller(in)
square [skweə]	Platz
neighbourhood ['neɪbəhʊd]	Nachbarschaft
yard [jɑ:d]	*englisches Längenmaß (= 0,914 m)*
soldier ['səʊldʒə]	Soldat(in)
administrator [əd'mɪnɪstreɪtə]	Verwalter(in), Leiter(in)
narrow ['nærəʊ]	eng, schmal
spacious ['speɪʃəs]	geräumig, weitläufig
trader ['treɪdə]	Händler(in)
bookie ['bʊki]	Buchmacher(in)
hangout ['hæŋaʊt]	Stammplatz, Stammlokal
to **pick up** [pɪk‿'ʌp]	abholen
to **hang* out** [ˌhæŋ‿'aʊt]	herumlungern
to **run** [rʌn]	*hier:* führen, leiten
bakery ['beɪkri]	Bäckerei
bicycle ['baɪsɪkl]	Fahrrad
to **drop in** [drɒp‿'ɪn]	vorbeischauen
customer ['kʌstəmə]	Kunde/Kundin
gambling ['gæmblɪŋ]	(Glücks-)Spiel
pavement ['peɪvmənt]	Bürgersteig, Gehweg
cotton ['kɒtn]	Baumwolle
invention [ɪn'venʃn]	Erfindung
to **have to do sth.** [ˌhæv tə 'du:]	etw tun müssen
weekday ['wi:kdeɪ]	Wochentag, Arbeitstag
decimal point [ˌdesɪml 'pɔɪnt]	Komma(stelle)
bet [bet]	Wette
⟨**opening price**⟩ ['əʊpnɪŋ ˌpraɪs]	Eröffnungskurs
⟨**closing price**⟩ ['kləʊzɪŋ ˌpraɪs]	Schlusskurs
beggar ['begə]	Bettler(in)
to **place** [pleɪs]	setzen, platzieren
to **break*** [breɪk]	(zer)brechen, knacken
headphones ['hedfəʊnz]	Kopfhörer
to **touch** [tʌtʃ]	berühren, anfassen
excitement [ɪk'saɪtmənt]	Aufregung
knob [nɒb]	Knopf, Knauf
beep [bi:p]	Piepsen
rupee [ru:'pi:]	*indische Währung*
note [nəʊt]	Banknote
paper ['peɪpə]	*hier:* Zeitung
Russian ['rʌʃn]	russisch, Russisch

people with -or / -er

sailor	driver
doctor	waiter
administrator	writer
visitor	trader
actor	customer
…	…

What's for lunch? Fish and chips, lamb, vegetables, …

Who was the inventor of the telephone, the computer, …?

The British were soldiers and administrators in India.

That's a very narrow road – there's only room for one car.

The house is spacious = the rooms are big.

We've got two bakeries in our neighbourhood.

Always two parts: glasses, sunglasses, headphones, scissors, jeans, trousers, shorts, boots, …

'Bike' is short for bicycle.

Lots of homeless people are beggars.

You can't hear people with your headphones on.

building words

neighbour	neighbourhood
exciting	excitement
cool	coolness
to gamble	gambling
to invent	invention
to define	definition

Can you find some more examples?

4

	Sputnik ['spʌtnɪk]	*erster Satellit im Weltall (1957)*
	Gagarin [gə'gɑ:rɪn]	*russischer Kosmonaut (1934–1968), erster Mensch im Weltall (1961)*
	to **gamble** ['gæmbl]	(um Geld) spielen
	public ['pʌblɪk]	öffentlich
	to **look** [lʊk]	aussehen
	to **be disappointed** [ˌdɪsə'pɔɪntɪd]	enttäuscht sein
	to **be unlucky** [ʌn'lʌki]	Pech haben
	to **fool** [fu:l]	zum Narren halten, hereinlegen
	to **stuff** [stʌf]	füllen, stopfen
	(ten) times [ˌten 'taɪmz]	(zehn)mal
	once [wʌns]	einmal
	walking stick ['wɔ:kɪŋ ˌstɪk]	Gehstock, Spazierstock
	rule [ru:l]	Herrschaft
	liar ['laɪə]	Lügner(in)
	canvas ['kænvəs]	Segeltuch
	to **get back** [get 'bæk]	zurückkommen, ankommen
	to **be scared** ['skeəd]	Angst haben, verschreckt sein
	discovery [dɪ'skʌvri]	Entdeckung
	to **protect** [prə'tekt]	(be)schützen
	to **fall asleep** [ˌfɔ:l‿ə'sli:p]	einschlafen
	war [wɔ:]	Krieg
	for [fɔ:]	... lang
	to **smash** [smæʃ]	zerschlagen, zerschmettern
1	to **go with** ['gəʊ wɪð]	passen zu
	businesslike ['bɪznɪslaɪk]	geschäftstüchtig, nüchtern

Grandfather can't read the paper without his glasses.

She was disappointed because her dad couldn't come to the concert.

to be unlucky ≠ to be unhappy

once, twice, three times, four times, five times, ... times

Asterix and Obelix were against the Romans. They often fooled the Roman soldiers.

franz protéger *lat* protegere
engl to protect

We know that the Vikings were very war-like people.

STEP C

1	to **belong to** [bɪ'lɒŋ tʊ]	gehören (zu)
2	**scrambled eggs** [ˌskræmbld‿'egz]	Rührei
	crisp [krɪsp]	knusprig
	muffin ['mʌfɪn]	weiches Brötchen, kleiner Kuchen
	whatever [wɒt'evə]	was (auch immer), egal was
	you're welcome [ˌjɔ: 'welkəm]	bitte sehr, nichts zu danken

Everybody knows you can't make scrambled eggs without breaking eggs.

What's for breakfast? Muffins, tea, butter, ...

TRACK 2

+**top** [tɒp]	obere(r/s)
+**Mayflower** ['meɪflaʊə]	*Name eines Schiffes*
+**settler** ['setlə]	Siedler(in)
+**Massachusetts** [ˌmæsə'tʃu:sɪts]	*amerikanischer Bundesstaat*
+**gift** [gɪft]	Geschenk
+**Pilgrim** ['pɪlgrɪm]	Pilger(in)
+**religious** [rɪ'lɪdʒəs]	religiös
+**Puritan** ['pjʊərɪtn]	Puritaner(in)
+**the Netherlands** ['neðələndz]	Niederlande
+**Speedwell** ['spi:dwel]	*Name eines Schiffes*
+to **join so.** [dʒɔɪn]	sich jmdm. anschließen
+**New England** [ˌnju: 'ɪŋglənd]	Neuengland *(Region im Nordosten der USA)*
+**Thanksgiving** [ˌθæŋks'gɪvɪŋ]	*Erntedankfest (4. Donnerstag im November)*
+to **grow** [grəʊ]	anbauen
+**harvest** ['hɑ:vɪst]	Ernte
+**feast** [fi:st]	Festmahl, Bankett
+**holiday** ['hɒlədeɪ]	Feiertag

The Pilgrims came from Britain. There were more settlers from other countries, for example the Netherlands.

The settlers lived in colonies on the east coast.

The Puritans didn't want to live in colonies.

Many people say Holland for the Netherlands, but Holland is only part of the country.

The New England states are in the north-east of the USA.

Thanksgiving is a very important feast for the Americans.

VOCABULARY

	+**turkey** ['tɜ:ki]	Truthahn	A turkey is not a bird from Turkey!
2	+**yourselves** [jɔ:'selvz]	euch (selbst)	Enjoy yourselves! = Have a good time!
	+**ocean** ['əʊʃn]	Ozean, Meer	An ocean is a large sea.
	+**month** [mʌnθ]	Monat	
	+**score** [skɔ:]	Punkte, Spielstand	In matches you score points or goals.
4	+**snail-mail** ['sneɪlmeɪl]	Schneckenpost	
	+**if** [ɪf]	ob	
	+**just** [dʒʌst]	genau	
	+**rigging** ['rɪgɪŋ]	Tauwerk, Takelage	

CHECK-OUT

2	**rainy** ['reɪni]	regnerisch	There is a lot of rain in the north-west. It is a rainy area.
	palace ['pælɪs]	Palast	A palace is a large house for a king or queen.
3	+to **step off** [step‿'ɒf]	aussteigen	
4	**Dutch** [dʌtʃ]	holländisch, niederländisch	
	James Cook [ˌdʒeɪmz 'kʊk]	*britischer Seefahrer (1728–1779)*	
	to **do well** [du: 'wel]	erfolgreich sein	
	to **drive* off** [draɪv‿'ɒf]	vertreiben	

COGNATE WORDS

accent ['æksnt]	Akzent
barrack ['bærək]	Kaserne, Baracke
bungalow ['bʌŋgləʊ]	Bungalow
businessman ['bɪznɪsmæn]	Geschäftsmann
butter ['bʌtə]	Butter
chewing gum ['tʃu:ɪŋ ˌgʌm]	Kaugummi
+**colony** ['kɒləni]	Kolonie
communication [kəˌmju:nɪ'keɪʃn]	Übertragung, Kommunikation
+**corn** [kɔ:n]	Getreide, Korn
doctor ['dɒktə]	Arzt/Ärztin, Doktor
electronic [ˌelek'trɒnɪk]	elektronisch
function ['fʌŋkʃn]	Funktion, Aufgabe
generation [ˌdʒenə'reɪʃn]	Generation
+**God** [gɒd]	Gott
to **improvise** ['ɪmprəvaɪz]	improvisieren
+**Indian** ['ɪndiən]	Indianer(in)
lead singer [ˌli:d 'sɪŋə]	Leadsänger(in)
legal ['li:gl]	gesetzlich, legal
magic ['mædʒɪk]	magisch, zauberhaft
mechanic [mɪ'kænɪk]	Mechaniker(in)
military ['mɪlɪtri]	militärisch, Militär-
nomad ['nəʊmæd]	Nomade / Nomadin
optimistic [ˌɒptɪ'mɪstɪk]	optimistisch
policeman [pə'li:smən]	Polizist
popularity [ˌpɒpjə'lærəti]	Beliebtheit, Popularität
to **practice** ['præktɪs]	ausüben, praktizieren
regular ['regjələ]	regelmäßig
to **repair** [rɪ'peə]	reparieren
schoolboy ['sku:lbɔɪ]	Schuljunge
serious ['sɪəriəs]	ernsthaft, seriös
service ['sɜ:vɪs]	Dienst(leistung), Service
set [set]	Satz, Garnitur
to **sink*** [sɪŋk]	sinken, (ab)fallen
sketch [sketʃ]	Sketch, Szene
sort [sɔ:t]	Sorte, Art
statue ['stætju:]	Statue, Standbild
studio ['stju:diəʊ]	Studio
system ['sɪstəm]	System
temple ['templ]	Tempel
toast [təʊst]	Toast(brot)
verandah [və'rændə]	Veranda
whisky ['wɪski]	Whisky
workshop ['wɜ:kʃɒp]	Werkstatt

UNIT 5

Getting fit and having fun

DANCING / AEROBICS

What you'll need – Good dance shoes or trainers that support your feet well, and comfortable clothes.

Time out – A class two or three times a week will probably be more than enough for you. Some people find that a workout once a week is fine.

It will – Improve your shape and all-round fitness.

Go for it if – You like exercising to music; you want to get really fit. If you're too shy to exercise in public, you can buy an aerobics or dance video to use at home.

FOOTBALL

What you'll need – If you're really serious about it, you'll need proper football boots. But if you are just doing it for fun, trainers and sporty clothes are fine.

Time out – It's up to you, but if you really want to go for it, you'll have to find a team to play for and you can expect to train a couple of times a week.

It will – Improve your fitness and stamina.

Go for it if – You love watching football; you'd like to play in a team; you don't mind running around a muddy football pitch on a wet Sunday afternoon.

SWIMMING

What you'll need – A comfortable swimsuit or pair of trunks, and a towel. If you're serious about it, you should buy a pair of goggles too.

Time out – It's up to you. For some it's enough go to the pool once or twice a week, but others become real water babies and join a swimming club. This can mean training several times a week.

It will – Tone up your legs, stomach, arms and bottom, and give your heart and lungs a good workout.

Go for it if – You enjoy splashing about in water. If you can't swim yet, it's never too late to learn!

1 Collecting and organizing words

Copy and complete the grid with words from the article. Add three more sports to your list, and use your dictionary to help you with new words.

Sport	Place	Equipment
aerobics	gym, at home	music, good trainers
football	…	…

2 Parts of the body

Collect words for parts of the body. Draw a person or cut a picture out of a magazine and stick it in your exercise book. Name the parts of the body.

3 Fitness freak or yo-yo player?

Work in pairs. Find out how sporty your partner is. Ask questions about …

- what sports your partner likes watching,
- whether he / she does any sports or plays any games,
- how your partner feels about sport.

TENNIS

What you'll need – Two or three tennis balls, a good racket and, of course, a partner! Your trainers and comfy clothes are all you need to wear, but you can spend a lot of money if you really want to look good on the tennis court!

Time out – It's up to you. You can spend as much or as little time as you want to. But the more you play, the better you become.

It will – Make your leg muscles stronger and burn up calories.

Go for it if – You enjoy competitive sports and trying to beat someone; you've got quite good coordination. It helps if you play with someone who is more or less the same level as you.

HORSE-RIDING

What you'll need – Well, a horse is a good start! You also need comfortable clothes, sensible shoes and a riding hat, plus boots if you're going to go riding regularly.

Time out – Riding can be expensive, so it isn't the kind of thing you can do four or five times a week. Once a week is probably the most you can expect, and riding is more of a summer sport than a winter one.

It will – Tone up your thighs and take you outside into the fresh air.

Go for it if – You love horses, and you don't want to work out in a gym.

GYMNASTICS

What you'll need – A leotard is the basic uniform for gymnasts, but even shorts and T-shirt are fine when you start. You don't need fancy trainers as most gymnastic work is done in bare feet.

Time out – If you're serious about gymnastics and want to enter competitions, etc. then you'll have to train two or three times a week. If it's just for fun, then once or twice a week is plenty.

It will – Improve your posture and suppleness, and tone up your whole body from head to toe.

Go for it if – You've got good rhythm, and you're good at bending or stretching. Always warm up properly. If you're too ambitious at first, you might hurt yourself.

5

From *Bliss* magazine

4 +It's good for you!

Think of eight tips people could give the yo-yo player in the cartoon on page 72. Use the ideas below.

Horse-riding Dancing and aerobics Playing football Skating Playing with a yo-yo Gymnastics Swimming Playing tennis	is good	for if you don't like the idea of if you enjoy	relaxing. doing workouts in a gym. being outdoors in the fresh air. playing in a team. improving your all-round fitness. splashing about in water. burning up calories. running around muddy pitches.

5 Go for it!

Think of a sport you know quite well and write about it. Say what you'll need, how often you should do it, what it will do for you, and what kind of person would be good at it. If possible, add a tip.

Marathon Man or mummy's boy?

Ken is out of shape. He wants to get fit, but isn't sure how. One day he has an idea ...

G 26 1 You make the rules

a) *Copy the grid and add more examples of structures from the dialogue.*

will-future	going to-future	present progressive	simple present
I'll take part in the New York Marathon.	I'm going to take part in the New York Marathon.	I'm taking part in the New York Marathon in October.	Do you want to come?

b) *Look at the examples you collected under 'present progressive' and 'simple present'. In which of the sentences is the speaker not talking about the future? Cross them out.*

c) *Now look at the other examples in the grid. In which sentences is the speaker …*

- talking about something on a timetable?
- deciding to do something while speaking?
- talking about an expectation?
- warning someone?
- talking about something already fixed?
- seeing a sign of what is going to happen soon?
- making a promise?
- talking about what he has already decided to do?

d) *When do you use each of the four structures for the future? Make some general rules. (This is a grey area, so keep your eyes and ears open to how speakers of English talk about the future.)*

G 26 2 Ken's plans

a) *Talk about Ken's diary with a partner. Ask and answer questions about what he is doing, and when.*

Example: What is Ken doing on Monday? – He's flying to Los Angeles in the morning. Then he's ...

Monday 6:40 am – Fly to Los Angeles (AA 196) 3 pm – Make running shoe advertisement Evening – Don't forget to call Mom !!!!!	**Friday** 5:30 am – Do press-ups, knee-bends, sit-ups, handstands Morning – Collect new exercise bike from store 6:30 pm – Titanic II (Kennedy Movie Theater)
Tuesday 5:30 am – Do press-ups 7 am – Power breakfast with sponsors 5 pm – Fly back to New York (AA 198)	**Saturday** 10 am – Meet CNN reporters for interview 11:30 am – Boston Marathon 8 pm – Watch interview on TV
Wednesday 5:30 am – Do press-ups and knee-bends 7 am – Make breakfast-in-bed for Mom 4 pm – See Dr Aziz about big toe	**Sunday** 9 am – Church with Mom 10 am – Fun Run in NY Central Park Afternoon – Answer letters from fans
Thursday 5:30 am – Do press-ups, knee-bends, sit-ups Morning – Take broken exercise bike back to store Afternoon – Buy new running shoes	**Notes** 

b) *Write your own fantasy diary. Then work in pairs. Tell each other about your busy weeks, and find the best time when you can meet.*

Example:

> Can we meet at 8 o'clock on Thursday evening?

> Sorry, but I'm rehearsing for my concert on Thursday evening.

5

G 26 3 Expectations

a) *What do you think Ken will be like in 30 years? Choose from the ideas below, and explain why.*

He'll (probably) be ...	fatter / fitter / dead / married / famous / a nobody / ...?
He'll (probably) have ...	grey hair / long hair / no hair / a family / a girlfriend / no friends / ...?

b) *Who are the big sports stars at the moment? Say how you think they will change as they get older.*

G 26 4 Warnings and promises

What is Ken's mother saying in pictures 1–3? (She always tried to protect him when he was little.) And what is Ken saying in pictures 4–6? (He was always very helpful.) Use the verbs below.

Example:

1. Be careful, or you'll fall off!

be sick	answer	drop
fall off	carry	mend

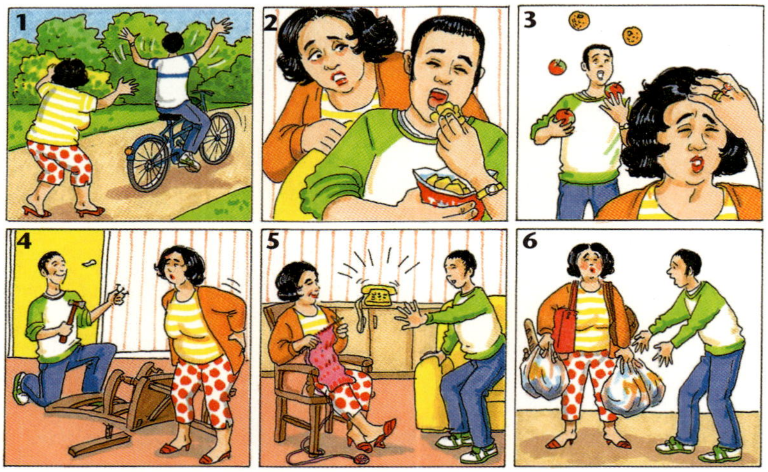

5

G 26 5 Will or going to?

What do they say? Start with 'I'll' or 'I'm going to', and choose from the verbs on the right.

1. Ken wants muesli for breakfast. His mother asks him why he is cutting apples. What does he say?

   Example: "I'm going to make muesli."

2. The next morning Ken is in a hurry to leave the house, so his mother offers to get his breakfast ready for him. What does she say?
3. Ken has just drunk the last bottle of orange juice. It's his mother's shopping day today. What does she offer to do?
4. Ken has bought some flowers for Mother's Day. A friend wants to know who they are for. What does Ken tell his friend?
5. Ken's big toe hurts and is very red. Dr Aziz tells him he needs a new pair of running shoes. What does Ken tell his mom the next day?
6. Ken forgot to bring his water bottle to the Marathon, and it starts in two minutes. One of his fans has got an extra water bottle. What does she tell him?
7. Ken would like to become a member of a New York tennis club. His mother wants to know which club he has chosen. What does she ask?
8. When Ken tells her it's 'The Manhattan Celebrity Tennis Club', she suddenly decides she wants to be a member too. What does she tell Ken?

join
make
give
buy

G 27

6 Tips from the trainer

Say it another way with 'if': Start with 'If you (+ verb), ...', or 'If you don't (+ verb), ...'.

Example: You must train harder, or you won't be fit enough for the race.
If you train harder, you'll be fit enough for the race.
If you don't train harder, you won't be fit enough for the race.

1. Do what I tell you, and then you'll win the Marathon.
2. You mustn't take drugs, or they'll throw you out of the race.
3. I hope you believe in 'fair play', or I won't work with you.
4. Eat lots of pasta, or you won't have enough energy for the race.
5. But don't eat a big meal before the race, or you'll be too full to run!
6. Warm up before the race, or you'll damage a muscle.
7. Go to bed early, and then you won't be so tired the next day.

SAVE

If you start with 'if', use a comma between the clauses.

You don't need a comma if your 'if' is in the middle.

G 28

7 ⟨That's a tricky one!⟩

a) Four people are taking part in a radio quiz called 'That's a tricky one!' They are describing what they would do in difficult or tricky situations. *Note down what you think the situation is.*

A: Well, I wouldn't eat the cake for a start. If I did, I'd probably be sick! I'd tell him, of course, but I'd try to be polite about it. Salt looks just like sugar, doesn't it? Mistakes like that can happen to anyone.

B: Hm ... that's a tricky one. On the one hand, I wouldn't want to hurt her, so I'd probably say something like, 'Yeah, it looks great.' That wouldn't be a complete lie, because it would look great on a supermodel.

C: I'd ask the shop to mend it, and if that wasn't possible, I'd buy him a new camera. I wouldn't tell him anything. He wouldn't know the difference. But I don't know what I'd do if it was really expensive and I didn't have enough money for a new one.

D: I'd help, of course. I'd use my mobile phone to call an ambulance, and then I'd wait at the scene of the accident until it came. I'd have a problem if they were badly hurt. I can't stand the sight of blood, you see.

b) *Ask your teacher what he or she would do in the same situations. Then say what you would do.*

c) *Work in pairs. Take turns asking and answering the questions.*

What would you do if ...

- you opened your schoolbag and found a snake?
- you hit a tennis ball through the window of a teacher's car?
- a bully asked you to give him your pocket money?
- you woke up tomorrow with funny red spots all over your body?
- a friend asked you to do her homework for her?

I'd probably ...
I wouldn't ...
I might ...
And what about you ...?
It depends. If ..., then I'd ...

SAVE

If Ken **wins** the Boston Marathon, he **will pay** his trainer more money.
(reale Möglichkeit)

If Ken **won** a billion dollars, he **would put** it all in the bank.
(irreale Bedingung)

YOU

8 ⟨Would you really?⟩

Would you ever do these things? In what situations would you do them?

tell a lie – kiss a police officer – paint your face white – do someone else's homework – wear a red nose

The mile

1 A natural athlete

What kind of person is 'a natural athlete'?

Choose from the expressions on the right.

competitive — very fit — hates losing
lazy — ambitious — doesn't need to train
a good loser — trains hard — gives up early

2 Listening comprehension: The mile

a) *Before you read, listen to the first part of the story 'The mile'. Make notes about:*

- George (the narrator) and Arthur Boocock
- 'the mile', and why George takes part in it.

b) *Talk about what you have found out. What do you think will happen next?*

3 While you read

Go through the story and try to guess which words mean the same as these:

Elend – herumwandern – Laufbahn – Kerl
Kartoffelchips – die Nase voll haben – Durchsage
Wettbewerbsteilnehmer – überrascht – ignorieren
Schatten – spurten – anfeuern

Mum was reading my school report for the third time. I didn't say anything. I just stared at my gammon and chips. What could I say? Mum looked so disappointed. "I mean, you didn't even do well at sport, did you? 'Sport – he is not a natural athlete.' Didn't you do anything right this term?"

I smiled to myself. No, I'm not a natural athlete, but I'd done one thing right this term. I'd shown Arthur Boocock that he couldn't push me around any more.

That's why everything else had gone wrong. That's why I had such a bad report. That's why this last term was so miserable, because of Arthur Boocock.

I didn't like him. He's a right bully, but because he's a bit older and is good at sport and running and things, everybody does what he says. Arthur holds the school record for the mile. Mr Melrose is in charge of athletics and he says Arthur could run for Yorkshire one day if he trains hard enough.

Arthur hit me every time he saw me. Sometimes he hit me in the stomach, sometimes on the back of my neck. Then he started taking my pocket money. He used to say, 'Oh, you don't want that, do you?' and I said, 'No, you have it, Arthur.'

I was really scared of him. He made my life a misery. I hated going to school, and when I could, I stayed at home by pretending to be sick.

I suppose that's when I started to get behind with my schoolwork, but anything was better than being bullied by Arthur Boocock. And when I did go to school, I stayed in the classroom at playtime, or I made sure I was near the teacher who was on playground duty.

Of course, Arthur thought it was all very funny. He tried to hit me when the teacher wasn't looking – and that was often.

Dinnertime was the worst because we had an hour free before the bell went for school dinners, and no one was allowed to stay inside. It was a school rule. That was an hour for Arthur to bully me. I used to try and hide but he always found me.

Soon I stopped going to school dinners. I'd get some chips, or a Cornish pasty, and wander around. Sometimes, I'd go into town and look at the shops, or else I'd go to the park. Anything to get away from school and Arthur Boocock. That's how I met Archie.

There's a running-track in the park, a proper one with white lines and everything, and one day I spent all dinnertime watching this old bloke running round. That was Archie. I went back the next day and he was there again, running round. I got talking to him.

"Hey, mister, how fast can you run a mile?" I was holding a bag of crisps, and he came over and took one. He smiled at me.

"How fast can *you* run a mile?"

"I don't know, I've never tried."

He smiled again. "Well, now's your chance. Come on, get your jacket off."

He was ever so fast and I found it hard to keep up with him, but he told me I'd done well. I used to run with Archie every day after that. He gave me an old tracksuit top, and I changed into my shorts and

4 A closer look

a) *Note down the key facts of the story. Then use your notes to give a short summary.*
b) *Look at the speech bubbles below. Who do you think is talking to whom? Find facts in the story to explain why you think so. (In some cases different answers are possible.)*

I'd like to enter the open mile, please.

Congratulations! You did really well!

I hope you get a better report next term.

Would you like some more orange?

Oh, did that hurt? … It's all right if I take this, isn't it?

It's just a matter of training.

I don't feel well. Can I stay at home today?

Your homework is not good enough!

5 A step further

Is bullying a problem at your school? What can – or should – people do about bullies like Arthur?

6 Creative writing

Choose either a) or b). a) Mr Melrose meets George and Arthur at the end of the race. *Write a short dialogue between them.*

b) *Write a different ending for the story. Start with the line:*

I surprised a lot of people that day. …

trainers, and chased round the track after him. Archie said I was getting better and better.

"You'll run for Yorkshire one of these days." I laughed and told him to stop teasing me. He gave me half an orange. He always did after running.

"Listen, boy, I'm serious. It's all a matter of training. Anybody can be good if they train hard enough. See you tomorrow."

That's when I got the idea. I decided to go in for the mile in the school sports at the end of term. Anybody could enter the mile.

There were three weeks to the end of term, and in those three weeks I ran everywhere. I ran to school. I ran with Archie every dinnertime. I went back and ran on the track after school. Then ran home. If my mum wanted anything from the shops, I ran there. I got up really early in the mornings and ran before breakfast.

I was always running. I got into trouble at school for not doing my homework properly, but I didn't care. All I thought about was the mile.

I had daydreams about it. Always me and Arthur, neck and neck. Just me and Arthur against each other. I was sick of him and his bullying.

Arthur did well at sports day. He won the high-jump and the long-jump, the half-mile and the four-forty. Then there was the announcement for the mile. "Will all those competitors who would like to enter the open mile please go to Mr Melrose."

I hadn't told anybody that I was going to enter, so everybody was very surprised to see me when I went over in my shorts and running shoes – especially Melrose. Arthur thought it was really funny.

"Well, look who it is. Do you want me to give you half a mile start?"

I ignored him, and waited for Melrose to start the race. I surprised a lot of people that day, but nobody more than Arthur. I stuck to him like a shadow. When he went forward, I went forward. If he dropped back, I dropped back. This went on for about half the race. He kept giving me funny looks. He couldn't understand what was happening.

"You won't keep this up. Just watch."

And he suddenly spurted forward. I followed him, and when he looked round to see how far ahead he was, he got a shock when he saw he wasn't.

It was just like my daydreams. Arthur and me neck and neck, the whole school cheering us on, both of us heading for the last bend. I looked at Arthur and saw the tears rolling down his cheeks. He was crying his eyes out. I knew at that moment I'd beaten him. I don't mean I was winning the race. I didn't care about that. I knew I'd beaten him – Arthur. I knew he'd never hit me again.

That's when I walked off the track. I didn't see any point in running the last two hundred yards. I suppose that's because I'm not a natural athlete.

"'Sport – he is not a natural athlete.' Didn't you do anything right this term?"

My mum was still reading my report! I started to eat my gammon and chips. They'd gone cold.

From *The Puffin Book of School Stories* by George Layton (abridged)

1 Excuses, excuses

a) *Listen to the four dialogues and find the right picture. (Two pictures have nothing to do with the dialogues.)*

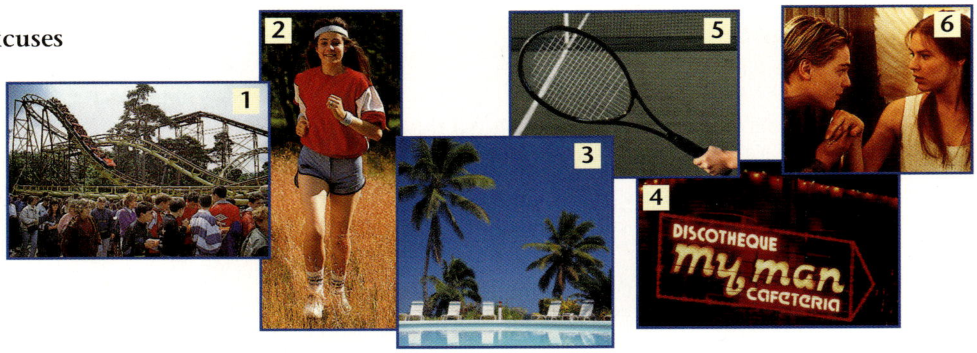

b) *Which two people decline the invitations? What are their reasons or excuses?*

c) *Practise invitations with a partner. Use the pictures for ideas and the phrases below.*

Inviting
I was wondering if you'd like to …
Would you like to …?
How / What about …?
Why don't we …?
Do you fancy (+ noun / +gerund) …?

Thanking
Thank you very much.
Thank you for inviting me.
That's very kind of you.
Thanks.

Declining
That's very kind of you but …
I'm afraid I can't because …
I'd rather not, thanks, because …
I'd love to but …

Accepting
I'd love to.
Yes, that sounds fun.
What a good idea.
That would be great.
That'd be great / nice.

Giving a reason
I'm busy on …
I'm visiting my cousins.
I won't be here on …
I've planned something else.

G 29

2 When or if?

a) *Can you explain the difference between these two sentences? (If you aren't sure, check the* SAVE *box.)*

I'll watch the Marathon if I go to New York.
I'll watch the Marathon when I go to New York.

SAVE

when – *it's a matter of time*
if – *it's not sure*

Remember: Only put 'will' or 'won't' in the main clause.

b) *Make sentences with 'when' or 'if'.*

Example: Ken is going shopping. In town, he'll look for a ring.
When Ken goes shopping, he'll look for a ring.

1. He'll find a nice ring and ask about the price.
2. Maybe the ring will be too expensive. Then he'll choose a cheaper one.
3. As soon as Ken gets home he will phone his girlfriend.
4. It is possible that she won't be at home. Then he'll watch sport on TV.
5. But she might be at home after all. Then Ken will invite her to dinner.
6. Ken hopes she will accept, and then he'll take her to a nice restaurant.
7. As soon as the meal is finished, Ken will ask her to marry him.
8. It's possible, of course, that she will decline. Then Ken will be very disappointed.

WP

3 Verb-noun collocations

Which verb goes with which group of nouns?

do make take have tell catch spend

1. lunch, a break, a holiday
2. a photo, turns, advice
3. homework, aerobics, a test
4. a story, a lie, a joke
5. a mistake, a plan, a promise
6. a ball, a bus, a cold
7. hours, money, the summer holidays

Collocations are pairs or groups of words that usually go together. Try to learn words together with their 'partners'.

4 Vocabulary tips

LEARNING TO LEARN

a) *Read about how these pupils learn French vocabulary. Which pieces of advice are the most useful for you? Can you add any more?*

Caroline

I use flash cards, with the English word on one side and the French translation on the back. I test myself regularly.

Mark

I always revise vocabulary with my girlfriend. She reads the French word, and I write down the English word. Then I test her.

Megan

I write the words in big letters on pieces of paper and stick them all over my room.

Sanjay

I draw a plan of my flat. Then I choose a room for each of the words. For example, if I wanted to learn the French word for 'joke', I would write it in my brother's room because he likes telling jokes.

Glen

I try to write a story with all the words. Writing the words helps me to remember them.

Selima

I repeat the words very loudly. Sometimes I rap the words to music.

Tony

I write sentences or little dialogues with the words and record them on a cassette. I listen to the cassette on my walkman while I'm doing something else.

5

b) *Below are some words you have met in this unit. Try Sanjay's tip and put the words in rooms. Then find out where the words are in your partner's flat or house. Talk about why you chose those rooms.*

to make a promise – comfortable – serious – pancakes – muddy – several – racket
towel – plenty – umbrella – disappointed – muscles – blood – get married

c) *Now write a story with all of the words.*

1 Healthy living

a) *Read the article below and match the advice on the right with the questions on the left.*

There are lots of ways to make sure you stay healthy. One good way is to work out how healthy you are now, then look at your lifestyle to see if there are things you can do to improve your health.

Ask yourself

1. Are you too thin or too heavy?
2. Do you get angry easily, or do you find it difficult to relax?
3. Do you smoke, drink alcohol or take drugs?
4. Do you eat a healthy diet? Do you have fruit and vegetables at least five times a day?
5. Do you exercise regularly?
6. Are you getting enough sleep?

What you can do about it

a. Get more rest and more exercise. Talk through your problems with someone. You will find that really helps. Try to stay away from stressful situations.
b. Write down what you eat. Eat lots of energy food like bread, pasta, potatoes, rice, plus fruit and vegetables – but chocolate cake now and then won't hurt!
c. Find out about different sports in your area: It's a great way to make friends. Try to walk or go by bike instead of the bus.
d. Change what you eat or how much you eat. Maybe you will need to eat more, or maybe you should eat fewer sweets. Also look at how much you exercise.
e. Compare how long you sleep with how you feel in the morning. The less sleep you get, the worse you feel.
f. Ask yourself why you are doing it. Is it because your friends do? Try to stop because it's not good for you.

From *National Health Service* Homepage

b) *Complete the pieces of advice with information from the article.*

1. If you don't exercise regularly, you ...
2. You will need to go bed earlier if ...
3. If you are too thin, ...
4. If you smoke, ...
5. You should eat fewer sweets if ...
6. If you get angry too easily, ...
7. It will really help if ...
8. Your diet is not healthy if ...

WP 2 Verbs and nouns

a) The words on the right can be verbs or nouns. There are eleven in the article above. *Find them and say whether they are verbs or nouns in that context.*

exercise	drink	sleep	talk
rain	rest	walk	run
change	look	stop	diet
smile	laugh	wait	stay
dream	ring	answer	visit

b) *Change the sentences below so that the verbs become nouns, and the nouns become verbs. (With some nouns you should add the verbs 'have a', 'go on', 'get' or 'give'.)*

Example: 1. Would you like to drink something?
Would you like to have a drink?

2. There will be a lot of rain tomorrow.
3. I don't exercise enough.
4. I sleep a lot.
5. And I also have a lot of dreams.
6. He hasn't given me an answer.
7. Ken talked about his life as a marathon runner.
8. Have a look at the article.
9. Only go on a diet if it is really necessary.

Ken's interview

It is 30th June. A reporter is interviewing Ken on television.

Interviewer: Tell us about your experience as a marathon runner, Ken.

Ken: Well, I started training last August, and I've taken part in eight marathons already. I'm going to take part in three more this year.

Interviewer: How many have you won?

Ken: Only one so far, but I'm sure I'll win the next three.

Interviewer: What about training? How many miles do you run a month?

Ken: About 400 miles a month.

Interviewer: So you will have got through a lot of running shoes already.

Ken: That's right. I need a new pair every month. Of course, I wear MIDAS running shoes ...

Interviewer: No advertising, please, Ken! Tell us the real secret of your success.

Ken: Carrot juice and bananas! You know, since Thanksgiving, I've been eating about 300 bananas a month and I feel great! I'll be able to run until I'm 80!

Interviewer: Really?! Well, I hear that you're writing a recipe book. How is it going?

Ken: Not too well, I'm afraid. I've only written about five pages, but I hope to finish it next April.

Interviewer: I'm looking forward to it! You live in Chicago now, right?

Ken: That's right. We moved to Chicago last February. I've always wanted to live there.

Interviewer: We? Is there someone else in your life, Ken?

Ken: Yes, there is. My new girlfriend and I are getting married next month.

Interviewer: Congratulations! One last question: Do you think you'll break the world record this year?

Ken: I'd like to, but it's impossible. Maybe next year.

5

G 30

1 By the end of the year

a) *What two things will Ken not have done by the end of the year?*

b) *Ask and answer questions about what Ken will have done by the end of the year.*

1. take part in / marathons (How many ...?)
2. run / miles (How many ...?)
3. buy / running shoes (How many ...?)
4. eat / bananas (How many ...?)
5. live / Chicago (How long ...?)
6. be married (How long ...?)

SAVE

future perfect =
will + have + *past participle*

By the end of the year Ken **will have taken part** in lots of marathons, but he **won't have won** all of them.

2 Looking into the future

Work in pairs. Find out what your partner thinks he / she will probably have done by the age of 20.

leave school – start a job – meet Mr Right / Ms Right – get married – start a family – become famous

break a world record – make lots of money – write his/her life story – see the world – ...

Do you think you'll have left school?

Yes, I expect so.

I hope not.

I might have.

No, I don't think so.

3 Connecting words

Think of ways to finish the sentences.

1. Ken will go on running as long as ...
2. Some runners take part in marathons until ...
3. Ken's mother will be really disappointed if ...
4. Although Ken had problems with his big toe, ...
5. His fans will buy his recipe book as soon as ...
6. Ken has to stop to drink water while ...
7. When Ken's running shoes get too old, ...
8. Ken has moved to Chicago because ...
9. After Ken gets married, ...

4 ⟨I wish⟩

Write your own 'I wish' poem.
Think about:

- what you wish you were,
- where you wish you lived,
- what you wish you had,
- what you wish you could do,
- what you wish you didn't have,
- what you wish you didn't have to do,
- anything else you wish!

I wish ...

I wish I were rich
But I'm poor.
I wish I were young
But I'm old.
I wish I could live where it's sunny and hot,
But I live where it's rainy and cold.
I wish I had wings
But I haven't.
I wish I could fly
But I can't.
I wish that my wishes were more than just wishes.
But I'm sorry to say that they aren't.

5

5 What's the sport?

A rugby

B tossing the caber

C basketball

D cricket

a) *Match the description to the sport.*

1. There are two teams, with five players in each team. They play with a ball on a court, and try to score by throwing the ball through the opponent's goal (a net with a hole in it).
2. In this traditional Scottish sport, the competitor throws a piece of wood about 17 foot long so that it turns over in the air and falls on the ground with its small end nearer the thrower.
3. There are two teams of eleven players each. The bowler (the person who throws the ball) tries to hit the wicket behind the person with the bat to get him out. If the batter hits the ball, he and a player opposite him change places as often as possible before an opponent hits a wicket with the ball.
4. Two teams, with 13 or 14 players on each side, play with an oval ball on a large field. Players kick, carry or throw the ball, but they can't pass it forward. They score goals by carrying or kicking it over the opponent's goal line.

b) *Find out about an interesting or unusual sport, and write a description.*

WP 1 Parts of the body

Say what you can do with each part of the body.

Example: You can walk or run with your legs. You can bend them.

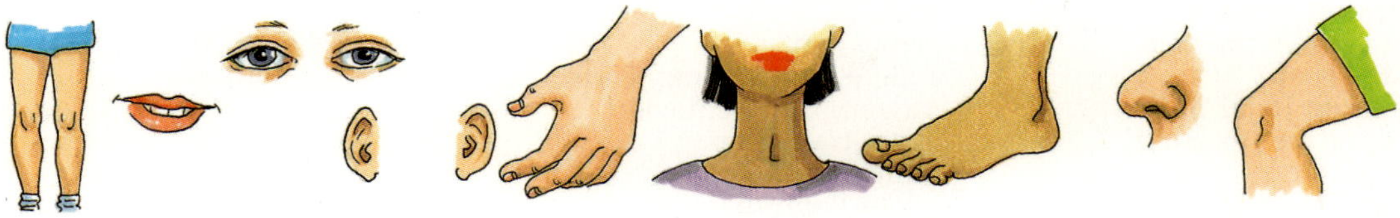

2 In the future

Use the words on the right to write answers. Which future tense do you need?

1. Do you want to come to the disco with me? (Sorry, I / wash my hair / tonight)
2. These boxes are really heavy. (Give them to me. I / carry / them)
3. Have you got a timetable? (Yes, the train / leave / at 14.45)
4. Have you got a football match on Sunday? (Yes, we / play / against Wigan)
5. Why are you going out? (I / post / a letter)
6. What are your plans for the weekend? (I don't know what / I / do)
7. Look at this new skateboard trick. (Watch out, or you / break / your neck!)
8. Remember to bring your swimming things. (Don't worry, I / not / forget)

3 If ...

Put the verb in the right form.

1. If you ... serious about football, you ... proper football boots. (be / need)
2. If you ... a sports club, then I ... it, too. (join / join)
3. We ... play football in the gym if it ... this afternoon. (play / rain)
4. George ... to run for Yorkshire if he ... hard enough. (be able to / train)
5. I ... you my tennis racket if you ... it properly. (not lend / not look after)

YOU 4 ⟨What will (or would) you do?⟩

Decide which of the things below could really happen to you next Monday. If they are probable, say what you will/won't do if they happen. If they aren't probable, say what you would/wouldn't do if they happened.

YOU 5 +A perfect future

Write sentences about what you hope you will have done by the time you are 20, 40, 60 and 90.

Example: By the time I'm 20 I hope I will have learned to drive.

CHECK-IN

A	to **get fit** [ˌget ˈfɪt]	fit werden
	to **support** [səˈpɔːt]	unterstützen
	workout [ˈwɜːkaʊt]	Training
	to **improve** [ɪmˈpruːv]	verbessern
	shape [ʃeɪp]	äußere Erscheinung, Form
	time out [taɪm‿ˈaʊt]	Auszeit; *hier:* Zeitbedarf
	to **exercise** [ˈeksəsaɪz]	üben, trainieren
	shy [ʃaɪ]	schüchtern
	in public [ˈpʌblɪk]	in der Öffentlichkeit
	to **go for sth.** [ˈgəʊ fɔː]	etw. anpacken, ausprobieren
	proper [ˈprɒpə]	passend, geeignet
	it's up to you [ˌʌp tə ˈjuː]	es liegt an dir / Ihnen
	a couple (of) [ˈkʌpl‿əv]	ein paar
	stamina [ˈstæmɪnə]	Durchhaltevermögen, Ausdauer
	to **mind** [maɪnd]	etw dagegen haben
	muddy [ˈmʌdi]	schmutzig, schlammig
	pitch [pɪtʃ]	(Fußball-)Feld, (Sport-)Platz
	swimsuit [ˈswɪmsuːt]	Badeanzug
	trunks [trʌŋks]	Badehose(n)
	towel [ˈtaʊəl]	Handtuch
	goggles [ˈgɒglz]	Schutzbrille
	to **join** [dʒɔɪn]	beitreten, Mitglied werden
	several [ˈsevrl]	einige, mehrere
	to **tone up** [ˌtəʊn‿ˈʌp]	stärken, festigen
	stomach [ˈstʌmək]	Magen, Bauch
	bottom [ˈbɒtm]	Po
	to **splash** [splæʃ]	plantschen, spritzen
B	**racket** [ˈrækɪt]	(Tennis-)Schläger
	comfy *coll.* [ˈkʌmpfi]	komfortabel, bequem
	court [kɔːt]	(Tennis-)Platz, Spielfeld
	little [ˈlɪtl]	wenig
	the … the [ðə … ðə]	je … desto
	muscle [ˈmʌsl]	Muskel
	to **burn up** [ˌbɜːn‿ˈʌp]	verbrennen, verbrauchen
	competitive [kəmˈpetɪtɪv]	konkurrierend, Wettkampf-
	to **beat*** [biːt]	schlagen, besiegen
	gymnastics [dʒɪmˈnæstɪks]	Turnen
	leotard [ˈliːətɑːd]	Trikot, Gymnastikanzug
	gymnast [ˈdʒɪmnæst]	Turner(in)
	fancy [ˈfæntsi]	ausgefallen
	bare [beə]	nackt, bloß
	to **enter** [ˈentə]	melden, sich beteiligen an
	competition [ˌkɒmpəˈtɪʃn]	Wettkampf, Wettbewerb
	plenty [ˈplenti]	reichlich, im Überfluss
	posture [ˈpɒstʃə]	(Körper-)Haltung
	suppleness [ˈsʌplnəs]	Elastizität, Flexibilität
	body [ˈbɒdi]	Körper
	toe [təʊ]	(Fuß-)Zehe
	bending [ˈbendɪŋ]	Beugen
	ambitious [æmˈbɪʃəs]	ehrgeizig
	might [maɪt]	könnte(n), dürfte(n)
	horse-riding [ˈhɔːsˌraɪdɪŋ]	Reiten
	sensible [ˈsensɪbl]	vernünftig
	thigh [θaɪ]	Oberschenkel
1	**grid** [grɪd]	Netz, Gitter
4	+**skating** [ˈskeɪtɪŋ]	Schlittschuhlaufen, Rollschuhlaufen

What can you often hear in classroom? "Don't be shy – come and try!"

'a couple of' often goes with minutes, hours, days, …

They stayed in Australia for a couple of weeks.

I used my friend's towel and he didn't mind.

These are plural words because they come in pairs: jeans, shorts, trousers, trunks, glasses, headphones, scissors, goggles, …

Swimming and splashing in a river can be fun. But you can come out all muddy.

The more you practise, the better you become.

Longer words often have a shorter form (to make them easier):

information	info
electronic mail	e-mail
comfortable	comfy
gymnasium	gym
…	…

The Greek word 'gymnos' means 'bare'.

You can win prizes in competitions.

Can you name ten parts of the body: toe, arm, …?

Bending exercises are good for the suppleness of your body.

You might be right, but I don't think so.

GB	D
sensible	vernünftig
sensitive	sensibel

	+**outdoors** [ˌaʊtˈdɔ:z]	im Freien, draußen

STEP A

	out of shape [ˌaʊt‿əv ˈʃeɪp]	außer Form
	couch potato [ˈkaʊtʃ pəˌteɪtəʊ]	jmd, der ständig vor dem Fernseher sitzt
	matter [ˈmætə]	Sache, Angelegenheit
	pancake [ˈpænkeɪk]	Pfannkuchen
	mom *(AE)* [mɒm]	Mama, Mutti
	Hawaii [həˈwaɪi:]	*Inselgruppe im Pazifischen Ozean*
	to **register** [ˈredʒɪstə]	sich eintragen, einschreiben
	umbrella [ʌmˈbrelə]	(Regen-)Schirm
	race [reɪs]	(Wett-)Rennen
	to **get sth.** [get]	etw holen
	congratulations [kənˌɡrætʃʊˈleɪʃnz]	Gratulation, Glückwunsch
	to **get married** [ˌget ˈmærid]	heiraten
1	**expectation** [ˌekspekˈteɪʃn]	Erwartung, Aussicht
	promise [ˈprɒmɪs]	Versprechen, Zusicherung
2	**press-up** [ˈpresʌp]	Liegestütz
	knee-bend [ˈni:bend]	Kniebeuge
	sit-up [ˈsɪtʌp]	Klappmesser
	exercise bike [ˈeksəsaɪz ˌbaɪk]	Heimtrainer
	Kennedy Movie Theater [ˌkenədi ˈmu:vi ˌθɪətə]	*Name eines Kinos*
	CNN [ˌsi:enˈen]	*amerikanische Fernsehstation*
	Boston [ˈbɒstn]	*Hauptstadt von Massachusetts*
	Central Park [ˈsentrl ˌpɑ:k]	*größter Park in New York*
3	to **be married** [ˈmærid]	verheiratet sein
5	**to offer (to do sth.)** [ˈɒfə]	anbieten (etwas zu tun)
	celebrity [səˈlebrəti]	Berühmtheit
⟨7⟩	**tricky** [ˈtrɪki]	kompliziert, schwierig
	sugar [ˈʃʊgə]	Zucker
	lie [laɪ]	Lüge
	sight [saɪt]	Anblick
	blood [blʌd]	Blut
	ambulance [ˈæmbjələns]	Krankenwagen
	snake [sneɪk]	Schlange
	spot [spɒt]	Fleck, Pickel
⟨8⟩	**to kiss** [kɪs]	küssen
	officer [ˈɒfɪsə]	(Polizei-)Beamter / -beamtin

STEP B

1	**lazy** [ˈleɪzi]	faul
	loser [ˈlu:zə]	Verlierer(in)
	to **give up** [gɪv‿ˈʌp]	aufgeben
2	**narrator** [nəˈreɪtə]	Erzähler(in)
A	**report** [rɪˈpɔ:t]	(Schul-) Zeugnis
	gammon [ˈgæmən]	geräucherter Schinken
	term [tɜ:m]	Trimester, Semester
	to **be in charge of sth.** [ɪn ˈtʃɑ:dʒ‿əv]	die Aufsicht haben über etw
	Yorkshire [jɔ:kʃə]	*Grafschaft in Nordengland*
	to **hit*** [hɪt]	schlagen, stoßen
	neck [nek]	Hals, Genick
	to **get behind** [get bɪˈhaɪnd]	in Rückstand geraten

mother – mummy – mum *(BE)* / mom *(AE)*

Hawaii is one of the 50 states of the USA.

Races → → and matches → ← are competitive.

Do some … Practise … Use a / an … Play … Go …	press-ups jogging knee-bends stretching tennis bending swimming exercise bike gymnastics for a walk …

Too much sugar is not good for your health.

A lot of people are afraid of snakes.

When you talk to a policeman or a policewoman, you say "Officer".

He's very lazy: he doesn't do any sports.

A loser is a person who is always unsuccessful.

	playtime ['pleɪtaɪm]	*(Schule)* Pause
	to **be on duty** ['dju:ti]	im Dienst sein, Aufsicht haben
	dinnertime ['dɪnəˌtaɪm]	Essenszeit
	to **be allowed to** [ə'laʊd tʊ]	dürfen
	used to do sth. [ˌju:st tə 'du:]	pflegte zu tun, machte früher
	pasty ['pæsti]	(Fleisch-)Pastete
	running-track ['rʌnɪŋ ˌtræk]	Aschenbahn
	bloke *coll.* [bləʊk]	Kerl, Typ
	to **get talking** [get 'tɔ:kɪŋ]	ins Gespräch kommen
	crisp [krɪsp]	Kartoffelchip
	to **keep up** [ki:p‿'ʌp]	Schritt halten, mithalten
	tracksuit ['træksu:t]	Jogginganzug
B	**to tell so. to do sth.** [tel]	jmdm. sagen, dass er/sie etw. tun soll
	to **tease** [ti:z]	auf den Arm nehmen, necken
	to **go in for** [gəʊ‿'ɪn fɔ:]	sich beteiligen an (Wettbewerb)
	to **get into trouble** ['trʌbl]	in Schwierigkeiten geraten
	daydream ['deɪdri:m]	Tagtraum
	high-jump ['haɪˌdʒʌmp]	Hochsprung
	long-jump ['lɒŋˌdʒʌmp]	Weitsprung
	⟨**four-forty**⟩ [ˌfɔ: 'fɔ:tɪ]	eine Viertelmeile (*440 yards*)
	announcement [ə'naʊnsmənt]	Ankündigung, Ansage
	competitor [kəm'petɪtə]	Wettkämpfer(in), Mitbewerber(in)
	to **keep doing sth.** [ˌki:p 'du:ɪŋ]	etw. immer wieder, ununterbrochen tun
	to **drop back** [drɒp 'bæk]	zurückfallen
	look [lʊk]	Blick, Anblick
	ahead [ə'hed]	voran, voraus
	to **keep sth. up** [ki:p‿'ʌp]	etw. (durch)halten
	to **cheer** [tʃɪə]	jubeln, Beifall klatschen
	to **head for** [hed]	zugehen auf
	bend [bend]	Biegung, Kurve
	tear [tɪə]	Träne
	cheek [tʃi:k]	Wange, Backe
	to **see no point in sth.** [ˌsi: nəʊ 'pɒɪnt‿ɪn]	etw. für sinnlos halten
4	**summary** ['sʌmri]	Zusammenfassung
	key [ki:]	Schlüssel(-)
	speech bubble ['spi:tʃ ˌbʌbl]	Sprechblase
	whom [hu:m]	wem, wen
6	**either ... or** ['aɪðə ... 'ɔ:]	entweder ... oder

STEP C

1	**excuse** [ɪk'skju:s]	Entschuldigung
	Do you fancy ... ? [dju: 'fænsi]	Hättest du Lust ... ?
	to **decline** [dɪ'klaɪn]	ablehnen, ausschlagen
	rather ['rɑ:ðə]	eher, lieber, ziemlich
2	to **marry** ['mæri]	heiraten
3	**advice** [əd'vaɪs]	Rat(schlag), Empfehlung
	cold [kəʊld]	Erkältung, Schnupfen
4	to **revise** [rɪ'vaɪz]	wiederholen

TRACK 1

1	**healthy** ['helθi]	gesund
	sleep [sli:p]	Schlaf
	potato, *pl.* **-oes** [pə'teɪtəʊ]	Kartoffel

There's a time for nearly everything: breakfast-time, dinnertime, teatime, lunchtime, playtime, bedtime, ...

Look at that lazy bloke: sitting in front of the TV, eating crisps and pasties – a real couch potato, and in bad shape.

What people need for sports: balls, rackets, goggles, leotards, trainers, tracksuits, ...

You are teasing me again.
You drive me round the bend!

people with -or

competitor, narrator, author, doctor, ...

The 'key' to stamina, suppleness and good shape: exercise.

What people say in comics is in

speech bubbles.

verb	noun
to decline	a / the decline

Other examples: test, sleep, excuse, look, daydream, promise, exercise, hit, beat, run, ...

These two rings mean that two people are married.

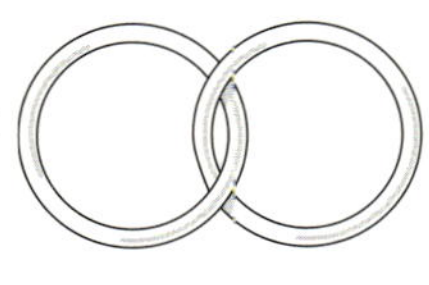

Nouns without a plural form: rice, salt, sand, chalk, ...

franz succès *lat* successus
engl success

rice [raɪs]	Reis
fruit [fru:t]	Obst, Früchte
instead of [ɪn'sted‿əv]	anstelle von, statt

TRACK 2

	to **get through** ['get θru:]	*hier:* verschleißen
	+**advertising** ['ædvətaɪzɪŋ]	Werbung, Reklame
	+**secret** ['si:krət]	Geheimnis
	+**success** [sək'ses]	Erfolg
	+**recipe** ['resɪpi]	(Koch-)Rezept
	+**impossible** [ɪm'pɒsəbl]	unmöglich
3	+**although** [ɔ:l'ðəʊ]	obwohl, obgleich
⟨4⟩	**wing** [wɪŋ]	Flügel
5	+**tossing the caber** [ˌtɒsɪŋ ðə 'keɪbə]	Baumstammwerfen
	+to **score** [skɔ:]	Punkte erzielen
	+**opponent** [ə'pəʊnənt]	Gegenspieler(in), Gegner(in)
	+**goal** [gəʊl]	Tor
	+**wood** [wʊd]	Holz
	+**thrower** ['θrəʊə]	Werfer(in)
	+**bowler** ['bəʊlə]	*(Kricket)* Werfer(in)
	+**wicket** ['wɪkɪt]	Krickettor
	+**bat** [bæt]	Schlagholz
	+**batter** ['bætə]	Schlagmann
	+**large** [lɑ:dʒ]	groß
	+**forward** ['fɔ:wəd]	vorwärts, nach vorn

CHECK-OUT

⟨4⟩	to **star** [stɑ:]	die Hauptrolle spielen

COGNATE WORDS

to **accept** [ək'sept]	annehmen, akzeptieren
aerobics [eə'rəʊbɪks]	Aerobic, rhythmische Gymnastik
all-round fitness [ˌɔ:lraʊnd 'fɪtnəs]	Rundum-Fitness
apple ['æpl]	Apfel
athlete ['æθli:t]	Leichtathlet(in), Sportler(in)
athletics [æθ'letɪks]	Leichtathletik
basic ['beɪsɪk]	grundlegend, Grund-, Basis-
calorie ['kælri]	Kalorie
coordination [kəʊˌɔ:dɪ'neɪʃn]	Koordination
carrot juice ['kærət ˌdʒu:s]	Karottensaft
to **copy** ['kɒpi]	kopieren, abschreiben
+**cricket** ['krɪkət]	Kricket
diet ['daɪət]	Diät
energy ['enədʒi]	Energie
fan [fæn]	Anhänger(in), Fan
fat [fæt]	fett, dick
flash card ['flæʃ ˌkɑ:d]	Illustrationstafel, Flashcard
foot [fʊt]	Fuß *(engl. Längenmaß, ca. 30cm)*
fresh [freʃ]	frisch
future ['fju:tʃə]	Zukunft
handstand ['hændstænd]	Handstand
to **ignore** [ɪg'nɔ:]	hinwegsehen, ignorieren
level ['levl]	Ebene, Niveau
lung [lʌŋ]	Lunge
miserable ['mɪzrəbl]	unglücklich, miserabel
misery ['mɪzri]	Qual, Misere
muesli ['mju:zli]	Müsli
mummy ['mʌmi]	Mami, Mutti
orange juice ['ɒrɪndʒ ˌdʒu:s]	Orangensaft
+**oval** ['əʊvl]	oval
to **pass** [pɑ:s]	(einen Ball) passen
pasta ['pæstə]	Teigwaren, Nudeln
plus [plʌs]	plus, extra
record ['rekɔ:d]	Rekord
+**rugby** ['rʌgbi]	Rugby
⟨**schoolbag**⟩ ['sku:lbæg]	Schultasche, -ranzen
sponsor ['spɒntsə]	Sponsor(in)
sporty ['spɔ:ti]	sportlich
to **spurt** [spɜ:t]	sprinten, spurten
stressful ['stresfʊl]	stressig
stretching ['stretʃɪŋ]	Strecken, Dehnen
structure ['strʌktʃə]	Struktur, Aufbau
⟨**supermodel**⟩ ['su:pəˌmɒdl]	Mannequin, Topmodel
swimming ['swɪmɪŋ]	Schwimmen
team [ti:m]	Mannschaft
to **train** [treɪn]	train
tip [tɪp]	Hinweis, Tipp
to **test** [test]	prüfen, testen
trainer ['treɪnə]	Trainer(in)
to **wander** ['wɒndə]	herumwandern
to **warm up** [ˌwɔ:m‿'ʌp]	aufwärmen
warning ['wɔ:nɪŋ]	Warnung
yo-yo ['jəʊjəʊ]	Jojo

UNIT 6

UFOs – the greatest mystery

Throughout history people have wondered about the possibility of life on other planets. Some people even believe that extraterrestrials have visited Earth in gigantic spaceships.

This idea has always been a source of inspiration to science fiction authors, poets, film producers, painters, musicians and cartoonists.

The sudden appearance of a UFO (Unidentified Flying Object) startles people. They think these extraterrestrials are greedy and aggressive.

A UFO

It came in the night,
All shining bright.
The thing let out a blinding glow,
It seemed to have nowhere to go.

Hovering slowly, it seemed to say,
Go away little girl, go away.
The glow turned red, then blue and green.
This is something I wish I hadn't seen.

(Poem by Deborah Stone of John Ball School, London)

The beings in the spaceships are often described as ugly monsters. Their heads are bald and too large for their bodies. They threaten our civilization with powerful laser beams and unknown technologies.

1 Listening comprehension: A UFO in New Zealand

There have been lots of reports of UFOs all over the world.

a) *Listen to a radio report about the landing of a UFO in New Zealand in 1999 and answer these questions:*

1. Where in New Zealand did it happen?
2. What were the children doing when the UFO landed?
3. What did the extraterrestrial (ET) look like?
4. What did the boy do and what happened to him?
5. What about the dog?
6. Why did the children race back to the house?
7. What did the police discover the day after?

b) *And what do* you *think about UFOs? Discuss.*

1. Do you believe in UFOs?
2. Can there be life on other planets?
3. What would you do if you saw a UFO?
4. How would you react if you met an ET?
5. What (famous) films about space travel, UFOs and ETs do you know?

Missions to Mars

- In the 1870s, the Italian astronomer Schiaparelli discovered 'canals' on Mars. He believed that there was water on the planet.
- In 1895, the American astronomer Lowell thought these canals were traces of an old civilization and he believed that if there was water, there must be life on Mars.
- With its unmanned spaceships 'Mariner' (1964–1971) and 'Viking' (1976) NASA was able to take the first photos of Mars and so the astronomers had to give up the 'canal theory'. Mars looked like the Moon: there were craters, nothing but craters.
- In 1996, NASA sent up 'Pathfinder', (a 'lander'). Inside was 'Sojourner' (a Mars rover like a microwave oven on a skateboard), with which they were able to take the first photos on the surface of Mars. (There were no traces of life.)
- In the next 25 years, NASA may be able to send a manned mission to Mars. This will be the most expensive journey ever and the astronauts will have to travel for six to seven months (one way!).

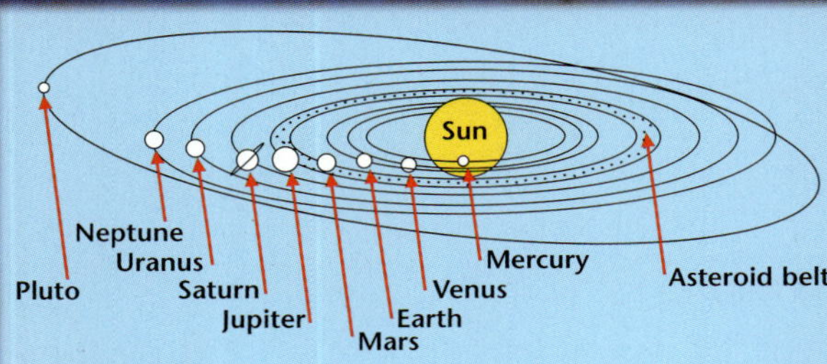

EARTH ⊕

Average distance from the sun: 93 million miles
Diameter: 7,926 miles
Time to revolve around the sun: 365 ¼ days
Time to rotate on its axis: 23 hours, 56 minutes, 4.1 seconds
Number of moons: 1

DID YOU KNOW? Earth's path around the sun is nearly 600 million miles long. To make the trip in one year, Earth travels more than 66,000 miles per hour.

MARS ♂

Average distance from the sun: 142 million miles
Diameter: 4,220 miles
Time to revolve around the sun: 687 days
Time to rotate on its axis: 24 hours, 37 minutes, 26 seconds
Number of moons: 2

DID YOU KNOW? Mars is the home of Olympus Mons, the largest volcano found in the solar system. It stands about 17 miles high, with a crater 50 miles wide.

From *World Almanac for Kids*, 1998

6

SAVE

can – am / is / are able to	was / were able to	will be able to
must – has / have to	had to	will have to
may – am / is / are allowed to	was / were allowed to	will be allowed to

With the Hubble telescope NASA was even able to draw a map of Mars.

G 33

1 Cartoon fun I: The 'be able' story

Well, this man was able to land safely on a prehistoric planet. And now there are lots of questions with 'be able'. a) *Can you ask (and answer) them?*

... to get gas? ... to survive? ... to live in prehistoric times

... to fly back? ... to find a gas station?

b) *What other questions can you think of?*

G 33 2 Cartoon fun II: A time machine

What questions can you ask the two men in this cartoon? Use forms of 'be able to', 'be allowed to' and 'have to'. Work with a partner and make funny dialogues.

Example:

– Were you able to talk to King Arthur?
– Yes, but I had to wait for him for five years and I wasn't allowed to take a photo of him.

"Leave it here … you can pick it up last Friday."

G 33/34 3 On board a spaceship

Imagine some very friendly extraterrestrials have invited you to go on a little trip in their spaceship. Their English is excellent. They tell you what you must or mustn't, can, may or may not do.

You must sit still for a while!

It's a touchscreen. You must touch it.

Yes, you may talk to our commander.

You may not walk around.

No, you mustn't switch on the laser beam!

You must fasten your seatbelt.

Press this button and you can open the door.

a) *After the trip you report to your friends:*

I had to sit still for a while. I …

b) *You can also report like this:*

They told me to sit still for a while. …

They	asked told warned showed	me	(not) to … how to …

c) *Now make some more sentences like this with 'where to', 'how to', 'what to', 'when to', etc.*

I	didn't know	where to go.
She	showed me	how to fasten my seatbelt.
He	explained	what to do.
They	told us	when to be back at the space station.
…	…	…

R 4 +In the year 2100 …

What can you predict about the year 2100? Make some positive and some negative statements about what will (won't) have happened on Earth. Here are some ideas to help you:

life	computers	learning
electricity	schools	space travel
homework	museums	forms of energy
families	hurricanes	technologies
love	teachers	civilization on Mars

Example: In the year 2100 life will have changed.

… will have become popular.
… will have changed.
… will have been invented.
… will have gone.
… will have become a problem.
… will have become easy.
… will have become less important.
… will have been built.
… will have become quite normal.
… will be nothing unusual.

5 Make your dream come true

a) Welcome to Disney World! *Match the texts below with the pictures in the brochure.*

Meet your favourite Disney characters.

Take a step into the future world.

Sail among the stars on Orbiter.

Come face to face with some horrible extraterrestrials.

Discover the reality of special effects.

b) *Think of your favourite adventure park. What would you write about the attractions for a brochure?*

G 35

6 Visitors from the past

Some young people from King Arthur's time have invented a time machine and travelled into the future. They are now in your house and they speak English. But they get into trouble with all the technical things. You must help them with commands and warnings. *Look at the examples. Can you add some more to the lists? Think of some funny ones.*

SAVE

Imperatives: *you tell people (animals) to do or not to do things. It's nicer with 'please'.*	Hello! Sit down, please. Don't sit on the TV!
Proposals: *you invite people to do something (together). You use 'let's'.*	OK, let's watch TV together. But let's not sit too close to it.

positive	negative	let's
Show me your time machine. …	Never touch the surface of CDs. …	Let's go and have a snack. …

7 The robot

Write down the story. Start like this:

A man is playing cards with his robot. The robot …

Watching brief

Before you read this short short story, think about this: You are in your garden and your new neighbour comes up to you. What would you say / ask / do?

It was just after the North Sea oil wells began to run dry that a man looked over my fence.
"Good evening. I'm your new neighbour."
His sudden appearance startled me. Still, I thought, he looked harmless. His eyes were bright blue. He was almost bald and his head looked too large for his frail body. He wore a black and white jacket over a sweater and black trousers. We shook hands, and he introduced himself as Alfred Bell.
"My friends call me Alfie," he added with a smile.
"Well, Alfie," I said, "perhaps you would care to come down to the Moon and Stars with me for a drink?"
"Just a minute," he said, "I'll get my torch."
It would be dark soon and the government wanted to save energy. For the same reason the moving pavements for pedestrians had been turned off, and we had to walk the mile to the pub. The Moon and Stars was filling up when we arrived, and we chose a table well away from the crowd of youths at the bar. They all wore black leather jackets and carried crash helmets.
"You're not from these parts," I told Alfie. "You haven't got the local accent."
He said: "You're a good observer. I don't stay in one place long enough to pick up local accents."
"You're a commercial traveller?" I asked.
"No, I'm, well, I suppose you would call me a surveyor."
Before I could ask him what sort of surveyor, he rose and said: "Let me buy you a drink."
I watched him go to the bar and take out a wallet. As he was putting it away his elbow was jogged by one of the youths. The wallet fell to the floor and, as Alfie bent to pick it up, I saw the youth grab Alfie's glass, drain it, and put it back on the counter. I jumped up.
"You stole my friend's drink," I shouted. The young man's companions crowded round me.
"What are you going to do about it?" they demanded.
I realized that we were outnumbered so I grabbed Alfie's arm and said: "Come on. Let's get out of here."

Before you read on: How would you react – as the man who is telling the story, as Alfie, as the young man? And what, do you think, will happen next?

We had gone a hundred yards when the youths passed us on their motorcycles. They then turned and came back. Alfie and I had to jump to the side to avoid being knocked down.
"Is it a game or do they mean us harm?" shouted Alfie. I looked at him in amazement.
"Where have you been?" I demanded. "We'll be lucky to escape with our lives!"
Alfie shook his head sadly. "It's up to me then," he said. The narrow lane under the trees became a tunnel of light as Alfie took a torch from his pocket. He pressed the button as the first rider approached, and a pencil of green light flashed across the road.
The engine of the machine stopped as if it had hit a stone wall. The rider flew over the handlebars and his head smashed into a tree. The effect on the riders behind was catastrophic. Within seconds a tangled mass of metal and broken bodies littered the road. Alfie switched off the beam and put the torch back in his pocket. "Let's go," he said.
When we parted in front of my house Alfie looked at me and said: "Least said soonest mended, eh?" I nodded and said: "We don't want trouble with the authorities, do we?"
"No. My people wouldn't like it if I drew attention to myself." Who, I wondered, were his people; and if he was a surveyor, just what was it that he was looking at? I was soon to find out.

Before you read on: Can you answer the author's questions?

6

That night I was awakened by the crash of breaking glass. It was followed by a horrible scream from the house next door. They've got Alfie, I thought. I flung on some clothes and ran next door. The lights were on and the front door was open. Alfie seemed all right but the two men lying on their backs on the floor were in a bad way. Each one had a hole in his chest and as I watched, their bodies disintegrated until nothing remained except two small piles of brown dust. Alfie dropped his torch weapon into a pocket of his dressing gown and said: "They broke in and attacked me. I had to defend myself."

"It means the failure of your mission?" I asked. He nodded sadly. "You understand quite well. People are much too greedy, much too aggressive on this planet. I see no hope of cooperation."
"You have to report back?" I asked.
"Yes, I have to report the result of my survey."
"Don't write us off," I said. "Call again sometime."
"When?" he asked. "In a few thousand years? In the year million?"
I was silent. I watched him go back into the bedroom. A few moments later I pushed open the bedroom door. The room was empty. Alfie had left as mysteriously as he had arrived.

Granville Wilson (adapted)

1 Reporting back

a) *Imagine you are Alfie and you have to report back. What would be the main points of your report? Start like this:*

I lived in a house in a small town in England. My neighbour was quite nice, so we went to a pub for a drink. I took my torch with me because …

b) *How do you know that this is a science fiction story? Give reasons.*

2 Alfie

Match the sentence parts.

1. The moving pavements were switched off, so they
2. The two friends were hopelessly outnumbered, so they
3. Alfie said he never stayed long in one place and so he
4. With his trick the young man
5. To avoid being knocked down they
6. With his torch weapon Alfie
7. When the two youths attacked Alfie he
8. Alfie said after his mission he
9. The result of his report was that people on Earth

… defend himself.
… jump to the side.
… walk the mile to the pub.
… cooperate with other civilizations.
… stop the motorcycle.
… leave the pub as fast as they could.
… report back.
… steal Alfie's drink.
… pick up local accents.

3 A positive ending

a) *What is Alfie's mission on Earth? Is it successful?*
b) *Who is responsible for the trouble with the riders in your opinion? Why?*
c) *Rewrite the ending of the story in a positive way. Here are some ideas:*

- Perhaps Alfie doesn't kill the two youths in his house, he just stops them. So they have the chance to learn.
- Perhaps Alfie gives the narrator a book about the peaceful civilization on his planet. So people on Earth can learn from it how to live peacefully together and be less greedy and aggressive.
- Maybe Alfie agrees and promises to call sometime, in a hundred years or so.
- Maybe Alfie invites his neighbour to come with him to show him what life is like on his planet.
- Think of other ways to show people on Earth that there is hope for the future.

1 How stupid!

Someone must have covered part of the text on the sign. *Can you help the monster and tell him what is missing? Which of the lines given on the right do you think …*

- makes sense?
- is nonsense?
- is funny / the funniest?
- you would choose?
- fits best?
- is in the original text (your teacher knows!)?

you can try
you mustn't try
you must be as tall as this sign
you needn't try
you may come
you are allowed
you may now begin
you aren't allowed
you can't win if you want
you have

2 ⟨A song: A spaceman[1] came travelling⟩ by Chris de Burgh

A spaceman came travelling on his ship from afar[2].
'Twas light years of time since his mission did start.
And over a village he halted[3] his craft[4].
And it hung[5] in the sky like a star, just like a star …

He followed a light and came down to a shed[6].
Where a mother and child were lying there on a bed.
A bright light of silver shone round his head.
And he had the face of an angel[7], and they were afraid.

Then the stranger[8] spoke, he said, "Do not fear[9].
I come from a planet a long way from here.
And I bring a message[10] for mankind[11] to hear."
And suddenly the sweetest music filled the air.

And it went La La …
Peace and goodwill[12] to all men, and love for the child …

This lovely music went trembling[13] through the ground[14],
And many were awakened on hearing that sound.
And travellers on the road, the village they found.
By the light of that ship in the sky, which shone all around.

And just before dawn at the paling[15] of the sky.
The stranger returned and said, "Now I must fly.
When two thousand years of your time has gone by.
This song will begin once again, to a baby's cry[16] …"

And it went La La …
This song will begin once again to a baby's cry.
And it goes La La …
Peace and goodwill to all men, and love for the child.
Oh the whole world is waiting, waiting to hear that song again,
There are thousands standing on the edge of the world.
And a star is moving somewhere, the time is nearly here.
This song will begin once again, to a baby's cry.

[1]['speɪsmæn] *Raumfahrer(in)* [2][ə'fɑː] *weit her* [3][hɒlt] *(an)halten* [4][krɑːft] *Schiff, Flugzeug* [5][hæŋ] *hängen* [6][ʃed] *Stall, Schuppen* [7]['eɪndʒl] *Engel* [8]['streɪndʒə] *Fremde(r)* [9][fɪə] *Angst haben* [10]['mesɪdʒ] *Nachricht, Botschaft* [11][mæn'kaɪnd] *Menschheit* [12][gʊd'wɪl] *guter Wille, Verständigungsbereitschaft* [13]['trembl] *zittern, vibrieren* [14][graʊnd] *Erde, Boden* [15][peɪl] *blass werden* [16][kraɪ] *Schrei*

3 A space poster

Work with a partner and make a space poster for your classroom. Cut out drawings and photos, write in words, collect material and use everything for a big poster.

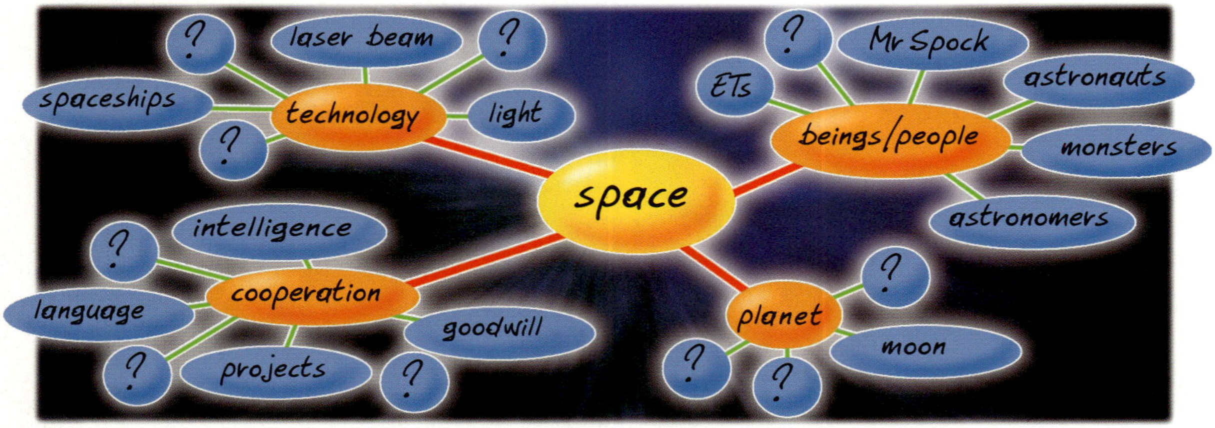

4 Grammar tips

LEARNING TO LEARN

Organizing language material in groups (not only in lists) can be very helpful. You already know :

Groups of four:

this	that
these	those

Groups of six:

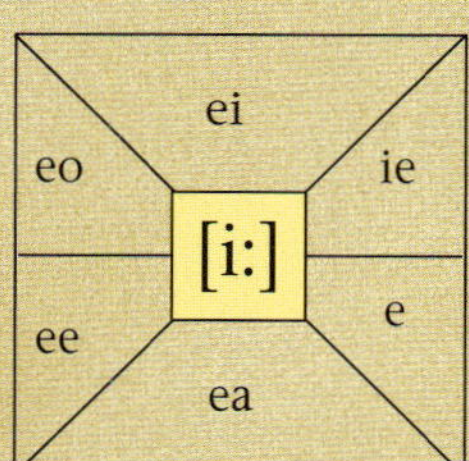

And here you have groups of three to show present, past and future:

YES

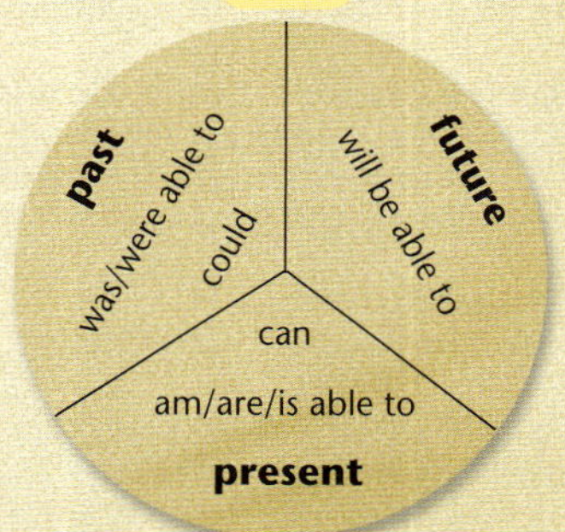

NO

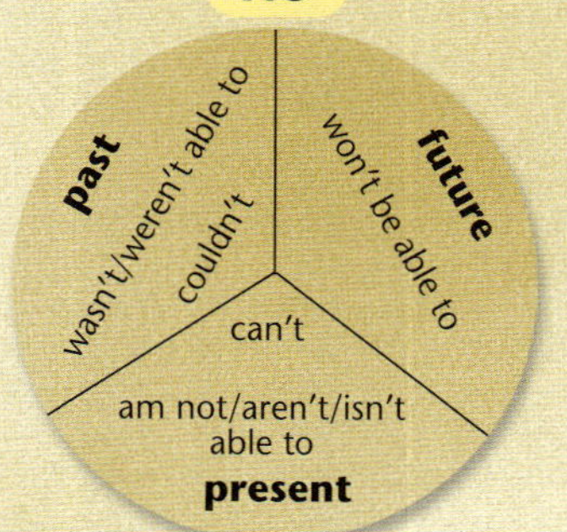

a) *Make more groups of three with these words:*

may	may not / mustn't	
am is are	am not isn't aren't	allowed to
could / might		
was were will be	wasn't/ weren't won't be	allowed to
must	needn't	
has to have to had to will have to	doesn't don't didn't won't	have to have to

b) *What else can you put in groups of three?*

6

UFOs in the past?

Lots of people all over the world believe that space travellers visited Earth in earlier times. They say that these early visitors did great things like building Stonehenge (see page 50) or making the sculptures on the Easter Islands or the Westbury white horse. And even Chris de Burgh mentions this idea in his song.
But it is more likely that these pictures, sculptures and prehistoric temples had something to do with myths and early religions. So we have to be very careful with all these UFO theories.

1 Could, shall, or should?

Put in the right positive or negative forms.

1. … I open the window? It's very hot in here.
2. You … do that! It's not nice.
3. … we read another science fiction story? I like them.
4. She … finish the book. There wasn't enough time.
5. … we play this game? It's fun.
6. You … always do your homework.
7. Space travellers … leave rubbish in outer space.
8. They … take it with them.
9. … we help the people in the Space Volunteer Project?

WP 2 More words

How many more words can you add?

1. poets, painters, …
2. space monster, spaceship, …
3. CD, UFO, …
4. travel, trip, …
5. sun, planet, …

6

3 Poem fun

Where there's a will, there's a won't.
Where there's a do, there's a don't.

Where there's a could, there's a couldn't.
Where there's a should, there's a shouldn't.

Where there's a had, there's a hadn't.
Where there's a did, there's a …

Write some more lines. Here are some ideas:

need does must
has was
can are

The man in black

On 11 September 1976, 58-year-old Dr Herbert Hopkins of Maine, who had taken part in hypnosis sessions with an alleged UFO contactee, received a visitor who said he was from the New Jersey UFO Research Organization (there is no such organization). The visitor wore a black suit, black shoes, black tie, black hat and white shirt. He had no hair. He wore lipstick, and his head moved in an unnatural way. He spoke in a monotone, and had psychic abilities. He told Dr Hopkins the contents of his pockets, and caused a coin first to change colour and then disappear, saying: "Neither you nor anyone else on this planet will ever see that coin again." After talking for a while about other things, he said very slowly: "My energy is running low – must go now – goodbye." He walked out of the house to where Dr Hopkins could see a strange blue light, too bright for a car. Both visitor and light then disappeared. Dr Hopkins did what his visitor had instructed: he erased his tapes and stopped all research in this field.

SAVE

past perfect

had + *participle* = had been / spoken / invited

first action	*then following action*
all over in the past	all over now

He came in. Then they sat down.
After he had come in, they sat down.

G 36

1 The story again

Complete the sentences and retell the story.

1. After Dr Hopkins had been involved in hypnosis sessions …
2. After Dr Hopkins had invited him in …
3. After the man had spoken to Dr Hopkins …
4. After he had told Dr Hopkins the contents of his pockets …
5. After the man in black had talked about some other things …
6. After he had walked out of the house …

2 Later

Go through the text and say what Dr Hopkins found out/reported/said/did/… later.

Example:
Later Dr Hopkins found out that there was no such organization.
Later he reported …

G 37

3 The mission

This is what some astronauts told their people and friends after their missions. There are always two sentences that go together, one with the past simple and one with the past perfect progressive.
Match them and write them down.

1. At last the countdown was on.
2. Ground control knew nothing about the trouble with one of our cameras.
3. It was a bit of a job to put the three satellites into orbit.
4. It was an exciting moment when the Soviet spacecraft and our shuttle docked.
5. We were able to repair the Hubble telescope in December 1993.
6. Our colleague Dr Shannon Lucid set the record for all American and all female astronauts.

a) We and our Soviet colleagues had been looking forward to it since our missions started.
b) We had been waiting for this launch for months.
c) The Hubble telescope had been sending back fuzzy photos since it was launched.
d) She had been flying with the Soviet Mir crew for 188 days.
e) But we had been training for this job for three months.
f) We had been trying to repair it since we were in orbit.

WP 1 Words that go together

Example: extraterrestrial, crash helmet, …

extra	crash	local
time	report	science
film	space	leather
radio	UFO	manned
next	laser	knock
frail	turn	sudden

appearance	fiction	back
producer	off	terrestrial
accent	door	body
helmet	down	theories
machine	traveller	report
mission	beams	jacket

2 Robots are so useful

A man has come to visit his old schoolfriend who is a robot expert. (We are in the year 2015.)
a) *Use forms of 'can', 'may', 'be able to', 'be allowed to' or 'have to'.*

Visitor: Your new robot is very good. He opened the door and said 'Hello' to me.
Expert: Ah, you mean Bernie? Yes, he … do all the practical jobs around the house. Tomorrow he … make your breakfast.
Visitor: When I was a little boy robots … do such jobs.
Expert: Well, things have changed and our new robots … do lots of jobs.
Visitor: … I test Bernie?
Expert: Yes, certainly!
Visitor: Hello, Bernie! *Comment allez-vous?*
Expert: Oh, sorry! Bernie … speak French. He … only understand and speak English. But next year he … speak French too. And before that he … learn to understand some local accents.
Visitor: Will there be a new generation of robots in the next few years?
Expert: Oh, yes, and they … do nearly everything for us.

YOU b) *Think of a robot you would like to have at home.*
– What should it be able to do (and what not)?
– What should it be allowed to do (and what not)?

Example:
My robot would be able to do my homework. It …

6

3 What they say is typical

Two utterances in each group are 'odd ones out'. a) *Say which ones and why.* b) *Rewrite the three groups with the 'right' utterances.*

at school	at home	with friends
Wake up, Jimmy. Time for school.	Don't wait for me, Dad!	Tell me about your grandma's new computer.
And now open your books, please.	Grandpa, turn the TV off, please.	Collect the exercise books, please.
OK. Now let's check your homework.	Susan, open the bathroom window!	Come on. Let's have an ice cream.
Hey, my bike is new. Don't go so fast on it.	Oh dear! Assembly starts in a minute. Let's go!	Let's meet at the cinema.
OK. You can rewrite the text after lunch break.	Hey, Susan. Look at all the new T-shirts in this shop here.	Mum, come quickly! Telephone for you!
	Jim, don't leave your schoolbag in the kitchen.	Can I borrow your pen?

CHECK-IN

A	**throughout** [θru'aʊt]	überall (in)
	to **wonder** ['wʌndə]	sich fragen, sich wundern
	possibility [ˌpɒsə'bɪləti]	Gelegenheit, Möglichkeit
	extraterrestrial [ˌekstrətə'restriəl]	außerirdisch, Außerirdische(r)
	earth [ɜ:θ]	Erde
	spaceship ['speɪsʃɪp]	Raumschiff
	source [sɔ:s]	Quelle, Ursprung
	producer [prə'dju:sə]	Produzent(in), Hersteller(in)
	painter ['peɪntə]	(Kunst-)Maler(in)
	appearance [ə'pɪərnts]	Erscheinen, Auftauchen
	unidentified [ˌʌnaɪ'dentɪfaɪd]	unbekannt, nicht identifiziert
	to **startle** ['stɑ:tl]	erschrecken, aufschrecken
	greedy ['gri:di]	gierig, gefräßig
	blinding ['blaɪndɪŋ]	blendend
	glow [gləʊ]	Glut, grelles Licht
	to **wish** [wɪʃ]	wünschen
	to **hover** ['hɒvə]	schweben
B	**being** ['bi:ɪŋ]	(Lebe-)Wesen, Geschöpf
	to **be described** [dɪ'skraɪbd]	beschrieben werden
	bald [bɔ:ld]	kahl, glatzköpfig
	to **threaten** ['θretn]	drohen, bedrohen
	laser beam ['leɪzə ˌbi:m]	Laserstrahl
	unknown [ʌn'nəʊn]	unbekannt
1	**New Zealand** [ˌnju:'zi:lənd]	Neuseeland
	to **race** [reɪs]	um die Wette rennen, rasen
	space travel ['speɪs ˌtrævl]	Raumfahrt

An extraterrestrial is a being from another planet.

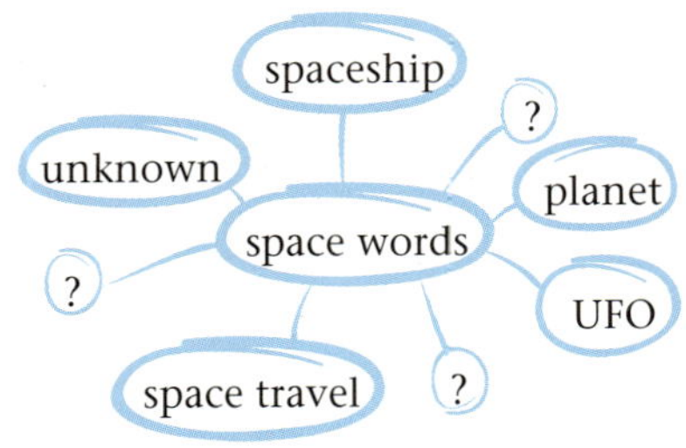

A person's appearance is what he or she looks like.

A greedy person is someone who wants a lot of money or other things.

Put on your sunglasses when the light is blinding.

She was startled by the blinding light.

franz décrire *lat* describere *engl* to describe

In some ways, New Zealand is like England.

Space travel is travelling from one planet to another.

6

STEP A

Giovanni Schiaparelli [ˌdʒi:əʊ'vɑ:ni ˌskæpə'reli]	*italienischer Astronom (1835-1901)*
Percival Lowell [ˌpɜ:sɪvl 'ləʊəl]	*amer. Astronom (1855-1916)*
trace [treɪs]	Spur
Mariner ['mærɪnə]	*Name eines Raumschiffs*
NASA ['næsə] (National Aeronautics and Space Administration)	*Nationale Luft- und Raumfahrtbehörde der USA*
to **be able to** ['eɪbl‿tə]	fähig sein, in der Lage sein
Pathfinder ['pɑ:θˌfaɪndə]	*Name einer landefähigen Marssonde*
Sojourner [sɒ'dʒɜ:nə]	*Name eines Erkundungsfahrzeugs für den Mars*
rover ['rəʊvə]	Vagabund; *hier:* Erkundungsfahrzeug
microwave oven [ˌmaɪkrəʊweɪv‿'ʌvn]	Mikrowellenherd
surface ['sɜ:fɪs]	Oberfläche
Edwin P. Hubble ['hʌbl]	*amerikanischer Astronom (1889-1953)*

He is not able to play tennis: he has got problems with his back.

You can cook food very quickly in a microwave oven.

It is very interesting to see the surface of Mars.

	prehistoric [ˌpriːhɪˈstɒrɪk]	vorgeschichtlich, prähistorisch
	gas *(AE)* [gæs]	Benzin
	to **survive** [səˈvaɪv]	überleben
	gas station *(AE)* [ˈgæs ˌsteɪʃn]	Tankstelle
2	to **wait for** [ˈweɪt fɔː]	warten auf
3	**touchscreen** [ˈtʌtʃˌskriːn]	Kontaktbildschirm, Tastenbildschirm
	to **fasten** [ˈfɑːsn]	befestigen, anschnallen
	seatbelt [ˈsiːtbelt]	Sicherheitsgurt
	to **press** [pres]	drücken
	button [ˈbʌtn]	Knopf, Schalter
4	+to **predict** [prɪˈdɪkt]	vorhersagen, prophezeien
	+to **invent** [ɪnˈvent]	erfinden
5	**Disney World** [ˈdɪzni ˌwɜːld]	*berühmter Vergnügungspark*
	horrible [ˈhɒrəbl]	schrecklich, entsetzlich
	Orbiter [ˈɔːbɪtə]	*Name eines Raumschiffs*

AE: gas – gas station
BE: petrol – petrol station

Stonehenge is a prehistoric monument.

It's a touchscreen.
You must touch it.

FASTEN YOUR SEATBELT!

to invent ⇔ inventor

I had a horrible dream last night: It was about a UFO.

Orbiter is a spaceship that goes into orbit.

STEP B

A	**watching brief** [ˈwɒtʃɪŋ ˌbriːf]	Beobachtungsauftrag
	neighbour [ˈneɪbə]	Nachbar(in)
	North Sea [ˌnɔːθ ˈsiː]	Nordsee
	well [wel]	(Öl-)Quelle, Bohrloch
	fence [fens]	Zaun
	harmless [ˈhɑːmləs]	ungefährlich, harmlos
	frail [freɪl]	zart, zerbrechlich
	sweater [ˈswetə]	Pullover
	to **introduce** [ˌɪntrəˈdjuːs]	vorstellen, bekannt machen
	Moon and Stars [ˌmuːn‿ən ˈstɑːz]	*Name eines Pubs*
	would you care to [ˌwʊd juː ˈkeə]	hätten Sie Lust (zu)
	torch [tɔːtʃ]	Taschenlampe
	government [ˈgʌvnmənt]	Regierung
	moving [ˈmuːvɪŋ]	beweglich
	pedestrian [pɪˈdestriən]	Fußgänger(in)
	youth [juːθ]	Jugendliche(r)
	crash helmet [ˈkræʃ ˌhelmət]	Sturzhelm
	parts *pl.* [pɑːts]	Gegend, Region
	observer [əbˈzɜːvə]	Beobachter(in)
	commercial traveller [kəˌmɜːʃl ˈtrævlə]	Handelsreisende(r)
	to **suppose** [səˈpəʊz]	denken, meinen, annehmen
	surveyor [səˈveɪə]	Gutachter(in)
	wallet [ˈwɒlɪt]	Brieftasche
	as [æz/əz]	als, während
	elbow [ˈelbəʊ]	Ellbogen
	to **jog** [dʒɒg]	anstoßen, antippen
	to **grab** [græb]	packen, schnappen
	to **drain** [dreɪn]	leeren
	counter [ˈkaʊntə]	Theke
	companion [kəmˈpænjən]	Begleiter(in), Kamerad(in)
	to **crowd** [kraʊd]	(sich) drängen
	to **demand** [dɪˈmɑːnd]	fordern, verlangen

Neighbours are people who live next door or near your house or flat.

franz introduire *lat* introducere
engl to introduce

Observers and surveyors collect information.

'-er' and '-or' tell you what people do:

-er	-or
producer	visitor
painter	surveyor
observer	director
…	…

6

	to **realize** ['rɪəlaɪz]	bemerken, erkennen, realisieren
	outnumbered [ˌaʊt'nʌmbəd]	zahlenmäßig unterlegen
	motorcycle ['məʊtəˌsaɪkl]	Motorrad
	to **be knocked down** [biː ˌnɒkt 'daʊn]	umgefahren werden
	to **mean so. harm** [ˌmiːn 'hɑːm]	jmdm. weh tun wollen
	amazement [ə'meɪzmənt]	Erstaunen, Verblüffung
	to **escape** [ɪ'skeɪp]	entkommen, entfliehen
	lane [leɪn]	Gasse, Sträßchen
	rider [raɪdə]	Fahrer(in)
	to **flash** [flæʃ]	aufblitzen, aufleuchten
	engine ['endʒɪn]	Motor
	handlebar ['hændlbɑː]	Lenkstange, Lenker
	within [wɪ'ðɪn]	in, innerhalb
	tangled ['tæŋgld]	verheddert
	to **litter** ['lɪtə]	verstreuen, übersäen
	to **part** [pɑːt]	sich trennen, auseinandergehen
	least said soonest mended [ˌliːst 'sed ˌsuːnəst 'mendɪd]	je weniger geredet wird, desto schneller wird es wieder gut
	to **draw* attention to** [ˌdrɔː ə'tentʃn]	Aufmerksamkeit ziehen auf
B	to **awaken** [ə'weɪkn]	aufwecken, aufwachen
	scream [skriːm]	Schrei, Heulen
	to **fling* on** [ˌflɪŋ‿'ɒn]	*(Kleidung)* schnell überwerfen, anziehen
	in a bad way [ˌbæd 'weɪ]	in einem schlechten Zustand
	chest [tʃest]	Brust
	to **disintegrate** [dɪ'sɪntɪgreɪt]	(sich) auflösen, zersetzen
	to **remain** [rɪ'meɪn]	zurückbleiben
	pile [paɪl]	Haufen, Stapel
	dust [dʌst]	Staub
	weapon ['wepən]	Waffe
	dressing gown ['dresɪŋ ˌgaʊn]	Morgenrock
	to **attack** [ə'tæk]	angreifen
	to **defend** [dɪ'fend]	verteidigen
	failure ['feɪljə]	Misserfolg, Scheitern
	to **nod** [nɒd]	nicken
	to **report back** [rɪˌpɔːt 'bæk]	sich zurückmelden
	to **write sth. off** [ˌraɪt‿'ɒf]	abschreiben
	to **push** [pʊʃ]	stoßen, schieben
3	to **promise** ['prɒmɪs]	versprechen
	hope [həʊp]	Hoffnung

STEP C

1	to **cover** ['kʌvə]	zudecken, abdecken
	sense [sens]	Sinn
	tall [tɔːl]	hoch, groß, lang

TRACK 1

	Easter Island ['iːstə ˌaɪlənd]	Osterinsel
	Westbury ['westbri]	*Ort in England*
	Chris de Burgh [ˌkrɪs də 'bɜːg]	*irischer Popmusiker*
	to **mention** ['mentʃn]	erwähnen
	likely ['laɪkli]	wahrscheinlich
1	**outer space** [ˌaʊtə 'speɪs]	der äußere Weltraum

You and your companions are outnumbered if the others are in a larger group.

A lane is a narrow road, often in the country.

Every car has an engine – some are more powerful than others.

to push

to pull

Be careful with words.
Don't use them as weapons.

verbnounverbnounverbnoun
to / a promise: hope, wonder, race, travel, crowd, demand, escape, flash, cover, …

opposites

likely	unlikely
dry	wet
known	unknown
married	unmarried
to defend	to attack
tall	small
to awaken	to fall asleep
sense	nonsense
least	most
identified	unidentified

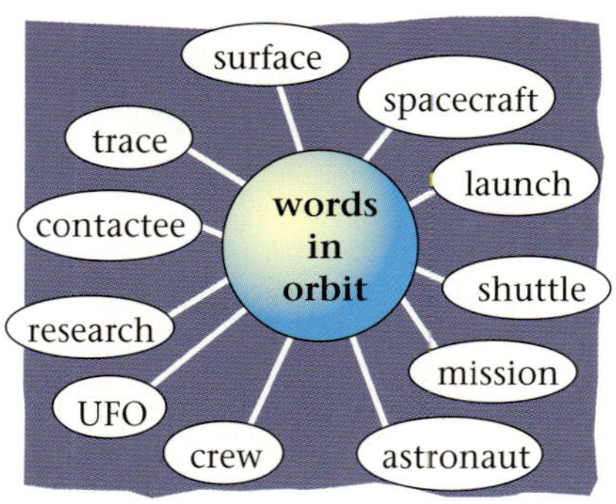

6

TRACK 2

+**Maine** [meɪn]	*amerikanischer Bundesstaat*
+**session** ['seʃn]	Sitzung, Treffen
+**alleged** [ə'ledʒd]	angeblich
+**contactee** [ˌkɒntæk'ti:]	jmd, der mit einem UFO Kontakt hatte
+**New Jersey** [ˌnju:'dʒɜ:zi]	*amerikanischer Bundesstaat*
+**research** [rɪ'sɜ:tʃ]	Forschung
+**suit** [su:t]	Anzug
+**lipstick** ['lɪpstɪk]	Lippenstift
+**psychic** ['saɪkɪk]	telepathisch
+**ability** [ə'bɪləti]	Fähigkeit
+**coin** [kɔɪn]	Münze
+to **disappear** [ˌdɪsə'pɪə]	verschwinden
+to **instruct** [ɪn'strʌkt]	anweisen, instruieren
+to **erase** [ɪ'reɪz]	entfernen, löschen
+**at last** [ət 'lɑ:st]	endlich
+**orbit** ['ɔ:bɪt]	(Erd-)Umlaufbahn
+**Soviet** ['səʊviət]	sowjetisch
+**spacecraft** ['speɪskrɑ:ft]	Raumfahrzeug
+**shuttle** ['ʃʌtl]	Transporter
+**female** ['fi:meɪl]	weiblich
+**launch** [lɔ:ntʃ]	Abschuss
+**fuzzy** ['fʌzi]	unscharf, verschwommen
+to **launch** [lɔ:ntʃ]	abschießen
+**Mir crew** ['mɪə ˌkru:]	Besatzung des Raumschiffs Mir *(russ.: Welt/Frieden)*

CHECK-OUT

3	**utterance** ['ʌtrns]	Äußerung
	to **rewrite*** [ˌri:'raɪt]	neu schreiben

COGNATE WORDS

aggressive [ə'gresɪv]	aggressiv, feindselig
astronaut ['æstrənɔ:t]	Astronaut(in)
astronomer [ə'strɒnəmə]	Astronom(in)
bar [bɑ:]	Bar, Kneipe
cartoonist [kɑ:'tu:nɪst]	Karikaturenzeichner(in)
catastrophic [ˌkætə'strɒfɪk]	katastrophal
civilization [ˌsɪvlaɪ'zeɪʃn]	Zivilisation
+**colleague** ['kɒli:g]	Kollege/Kollegin
command [kə'mɑ:nd]	Befehl, Kommando
commander [kə'mɑ:ndə]	Kommandant(in)
+**control** [kən'trəʊl]	Kontrolle
to **cooperate** [kəʊ'ɒpreɪt]	zusammenarbeiten
cooperation [kəʊˌɒpə'reɪʃn]	Zusammenarbeit, Kooperation
+**countdown** ['kaʊntdaʊn]	Countdown
crash [kræʃ]	Krachen, Krach
crater ['kreɪtə]	Krater
+**crew** ['kru:]	Besatzung
+to **dock** [dɒk]	anlegen, andocken
gigantic [dʒaɪ'gæntɪk]	gigantisch, riesig
+**hypnosis** [hɪp'nəʊsɪs]	Hypnose
inspiration [ˌɪntspr'eɪʃn]	Eingebung, Inspiration
intelligence [ɪn'telɪdʒnts]	Intelligenz
intelligent [ɪn'telɪdʒnt]	intelligent
to **kill** [kɪl]	töten, umbringen
lander ['lændə]	Landeeinheit
landing ['lændɪŋ]	Landung
machine [mə'ʃi:n]	Apparat, Maschine
manned [mænd]	bemannt
Mars [mɑ:z]	Mars
mass [mæs]	Menge, Masse
mission ['mɪʃn]	Auftrag, Mission
+**monotone** ['mɒnətəʊn]	monotoner Klang
mysteriously [mɪ'stɪəriəsli]	geheimnisvoll, mysteriös
myth [mɪθ]	Mythos
object ['ɒbdʒɪkt]	Gegenstand, Objekt
on board [ɒn 'bɔ:d]	an Bord
planet ['plænɪt]	Planet
robot ['rəʊbɒt]	Roboter
+**satellite** ['sætlaɪt]	Satellit
schoolfriend ['sku:lfrend]	Schulfreund(in)
science fiction [ˌsaɪənts 'fɪkʃn]	Sciencefiction
sculpture ['skʌlptʃə]	Skulptur
second ['seknd]	Sekunde; zweiter(r/s)
skateboard ['skeɪtbɔ:d]	Skateboard
+**tape** [teɪp]	(Ton-)Band
technology [tek'nɒlədʒi]	Technologie, Technik
telescope ['telɪskəʊp]	Teleskop, Fernrohr
theory ['θɪəri]	Theorie
UFO (unidentified flying object) [ˌju:ef'əʊ]	UFO (unbekanntes Flugobjekt)
unmanned [ʌn'mænd]	unbemannt
+**unnatural** [ʌn'nætʃrl]	unnatürlich

6

UNIT 7

Insiders, outsiders

1 Just like us?

Choose a person in one of the pictures. Write down a question you would ask this person if you met him/her. In groups, read out your questions and talk about what the people might answer.

2 Listening comprehension: A radio interview

a) *Listen to the radio interview. Match the topic with a picture on the left.*

b) *Listen again and note down:*

– the interviewer's first question.
– the reasons the boy gives in his answer.
– the advice he gives to young people.

c) *Is there a similar problem in your school or town? What should people do about it?*

3 The price of fashion

a) *Put the pieces back together to find two letters to the magazine 1015.*

A: think they have to be very thin to look good. A while ago I was reading an article about a young girl who

D: Dear 1015
I am writing about skinny models. They are a bad influence on girls who

H: shoes you're just supporting poverty in the Third World.
Faith Pitman, Lancashire

E: they only get slave wages. Overall, if you buy expensive trainers and

B: Dear 1015
I'm writing to tell everyone about the negative aspect of buying trainers and shoes.

I: Secondly, lots of people want to be fashionable, but buying designer trainers doesn't help the workers if

F: All in all, trainers cost only a few pounds to make, so the high prices are a rip-off.

C: helped girls like her. But soon after, when she was out on a walk, a model agency asked her to work for them. I think this is terrible, as it shows that

G: model agencies really look out for skinny girls.
Stephanie Lynch, Norfolk

J: was anorexic because of this. She went to a special school which

From *1015* in *The Times*

b) *Do you agree with the points the writers make? Why, or why not?*

4 Influences

a) *Look again at the people in the pictures. What do you think are the most important influences in their lives? Explain why you think so.*

money – friends – religion – school – parents – clothes – work – health – music – fashion magazines

b) *Write a report with the heading 'How times have changed'. Ask your parents about the influences on them when they were your age, and compare their lives as teenagers with yours.*

1 Listening comprehension: Selima

38/39

a) You are going to hear a second interview, this time with a British girl, Selima. *Before you listen, look at the interviewer's notes. What would they be as full sentences?*

Example: Selima's family are Muslim. Her parents are from India. …

b) *Now listen to the interview and find four mistakes in the interviewer's notes. Can you correct them?*

Example: The interviewer writes that …, but Selima tells him / says …

c) *Listen again and complete the sentences.*

Example: Selima's parents expect her to wear traditional clothes. They also expect her to …

Selima's parents	– expect her to …
	– want her to …
	– don't want her to…
	– have told her not to …
A boy	– has asked her to …
Selima's brother	– tells her not to …
	– wants her to …
Selima	– can't tell her brother to …

– family Muslim (parents from India)
– religion v. imp.
– S. happy in Britain – but doesn't feel British
– not interested in modern clothes
– angry because she can't invite boys home
– thinks it's v. imp. to have good relationship with parents
– doesn't want boyfriend
– is having trouble at school
– always does what parents want (but 'not a sheep')

SAVE

She says (that) …
She tells me (that) …

When you report what people say,

– be careful with the pronouns,
– don't change the tense if the reporting verb is in the present tense,
– you needn't repeat every word. You can give a summary with expressions such as 'tells … to' and 'offers to'.

2 What people said to Selima

38/39

Look at these examples of reported speech. What did people actually say?

1. Jasmit has asked me to go ice-skating with him.
2. I accepted his invitation.
3. Jasmit offered to lend me his sister's ice skates.
4. I refused his offer to lend me the ice-skates.
5. My mum wants me to help her make a curry tonight.
6. My brother wants me to listen to his bhangra music.
7. My parents tell me not to give boys my address.

Do you think you could … ?
You should …
Don't …
Would you like me to … ?
Thanks, but I've already got a pair.
Would you like to … ?
Yes, I'd love to.

3 What about you?

Work in pairs. Talk about what your family, your teachers and your friends expect/want you to do.

4 Quiz: Are you a fashion slave?

Decide which statements you agree with, then talk about them with a partner. Say whether you think he/she is a fashion slave.

1. I wear something different every day.
2. I haven't been to a clothes shop for years.
3. I usually wear what's in fashion.
4. I hardly ever buy designer clothes.
5. I'm really interested in clothes.
6. I spend money on clothes much too easily.
7. I often read fashion magazines to find out what's 'in'.
8. I always check the price before I buy something.
9. I've never followed fashions blindly.
10. I went to Paris last spring to see the latest fashion collections.
11. I didn't do well at school last term because I was worrying about my outfits.

"I wanted MIDAS trainers!"

G 40

5 What's the rule?

a) *Put these adverbs from the quiz into groups:*

– manner (how)
– place (where)
– time (when / how often)

every day	usually	to a clothes shop
last term	well	in the spring
often	really	for a long time
never	to Paris	much too easily
always	at school	hardly ever

b) *Look at the order of verbs and adverbs in the quiz. Would the order be different in German? Try to work out some rules for English sentences.*

G 40

6 Words in the right order

Put the words in the right order to complete the sentences.

1. Selima's father (speaks / very well / English).
2. He has (in London / for / been / twenty years / living).
3. Selima's mother (beautiful dresses / sometimes / her / makes / for).
4. Selima (usually / is / to her parents / very polite).
5. She (her brother / angry / with / sometimes / gets).
6. Her brother (wants / to / always / her / his bhangra music / listen to).
7. Jasmit and Selima (last Sunday / secretly / in the park / met).
8. Selima's parents asked: "Selima, why did you (late / so / home / come)?"

G 40

7 About you

Complete the sentences about yourself. Continue with an adjective, with an adverb and an adjective (e.g. quite hungry), or with a verb.

1. When I come home from school I am usually ...
2. When I come home from school I usually ...
3. I am sometimes ... before a test.
4. I sometimes ... before a test.
5. When I choose clothes I always ...
6. When I choose clothes I am always ...

"You'd tell me if it looked silly on me, wouldn't you?"

MIDAS

Cast: Mike, pupil 1, pupil 2, pupil 3, pupil 4

The scene takes place in a high school. Pupils are standing in the hall and talking. They are all wearing white T-shirts and black pants. Enter Mike wearing MIDAS shoes, MIDAS tear-away pants, MIDAS shirt and MIDAS hat.

Mike: Hi, guys! Like the clothes?
Pupil 1: Oh ... Barbie went shopping.
Pupil 2: More MIDAS stuff? Mike, aren't you just a little obsessed with the MIDAS thing?
Mike: Hey, I'm just keeping up with the latest style.
Pupil 3: You just got a new outfit last week!
Mike: Ah, but that was last week's style.
Pupil 4: Mike, one question.
Mike: Yeah?
Pupil 4: How much did you pay for that?
Mike: It was only two hundred and fifty bucks.
All: What? *(Murmurs.)*
Mike: There was a special offer.
Pupil 1: Mike, you paid two hundred and fifty bucks for that?
Mike: Hey, get off my back. Besides *(pause)* my Mom bought it for me.
Pupil 2: Your Mom's a sucker.
Mike: Maybe.
Pupil 3: Do you know how much it cost MIDAS to make all that?
Mike: I'm sure it cost them a lot. It's quality stuff.
Pupil 4: Actually, no. In total, your outfit probably cost ten dollars to make.
Mike: Ten bucks? So why would MIDAS price it so high?
Pupil 1: So they can make a huge profit.
Mike: Well, they probably had to pay their workers.
Pupil 3: More like slaves.
Pupil 4: Ever heard of sweatshops, Mike?
Mike: Sure.
Pupil 1: You have?
Mike: Yeah, of course. Everyone knows what they are ... uh ... stores ... for ... uh ... sweaters.
Pupil 2: It's only common knowledge.
Mike: Exactly.
Pupil 3: And no one supports them.
Mike: Why not?
Pupil 4: Especially when the workers have to work for less than the minimum wage.
Mike: Oh ... I like sweaters.
(Pupil 1 takes Mike's hat.)
Mike: Hey!
Pupil 1: You see this hat here? This probably cost two dollars to make.
Pupil 2: Fact number one:
Pupil 1: The minimum wage in Ontario is six dollars, eighty-five cents an hour. In southern China, where MIDAS produces a lot of its clothes, workers get twenty-five cents, American, an hour.
Mike: It's not my fault.
Pupil 3: Fact number two.
Pupil 1: A normal working day for us is eight hours. In the factories they work a ten to twelve hour day. And two to four hours overtime.
Mike: Well, at least they get money for that.
Pupil 4: That's not the case with many MIDAS workers. They don't receive any overtime pay and if they're lucky enough to get some extra cash, it's less than what the law says they should get.
Mike: Well, what can I do about it, huh?
Pupil 1: Final fact number four. If they don't feel like working overtime, or if the boss catches them talking on the job, they can lose a day's pay.
Mike: Fine. I'm sorry that the conditions aren't great. Just give me my hat! *(Pupil 1 throws hat away.)* Hey!
Pupil 2: *(takes off Mike's shoes)* Let's see how much it costs to make those shoes. The production and labour costs to make a pair of MIDAS Air Mercury shoes ...
Pupil 3: Two dollars and seventy-five cents, American.
Pupil 2: Cost for promotion and advertising:
Pupil 4: Four dollars.
Pupil 2: They pay almost twice as much for ads as they pay to make shoes.
Pupil 4: What do they sell for?
Pupil 1: Seventy dollars.
Mike: Well, they've got to make money somehow.
Pupil 2: Do you know how much profit MIDAS made last year?
Mike: No.
Pupil 2: Three hundred and ninety four million dollars.
Pupil 3: And these pants *(tears off Mike's pants)* ...
Mike: Why did you just take off my pants?
Pupil 3: These pants weren't made here in Toronto because MIDAS closed down the factory.

They sacked one hundred and twenty-five of their workers, and said they had no responsibility to them.

Mike: Fine! I get your point. Now give me my pants. I'm cold.

Pupil 4: Do you like hockey?

Mike: Sure. Why not? You've taken everything ELSE I own.

Pupil 4: Did you know that MIDAS is the owner of Bayer skates?

Mike: *(sarcastically)* You don't say!

Pupil 4: Yep. And last year MIDAS decided to close down its factory in Cambridge. That means four hundred of their employees will lose their jobs.

Mike: Why would MIDAS do that?

Pupil 4: Why pay extra, when you can do it cheaper in a sweatshop in Asia or Eastern Europe?

Pupil 1: Do you see our point?

Mike: Yes.

Pupil 2: And that would be?

Mike: That sweatshops don't sell sweaters.

Pupil 3: And …?

Mike: That I should realize the labour behind the label. *(Mike takes off his MIDAS shirt.)*

Pupil 4: And …?

Mike: That I'm very cold without clothes on.

(All the pupils exit. They take Mike's clothes with them and leave him on stage in his boxers and socks. He looks around.)

Mike: Guys …

All (off stage): What?

Mike: Can I have my clothes back? *(pause)* Please?

(Pupils throw a different set of clothes back on stage. Blackout.)

Curtain.

Adapted from the play *Swoosh* by Blair Francey

1 Thinking about the themes

a) *Describe what the play is about in no more than three sentences.*

b) *What is your opinion of Mike?*

I feel sorry for him because …
I don't feel sorry for him because …

c) *Say what you think would happen if …*

1. people like Mike stopped buying MIDAS clothes.
2. MIDAS paid higher wages to its workers in Asia and East Europe.
3. MIDAS closed down its factories in Asia and East Europe.
4. people only bought products from rich countries.

2 A summary

Complete the summary of the play with words from the box.

MIDAS is a play about a boy who always wears expensive … because he wants to keep up with the … . His friends are shocked when he says his outfit cost … . Actually, it was Mike's … who paid for it. The others tell him that the clothes are made in … . Mike thinks they are … . His friends begin to … his clothes and tell him what they really … to make. They explain that the prices are … not because the quality is …, and in fact workers' wages are very … . They also give examples of the terrible … in the sweatshop, for example, the long hours and no … . They say that MIDAS does not act … towards its workers. If labour becomes too expensive, they close down their … . In the end, Mike shows he understands that his clothes are a … .

responsibly	factories
cost	low
designer labels	$250
high	mother
sweatshops	rip-off
overtime pay	tear off
latest styles	good
stores that sell sweaters	
working conditions	

3 A step further

a) Midas was a fabled king who turned everything he touched into gold. *Do you think MIDAS is a good name for fashion trainers? Why, or why not?*

b) *List the names of fashion trainers that are popular in your country. Do the names have anything in common? Why do you think the companies chose them? Think about the 'message' they give us.*

c) *Find out what actually happened to Midas. What can we learn from the story?*

1 Putting on a play

Put on the play MIDAS. *You can rehearse it in groups and perform it to each other in class. Or you can perform it to a wider audience – maybe during your school open day. Ask your teacher for tips and ideas.*

2 What's the word?

A verb is missing in each sentence. What should it be, and where should it go? Rewrite the sentences with the verb in the right form.

1. Could you me the time, please?
2. Do you English?
3. It's a secret, so please don't anyone.
4. Sorry, did you something?
5. He terrible jokes.
6. Actors need to clearly.
7. People are about me behind my back.
8. What a surprise! I don't know what to!

3 Don't say no!

Play this game in groups. One of you sits in the 'hot seat'. The others ask questions, but you must try not to say 'yes' or 'no'. If you do, someone else takes the hot seat. The person who stays in the hot seat the longest is the winner.

Tips for the hot seat	
Yes	No
Absolutely! Of course! Sure. I agree. I do. / I am. / …	Never! I'm not sure. Not exactly. I'd rather not say. I don't. / I'm not. / …

4 I'd rather not say

a) *Read the poem on your own. Decide which words you need to stress. Then read the poem aloud with a partner.*
b) *Why do you think the person doesn't want to answer the questions? Would you feel the same way?*
c) *Write five more lines for the poem. Think of four questions people often ask you, and end with "I'd rather not say".*

Personal questions

Where were you born?
I'd rather not say.
Where are you from?
I'd rather not say.
How tall are you?
How old are you?
How much do you weigh?
I'd rather not say.
How much rent do you pay?
I'd rather not say.
How much do you make?
I'd rather not say.
Why aren't you married?
I'd rather not say.
Why don't you have children?
Where were you last night?
Why weren't you home?
Did you stay out late?
Did you come home alone?
Did you have a good time?
Did you see a good play?
Did you go to a concert?
I'd rather not say.

From *Jazz Chants* by Carolyn Graham

7

Conversation skills
LEARNING TO LEARN

5 At the airport
Describe what is happening in the picture.

Useful phrases: Meetings and greetings

Hi, there!	Welcome to …
Hello, my name's …	It's nice to meet you.
How d'you do?	Pleased to meet you.
How are you?	Fine, thanks. And you?
Hi, how're you doing?	Not too bad.
How was the flight?	Great to see you again!

6 Listening comprehension: Greetings

a) Tobias, an exchange pupil from Germany, is meeting his American host family. *Listen and say which of the phrases from exercise 5 they use.*

b) *Listen again and note down more phrases you can use when you meet someone after a journey.*

c) *Work in groups. Write a dialogue between a host family and an exchange pupil who are meeting for the first time.*

7 Listening comprehension: The art of conversation

Listen to two conversations. Decide which is the more successful conversation, and try to explain why.

8 Tell me more!

a) *Complete the sentences about yourself. They needn't be true.*

1. I live in …
2. I can …
3. On the way to school this morning, I …
4. On Saturday I'm going to …
5. The most interesting thing I own is …
6. I'm not who you think I am. I'm really …

b) *Work in pairs. Read your sentences to each other. Show interest in what your partner says, and ask him or her to tell you more.*
Example:

– I live in a castle.
– Do you? How interesting! What's it like?

Useful phrases: Showing interest

Do you? / Can you? / Did you?
Is that so?
Really?
How interesting!
Tell me more!
What happened next?
Tell me about it!

9 Listening comprehension: Saying it the right way

a) *Read the sentences aloud. Then listen carefully and say which sentence you hear.*

	A	B
1.	I don't know, Carlos.	I don't know Carlos.
2.	Don't, stop!	Don't stop!
3.	I'm afraid, I can't!	I'm afraid I can't.
4.	Why, is it broken?	Why is it broken?
5.	I'm sorry, I can't come.	I'm sorry I can't come.
6.	I don't, no.	I don't know.

b) *Match the sentences below with their answers in a).*

1. You can't use my CD player.
2. Do you spend a lot of money on clothes?
3. We're flying at 10,000 feet. Let's jump now!
4. Carlos says you know him.
5. I'm going to push you into the water.
6. Here, I've bought you a ticket for the school play.

1 Funny fashions

a) *Put the photos in the order of when the fashions appeared.*

b) *Talk about the fashions. Say which you think is the …*

silliest | funniest | nicest | ugliest | strangest | most sensible

c) *Ask your teacher for his/her opinion about the fashions.*

2 A fashion report

Write a report about what is in fashion today. Describe the clothes that are popular and the sorts of people who wear them. You can add pictures from magazines, or draw the clothes yourself. Also say what you think the next fashion will be.

3 Which ones?

Write dialogues with 'Which one(s)?' and 'The one(s) with the …' or 'The … one(s).'

Example: 1. A: Can I clean the windows with that T-shirt?
B: Which one?
A: The one with all the holes.

7

1. Can I clean the windows with that T-shirt?
2. I love those shoes!
3. I've already got jeans like those.
4. That hat would look good on you.
5. You can't wear that skirt to school.
6. Those glasses are funny.

The focus group

A jeans company is doing a market survey. The marketing assistant, Jason Reed, interviewed a group of teenagers in a 'focus group' and sent this fax to his boss.

I don't care about the name as long as the jeans look good.

I can choose what I wear.

I bought four pairs last year.

I'm not allowed to wear jeans. It's against my religion.

Where are your factories?

I only buy jeans that are on sale.

What? Then I won't buy your jeans any more! I've heard awful things about your sweatshops in China.

I never wear jeans.

To: Ashley Cooper, Marketing Manager
From: Jason Reed
Re.: Market survey

Sorry you couldn't come to the focus group this morning. Here's what I found out:

- Most teenagers said that they could choose what they wore, without their parents' advice.
- More than half said they had bought more than three pairs of jeans last year.
- A few said they never wore jeans at all.
- One Asian woman told me she was not allowed to wear jeans because it was against her religion.
- Jeans customers seem to fall into three groups: The 'price shoppers' said they only bought jeans if they were cheap or on sale. The 'individualists' said they didn't care about the label or price as long the jeans looked good. Finally, there were the 'copycats', who only stuck to designer labels – not always ours!
- It seems that we need to improve our image. One young man asked where our factories were. When I told him, he got angry and said he wouldn't buy jeans from us any more because he had heard negative reports about sweatshops in China.

More details later.
Regards,
Jason

1 What type are you?

Jason Reed talks about three types of jeans customer. What are they? And what type are you?

2 Changing the verb

G 41

a) *Look at how the tenses of the verbs change when Jason reports what people said. Are the rules different for French or German?*

b) *One group told Jason that they 'only stuck to designer labels'. What do you think the people actually said? (Different answers are possible.)*

SAVE

direct speech	–	reported speech
is / are	–	was / were
can	–	could
will	–	would
buy	–	bought
bought	–	had bought
have bought	–	had bought
had bought	–	had bought

3 Reporting what people said

G 41

Example: 1. Jason Reed: "I'm collecting information for a survey."
Jason said he was collecting information for a survey.

2. Selima: "Jeans are really boring!"
3. Kate: "My parents don't give me enough money to buy clothes today."
4. Peter: "I wear jeans every day."
5. Lee: "I saw a great advertisement for jeans last night."
6. Nina and Wendy: "Look – we're wearing the same pair of MIDAS jeans!"
7. Tim: "I'm doing a project about the history of jeans this week."
8. Greg: "I can't understand why jeans are so expensive here."
9. Jason Reed: "I'll give you 20 euros for taking part in this survey."

SAVE

direct speech	–	reported speech
this week	–	that week
today	–	that day
yesterday	–	the day before
last night	–	the night before
tomorrow	–	the following / next day
here	–	there

G 42

4 Verbs for reporting

say	explain	invite	hint	answer
think	wonder	tell	warn	ask
describe	want to know	pretend	guess	lie

SAVE

questions

reporting verb + question word/whether/if

One young man **asked where** our factories were.

1. Which three verbs can you use to report questions?
2. Which two verbs can you use to show what someone said was not true?
3. Which verbs can have the word 'that' directly after them?

You can add more examples to your SAVE *boxes later.*

5 Questions and answers

A man from the organization 'Clean Clothes' interviewed some women who work in sweatshops.

a) *Match the questions and answers.*

1. What is your name?
2. How old are you?
3. Do you enjoy your work?
4. Do you have any breaks?
5. What are the conditions in the factory like?
6. How many hours do you work a week?
7. Do you earn the minimum wage?
8. Why don't you ask for more money?

a) No, I earn less. It isn't enough to live on.
b) 75 hours a week.
c) Because I don't want to lose my job!
d) No, but I'm happy to have a job!
e) Amanda.
f) Well, they are noisy, and the air is bad.
g) I'm 20.
h) Yes, but they are very short.

b) *Report the interview. Be careful with the word order when you report the questions.*

Example: The interviewer asked the woman what her name was. She told him that … .
Then he asked her … … He also wanted to know … When he asked …, she answered …

G 43

6 Say it a different way

a) *Say it without 'to' or 'for'.*

Example: 1. Selima mustn't give her address to boys.
Selima mustn't give boys her address.

2. Some parents buy expensive clothes for their children.
3. Jasmit sent some flowers to Selima.
4. Carlos lent some money to his friends.
5. Jasmit wrote a long letter to Selima.
6. She didn't show the letter to her parents.
7. Carlos says his school didn't teach anything to him.
8. Carlos told an interesting story to the interviewer.
9. The gang offered a job to Carlos.
10. Selima's brother played his new bhangra record to her.
11. Selima's mum made a beautiful dress for her.

SAVE

verbs with two objects

Can you give me your phone number?
Can you give your phone number to me?
Can you give it to me?

give	pay	play	make
buy	offer	lend	send
teach	show	tell	write

b) *Look at the examples in the* SAVE *box. Which is the direct object, and which is the indirect object? When does the indirect object come last? Can you make a rule?*

WP

1 The world of work

Match the words (a–l) with their meanings (1–12).

a) slave	b) wages	c) special offer	d) factory	e) employee	f) buck
g) rent	h) labour	i) to sack	j) overtime	k) profit	l) advertising

1. money you get for work
2. to tell a worker to leave his / her job
3. money you make when you sell something
4. place of production
5. person who has to work for no pay
6. a form of promotion
7. worker
8. you pay less than the normal price for it
9. money you pay for a place to live
10. dollar
11. work or workers
12. extra hours of work

2 Where do the adverbs go?

Put in the adverbs.

1. (never) I have been to China.
2. (quite) Designer clothes are expensive.
3. (often) Selima has to help her mum.
4. (last year) Maike went to England.
5. (really well) Now she speaks English.
6. (late) I shouldn't go to bed.
7. (a week ago) Jasmit wrote Selima a letter.
8. (also / every day) He phones her.

3 Meeting at the airport

a) *Put the parts of the dialogue in the right order.*

– It was fine, but too long. I'm quite tired.
– Oh, thanks very much, but I'm afraid it's quite heavy.
– Hi, Christina. I'm Mike Jones, Karen's father. Welcome to Washington!
– It's not too bad. Oh, there's Karen. She's waiting for us over there!
– Excuse me, are you Christina Becker?
– Oh, Mr Jones! Nice to meet you!
– That's right.
– Hey, just call me Mike, OK? So how was the flight?
– Let me take your bag.

b) *Go on with the dialogue between Christina, Mike and Karen. Write between five and ten lines.*

4 Reported speech

a) *Do you remember Mike and his friends at the high school in Toronto? Say what Mike **tells** the others.*

1. "I'm just keeping up with the latest style."
2. "You've taken everything else I own."
3. "Now give me my pants."
4. "Hey, get off my back!"

b) +*Say what Mike **told** the others.*

c) +*Report what people **asked** Mike.*

1. "How much did you pay for your outfit?"
2. "Have you ever heard of sweatshops?"
3. "What do they sell for?"
4. "Do you see our point, Mike?"

5 +Verbs with two objects

Put the words in the right order to complete the sentences.

1. Did Joe (you / his banjo / lend)?
   No, he didn't (me / to / lend / it)!
2. Has Jason (Ashley / the fax / sent)?
   Yes, he (it / him / to / sent) yesterday.
3. Who (those flowers / gave / you), Selima?
   Oh, a friend (me / them / to / gave).
4. Could (you / me / make / a cup of tea)?
   I'll only (for / one / make / you) if you say 'please'.

CHECK-IN

2	**similar** ['sɪmɪlə]	ähnlich, gleichartig
	agency ['eɪdʒntsi]	Geschäftsstelle, Büro, Agentur
	skinny ['skɪni]	mager, dürr
	influence ['ɪnfluəns]	Einfluss
	slave [sleɪv]	Sklave / Sklavin
	wage [weɪdʒ]	(Arbeits-)Lohn
	overall [ˌəʊvr'ɔ:l]	insgesamt, allgemein
	rip-off ['rɪpɒf]	Wucher, Nepp
	Norfolk ['nɔ:fək]	*Grafschaft in Ostengland*
	poverty ['pɒvəti]	Armut
	Lancashire ['læŋkəʃə]	*Grafschaft im Nordwesten Englands*
	fashionable ['fæʃnəbl]	modisch, schick
	anorexic [ˌænər'eksɪk]	magersüchtig
4	**health** [helθ]	Gesundheit

An agent works for an agency.

The two brothers are similar in appearance.

She's very skinny. She should eat more.

If something is a rip-off, it means that the price is much too high.

Did you know that there were slaves in America before the Pilgrims arrived?

Lots of people who live in poverty have health problems.

She always wears the latest fashion. Her clothes are very fashionable.

STEP A

1	**relationship** [ˌrɪ'leɪʃnʃɪp]	Beziehung, Verhältnis
	expression [ɪk'spreʃn]	Ausdruck
	ice-skating ['aɪsˌskeɪtɪŋ]	Schlittschuhlaufen
	ice skate ['aɪs ˌskeɪt]	Schlittschuh
	to **refuse** [rɪ'fju:z]	ablehnen, verweigern
	offer ['ɒfə]	Angebot
4	**statement** ['steɪtmənt]	Feststellung, Behauptung, Aussage
	whether ['weðə]	ob
	hardly ['ha:dlɪ]	kaum
5	**order** ['ɔ:də]	Reihenfolge
	to **work out** [wɜ:k‿'aʊt]	ausarbeiten, herausfinden

franz expression *lat* expressio *engl* expression

Ice-skating and rollerskating are very similar.

I don't know whether he is happy or unhappy.

STEP B

A	**cast** [kɑ:st]	(Rollen-)Besetzung, Ensemble
	pants *(AE)* [pænts]	Hose
	stuff [stʌf]	Zeug, Sachen
	to **be obsessed (by)** [əb'sest]	besessen sein (von)
	buck *(AE) coll.* [bʌk]	Dollar
	besides [bɪ'saɪdz]	außerdem
	sucker ['sʌkə]	*hier*: Idiot(in)
	huge [hju:dʒ]	riesig, gewaltig
	sweatshop ['swetʃɒp]	Ausbeuterbetrieb
	common ['kɒmən]	allgemein
	knowledge ['nɒlɪdʒ]	Wissen, Kenntnis
	Ontario [ɒn'teəriəʊ]	*Provinz in Ostkanada*
	southern ['sʌðən]	südlich, Süd-
	fault [fɔ:lt]	Fehler, Schuld
	factory ['fæktri]	Fabrik, Werk
	overtime ['əʊvətaɪm]	Überstunden
	at least [ət‿'li:st]	zumindest
	case [keɪs]	Fall, Sache
	pay [peɪ]	Bezahlung, Vergütung

The cast of characters is very important in a film.

She was obsessed by her new idea.

She has got a cupboard and a lamp beside her bed.

When you do or say or write something wrong, that's a mistake.
When you are responsible for something that is or has gone wrong, it's your fault.

Overtime is when you work more than your usual number of hours.

7

	extra cash [ˌekstrə 'kæʃ]	Zuschlag, Sonderzahlung	Laws tell you what you may or may not do, and what you must or must not do.
	law [lɔ:]	Gesetz	
	final ['faɪnl]	(aller)letzte/r/s	The final tests are at the end of the school year.
	condition [kən'dɪʃn]	Bedingung, Kondition	
	labour ['leɪbə]	Arbeit, Arbeitskräfte	*franz* labeur *lat* labor *engl* labour
	Mercury ['mɜ:kjri]	Merkur *(römischer Gott, Götterbote)*	
	promotion [prə'məʊʃn]	Förderung, Unterstützung	
	advertising ['ædvətaɪzɪŋ]	Werbung, Reklame	Businessmen and business-women know that advertising pays.
	somehow ['sʌmhaʊ]	irgend wie	
	to **tear (off)** [teər]	(ab)reißen	
	Toronto [tə'rɒntəʊ]	*Hauptstadt von Ontario*	
	to **own** [əʊn]	besitzen	
B	to **sack** *coll.* [sæk]	*hier:* entlassen	
	responsibility [rɪˌspɒnsə'bɪləti]	Verantwortung	Nouns ending in -ility: responsibility, possibility, …
	to **get so.'s point** *coll.* [pɔɪnt]	jmdn verstehen	
	yep *coll.* [jep]	ja	
	Cambridge ['keɪmbrɪdʒ]	*Ort in Kanada*	
	employee [ɪm'plɔɪi:]	Arbeitnehmer(in), Angestellte(r)	
1	**opinion** [ə'pɪnjən]	Meinung, Ansicht	*franz* opinion *lat* opinio *engl* opinion
	to **feel sorry for** [fi:l 'sɒrɪ]	bemitleiden	
3	**fabled** ['feɪbld]	sagenhaft, fabelhaft	
	to **turn into** ['tɜ:nˌɪntʊ]	(sich) verwandeln in	

STEP C

1	**during** ['djʊərɪŋ]	während	
2	to **be missing** ['mɪsɪŋ]	fehlen	
	surprise [sə'praɪz]	Überraschung	
4	to **be born** [bɔ:n]	geboren sein	
	to **weigh** [weɪ]	wiegen	
	rent [rent]	Miete	
5	**skill** [skɪl]	Fähigkeit, Fertigkeit	
	greeting [gri:tɪŋ]	Begrüßung, Gruß	
	How d'you do? [ˌhaʊ djʊ 'du:]	Guten Tag! Sehr erfreut!	
	Pleased to meet you. [pli:zd]	Angenehm. Sehr erfreut.	
6	**exchange** [ɪks'tʃeɪndʒ]	Austausch	
	host [həʊst]	Gastgeber(in)	
9	**foot** [fʊt]	Fuß *(engl. Längenmaß, ca. 30 cm)*	

verb / noun

to / a	sack	touch, present, surprise, rent, exchange, …

When babies are born, they are always weighed.

After a visit: send your host a 'thank you' letter. They will be very pleased.

TRACK 1

1	to **appear** [ə'pɪə]	erscheinen, auftauchen	to appear → ← to disappear

TRACK 2

	+**survey** ['sɜ:veɪ]	Umfrage, Untersuchung	Surveys are important in business.
	+**focus group** ['fəʊkəs ˌgru:p]	Gruppengespräch, Gesprächsgruppe	A focus group is a discussion where people are asked what they think about a product.

7

	+**copycat** ['kɒpikæt]	Nachahmer(in)	Many things are cheaper in a sale.
	+to **stick to sth.** [stɪk]	etw treu bleiben, bleiben (bei)	
4	+to **lie** [laɪ]	lügen	A copycat is someone who does exactly the same as another person.
5	+to **earn** [ɜ:n]	verdienen	
	+**manufacturer** [ˌmænjə'fæktʃərə]	Hersteller(in), Produzent(in), Fabrikant(in)	to earn = to get money by working

COGNATE WORDS

absolute [ˌæbsə'lu:t]	völlig, absolut	**interest** ['ɪntrəst]	Interesse
aspect ['æspekt]	Gesichtspunkt, Aspekt	**label** ['leɪbl]	Etikett, Label
+**assistant** [ə'sɪstnt]	Assistent(in), Mitarbeiter(in)	+**manager** ['mænɪdʒə]	Manager(in)
blackout ['blækaʊt]	Verdunkelung, *hier:* Stromausfall	+**marketing** ['mɑ:kɪtɪŋ]	Vertrieb, Absatz, Marketing
blind ['blaɪnd]	blind	**minimum** ['mɪnɪməm]	Minimum
+**boss** [bɒs]	Chef, Boss	**modern** ['mɒdn]	modern, zeitgemäß
boxers *pl.* ['bɒksəz]	Boxershorts	**murmur** ['mɜ:mə]	Gemurmel
collection ['kəlekʃn]	Sammlung, Kollektion	**Muslim** ['mʊzlɪm]	moslemisch, mohammedanisch
conversation [ˌkɒnvə'seɪʃn]	Gespräch, Konversation	**outfit** ['aʊtfɪt]	Kleidung, Ausstattung
to **cost*** [kɒst]	kosten	**outsider** [ˌaʊt'saɪdə]	Außenseiter(in)
designer [dɪ'zaɪnə]	Designer(in)	to **produce** [prə'dju:s]	herstellen, produzieren
+**euro** ['jʊərəʊ]	Euro *(europäische Währung)*	**production** [prə'dʌkʃn]	Herstellung, Produktion
to **exit** ['eksɪt]	hinausgehen, von der Bühne ab gehen	**profit** ['prɒfɪt]	Gewinn, Profit
		quality ['kwɒləti]	Qualität
		religion [rɪ'lɪdʒn]	Religion
		sarcastic [sɑ:'kæstɪk]	sarkastisch
+**fax** [fæks]	(Tele-)Fax	**skate** [skeɪt]	Rollschuh, Schlittschuh
+**gang** [gæŋ]	Gang, Bande		
+**image** ['ɪmɪdʒ]	Bild, Image	**teenager** ['ti:neɪdʒə]	Teenager, Jugendliche(r)
in total [ɪn 'təʊtl]	insgesamt, total		
+**individualist** [ˌɪndɪ'vɪdʒuəlɪst]	Individualist(in)	**Third World** [ˌθɜ:d 'wɜ:ld]	Dritte Welt
		+**type** [taɪp]	Typ, Art
insider [ˌɪn'saɪdə]	Eingeweihte(r), Insider(in)	**wide** [waɪd]	weit

7

A dictionary guide

If you want to look up a new word in the dictionary, you must know the alphabet. If there are two words with the same second letter, you must look at the next one after that.
Example:
dance – dark –
date – different –
difficult – door –
down – drink –
drive – dry

Guide words at the top of the page show you the first and last words printed on that page.

To find the word you are looking for, you must find the right page first. Here are the guide words on four pages:
galvanization – 444 – gander
roast – 965 – rocket
plaque – 835 – play
hoop-la – 529 – hopping mad

On which pages can you find these words: gangster, hop, rock, plan, game, robot, road, hopscotch, plate, rocky?

descriptive **140** **destabilize**

f; **beyond** ~ unbeschreiblich; **of every** ~ jeder Art; **answer to a** ~ e-r Beschreibung entsprechen; **de•scrip•tive** [dɪ'skrɪptɪv] *adj* 1. beschreibend 2. anschaulich; ~ **writ-ing** Beschreibung *f*
des•ecrate ['desɪkreɪt] *tr* (REL) entweihen; **des•ecra•tion** [ˌdesɪ'kreɪʃn] *s* Entwe… hung *f*
de•seg•re•gate [ˌdiː'segrɪgeɪt] *tr* di… sentrennung aufheben in; **de•seg…** …[ˌ…segrɪgeɪʃn] *s* Aufhebu… …esegregation *f*
…sɪtaɪz] *tr* … 2. (MI…
…lichtunempfi…
sibilisieren
de•sert¹ [dɪ'zɜː…
…lassen; **~ed stre…**
desertieren
des•ert² ['dezə…
…fruchtbar; W…
…en, … Straß… *adj* … …ur *m;* **de…** …keɪʃn] *s* …bildung *f* …(böswilliges) …nenflucht *f* …dienste *npl,* ver… …**rding to one's** ~ …en; **get one's (just)** ~ …was man verdient hat
de•serve [dɪ'zɜːv] *tr* verdienen; **he ~s to be punished** er verdient es bestraft zu werden; **de•serv•ed•ly** [dɪ'zɜːvɪdlɪ] *adv* verdientermaßen, gebührend; **de•serv-ing** [dɪ'zɜːvɪŋ] *adj* verdienstvoll
de•sign [dɪ'zaɪn] I. *s* 1. Zeichnung, Skizze *f* 2. Entwurf, Plan *m* 3. Konstruktion *f* 4. Design *n;* Muster *n* 5. (*fig*) Absicht *f,* Vorhaben *n;* **by** ~ mit Absicht, absichtlich; **at the** ~ **stage** im Stadium der Konstruktion; **have ~s on** [*o* **against**] etw im Schilde führen gegen II. *tr* skizzieren; entwerfen; konstruieren; ~ **for s.th.** für etw vorsehen III. *itr* planen
des•ig•nate¹ ['dezɪgneɪt] *tr* 1. be-, kenn-… …ernennen (*s.o. as* …
…kennzeichnung *f* … (nach Sub-…
…ennung *f* …**a•tion** … Name … Er-…
de•sign•ed•ly [dɪ'zaɪnɪdlɪ] … vorsätzlich
de•signer [dɪ'zaɪnə(r)] *s* 1. … *m(f)* 2. Konstrukteur(in) *m(f)* … Dekorateur(in) *m(f);* ~ **drug** D… *f;* **de•sign•ing** [dɪ'zaɪnɪŋ] I. … verschlagen II. *s* Entwerfen *n* … …struieren *n*
…sir•able [dɪ'zaɪərəbl] … wün-…
schens-, begehrens-, erstrebenswert 2. (*Haus*) reizvoll, attraktiv; **de•sire** [dɪ'zaɪə(r)] I. *tr* 1. wünschen 2. begehren, verlangen … **…ves much to be ~d** … übrig II. *s* 1. … …langen, Be-…
…ˈzaɪərəs] *adj:* **be** … …haben zu … **…ir•ous** … Wunsch
de•sist [dɪ'zɪst] *itr* Abstand … von)
desk [desk] *s* 1. Schreibtisch … schäft) Kasse *f* 3. (*Presse*) … (*Hotel*) Empfang *m;* **ask** … **formation** ~ sich bei der Au… …digen; **desk lamp** *s* Schre… …*n;*
desk•top pub•lish•ing … …blɪʃɪŋ] *s* (EDV) De… …trostlich
…work *s* Büro… …zələt] *adj* 1. …dos 2. (*Mensch*) tieftraurig, … betrübt; **deso•la•tion** [ˌdesə'leɪʃn] *s* 1. Verwüstung *f* 2. Öde, Trostlosigkeit *f* 3. Verlassenheit, Einsamkeit *f*
des•pair [dɪ'speə(r)] I. *itr* verzweifeln (*of* an); ~ **of s.th.** alle Hoffnung auf etw aufgeben II. *s* Verzweiflung, Hoffnungslosigkeit *f* (*at* über); **in** ~ verzweifelt; **give up in** ~ verzweifeln, aufgeben; **be the** ~ **of s.o.** jdn zur Verzweiflung bringen; **des•pair-ing** [-ɪŋ] *adj* verzweifelt
des•per•ado [ˌdespə'rɑːdəʊ] <*pl* -ado(e)s> *s* Bandit, Desperado *m*
des•per•ate ['despərət] *adj* 1. verzweifelt 2. zum Äußersten entschlossen 3. (*Lage*) hoffnungslos, ausweglos 4. (*fig*) extrem; **get** ~ verzweifeln; **des•per•ation** [ˌdespə'reɪʃn] *s* Verzweiflung *f;* **in** ~ aus Verzweiflung; **drive to** ~ zur Verzweiflung bringen
des•pic•able [dɪ'spɪkəbl] *adj* verabscheuungswürdig, widerwärtig
des•pise [dɪ'spaɪz] *tr* verachten, verschmähen
des•pite [dɪ'spaɪt] *prep* trotz
de•spoil [dɪ'spɔɪl] *tr* berauben (*of s.th.* e-r S), plündern
de•spon•dent [dɪ'spɒndənt] *adj* mut-, hoffnungslos, niedergeschlagen
des•pot ['despɒt] *s* Despot *m a. fig;* **des-potic** [dɪ'spɒtɪk] *adj* despotisch, tyrannisch; **des•pot•ism** ['despətɪzəm] *s* Despotismus *m,* Tyrannei *f*
des•sert [dɪ'zɜːt] *s* Nachtisch *m,* Dessert *n;* **des•sert•spoon** [dɪ'zɜːtˌspuːn] *s* Dessertlöffel *m*
de•sta•bil•iz•ation [ˌdiːˈsteɪbəlaɪz'eɪʃn] *s* Destabilisierung *f;* **de•sta•bil•ize**

(PONS Schülerwörterbuch)

Headwords are the main entries printed in thicker, or bold type down the left-hand side of each column.

Each headword is followed by its meaning or definition. Different meanings for a word are listed by numbers.

You will always find the phonetic transcription of your word and one or more German translations. It is important to know the symbols and abbreviations used in your dictionary. These are usually explained at the front.
Example:
n = noun,
adj = adjective,
jdn = jemanden,
~ = same word,
etc.

Now look up these words. But first put them in alphabetical order: trouble, operation, cheese, roundabout, drama, cyclist, numbering, invitation.

7

A dictionary game

You need a dictionary and a partner. Give your partner a word. He or she must look it up and say the number of the page on which that word can be found. Both you and your partner start with 5,000 points. Now your partner tells you that your word is on page 250. So you must subtract 250 from 5,000 and go on from 4,750. Take turns. The winner is the first person to get down to the lowest possible number or to zero.

UNIT 8

Emergency

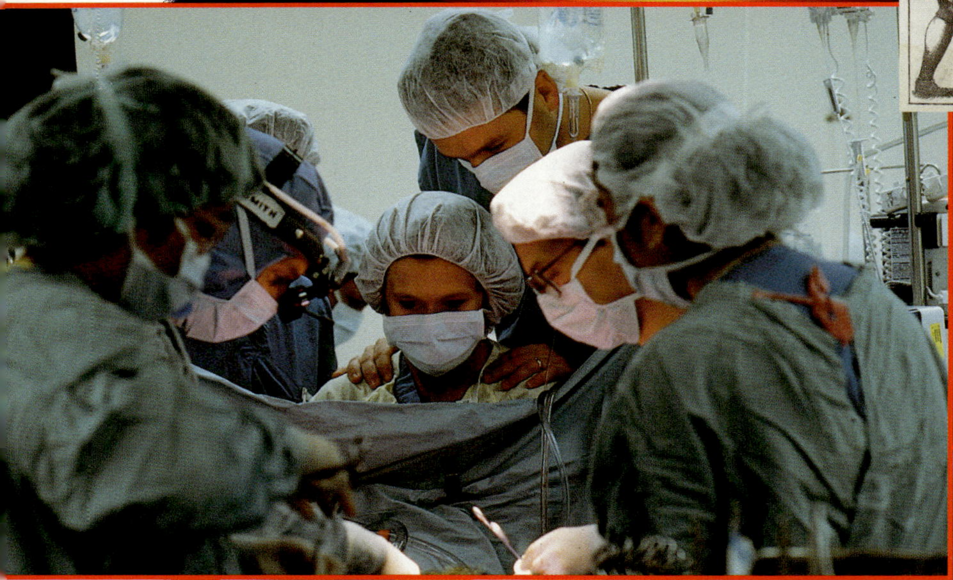

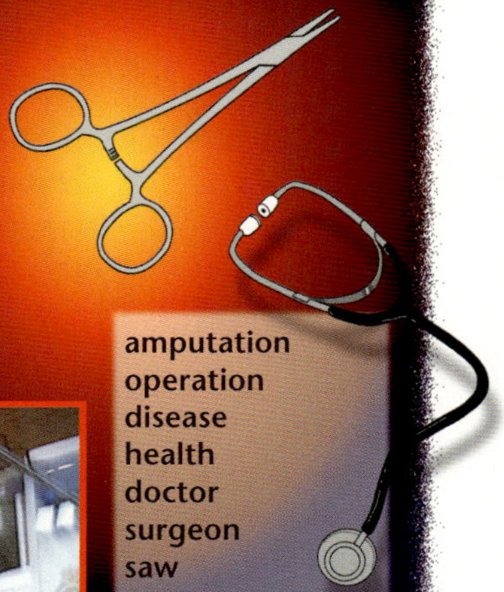

amputation
operation
disease
health
doctor
surgeon
saw
scalpel
pain
anaesthetic
accident
insurance
diagnosis
X-rays
medicine
antibiotics
nurse
emergency
paramedic
illness
vaccination
hygiene
operating theatre
ambulance

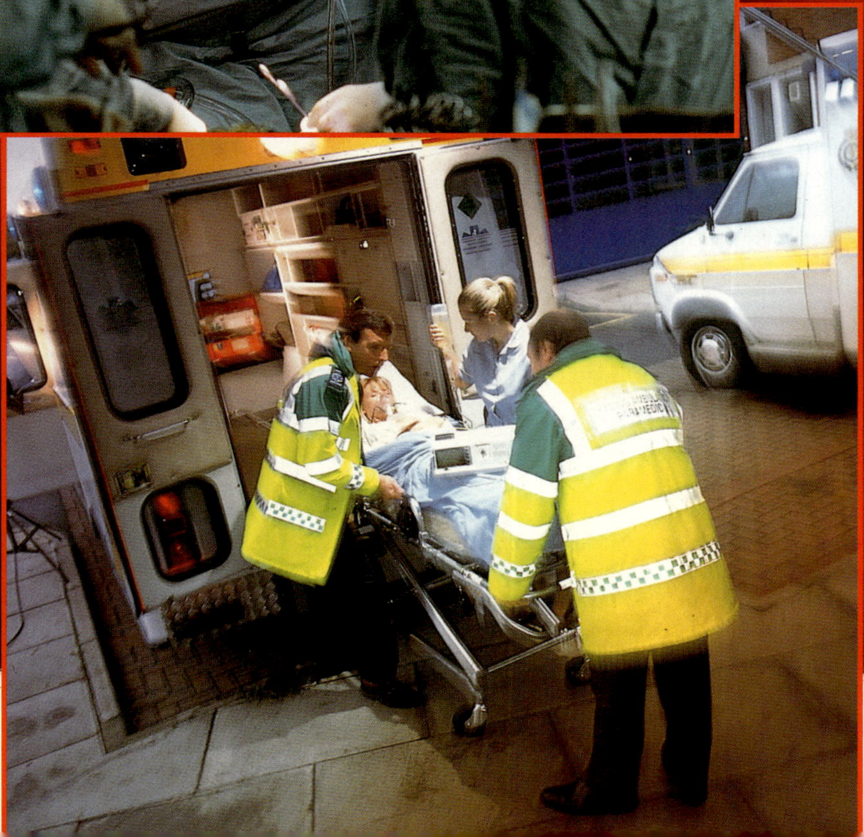

1 How hospitals have changed

Were they 'the good old days' or 'the bad old days'? *Compare the pictures on page 122 and talk about how hospitals have changed. The list of words will help you, so first make sure you know what they mean and how to say them.*

2 Life – a risky business

Some risks are part of life. There are other risks that people choose to take, even though they know about the dangers to their health. This grid shows just how risky some activities are:

From *National Health Service* Homepage

Activity	Absolute risk of death in one year
Injecting illegal drugs	1 in 50 (high)
Smoking ten cigarettes a day	1 in 200 (quite high)
Mountain climbing	1 in 1,500 (low)
Driving a car	1 in 8,000 (very low)
Playing football	1 in 25,000 (minimal)

a) *Work in pairs. For each activity, design and complete a table with the headings below. Then find another pair and compare your tables.*

Why people do it
Possible health benefits
Health risks

b) *What can mountain climbers do to prevent accidents? What about football players? Say what advice you would give them so that they could reduce the risk of an accident.*

c) You and a friend are climbing a mountain. You are almost at the top when it begins to snow heavily. Suddenly your friend slips on a rock and falls. He is in a lot of pain and cannot walk. *What would you do in this situation? What should your friend do?*

3 Exciting sports

a) *Talk about the activities in the photos. Have you ever done any of them, or do you know anyone who has? If so, tell the class about it.*

b) *What do you think is the attraction of sports like these?*

sky-diving

ski-jumping

free-climbing

8

Be prepared

The United States is often hit by natural disasters such as tornadoes, hurricanes and earthquakes. They cannot be prevented, but if you are in an area where they often happen, you should be prepared.

SAVE

Kansas **is** often **hit** by tornadoes.
(be + past participle)
Some disasters **cannot be prevented**.
(modal + be + past participle)

1 Ready or not?

Are you prepared for an emergency? Read the checklist and find out.

A disaster can happen any time. Here is a checklist of things that should be done ahead of time in case there is an emergency. Give yourself ten points for each statement that is true for your family. Then add up the points and see how well (or badly!) prepared you are for emergencies.

100	Excellent! Your family is ready for anything!
80 - 90	Good. Your family is better prepared than most.
60 - 70	OK. You need to do a few more things.
40 - 50	Not so good. Lots of preparation still needs to be done.
0 - 30	Poor. Start getting ready right away!

- The telephone number to call to report emergencies is written on or next to our phone.
- A fire escape plan has been made. There are at least two ways to get out of every room.
- Our family has a Safety Kit where things such as a first aid kit, flashlight, can opener, battery-powered radio, extra batteries, bottled water, blankets and other important things are kept in one place. This place is known to everyone.
- Our house number can easily be seen from the street.
- The batteries in our smoke detector(s) are checked every month.
- The matches are kept in safe places, and cannot be reached by children.
- We all know how to help someone who has been badly injured, or is having a heart attack.
- We all know what to do if our home is hit by a flood, a tornado, a hurricane or an earthquake.
- We all know how to keep warm if the heating is lost in a winter storm.
- We all know what to do if someone has been bitten by a poisonous snake or spider.

From *The Be Ready Book* by The American National Red Cross (adapted)

2 Emergency plans

The Taylor family from Kansas have done all the things on the checklist. Their son, Nathan, is explaining why each point is important. *What do you think he says?*

Example: The emergency number is written on the phone in case … / because … / so that … / otherwise …

8

G 44

3 The passive

a) The passive in English is made with a form of 'to be' (which shows the tense) and the past participle. *Collect examples of the passive in the checklist. There are …*

- six examples in the simple present,
- three examples in the present perfect,
- four examples with modal verbs (one of them is with 'to').

b) *What preposition is used in passive sentences if we need to say who/what does the action?*

c) *In what sort of texts do you often find passive forms? Can you explain why?*

d) *Work out how to make passive sentences in the present progressive, simple past and will-future. Give some examples.*

G 44

4 Newspaper headlines

Talk about the headlines with a partner. Remember to make full sentences with the auxiliary verbs 'was', 'has been' or 'have been'. Use the phrases in the box to react to the news.

Example: Guess what! A rat has been found in the kitchen of the White House!

Useful phrases: Reacting to news

How awful / wonderful / exciting!
It's always the same old story.
What great news!
Is that some kind of a joke?

DINOSAUR BONES DISCOVERED IN GRAND CANYON

Rat found in White House kitchen

Kansas Hit by Tornado

UFO SEEN OVER LAS VEGAS

Alligator Attack: German Tourist Eaten

TWENTY PEOPLE KILLED, HUNDREDS INJURED IN CALIFORNIA EARTHQUAKE

SEABIRDS RESCUED FROM OIL SLICK

Madonna's Jewelry Stolen

G 44

5 Creekville

a) The American state of Kansas is often hit by tornadoes. *Describe the damage that was done by a tornado to the small town of Creekville a few years ago. Use passive forms of the verbs below.*

Example: The church roof was badly damaged.

smash	damage
burn down	break
bring down	steal
cut	throw

HV

b) The town's mayor, Stan O'Hare, was interviewed two weeks later. *Listen and find out:*

- What was found soon after the tornado?
- Where was it found? How did it get there?
- What has been done since the tornado?
- What is still being done?

c) *Write a newspaper article about the tornado. Say what damage the tornado did and what has been done in the town since it was hit. You can use ideas from a) and b), and add your own details. Remember to give the article a headline.* *(See page 129 for tips!)*

G 44

6 Passive verbs – different tenses

Write passive sentences. Be careful with the tenses.

1. People (not usually warn) about tornadoes ahead of time, but tornadoes (can see) from miles away.
2. Creekville Church (build) in 1895. Its roof (repair) at the moment, and the windows (already replace). A new floor (put in) tomorrow.
3. A play (perform) when Creekville Theater (hit) by the tornado, but nobody (hurt).
4. Mr O'Hare (interview) by CNN at the moment, and it (show) live all over the world.
5. Yesterday a boy (ask) about his pet alligator. It (not see) since the tornado.

G 45 7 Passive with and without 'by'

Put these sentences in the passive. Only use 'by' when you need to say who did the action.

1. Christian Barnard performed the first heart transplant in 1967.
2. Doctors discovered anaesthetics in the 1700s.
3. Wilhelm Röntgen discovered X-rays in 1896.
4. William Shakespeare wrote 'Romeo and Juliet'.
5. A reporter wrote an article about the Creekville tornado.
6. An earthquake has hit San Francisco.
7. They arrested the men who stole the TVs.
8. Creekville beat Orion at baseball yesterday.

SAVE

False teeth were invented **by the Romans.**
(The 'by-agent' is necessary.)

Rome wasn't built in a day.
(You don't need 'by the Romans'.)

G 46 8 Do-it-yourself

a) *Put in -self/-selves.*

1. Terry and Kate built their house ...
2. Terry put in the windows ...
3. And Kate made the doors ...
4. The work ... wasn't difficult and they even enjoyed ...
5. "Kate is going to help me with the garden," said Terry. "I don't want to do it ..."
6. "We didn't have to pay for the house ...," said Kate. "We had insurance."

SAVE

	NOT reflexive in English	
myself		
yourself		
himself	remember	hurry
herself	concentrate	meet
itself	imagine	move
ourselves	decide	feel
yourselves	relax	
themselves		

8

b) *Put in -self/-selves or each other.*

1. They helped ..., so it took only two hours.
2. But Terry hurt ... while he was putting in a window.
3. Terry broke the window too. He could have kicked ...!
4. Then Kate cut ... with a saw!
5. It happened while she and Terry were talking to ...
6. Now she's feeling very sorry for ...

They are looking at themselves.

They are looking at each other.

1 Before you read

The pictures below tell a story. *Work in pairs. Talk about the pictures and work out the best order. Then tell your story to the class.*

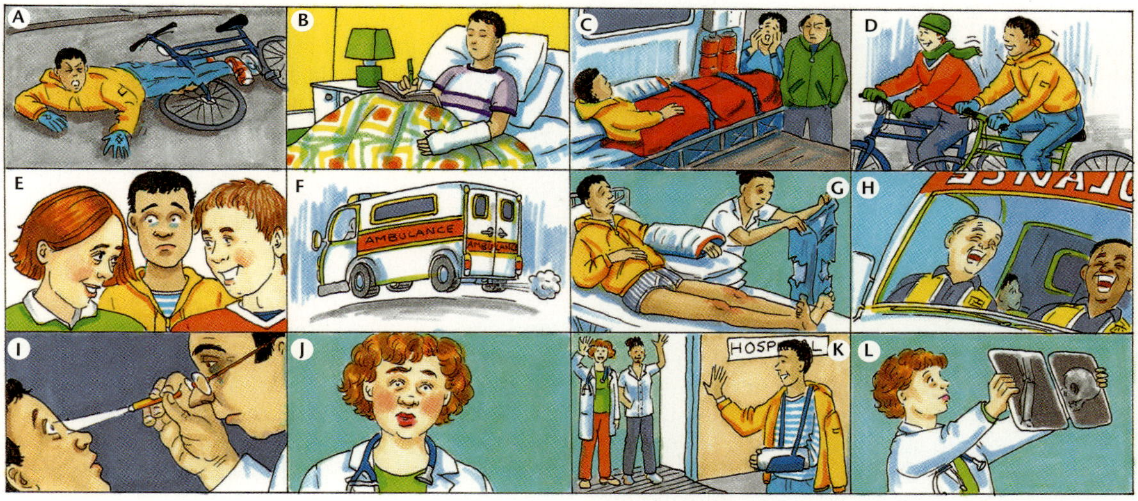

2 While you read

Read the story and compare the order of events with your story.

Crashing the pain barrier on a bike

Wednesday, 1st February
Have had a major accident and am stuck indoors, so decided to start my diary again.

Last Saturday started OK. Sam called and we went off on our bikes to visit a friend of ours, Joanna, as Sam had a cassette she wanted to copy. They disappeared upstairs, so I was left alone like a right idiot. Then Nick, another friend of ours, arrived and took my bike, so for a laugh I rode Sam's round the close. My legs were too short for Sam's bike and as I was going down the steep hill I suddenly couldn't find the brakes. At the bottom was a row of houses and a sharp left turn. I slid on some ice and hit the kerb. As I flew over the handlebars I heard a loud CRACK – and that was it.

The next thing I remember was the inside of the ambulance. The driver and his mate were laughing and telling jokes. I couldn't understand what had happened. My jeans were torn, my left arm was blown up in a plastic bag so I couldn't move it, and my head hurt like hell. Everything was coming and going, and I felt sick and faint. The ambulance didn't have the siren on. The paramedics said they only used that in real emergencies, or when they wanted a cup of tea in a hurry!

When we finally stopped and they opened the back doors there was Mum, crying, and Dad, white-faced. Dad started swearing and telling me what a stupid thing it was to do, and asked whether I did it on purpose to worry them, and why I didn't think about those things before I did them. Typical grown-ups! Mum told him to shut up. I wanted to get out of the ambulance by myself, just to show I was all right, but the paramedics pushed me back, wrapped me in a red blanket like I was 80, and carried me out in a sort of chair.

They said my arm was broken and the blown up plastic bag was to keep it still and stop it hurting. Mum clutched my good hand and Dad followed behind, muttering about Sam and how angry he was because of the scratches on his bike.

I was taken into a little white room and put on a hard bed. Nobody seemed to bother much about me, though somebody said something about a tetanus injection. Mum had to go out and ask if I could have something for the pain – but the nurses were too busy. At last a nurse came and put a thermometer in my mouth and held my wrist. If she wasn't as pretty as the nurses on telly, she was certainly as nice. She helped me to take my torn jeans off. My poor legs looked white and were covered in grazes. My heart nearly stopped when I thought she was going to take off my underpants. But she didn't.

A man came in and asked me questions about the accident, and some silly things like "What day is it?" and "Who is the Prime Minister?". He looked into my eyes with a light, stuck pins into my legs to see if I could feel, hit my ankles and then examined *every* last bit of me. He said he needed to check whether I had concussion. The 'silly questions' were to make sure that my brain was functioning OK.

After a lot of waiting, I was taken into another room where my skull and arm were X-rayed. Then more waiting. Began to want to be at home in my own bed.

Then a lady doctor came in and showed me the X-rays. Luckily my brain was OK. She said she couldn't understand why people didn't wear crash helmets when cycling, because 200 cyclists are killed and 24,000 are injured in England and Wales each year. If I wanted to get a motorcycle in the future, I would *have* to wear one. But even so, 469 motorcyclists are killed on the roads each year, and 26,000 injured. To stress the point, she said she spends most of every day putting together people who have had accidents, and that in any one year:

1 in every 24 motorcycle riders
1 in every 107 car drivers

are killed or involved in an accident. It doesn't even seem safe to walk around, as 1,300 pedestrians are killed and 49,000 injured each year. All this doesn't even include other types of accidents like drowning which kills over 200 children a year, or the 2 million-plus people who are treated by the hospital for home accidents each year: HELP!

Asked the doctor if *she* wore a crash helmet when she went out on her bike. She went pink and didn't answer. Mum gave me one of her special looks and said I seemed to be getting better.

Because I'd been knocked out, they said I might have to stay in hospital for the night. This frightened me at first, but then I thought it might be quite fun, especially if all my friends came to see me with presents. However, I was allowed home with my mum because everything seemed all right, but she was given instructions to bring me back if I began to throw up, had a bad headache, saw double, or became drowsy because of the knock on my head. They also told me to come back if the fingers of my broken arm became numb, or became white or blue. Sounded nasty, but didn't happen. The last four days have been boring – no fun playing Nintendo with one arm – which is why I am writing all this.

From *The New Diary of a Teenage Health Freak* by Aidan Macfarlane and Ann McPherson (adapted)

WP 3 Hospital words

Make a mind map of hospital words.

4 Quiz

Work in pairs. Write nine questions about the story. Then use your quiz to test another pair.

When ...?	What ...?	Who ...?
Why ...?	Where ...?	Which ...?
How many ...?	How long ...?	Whose ...?

YOU 5 What about you?

Have you ever had an accident? Tell the class about it.

6 Creative writing

a) *Write a diary entry about an accident you have had, or make one up.*
(To get ideas, you can ask your friends about accidents they have had.)

b) Sam comes to visit Peter while he is at home. *Work in pairs and write the dialogue between them.*

8

How to write a newspaper report — LEARNING TO LEARN

1 The headline

As you saw in Step A, headlines have their own special grammar. Look at these examples. What auxiliary verbs have been left out? What else has been changed?

GIRL MISSING **GIRL FOUND BY PARAMEDIC** **GIRL FINDS GOLD COINS**

2 The structure

Put the parts of the report in the right order.

1. **Headline**
2. **Introduction**
3. **Background**
4. **First events**
5. **Later events**
6. **Final events**
7. **Situation now**

Ⓖ When a friend of the injured girl rode to meet the ambulance at Deepdale Lane, Boston Spa, North Yorks, the paramedic Sue Forth decided to borrow the horse.

Ⓑ An ambulance worker took a friend's horse during an emergency call to rescue a schoolgirl who had been thrown from her horse.

Ⓕ The ambulance was trying to reach the schoolgirl, Rachel Stewart, when its wheels got stuck in mud.

Ⓒ Rachel is now back at home and has made a full recovery. Miss Forth, a paramedic for North Yorkshire ambulance service for five years, said: "You never forget how to ride."

Ⓔ Station Officer Phil Storr, the ambulance driver, followed on foot and carried Rachel, 13, of Clifford, for a mile to the ambulance.

Ⓐ Miss Forth, 26, a farmer's daughter, rode into the woods with heavy first aid equipment to find Rachel Stewart. Rachel was in shock after she had been thrown from her 22-year old horse Monty while going down a steep hill.

Ⓓ PARAMEDIC RESCUES GIRL, 13

From *The Daily Telegraph*

3 The tenses

Look at the tenses that are used in each part. Work out rules for how they are used in reports to …

– give the background to the event,
– talk about the events as they happened one after another,
– talk about the situation now.

Be extra careful with

- prepositions (in, on, at)
- tenses
- regular / irregular verbs
- verbs with 's' after he / she / it
- pronouns (he / him; who, which)
- 'to do' in questions and negatives
- comparison of adjectives (as good as ..., better than ...)
- spelling
- capital / small letters
- false friends (rock, spend, ...)
- style (telly / television, it's / it is)
- any other mistakes you often make; make a checklist

4 Your story

Choose a headline from page 125, ex. 4, and write a newspaper report of about 200 words. Do a first draft and check it for mistakes with the help of the list on the right. Then write your report. Remember to count the words.

5 Listening comprehension: What's the problem?

a) *You are going to hear three conversations at the doctor's. Listen and take notes. What are the symptoms of the patients, and how long have they had them?*

b) *What do you think is the matter with them? Why do you think so?*

c) *What advice would you give them? What exactly would you say?*

Useful phrases: Giving advice

You should / shouldn't …
Why don't you … ?
If I were you, I'd …
You could try …
You'd better (not) …

6 A visit to the doctor

a) *Look at the phrases below and decide who would say them – the doctor or the patient. Then copy them into your exercise book in two groups, and add your own ideas.*

b) *Work in pairs. Take turns in the roles of doctor and patient, and act out visits to the doctor.*

Let's have a look at you, then.
I feel faint and shivery.
Does it hurt when I do this?
What seems to be the matter?
You need lots of rest.
I don't think it's serious.
I've got a pain in my leg.
I'm going to give you a prescription.
My ankle hurts.
When did it start?
Have you got any other symptoms?
I've got a temperature.
Open your mouth and say 'aah'.
Well, it could be …
You should try to get more fresh air and exercise.
It hurts right here.
I've got a stomach ache.
How long have you had it?

WP

1 Find the words

Have a competition. Who can find the most words for these things in five minutes?

1. things you can wear
2. parts of the body
3. jobs
4. forms of transport
5. how concussion can make you feel
6. what concussion can make you do
7. what concussion can give you
8. two signs that you have a broken arm

2 Guess the object

a) *Can you guess what the objects are?*

1. They are made of plastic.
   They can be used as a form of payment.
   They aren't always accepted everywhere.

2. They are made of paper.
   You can put letters in them.
   Stamps are stuck on them.

3. You ride them, but they don't have wheels.
   They are not used as a form of transport.
   They are often found in gyms.

4. It can be found in a kitchen.
   It is made of metal.
   It is used to cut food.

5. It is made of plastic or wood.
   You can draw a straight line with it.
   It can be used to see how long something is.

6. It must be worn in a car.
   It needn't be worn in a bus.
   It could save your life.

b) *Write a quiz yourself. Think of six objects and write three clues for each object. Use as many passive forms as you can.*

3 In an emergency

List the things in the picture and write down why they are/would be useful in an emergency.

Example: Batteries are useful when electricity has been cut off.
A ladder can be used to ...

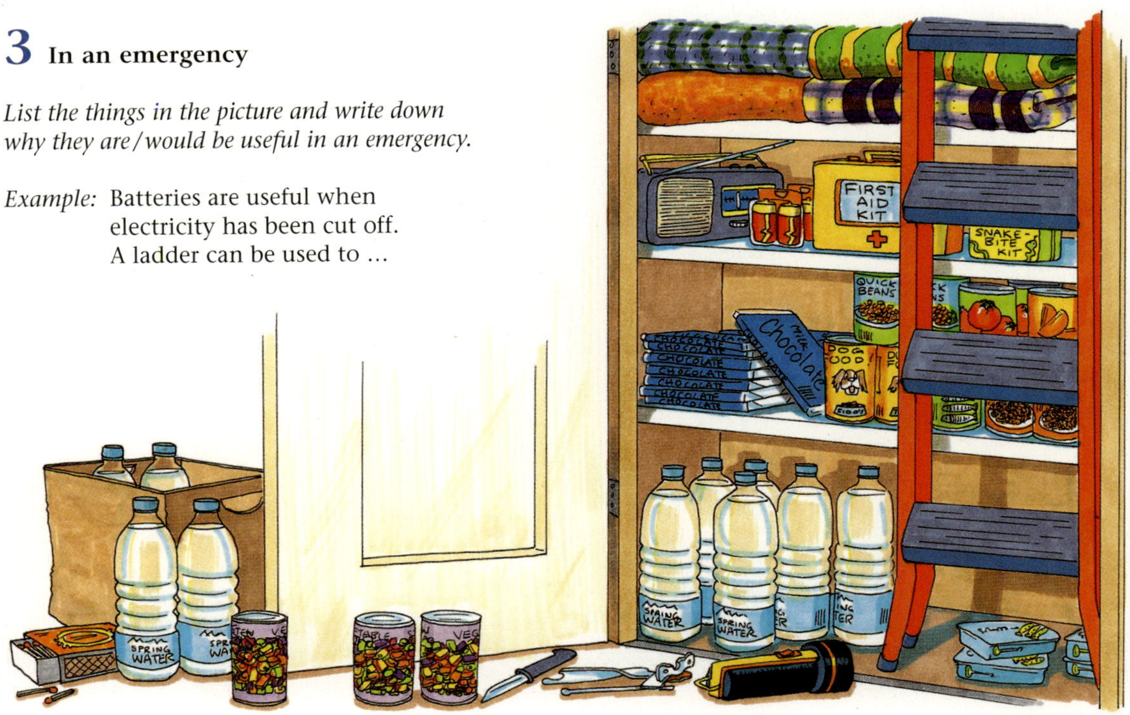

8

SAVE

Which past form is used when?

Present perfect	To talk about a finished action that happened in a time that is not over (e.g. this year, today). To talk about a situation that lasts up to the present. To talk about something that has a result or effect in the present.
Present perfect progressive	To talk about a recent long action / situation that lasts up to the present, especially when we say how long it has lasted. The situation itself / the time is more important than the result.
Simple past	To talk about a finished action that happened in a time that is over (e.g. last year, yesterday). To tell a story (often together with the past progressive or the past perfect).
Past progressive	To describe the background to another more important action / event.
Past perfect	To make clear which of two actions or situations happened first.

G 47

1 Past forms: What they are and when they are used

a) *Say what the past forms in the sentences are called. Use the information above to explain why the forms have been chosen in each case.*

Example: 1. The simple past tense is used because the time when Sam phoned (last week) is over.

1. Sam phoned Joanna twice last week.
2. Joanna has phoned Peter twice this week.
3. Peter has been lying in bed for the last four days.
4. Sam and Joanna taped the cassette Sam had brought.
5. Peter has had a major accident, so he is stuck indoors.
6. He slid on the ice and hit the kerb.
7. Peter was going down a steep hill when he suddenly couldn't find the brakes.
8. The last four days have been really boring for Peter.

b) *Change each sentence into a question, and then into a negative form.*

Example: 1. How often did Sam phone Joanna last week? / Sam didn't phone Joanna last week.

G 47

2 Signal words

Put the signal words in two groups: present perfect (unfinished time) and simple past (finished time).

ago	never	yet	always	when I was six	last year	already
since	in 1999	ever	at 2 o'clock	in my life	this year	before I was born

3 Man overboard!

Write out the story with the verbs in the right form. The 'P' shows that a passive form is needed.

I (travel) with my family by ship from Africa to England when a man (P: rescue) after he (be) in the water for eleven hours. The man (fall) overboard the night before during a party, but nobody (notice). The next morning we (have) breakfast when suddenly there (be) an announcement by the captain. "A man (fall) overboard, so we (decide) to turn the ship round and go back to look for him." A few hours later the man (P: spot) in the water. We all (watch) while he (P: rescue). When he (P: pull) out of the water, he (wear) his boots and nothing else. His life (P: save) by a wine bottle. He (stick) his thumb in the bottle, and this (prevent) him from drowning.

1 How are you?

a) *What does this poor man tell his doctor? Write down what he says he's got (4 things), and how he says he feels (2 things).*

b) *What does the doctor tell him? (3 pieces of advice)*

2 The odd one out

Find the odd one out and put it in the right group. Suggest a heading for each group.

1. wrist, ankle, arm, surgeon
2. tornado, headache, hurricane, flood
3. leg, paramedic, nurse, doctor
4. stomach ache, sore throat, earthquake, temperature

3 Antonyms and synonyms

a) *Find pairs of words in the box that are the opposite of each of the words below.*

1. right
2. speak
3. lose
4. healthy
5. break
6. poor

mend	sick	listen	win
repair	find	rich	ill
wrong	hear	left	good

b) *Write sentences with each of the words to show you know what they mean.*

4 Active to passive

a) *Change the sentences from active to passive.*

1. Someone has stolen Mike's car.
2. The police have arrested the men.
3. Sometimes hurricanes tear roofs off houses.
4. They are repairing the road.
5. They are going to close the hospital.
6. This means that some people will lose their jobs.
7. They are already sending patients to other hospitals.

+b) *Write the sentences in the passive – in two ways. Underline the one that sounds more natural.*

Example: 1. I was …
The prescription was …

1. The doctor gave a prescription to me.
2. They offered Stan O'Hare the job of Mayor of Creekville.
3. Will you send the newspaper article to me?
4. Someone has lent Mike Maryn a car.

5 What people do to themselves and each other

Write down what these people have just done to themselves or each other.

hit write buy cut

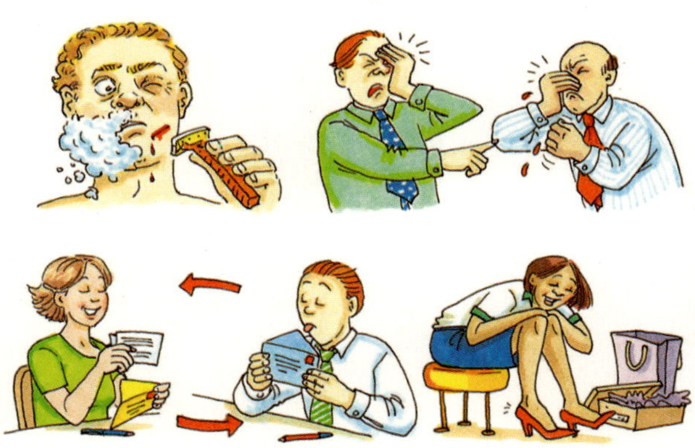

6 +Tricky tenses

Write the sentences with the verbs in the correct form.

1. We … English for nearly two years. We … in Class 7.
2. I … 'Titanic' three times this year.
3. We … television when suddenly we … a loud crack.
4. Liam … his new CD after he … his homework.
5. Peter … back to school two days ago.
6. She felt sick because she … chicken that … cooked properly.

hear see listen to learn go
not be watch eat start finish

CHECK-IN

	emergency [ɪ'mɜ:dʒnsi]	Notfall
	disease [dɪ'zi:z]	Krankheit
	surgeon ['sɜ:dʒn]	Chirurg
	saw [sɔ:]	Säge
	pain [peɪn]	Schmerz, Leid(en)
	insurance [ɪn'ʃʊərns]	Versicherung
	X-ray ['eksreɪ]	Röntgenaufnahme, -strahlen
	nurse [nɜ:s]	Krankenschwester, -pfleger
	paramedic [ˌpærə'medɪk]	Sanitäter(in)
	illness ['ɪlnəs]	Krankheit
	vaccination [ˌvæksɪ'neɪʃn]	Impfung
	operating theatre ['ɒpəreɪtɪŋ ˌθɪətə]	Operationssaal
	ambulance ['æmbjələns]	Krankenwagen
2	**business** ['bɪznɪs]	*hier:* Angelegenheit, Sache
	death [deθ]	Tod
	to **inject** [ɪn'dʒekt]	(ein)spritzen
	mountain climbing ['maʊntɪn ˌklaɪmɪŋ]	Bergsteigen
	benefit ['benɪfɪt]	Vorteil, Nutzen
	mountain climber ['maʊntɪn ˌklaɪmə]	Bergsteiger(in)
	to **prevent** [prɪ'vent]	verhindern, vermeiden
	to **reduce** [rɪ'dju:s]	verringern, reduzieren
	mountain ['maʊntɪn]	Berg
	to **slip** [slɪp]	(aus)rutschen, (aus)gleiten
3	**ski-jumping** ['ski:ˌdʒʌmpɪŋ]	Skispringen
	sky-diving ['skaɪˌdaɪvɪŋ]	Fallschirmspringen
	free-climbing ['fri:ˌklaɪmɪŋ]	Klettern ohne Ausrüstung

STEP A

	to **be prepared** [prɪ'peəd]	vorbereitet sein
	earthquake ['ɜ:θkweɪk]	Erdbeben
	Kansas ['kænzəs]	*amerikanischer Bundesstaat*
1	**ahead of time** [əˌhed‿əv 'taɪm]	im Voraus
	escape [ɪ'skeɪp]	Flucht
	kit [kɪt]	Ausrüstung
	such as ['sʌtʃ‿æz]	wie zum Beispiel
	flashlight *(AE)* ['flæʃlaɪt]	Taschenlampe
	can opener ['kæn ˌəʊpnə]	Dosenöffner
	battery-powered ['bætriˌpaʊəd]	batteriebetrieben
	bottled ['bɒtld]	in Flaschen (abgefüllt)
	blanket ['blæŋkɪt]	(Woll-)Decke
	smoke detector ['sməʊk dɪˌtektə]	Rauchmelder
	to **injure** ['ɪndʒə]	verletzen
	to **keep (warm)** [ki:p]	(warm) bleiben
	poisonous ['pɔɪznəs]	giftig
	snake [sneɪk]	Schlange
	spider ['spaɪdə]	Spinne
	right away [ˌraɪt‿ə'weɪ]	sofort
2	**in case** [keɪs]	falls
	otherwise ['ʌðəwaɪz]	sonst, ansonsten

In an emergency in Britain you dial 999.

Most illnesses are painful but the trouble is that some are not.

Before an operation the surgeons discuss the X-rays.

Write down a medical alphabet:

accident – bone – check – disease – emergency – …

Lots of injured people are in hospital because of the dangerous sports they do, such as mountain climbing, …

Mountain climbers need footwear that prevents them from slipping.

ski-jumping	–	ski jumper
sky-diving	–	sky diver
free-climbing	–	free climber

an escape	⇔	to escape
a nurse	⇔	to nurse
an X-ray	⇔	to X-ray
…		…

AE	BE
flashlight	torch
can opener	tin opener

Name a few things which are battery-powered: Walkman, radio, …

If you replace old batteries, don't throw them away. They are poisonous. Do you know how and where to dispose of them?

4	**headline** ['hedlaɪn]	Schlagzeile	Please do your homework. Otherwise we can't start the project tomorrow.
	Las Vegas [ˌlæs 'veɪgəs]	*Stadt in Nevada, USA*	
	bone [bəʊn]	Knochen	May I give your dog a bone?
	Grand Canyon [ˌgræn 'kænjən]	*Tal des Colorado River in Arizona, USA*	
5	**Creekville** ['kri:kvɪl]	*Kleinstadt in Kansas*	
6	to **replace** [rɪ'pleɪs]	ersetzen, austauschen	Can you replace this diskette, please? There's something wrong with it.
7	**Christian Barnard** [ˌkrɪstʃən bɑ:'nɑ:d]	*südafrikanischer Herzchirurg*	
	to **perform** [pə'fɔ:m]	durchführen	
	Orion [ə'raɪən]	*Name einer Baseballmannschaft*	
	to **invent** [ɪn'vent]	erfinden	
	Rome [rəʊm]	Rom	
8	**make yourself at home** [ˌmeɪk jɔ:ˌself‿ət 'həʊm]	machen Sie es sich gemütlich	
	mess [mes]	Unordnung, Durcheinander	My sister's bedroom is a mess.

Proverb
Rome wasn't built in a day.

STEP B

A	**major** ['meɪdʒə]	Haupt-, bedeutend(e/r/s)	
	indoors [ɪn'dɔ:z]	drinnen, zu Hause	
	close [kləʊs]	Straße, Hof	
	steep [sti:p]	steil	
	brake [breɪk]	Bremse	Check your brakes before you cycle down steep roads.
	kerb [kɜ:b]	Bordsteinkante	
	mate [meɪt]	Freund(in), Kumpel	
	to **blow* up** [ˌbləʊ‿'ʌp]	aufblasen, aufpumpen	
	hell [hel]	Hölle	
	faint [feɪnt]	schwach, matt	
	white-faced ['waɪtfeɪst]	mit weißem Gesicht	
	to **swear*** [sweə]	fluchen	
	on purpose ['pɜ:pəs]	absichtlich	
	to **shut up** [ˌʃʌt‿'ʌp]	den Mund halten	
	to **wrap** [ræp]	einwickeln, verpacken	
	to **clutch** [klʌtʃ]	greifen, packen, festhalten	
	to **mutter** ['mʌtə]	murmeln	
	scratch [skrætʃ]	Kratzer	
B	to **bother about** ['bɒðə‿əˌbaʊt]	sich kümmern um	
	wrist [rɪst]	Handgelenk	
	pretty ['prɪti]	hübsch	
	graze [greɪz]	Schürfwunde	
	underpants *pl.* ['ʌndəpænts]	Unterhose	Do you remember? Shorts, jeans, underpants, glasses, goggles, …
	Prime Minister [ˌpraɪm 'mɪnɪstə]	Premierminister(in)	
	pin [pɪn]	Nadel	
	ankle ['æŋkl]	Knöchel, Fußgelenk	
	to **examine** [ɪg'zæmɪn]	untersuchen	
	concussion [kən'kʌʃn]	Gehirnerschütterung	
	brain [breɪn]	Gehirn	Train your brain: use it or lose it!
	skull [skʌl]	Schädel	
	to **X-ray** ['eksreɪ]	durchleuchten, röntgen	
	cyclist ['saɪklɪst]	Fahrradfahrer(in)	Cyclists and motorcyclists wear crash helmets to protect their skulls.
	motorcyclist ['məʊtəˌsaɪklɪst]	Motorradfahrer(in)	
	to **involve** [ɪn'vɒlv]	einbeziehen, verwickeln	Was your brother involved in that accident?
	drowning ['draʊnɪŋ]	Ertrinken	
	to **treat** [tri:t]	behandeln, umgehen (mit)	A vet knows how to treat injured animals.
	to **knock so. out** [nɒk‿'aʊt]	jmdn. bewusstlos schlagen/werden lassen	
	to **frighten** ['fraɪtn]	erschrecken, Angst machen	

opposites

to shut up	–	to talk
to wrap	–	to unwrap
indoors	–	outdoors
faint	–	strong
…		…

words with wr... [r]

wrist	–	write
wrap	–	wrong

franz examiner *lat* examinare
engl to examine

8

	present ['preznt]	Geschenk
	to **throw up** *coll.* [θrəʊ‿'ʌp]	kotzen
	headache ['hedeɪk]	Kopfschmerz, Kopfweh
	drowsy ['draʊzi]	schläfrig
	numb [nʌm]	taub, gefühllos
	nasty ['nɑ:sti]	scheußlich, abscheulich
6	**entry** ['entri]	Eintrag

STEP C

1	**coin** [kɔɪn]	Münze
2	**recovery** [rɪ'kʌvri]	Genesung, Erholung
	mud [mʌd]	Schlamm, Matsch
	Clifford ['klɪfəd]	*Ortschaft in Nordengland*
	Deepdale Lane ['di:pdeɪl ˌleɪn]	*Straßenname*
	Monty ['mɒnti]	*hier: Pferdename*
4	**draft** [drɑ:ft]	Entwurf, Skizze
5	**flu** [flu:]	Grippe
	to **feel shivery** ['ʃɪvri]	frösteln
	sore throat [ˌsɔ: 'θrəʊt]	Halsschmerzen, Halsweh
	to **stick out** [stɪk‿'aʊt]	herausstrecken
	tongue [tʌŋ]	Zunge
6	**to have a look (at)** [ˌhæv‿ə 'lʊk]	(an)schauen, (an)gucken
	prescription [prɪ'skrɪpʃn]	Verordnung, Rezept
	stomach ache ['stʌmək‿ˌeɪk]	Magenschmerzen

TRACK 1

2	**payment** ['peɪmənt]	Zahlung
	stamp [stæmp]	Briefmarke
3	**ladder** ['lædə]	Leiter

TRACK 2

	+to **last** [lɑ:st]	andauern, anhalten
	+**recent** ['ri:snt]	kürzlich
3	+**thumb** [θʌm]	Daumen

CHECK-OUT

3	**ill** [ɪl]	krank
6	+**tricky** ['trɪki]	kompliziert, schwierig

You can have a(n) headache, earache, toothache, stomach ache, …

nasty = not nice

My new dictionary has got 30,000 entries.

There is a new £2 coin in Britain.

There is a lot of mud on the football field, but we can play the match.

illness

I'm down with flu / …
Look at my tongue …
He / She has got a …
I feel shivery …
You need an injection / …

	pay		payment
	ill		illness
from	drown	*to*	drowning
	invent		invention
	recover		recovery

– The play lasts about three hours, but it's very good.
– Yes, I know. I saw it recently.

People say hitchhikers 'travel with their thumbs'!

She has been very ill but has made a quick recovery.

That's a very tricky question. It's too difficult for me!

8

COGNATE WORDS

alligator ['ælɪgeɪtə] Alligator
amputation [ˌæmpjə'teɪʃn] Amputation
anaesthetic [ˌænəs'θetɪk] Betäubungsmittel, Narkose
antibiotic [ˌæntɪbaɪ'ɒtɪk] Antibiotikum
°**antonym** ['æntənɪm] Antonym
to **arrest** [ə'rest] festnehmen, verhaften
barrier ['bæriə] Schranke, Sperre, Barriere
checklist ['tʃeklɪst] Kontrollliste, Checkliste
to **concentrate** ['kɒntsntreɪt] (sich) konzentrieren
crack [kræk] Krach, Knall, Schlag
to **crash** [kræʃ] zusammenbrechen, (zusammen-) krachen
to **design** [dɪ'zaɪn] entwerfen, konstruieren
diagnosis [ˌdaɪəg'nəʊsɪs] Diagnose
false [fɔ:ls] falsch
finger ['fɪŋgə] Finger
flood [flʌd] Hochwasser, Überschwemmung
to **function** ['fʌŋkʃn] arbeiten, funktionieren
hospital ['hɒspɪtl] Krankenhaus, Klinik
hurricane ['hʌrɪkən] Wirbelsturm, Orkan
hygiene ['haɪdʒi:n] Gesundheitspflege, Hygiene
injection [ɪn'dʒekʃn] Spritze, Injektion
instruction [ɪn'strʌkʃn] Anweisung, Anleitung
medicine ['medsn] Medizin
minimal ['mɪnɪml] gering, minimal
operation [ˌɒpr'eɪʃn] Operation
risk [rɪsk] Gefahr, Risiko
risky ['rɪski] gefährlich, riskant
scalpel ['skælpl] Skalpell
siren ['saɪərən] Sirene
symptom ['sɪmptəm] Anzeichen, Symptom
°**synonym** ['sɪnənɪm] Synonym
temperature ['temprətʃə] Temperatur, Fieber
tetanus ['tetnəs] Wundstarrkrampf, Tetanus
thermometer [θə'mɒmɪtə] Thermometer
tornado, *pl.* **-oes** [tɔ:'neɪdəʊ] Wirbelsturm, Tornado
transplant ['trænsplɑ:nt] Transplantation

8

Read a London newspaper!

(after Unit 1)

These articles are from *Eastern Eye*, a London newspaper. Most of its readers are ethnic[1] Asians[2]. That means they or their parents or grandparents (or great-grandparents or ...) came to London from India, Pakistan, China[3] or another Asian country.

1. Before you read

Work in pairs or groups. Each reads only one of the two articles, and gets ready to tell the other person or group about it.

WHITE GIRLS TAKE GCSE[4] BENGALI[5]

TWO white schoolgirls could soon be able to understand their classmates'[6] Bengali gossip[7]. They have become the first non-Asians[8] to study for a GCSE in the language[9].

Hayley Pack and Hannah Moxon, both 15, joined[10] an after-school class at the City of Portsmouth Girls' School so that they could pick up their Asian pals'[11] native[12] patter[13].

"It's easier than I thought it would be, but perhaps that's because I want to learn it, so I'm more interested," said Hayley.

Hannah said they were still only starting. "We've been only in the class since the beginning of term, so we can't manage[14] a full conversation[15] yet. We can say things like our name and ask people how they are," she said.

Technology teacher Joanna Lofts has also signed up[16] for the Bengali lessons. She is teaching at a school where 150 of the 1,000 pupils are from ethnic minorities[17].

Judith Kilpatrick, the school's Head, said that many non-Asian girls were studying Bengali, but it was the first time pupils wanted to try for a formal qualification[18] in it.

Shopna Begun, 15, was excited about how her classmates were doing. "They have really learned a lot. Soon I won't be able to say anything without them knowing[19]," she said.

Do you think Sharon is taking this a bit too far ..?

BROTHER AND SISTER TEAM ARE YOUNGEST IN UNI[20]

Iksander and Noraisha have begun studying at Warwick

PURE[21] GENIUS[22]

by SALEEM USMANI

A brother and sister have made history: they have become the first siblings[23] ever to start at a British university.

Iksander Yusof, 12, and his sister Noraisha recently[24] began the new term at Warwick[25] University. They are both studying maths.

But they don't think they are anything special – their 14-year-old sister Sufiah is already in her second year at Oxford[26], and they expect that their 4-year-old sister Zuleika will pass A-level[27] Maths before she is six. The Yusof children have astounded[28] all the experts.

They are studying the teaching methods[29] of their parents.

Mathematician[30] Farooq Yusof and his chemistry[31] teacher wife[32] Halimahton taught their children at home, and believe that all children could do well at school if they got the same chances[33].

The Yusofs are Muslims[34], and they follow a routine[35] of prayer[36], exercise and learning every day. The children are not only mathematical[37] geniuses – they are all excellent tennis players. Noraisha won the Northamptonshire[38] women's title when she was just 12. She said, "I don't think it is a problem coming to university this young. I have already done my A-levels, so what else could I do?" Mr Yusof is now working on a book about his wonderful teaching methods.

Both articles from *Eastern Eye* (adapted)

[1]['eθnɪk] *ethnisch, Volks-* [2]['eɪʃn] *Asiate/Asiatin* [3]['tʃaɪnə] [4][ˌdʒi:si:es'i:] (= General Certificate of Secondary Education) *Abschlussprüfung* [5][beŋ'gɔ:li] *indische Sprache* [6]['klɑ:smeɪt] *Klassenkamerad(in)* [7]['gɒsɪp] *Klatsch* [8][nɒn] *nicht-* [9]['læŋgwɪdʒ] *Sprache* [10][dʒɔɪn] *sich anschließen, anmelden* [11][pæl] *Kumpel* [12]['neɪtɪv] *muttersprachlich* [13]['pætə] *Geplapper* [14]['mænɪdʒ] *schaffen* [15][ˌkɒnvə'seɪʃn] *Gespräch* [16][ˌsaɪn‿'ʌp] *sich einschreiben, sich anmelden* [17][maɪ'nɒrəti] *Minderheit* [18][ˌkwɒlɪfɪ'keɪʃn] [19]*ohne, dass (sie)* [20]['ju:ni] = university [ˌju:nɪ'vɜ:səti] [21][pjʊə] *reine(r/s), echte(r/s)* [22]['dʒi:niəs] *Genie* [23]['sɪblɪŋ] *Geschwister* [24]['ri:sntli] *kürzlich, vor kurzem* [25]['wɒrɪk] [26]['ɒksfəd] *berühmte Universität* [27]['eɪlevl] *höhere Abschlussprüfung* (= Abitur) [28][ə'staʊnd] *erstaunen* [29]['meθəd] [30][ˌmæθmə'tɪʃn] *Mathematiker(in)* [31]['kemɪstri] *Chemie-* [32][waɪf] *Ehefrau* [33]['tʃɑ:ns] [34]['mʊzlɪm] [35][ru:'ti:n] [36][preə] *Gebet* [37][ˌmæθ'mætɪkl] [38][ˌnɔ:'θæmptənʃə] *Grafschaft in Mittelengland*

2. After you read one of the articles
Look at the heading and the picture of the other article. Write out some questions to ask about that article. Here are some ideas:

What is ... ?	Who are ... ?	Why did ... ?
Why are ... ?	What do ... think of ... ?	
How do ... ?	Is / Are ... really ... ?	
How did ... ?	What is ... taking too far?	

Then ask the other person or group about it.

3. Discussing the topics
Now that you know what both articles are about, talk about what the people are doing. Is it a good idea/a bad idea to ... ?

Cinema poem

by Roger McGough *(after Unit 2)*

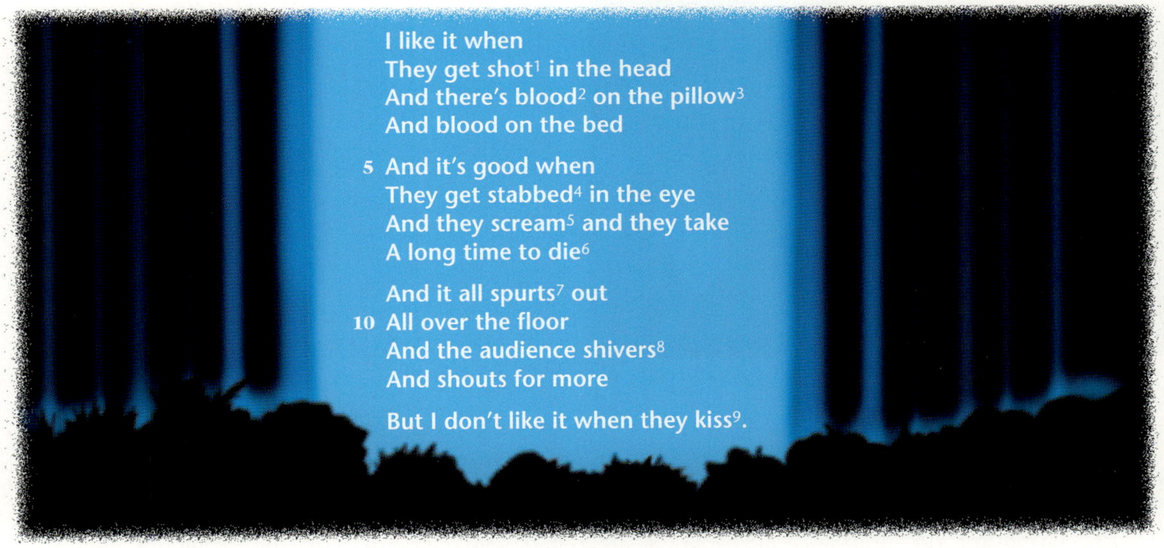

I like it when
They get shot[1] in the head
And there's blood[2] on the pillow[3]
And blood on the bed

And it's good when
They get stabbed[4] in the eye
And they scream[5] and they take
A long time to die[6]

And it all spurts[7] out
All over the floor
And the audience shivers[8]
And shouts for more

But I don't like it when they kiss[9].

1. *The speaker uses the word 'they' a lot. How many times? And who are 'they'?*
2. *What does he/she like – and not like?*
3. *Do you get an idea what kind of person the speaker is? Say what your ideas are.*
4. *Talk in groups about what kind of movies you like – and don't like.*
5. *Pick out the rhyme words. Can you think of more rhymes like these?*
6. *What about the rhythm of the poem? Is is regular or irregular?*
7. *Write your own little 'cinema poem'. (You can use this one as a model.)*

[1][ʃu:t] *schießen*
[2][blʌd] *Blut*
[3]['pɪləʊ] *(Kopf-)Kissen*
[4][stæb] *stechen*
[5][skri:m] *schreien*
[6][daɪ] *sterben*
[7][spɜ:t] *spritzen*
[8]['ʃɪvə] *zittern, beben*
[9][kɪs] *küssen*

Johnny Depp – in his own words

(after Unit 2)

1. Before you read

Have you heard of Johnny Depp?
- *If you have, say what you would like to know about him.*
- *If not, look at the photo. Guess what kind of a person he is.*

For all of you: Look quickly through the article (it's part of what he said in an interview) and its headings. Has it got the kind of information you want? If so, read on!

On his family

My mom was a waitress[1] when I was growing up in Florida. I remember my parents fighting and us kids wondering[2] who was going to go with whom if they got divorced[3].

On school

I was not the most popular kid in school. I always felt like a total and absolute freak. In high school I was bored and I hated it. I hung around[4] with bad crowds. We'd break into the school and destroy a room or something. I used to steal things from stores. I did every kind of drug there was by 14. Then you see where that's going and you get out.

On music

My mom bought me an electric guitar, I was about 12 years old. Then I locked[5] myself in my room for a year and taught myself how to play and then I started playing in little garage bands. I dropped out of high school and played rock'n'roll clubs in Florida. Then we went to Hollywood. It was horrible[6]. There were so many bands it was impossible to make any money.

On his first role, in the horror film 'Nightmare[7] on Elm Street'

I was just totally not what Wes Craven had written for the story. He had written the part of a big, blond, football player guy[8]. And I was small and thin, with hairspray and earrings[9]. But the director's daughter[10] saw me at the interview and ... five hours later my agent called me and said, "You are an actor".

On being a teenage star in the soap series[11] '21 Jump Street'

There are 365 days in the year, but for 275 of those days I'm saying someone else's words. And they're bad words. It was the first time I had any money, but I'd see all these commercials[12] about me. I felt like a box of cereal[13].

On his plans for the future

It's not my goal[14] to be the biggest box-office star in the world. If I ever look at something I did and say, 'That was great', I'll immediately[15] jump in the river.

2. After you read

a) *Has the article answered all of your questions? What new information have you now got?*
b) *From what you now know: Do you like Johnny Depp? Say why.*
c) *In what way (or ways) is he like you or your friends?*
d) *In what way (or ways) is he different?*
e) *Would you like his kind of life? Say why, or why not.*

[1] ['weɪtrəs] *Kellnerin* [2] ['wʌndə] *(sich) wundern* [3] [ˌget dɪ'vɔ:st] *sich scheiden lassen* [4] [ˌhæŋ‿ə'raʊnd] *herumhängen* [5] [lɒk] *einschließen* [6] ['hɒrəbl] *schrecklich, entsetzlich* [7] ['naɪtmeə] *Alptraum* [8] [gaɪ] *Kerl* [9] ['ɪərɪŋ] *Ohrring* [10] ['dɔ:tə] *Tochter* [11] ['səʊp ˌsɪəri:z] *Seifen(opern)serie* [12] [kə'mɜ:ʃl] *Werbespot* [13] ['sɪəriəl] *Getreide* [14] [gəʊl] *Ziel* [15] [ɪ'mi:diətli] *sofort, unmittelbar*

Autobahnmotorwayautoroute

by Adrian Mitchell (after Unit 3)

1. Before you read

a) *Check what these adjectives mean:*
gleaming[1] gigantic[2] circular[3]
Then find typical nouns for them.

b) *Think of things in your kitchen or living room to go with these words:*
frozen[4] ... instant[5] ...
a colour ... a hi-fi[6] ...
Write down all your phrases.

2. Whatdoesitmean?

a) *Try to explain the strange title.*

b) *Look through the poem to find more 'words' like the title. Can you break them up into their parts?*

3. Getting the idea

a) *Read the poem very quickly to yourself (at 100 miles an hour?). You don't need to understand everything at first, but just get the general idea.*

b) *Talk to a partner about it. What do you think it's about?*

⟨c)⟩ *Can any of the artists in the class draw a picture to go with the poem?*

4. Looking more closely

a) *Look at your phrases from exercise 1. Then check the poem for the way the poet uses the same seven words. Say what you think of the poet's phrases. Talk about them with a partner:*
I think this phrase is silly / crazy / nonsense / strange / clever / original / interesting / ...

b) *Read the poem again, this time more slowly, and in pairs. Talk about these questions:*
- *Why is the 'ring' (l. 2) revolving slowly (ll. 5, 9)?*
- *The English word for* Kreisverkehr *is 'roundabout'. Is that all it means in ll. 12/13?*
- *What are the people using their car(s) for in ll. 16-22?*
- *What do you think the last line means?*

Around the gleaming map of Europe
A gigantic wedding[7] ring
Slowly revolves[8] through Londonoslowestberlin
Athensromemadridparis and home again,
Slowly revolving.

That's no ring,
It's the Great European Limousine[9],
The Famous Goldenwhite Circular Car

Slowly revolving

All the cars in Europe have been welded[10] together
Into a mortal unity[11],
A roundaboutgrandtourroundabout
Trafficjamroundabout again,
All the cars melted[12] together,
Citroenjaguarbugattivolkswagenporschedaf.

Each passenger, lugging[13] his
Colourpiano, frozenmagazines, hi-fidog,
Clambers[14] over the seat in front of him
Towards what looks like the front of the car.
They are dragging[15] behind them
Worksofart, lampshades[16] made of human[17] money,
Instant children and exploding[18] clocks.

But the car's a circle
No front, no back
No driver no steering wheel[19] no windscreen[20]
no brakes[21] no

[1]['gli:mɪŋ] *glänzend* [2][dʒaɪ'gæntɪk] [3]['sɜ:kjələ] *kreisförmig* [4]['frəʊzn] *gefroren* [5]['ɪntstənt] *Fertig-, Pulver-* [6]['haɪfaɪ] [7]['wedɪŋ] *Hochzeits-, Ehe-* [8][rɪ'vɒlv] *sich drehen* [9][ˌlɪmə'zi:n] [10]['weldɪd] *zusammengeschweißt* [11][ˌmɔ:tl 'ju:nəti] *tödliche Einheit* [12]['meltɪd] *zusammengeschmolzen* [13][lʌg] *schleppen* [14]['klæmbə] *klettern* [15][dræg] *schleppen, ziehen* [16]['læmpʃeɪd] *Lampenschirm* [17]['hju:mən] *menschlich* [18][ɪk'spləʊd] *explodieren* [19]['stɪrɪŋ] *Lenkrad* [20]['wɪndskri:n] *Windschutzscheibe* [21][breɪk] *Bremse*

5. Comparing

a) *Compare this poem with the longer one in Unit 3, Step B (pp. 44/45):*
- *In what way is it the same?*
- *In what way or ways is it different?*

Think of:
- subject (what it's about),
- sections (long / short),
- rhyme / no rhyme,
- normal language / strange language.

b) *Which one do you like better? Say why.*

+England and the sea

(after Unit 4)

a) In her project, 'The story of English', Tara Modi went on to explain how English became a world language. Here are some more of her posters. They are about some very important people.

QUEEN ELIZABETH I

Born 1533, queen from 1558–1603. Her father was Henry VIII – the king who had six wives[1]. One of the reasons he had so many wives was that he wanted a son – he didn't think a queen could be strong. But he was wrong: Elizabeth was better than any king they ever had. She wanted to make England strong at sea as well as at home. Her main problem was the King of Spain. Ever since a Spanish ship discovered America for the Europeans in 1492, the Spanish[2] had been starting colonies in the 'New World'. Elizabeth wanted English sailors to do the same. One of her favourites, Sir Walter Raleigh[3], started three colonies on some islands of North America in the years 1585–87. They failed[4], but later colonies were more successful. When she died in 1603, England was the strongest country in Europe.
And English culture was better than ever. Shakespeare was among the many writers, artists and musicians who were active in Elizabethan[5] England.

FRANCIS DRAKE[6]

He was born near Plymouth in 1543. At the age of 18 he was working on a ship. Two years later he made his first trip across the Atlantic, and fought against Spanish ships. At 24 he was the captain of a ship. From 1577–80 he made a round-the-world voyage[7].

"Arise[8], Sir Francis!" On board his ship, Queen Elizabeth shows that she is very happy with Drake and the treasures he has brought back to England from his voyages.

1588: Drake was playing bowls[9] when the news came that the Spanish Armada[10] – a huge fleet[11] – was sailing up the Channel[12]. "There is time to finish the game and beat[13] the Spanish too," said Drake.

Of the 130 Spanish galleons[14], only 54 got back to Spain. The English ships were much smaller, but faster. And Drake was clever: he sent 'fire-ships' into the Spanish fleet to confuse them.

JAMES COOK

Born in Yorkshire in 1728. His parents were poor. At 17 he went to work in a shop in a seaside town. A year later, he went to sea. He joined the Navy[15] in 1755, and went to Canada to fight against the French. Cook made new maps of the coast, and so helped to win the war.
Cook was a great explorer[16]. He made three long voyages which took him to Australia, New Zealand and Antarctica[17]. He took scientists with him to study the strange plants[18] and animals of the countries he visited.

1770: Putting up the British flag in Australia

HORATIO NELSON[19]

Born in Norfolk in 1758. His uncle, a captain in the Navy, sent him on a voyage to the West Indies at the age of 12. When he came back, he became captain of a coastal ship – at the age of 14! Then he sailed to the Arctic[20] and the East and West Indies.
He fought many battles[21] at sea, and lost his right eye in one. "England expects that every man will do his duty[22]," he said at the Battle of Trafalgar (1805), when Britain was fighting against Napoleon[23]. Nelson's ship was hit, but they went on fighting, and the British fleet won in the end. Near the end of the battle, Nelson himself was hit. His last words: "Thank God I have done my duty."

Nelson in Trafalgar Square

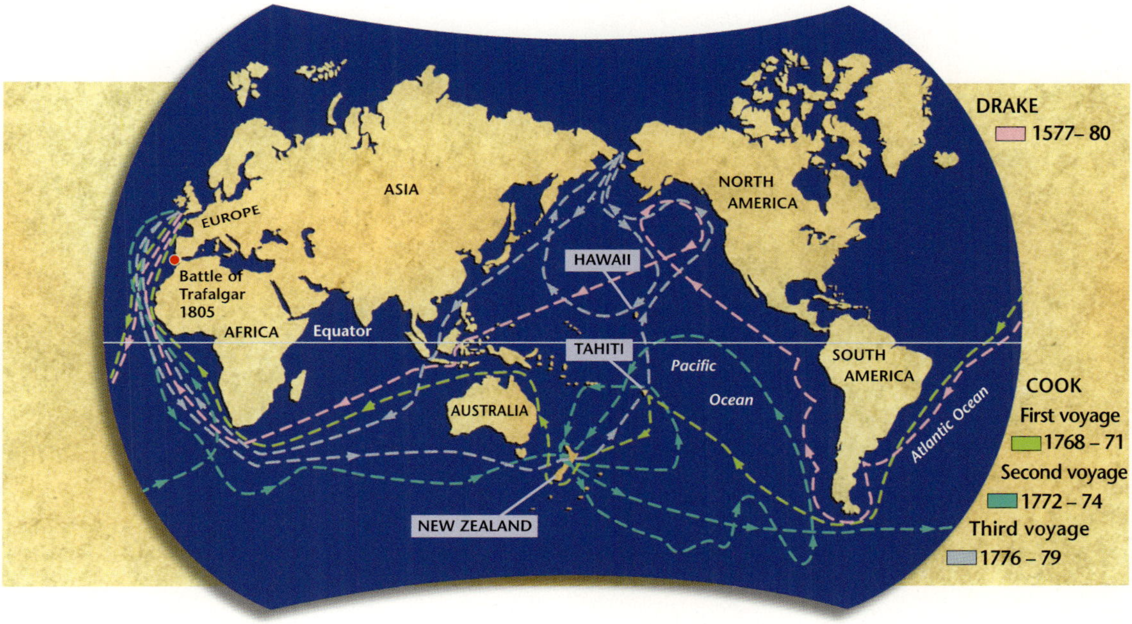

b) Tara asks her parents what they think of her project.

Dad: Not bad, Tara. But aren't you making Drake too much of a hero?

Tara: Well, he *was* a hero, wasn't he? He made Britain a great sea power.

Mum: That's right, Tara. And that's how the British Empire[24] started.

Dad: Yes, but think of how he did it. He attacked Spanish ships just for their gold and jewels[25]. That means he was a pirate[26]. And he bought and sold slaves[27].

Mum: But the Spanish were just as bad!

Dad: Don't forget that Drake attacked a Spanish ship before the king sent the Armada to England.

Tara: Did he? But I'm not going to put that in my project. It doesn't change the main facts ... What about Captain Cook? Is there anything important missing?

Dad: You should say how he died. Some natives killed him in Hawaii[28]. You see, he wasn't welcome in everybody's country!

Tara: Hmm ... Any more ideas about Lord Nelson?

Mum: Well, you have the main thing: he kept Britain strong and free. You could add that defeating Napoleon was good for Europe too.

Dad: But did you know that Nelson didn't always let other countries be free? For example, his job in the Caribbean was to stop the trade[29] between the people of the islands and the USA, which had just broken away from Britain.

Mum: All that may be true. But they all helped to build the Empire.

Dad: Build the Empire? You mean they conquered[30] other countries so that British traders could get richer and richer!

Mum: But don't forget: it's because of the Empire that we're a family.

1. *Why did Tara put Queen Elizabeth and Francis Drake on the same poster?*
2. *Look at Tara's posters, and find out about the early lives of the three men. What was the same for all three?*
3. *Now compare what they did as grown-ups. What is the same? What is different?*
4. *Make a list of the countries they travelled to. Then check the world map at the back of this book. What do you notice?*
5. *Look again at the bit about Queen Elizabeth and Sir Walter Raleigh. What do you already know about the 'more successful' later colonies?*
6. *Read the dialogue. From what you know of Tara's family (see Unit 1!), try to explain why her mother and father think differently about British history.*

[1][waɪvz] *Ehefrauen* [2]['spænɪʃ] [3][ˌwɒltə 'rɔ:li] [4][feɪl] *scheitern* [5][ɪˌlɪzə'bi:θn] [6][ˌfrɑ:ntsɪs 'dreɪk] [7]['vɔɪɪdʒ] *Seereise* [8][ə'raɪz] *(sich) erheben* [9][bəʊlz] *Bowling* [10][ɑ:'mɑ:də] [11][fli:t] *Flotte* [12]['tʃænəl] *Kanal* [13][bi:t] *schlagen, besiegen* [14]['gæliən] [15]['neɪvi] *(Kriegs-)Marine* [16][ɪk'splɔ:rə] *Forschungsreisende(r)* [17][æn'tɑ:ktɪkə] [18][plɑ:nt] *Pflanze* [19][həˌreɪʃiəʊ 'nelsn] [20]['ɑ:ktɪk] [21][bætl] *Schlacht* [22]['dju:ti] *Pflicht, Aufgabe* [23][nə'pəʊliən] [24]['empaɪə] *Weltreich* [25]['dʒu:əl] [26]['paɪərət] [27][sleɪv] *Sklave* [28][hə'waii:] [29][treɪd] *Handel* [30]['kɒŋkə] *erobern*

Language lyrics

by Joyce Trickett

(after Unit 4)

Have you noticed all the accents
that our language now contains[1]?
It's a fascinating[2] mish-mash
like a large Hungarian[3] Goulash
richly spiced[4] and multi-flavoured[5],
(Greeks, Italians, Dutch and Danes)
DIALECTABLE[6] – delicious[7], multi-savoured[8].

Early settlers[9] brought a mixture[10]
of the Cockney[11], Irish brogue[12],
Scots and Welsh and English Shires[13],
cold North Lands and Spanish fires.
German, French and Oriental[14],
convict[15], freeman, soldier, rogue[16] –
All garnish[17] to our Speech Pot, ornamental[18].

Thus[19] evolved[20] our own Australian,
lazy[21] language, easy, warm;
gold-rush time to modern day,
slang[22] and twang[23] from U.S.A.
Place-names from aborigines.
Ever changing voice and form,
our language grows from all of these.

[1][kən'teɪn] *enthalten, einschließen* [2]['fæsɪneɪtɪŋ] *faszinierend* [3][hʌŋ'geəriən] *ungarisch* [4][spaɪst] *gewürzt* [5][ˌmʌlti'fleɪvəd] *mit vielen unterschiedlichen Aromen* [6][ˌdaɪə'lektəbl] *mit Dialekten* [7][dɪ'lɪʃəs] *köstlich* [8][ˌmʌlti'seɪvəd] *mit vielen Gerüchen, Düften* [9]['setlə] *Siedler(in)* [10]['mɪkstʃə] *Mischung* [11]['kɒkni] *Jargon und Aussprache der gebürtigen Londoner* [12][brəʊg] *(irischer) Akzent* [13][ʃaɪə] *Grafschaft* [14][ˌɔ:ri'entl] [15]['kɒnvɪkt] *Sträfling* [16][rəʊg] *Gauner, Schurke* [17]['gɑ:nɪʃ] *garnieren* [18][ˌɔ:nə'mentl] *dekorativ, schmückend* [19][ðʌs] *so, auf diese Weise* [20][ɪ'vɒlv] *sich entwickeln, entstehen* [21]['leɪzi] *faul* [22][slæŋ] *Slang, Jargon* [23][twæŋ] *Näseln*

1. *Go through the poem quickly to find out where the writer lives. What do you know about that country?*
2. *How do you know she likes it that her language is a mixture? Find the words and phrases that make it sound a very good thing.*
3. *There is no such word as 'dialectable'. It is a mixture of 'delectable'* (köstlich) *and – what?*
4. *Why is her language such a mixture?*

The spoken word

by Annette Kosseris

(after Unit 4)

Words are weapons[1],
Use them with care!
A change of inflection[2]
can bring despair[3] ...

Words can cut,
yet words can melt[4]
the hardest heart,
when they're heart-felt[5].

Words can encourage[6],
words can excite!
But be aware[7] –
Words can bite[8]!

Words are powerful,
so be fair;
always choose
your words with CARE!

[1]['wepən] *Waffe*
[2][ɪn'flekʃn] *Abwandlung (der Stimme)*
[3][dɪ'speə] *Verzweiflung*
[4][melt] *dahinschmelzen*
[5]['hɑ:tfelt] *aufrichtig, tief empfunden*
[6][ɪn'kʌrɪdʒ] *ermutigen*
[7][ə'weə] *bewusst (sein)*
[8][baɪt] *beißen*

1. *What kinds of words can 'cut' (l. 5)? Can you give some examples?*
2. *And can you give an example of words that can 'melt the hardest heart' (ll. 6–7)?*
3. *And what about an example each for all the things in the third verse?*

And for both poems: *Can you work out the rhyme schemes? Use small letters (a, b, c, ...) for each kind of rhyme.*

Liz McColgan – A sports profile[1]

(after Unit 5)

***Liz McColgan** is one of Britain's leading athletes. She is a London Marathon champion[2], and has won an Olympic silver medal[3] for the 5,000 metres.*

"I've been sporty for as long as I can remember. I really loved sports at school – I was into everything. My PE teacher was Phil Kearns. I always got on really well with him. I was pretty quiet and didn't have that many friends at school. I joined all the sports clubs. I think one of the reasons for this was the fact that my family was pretty[4] poor – we did not have much money at home and so I made my own entertainment[5]. Sport was fun, sociable[6] and cost nothing.

After a few months at school, the cross-country season came along. Phil said: 'Right. Out you go. You run round that field.' I found out I loved running – I always came first or second. Phil was a mad marathon runner himself and noticed some of us were good.

He sent us to the local athletics club, the Hawkhill Harriers, where a good friend of his, Harry Bennet, was one of the coaches[7]. When I got better, Phil drove me to interschool[8] matches, not just me either[9] – four or five of us. This was in his own time, in his own car. As 80 per cent of us were from poor backgrounds[10] this was great – we couldn't afford[11] the bus fare[12]. Phil did so much outside school. It is great to have teachers like Phil who notice talent[13]. School is just the starting point.

Phil always keeps in touch, he sends me letters of congratulation when I've run well and also drops me a line[14] when I've not done so well – with a little message of encouragement[15]. It's really heartwarming."

***Phil Kearns** has taught at St Saviours High School, Dundee[16], Scotland, since it opened in 1973. He is now assistant head and PE teacher.*

"Liz's brothers came to us before her and they were all very good at sport. So when she arrived I said: 'Great! She'll be good at sport.' I wasn't wrong.

I think she had a love-hate relationship with running until she realised she was really good at it. I knew she'd be good, but it was not until Harry Bennet, her trainer at the club and a very close friend of mine, phoned me and said how good she was that I got really excited about her. Liz's body is ideal for running, she has a very high oxygen[17] intake[18].

Plus she has this determination[19] – she always really wanted to win.

Liz was quite shy and not very forward[20] in school life. I think she found it difficult to adjust[21] to secondary school, preferring[22] the primary school method[23] of having one teacher you can really get used to. Liz is very open, she always was. She never hides what she's thinking. I'm very happy about that. I think sport can be a great help. The discipline[24] of training prepares you physically[25] and mentally[26].

It can act as an avenue[27] for your social[28] life too, as you meet likeminded[29] people.

I always encouraged[30] Liz to get up on the stage to accept awards and even sing opera[31] because I knew she'd have to get used to it. If you are a professional[32] athlete you must also be a performer."

From *The Guardian Education*

1['prəʊfaɪl] *Kurzbiographie* 2['tʃæmpiən] 3['medl] 4['prɪti] *ziemlich* 5[ˌentə'teɪnmənt] *Unterhaltung* 6['səʊʃəbl] *gesellig* 7[kəʊtʃ] *Trainer(in)* 8['ɪntəsku:l] *zwischen ...* 9['aɪðə] *auch nicht* 10['bækgraʊnd] *Hintergrund* 11[ə'fɔ:d] *(sich) leisten können* 12[feə] *Fahrgeld* 13['tælənt] 14[ˌdrɒp‿ə 'laɪn] *Verbindung aufnehmen* 15[ɪn'kʌrɪdʒmənt] *Ermutigung* 16[dʌn'di:] 17['ɒksɪdʒən] *Sauerstoff* 18['ɪnteɪk] *Aufnahme* 19[dɪˌtɜ:mɪ'neɪʃn] *Entschlossenheit* 20['fɔ:wəd] *selbstbewusst* 21[ə'dʒʌst] *(sich) einstellen* 22[prɪ'fɜ:] *vorziehen* 23['meθəd] 24['dɪsəplɪn] 25['fɪzɪkli] *physisch, körperlich* 26['mentli] *mental, geistig* 27['ævənju:] *hier: Zugang* 28['səʊʃl] 29[ˌlaɪk'maɪndɪd] *gleichgesinnt* 30[ɪn'kʌrɪdʒ] *ermutigen* 31['ɒprə] 32[prə'feʃnl]

1. a) *Make a grid like the one on the right and fill in the information Liz and Phil give about themselves and each other.*
   b) *Find the points where they agree with each other or say the same thing in different ways.*
   c) *Find the points that only one of them talks about. Why do you think the other does not talk about these things?*
2. *What do you think makes a good sportsperson – and a good teacher? Discuss this in groups, write down your ideas, and then compare.*

	Liz	Phil
What Liz says about:		
What Phil says about:		

Space Oddity

by David Bowie

(after Unit 6)

"Ground Control to Major[1] Tom,
Ground Control to Major Tom,
Take your protein[2] pills and put your helmet on.

Ground Control to Major Tom
Commencing[3] countdown, engines on
Check ignition[4] and may God's love be with you.

Ten, Nine, Eight, Seven, Six, Five,
Four, Three, Two, One, Liftoff[5]

This is Ground Control to Major Tom,
You've really made the grade[6]
And the papers want to know whose shirts you wear
Now it's time to leave the capsule[7] if you dare[8]."

"This is Major Tom to Ground Control,
I'm stepping through the door
and I'm floating[9] in a most peculiar[10] way
and the stars look very different today.

For here am I
Sitting in a tin can[11]
Far above the world.
Planet Earth is blue
And there's nothing I can do.

Though I'm past one hundred thousand miles,
I'm feeling very still.
And I think my spaceship knows which way to go.
Tell my wife I love her very much – she knows."

"Ground Control to Major Tom
Your circuit's[12] dead, there's something wrong.

Can you hear me Major Tom?
Can you hear me Major Tom?
Can you hear me Major Tom?
Can you ...?"

"Here am I
Floating round in my tin can,
Far above the Moon,
Planet Earth is blue
And there is nothing I can do."

1. *Don't read the words as you listen to the song the first time. Just try to get the atmosphere!*
2. *If you have listened to the song for the atmosphere, can you now guess what it is about? Then listen again to check. (You can read the words now if you want.)*
3. *Who are the two people who speak in this song? And where are they?*
4. *In lines 1–12, some things are serious and necessary, and some things are rather silly. Find examples of each.*
5. *What goes wrong? And how do you know something is wrong?*
6. *Lines 17–21 and 33–37 are nearly the same. But what are the differences? And do the words mean something different the second time?*
7. *David Bowie wrote this song in 1969 shortly after Stanley Kubrick's film '2001: A Space Odyssey' came out. What connection(s) can you find? And why were they both so interested in space travel at the time?*

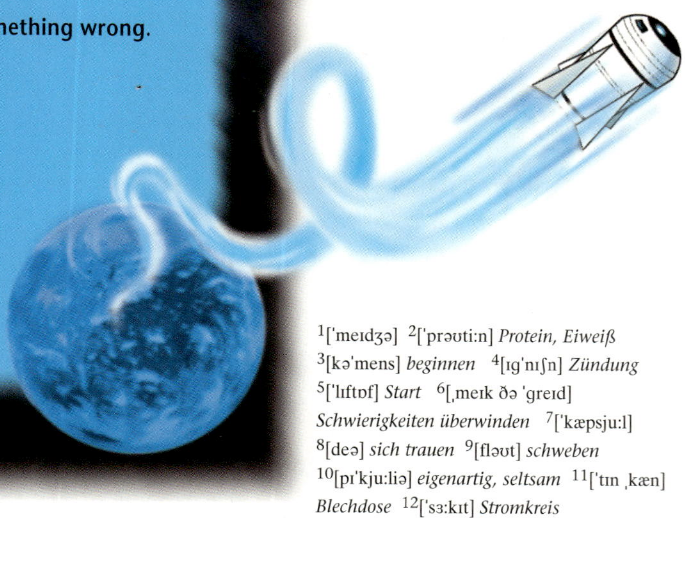

[1] ['meɪdʒə] [2] ['prəʊti:n] *Protein, Eiweiß* [3] [kə'mens] *beginnen* [4] [ɪg'nɪʃn] *Zündung* [5] ['lɪftɒf] *Start* [6] [ˌmeɪk ðə 'greɪd] *Schwierigkeiten überwinden* [7] ['kæpsju:l] [8] [deə] *sich trauen* [9] [fləʊt] *schweben* [10] [pɪ'kju:liə] *eigenartig, seltsam* [11] ['tɪn ˌkæn] *Blechdose* [12] ['sɜ:kɪt] *Stromkreis*

Holidays in space

(after Unit 6)

The American space agency which put the first man on the moon, NASA, has made an important decision[1].

NASA has, after many years of argument, agreed to think about sending tourists into space. Just imagine, instead of queuing[2] at Luton Airport for a fortnight[3] in the sun, you could be putting on your spacesuit and helmet at Edwards Air Force Base[4] ready for a trip around the planet.
But is it really likely to happen? A survey[5] in Japan[6] showed that ordinary[7] people would pay up to £4,000 each for a flight into space. At that kind of price, passenger-carrying spaceplanes would make a handsome[8] profit[9] for NASA.
The idea is that day trips into space would make enough money for the scientific[10] research[11] that is needed to develop[12] a manned flight to Mars. The smallest spaceplane would carry the pilot and one passenger. It would spend two minutes in space before it was pulled back to earth by gravity[13]. The whole trip, from blast-off[14] to landing, would take half an hour.

So stop buying clothes and music, and start saving all your money now, so that you can buy a ticket for a journey which is out of this world.

Max Glaskin

From *1015* in *The Sunday Times*

1. *Find the words in the article that mean:*
   a) what someone decides,
   b) something hard that you can wear on your head,
   c) (in business) more money than you paid in,
   d) the work that scientists do,
   e) what keeps you down on earth.
2. *Why has NASA now agreed to the idea of tourists in space?*
3. *'Out of this world' has a second meaning. Can you guess what it is?*
4. *Are you going to "stop buying clothes and music, and start saving all your money now ..."? Why, or why not?*

[1][dɪ'sɪʃn] *Entscheidung* [2][kju:] *Schlange stehen* [3]['fɔ:tnaɪt] *14 Tage* [4][beɪs] *Basisstation* [5]['sɜ:veɪ] *Untersuchung* [6][dʒə'pæn] [7]['ɔ:dnri] *gewöhnlich* [8]['hændsəm] *stattlich, ansehnlich* [9]['prɒfɪt] [10][ˌsaɪən'tɪfɪk] *wissenschaftlich* [11][rɪ'sɜ:tʃ] *Forschung* [12][dɪ'veləp] *entwickeln* [13]['grævəti] *Gravitation, Schwerkraft* [14]['blɑ:stɒf] *Abschuss, Start*

Spice girl

(after Unit 7)

Original Spice Michelle Stephenson went back to uni[1] instead of hitting the high life. Regrets[2]? She has a few …

Show business was my first love. From the age of five I was a show-off[3]. I would sing and dance round the house and I always performed in school plays. My parents sent me to stage school when I was 12 which was fantastic. I'd have school lessons in the afternoon, but the mornings were totally devoted[4] to singing, acting and dancing. I was even involved in the National Youth Theatre in the evenings.

Girl band

I never doubted[5] I'd end up working in the entertainment business. In 1994, while I was studying drama in my first year at university, I saw an ad in the showbiz paper *The Stage* for girls to join a new girl group.

I went along to a recording studio in London and auditioned[6] for a *Take That* style girl band. It was the brainchild[7] of a father and son team, Chris and John Herbert. I sang Dina Carroll's *Don't be a Stranger*[8].

'I was their first choice[9] for the group which was originally called *Touch*.'

First choice

I was over the moon when I got a call from Chris saying I was their first choice for the group which was then called *Touch*. The competition had been tough[10]. More than 1,000 girls had auditioned in all. Soon after, I was introduced to the other girls who were going to be in the group with me: Victoria, Geri, Mel B and Mel C. Emma wasn't on the scene then – I was the sweet one.

We all moved into a big house in Maidenhead in Berkshire and had a whale of a time[11]. Every day was spent singing, dancing and recording. The songs were very poppy[12], but you wouldn't recognise[13] them. Songs like *Wannabe* and *Say You'll Be There* came later. There have been lots of stories in the press about Geri falling out[14] with Mel B. I never saw anything like that. We had to get on well because we saw each other every minute of the day.

Holiday job

We went everywhere together. Geri used to drive us around in her car. It was such a laugh – we were five girls living it up away from home.

The *Spice Girls* are known for their outrageous behaviour[15], but is wasn't really like that then. We were quite normal actually.

Even though I was having lots of fun with the band, I knew I'd go back to university after the summer. For me, being in the group was a holiday job. I'd always intended[16] to finish my degree[17].

Big time

One of the Sunday papers said recently[18] that I left because my mum was ill. But the main reason was that I wanted to return to university.

The girls were upset[19] I was going, but I think they understood. I never kept it a secret[20] that I wanted to go back to college. And luckily, there were no hard feelings. I missed them a lot when I first left, but soon university life took over. I phoned them a few times and discovered I'd been replaced by Emma, but gradually[21] we lost touch.

I was really pleased when I first saw them on *Top Of The Pops*. I always knew they'd do well. But I don't regret leaving. I've formed my own band called Renoma, and we've a single out soon which I hope will get into the charts. Friends are surprised when they discover I was a Spice Girl, but I'm really proud to say I was involved[22] with them.

1. *What made Michelle a good Spice Girl? Make a list of her qualifications for the job.*
2. *What do you learn here about the background of this well-known pop group?*
3. *Why did Michelle leave the group? And how does she feel about it today?*

[1][ju:ni] = university [2][rɪ'gret] *Bedauern* [3][ˌʃəʊ'ɒf] *Angeber(in)* [4][dɪ'vəʊt] *widmen, verwenden* [5][daʊt] *zweifeln* [6][ɔ:'dɪʃn] *vorsingen (lassen)* [7]['breɪntʃaɪld] *Idee, geistiges Produkt* [8]['streɪndʒə] *Fremde(r)* [9][tʃɔɪs] *Wahl* [10][tʌf] *hart, schwierig* [11][weɪl] *sich prima amüsieren* [12]['pɒpi] [13]['rekəgnaɪz] *wiedererkennen* [14][ˌfɔ:l'aʊt] *sich streiten (mit)* [15][ˌaʊt'reɪdʒəs bɪ'heɪvjə] *ausgefallenes Benehmen* [16][ɪn'tent] *beabsichtigen* [17][dɪ'gri:] *akademischer Grad, Studium* [18]['ri:sntli] *kürzlich* [19][ʌp'set] *betrübt, geknickt* [20]['si:krət] *Geheimnis* [21]['grædʒuəli] *allmählich* [22][ɪn'vɒlv] *beteiligt (an)*

Finding out

by Nicholas Evans

(after Unit 8)

It was clever the way they handled[1] her finding out about the leg, Grace thought. Because looking back on it, she couldn't actually pinpoint[2] the moment that she knew. She supposed they had it down to a fine art, these things, and knew exactly how much dope[3] to pump[4] into you so you didn't freak out[5]. She was aware[6] something had happened down there even before she could move or speak again. There was this strange feeling and she noticed how the nurses seemed busier there than anywhere else. And it just seemed to slip into her consciousness[7] like many other facts as they hauled[8] her out of that tunnel of glue[9].

"Going home?" She looked up. Leaning in at the door was the woman who came each day to see what you wanted to eat. She was vast[10] and friendly, with a booming[11] laugh capable[12] of passing through bricks[13] and mortar[14].

Grace smiled and nodded.

"Alright[15] for some," the woman said. "Means you don't get to eat my Christmas dinner, mind."

"You can save me some. I'm coming back the day after tomorrow." Her voice sounded croaky[16]. She still had a Band-Aid[17] over the hole they had made in her neck for the respirator tube[18]. The woman winked[19].

"Honey, I'll do just that."

She went and Grace looked at her watch. It was still twenty minutes till her parents were due[20] and she was sitting on her bed, dressed[21] and ready to go. They had moved her into this room a week after she'd come out of the coma[22], freeing her at last from the respirator and she could speak rather than just mouth. The room was small, with a terrific[23] view of the parking lot[24] and painted that depressing[25] shade[26] of pale[27] green they must make specially for hospitals. But at least there was a TV and with every surface cluttered[28] with flowers, cards and presents, it was cheerful enough.

She looked down at her leg where the nurse had neatly[29] pinned up[30] the bottom half of her gray sweatpants. She'd once heard someone say that if you had an arm or a leg cut off, you could still feel it. And it was absolutely true. At night it itched[31] so badly it drove her crazy. It itched right now. The weird[32] thing was that even so, even as she looked at it, the funny half-leg they'd left her with didn't seem to belong[33] to her at all. It was someone else's. Her crutches[34] were propped[35] against the wall by a bedside table and peeping around[36] them was the photograph of Pilgrim. It was one of the first things she'd seen when she came out of the coma. Her father had seen her looking at it and told her the horse was okay and that made her feel better.

From *The Horse Whisperer*

1. *From whose point of view is this part of the story told?*
2. *You probably didn't understand the first sentence when you read it first. Say at what point you understood …*
   a) who 'they' (l. 1) were,
   b) what was wrong with Grace,
   c) how it had happened. *(Give line numbers.)*
3. *What do you learn about her medical treatment?*
4. *Try to explain the phrase 'tunnel of glue' (l. 11).*
5. *What kind of a person do you think Grace is? Give reasons for your opinion.*
6. *For those who have seen the film (or read the book): Explain to your classmates what all this has to do with the main story.*

[1]['hændl] *mit einer Sache umgehen* [2]['pɪnpɔɪnt] *genau festlegen* [3]['dəʊp] *Rauschgift, Droge* [4][pʌmp] [5][ˌfri:k'aʊt] *ausflippen* [6][ə'weə] *bewusst (sein)* [7][ˌslɪp'ɪntə 'kɒntʃəsnəs] *ins Bewusstsein schleichen* [8][hɔ:l] *zerren* [9][glu:] *Klebstoff* [10][vɑ:st] *riesig* [11][bu:mɪŋ] *dröhnend* [12]['keɪpəbl] *fähig (sein)* [13][brɪk] *Ziegel* [14]['mɔ:tə] *Mörtel* [15][ˌɔ:l'raɪt] *in Ordnung* [16]['krəʊki] *krächzend* [17]['bændeɪd] *Verband* [18]['respreɪtə ˌtju:b] *Beatmungsröhre* [19][wɪŋk] *blinzeln, zwinkern* [20][dju:] *planmäßig ankommen* [21][dres] *ankleiden, anziehen* [22]['kəʊmə] [23][tə'rɪfɪk] *sagenhaft, toll* [24]['pɑ:kɪŋ ˌlɒt] *Parkplatz* [25][dɪ'presɪŋ] *deprimierend* [26][ʃeɪd] *Schattierung, Nuance* [27][peɪl] *blass* [28]['klʌtə] *anhäufen* [29]['ni:tli] *ordentlich, sauber* [30][ˌpɪn'ʌp] *hochstecken* [31][ɪtʃ] *jucken, brennen* [32][wɪəd] *seltsam* [33][bɪ'lɒŋ] *gehören* [34][krʌtʃ] *Krücke* [35][prɒp] *anlehnen* [36][ˌpi:pə'raʊnd] *(sich) verstohlen hervorgucken*

School moviemakers

Project

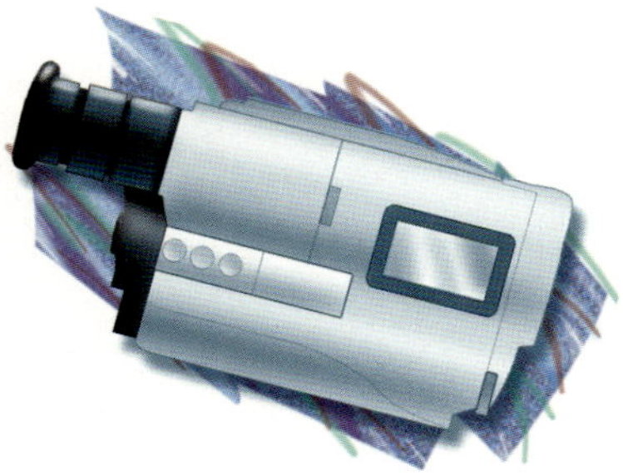

From time to time people want to know something about your school and the activities that go on there. And giving a talk (or listening to one) can sometimes be boring. So how about making a video instead? Then you could

- put on a video show at your next school fete,
- start a video chronicle about your school and add a cassette every year,
- send it to your partner school in Britain, the USA or elsewhere in the world,
- give a copy of it to all school leavers.

But you are sure to find more things you can use a video about your school for. How about making a list?

Preparations: a plan and a storyboard

First of all, make a plan. Discuss what might be interesting to other people. You will find some ideas on the two pages here. You can leave some of them out if you want to or add your own ideas. After that, decide who is going to do what. It may be a good idea to work in two or three groups. Then you need a storyboard. Write and/or draw all the information you want to give in frames on a sheet of paper. Add the people you are going to talk to and the places you are going to show. Decide how you are going to structure the video (a beginning, a middle and an end!) and how material can be presented.

Possible scenes or parts of the video

1. You may want to start with a short description of the school's past. You should think of the following points:
   - Who or where can you get information from?
   - How are you going to record your information?
   - How can you make your description more lively (background, reading text or speaking freely, clothes, how can photos be presented, etc.)?

2. Then you will want to show the school as it is today. You can
   - give facts and figures
   - show the subjects that are taught at your school
   - interview teachers
   - describe classrooms and other parts of your school
   - ask pupils for their opinions of subjects, teachers, the school, etc.

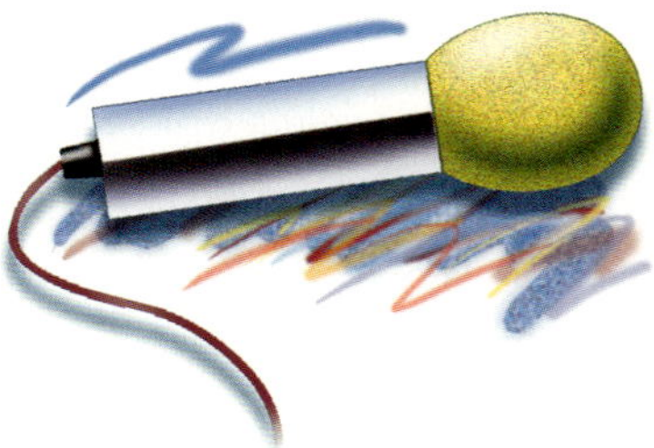

3. You can show what everyday school life is like.
   - Describe a normal day at school.
   - Spend a whole day with one pupil and film what he/she does. But don't forget to ask permission (pupils and teachers) before you start.
   - Do this with pupils in different classes/age groups.

4. Show how pupils get to school every day.
   - Find out where they come from (village, town, part of the town).
   - How many kilometres / metres do they have to travel / walk to school?
   - How long does it take them to get to school?
   - Who walks, cycles, uses public transport or is brought by car?

5. Film what pupils do in breaks between lessons.
   - Do this with various classes in the short and longer breaks.
   - What do the girls do? What do the boys do? What do they do together?

6. What happens in the afternoons at school?
   - Find out who stays at school after lessons (pupils, teachers, others).
   - What do they do (school work, repair work, cleaning, clubs, sports, activities, etc.)?
   - Interview the people who are there in the afternoon.

7. 'Old boys and girls'
   - Do you know any 'old boys' or 'old girls' who have become famous in some way or other sportsmen / sportswomen, actors, writers, local politicians, people with exciting jobs, people who collect unusual things or have strange hobbies ... ?
   - Find out about them and interview them.

8. And finally you could give a summary of what you think about school.
   - What is good about it? What is not so good?
   - Perhaps you can make some suggestions: how to make your school a more attractive place.

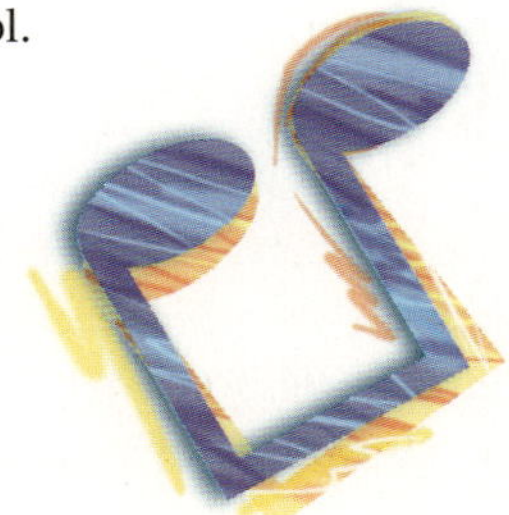

The final version

When you have done all this, or some of these things, look through all the material that you have filmed / collected and discuss it. When you have decided what should be used and what shouldn't, you can edit the material and put together the final version.
Then you need a good title. *Our School* is not a good title. Goethe goes to Hollywood might be a better one!
Try finding a good title by brainstorming in a group.
Don't forget to add some background music, perhaps different kinds of music for different parts of the video.
And what about sound effects?
Just one more thing: a video film shouldn't be too long or it becomes boring. And it should be fun.
So have fun making your school movie!

Translation

Wie du schon aus **Swift 1** weißt, kannst du mit diesen Übersetzungsübungen überprüfen, ob der Wortschatz und die Grammatik, die du in den einzelnen *Units* gelernt hast, ‚sitzen'. Wenn du nicht mehr weiter weißt, hilft oft ein Blick in die Texte der jeweiligen *Unit* oder in die entsprechenden Kapitel im Grammatikanhang. In den Kästchen zwischen den Übersetzungsübungen findest du Tipps, die dir zeigen, worauf du beim Übersetzen besonders achten musst. Viel Spaß!

T Im Deutschen macht es meist keinen Unterschied, ob du, wenn du über Vergangenes berichtest, Präteritum oder Perfekt verwendest, vor allem süddeutsche Sprecher(innen) gebrauchen häufig das Perfekt.

Gestern ging ich ins Kino. Dort traf ich meine Lehrerin.
Gestern bin ich ins Kino gegangen. Dort habe ich meine Lehrerin getroffen.

Im Englischen darf man zum Ausdruck abgeschlossener Handlungen der Vergangenheit jedoch nur das *simple past* verwenden.

Yesterday I went to the cinema. I met my teacher there.

1 Ein aufregender Tag beim Notting Hill Carnival — Unit 1 Step A

Maike hat ihren Eltern über ihre Erlebnisse vom Notting Hill Carnival einen Brief geschrieben und übersetzt Auszüge davon für Liz.

Der Carnival war einfach großartig! Einiges ist zwar schief gelaufen, aber am Ende war alles OK! Ich bin schon früh aufgewacht, weil ich so aufgeregt war. Ich habe mein coolstes Outfit angezogen, aber meine bequemsten Schuhe, weil man da stundenlang herumläuft und tanzt.
Jimmy und ich wollten uns mit Liz, Kevin und Tessa an der U-Bahnstation *Queensway* treffen, aber wir haben sie zuerst gar nicht gesehen, weil dort so eine Menschenmenge war. Ich habe Angst um mein Geld und meine Fahrkarte gehabt und so habe ich sie Tessa gegeben, damit sie sie in ihre Tasche steckt. Liz und ich sind vorne gegangen und die anderen haben versucht, mit uns Schritt zu halten, aber auf einmal konnten wir sie nicht mehr sehen. Das war sehr schlecht, weil sie alle drei Handys hatten, und wir keines! Aber es ist am Ende doch gut ausgegangen. Wir standen gerade dort, wo der Umzug anfängt, und ich habe nach jemandem mit einem Handy gesucht, als ein Mann auf einem Umzugswagen mich gefragt hat: „Bist du aus Deutschland?" Ich habe ja gesagt und da hat er Liz und mich auf den Wagen geholt und uns Deutschland-Fähnchen in die Hand gedrückt. So waren wir plötzlich Teilnehmer am Umzug. Wir wussten, dass die anderen sich den Umzug ansahen, und sie haben uns sofort gesehen, als wir um die Ecke *Great Western Road* bogen. Kevin hat sogar Fotos von uns gemacht.

T Was oben zum Ausdruck abgeschlossener Handlungen der Vergangenheit gesagt wurde, gilt auch für Fragen. Ist das Fragewort nicht Subjekt des Satzes, muss bei Vollverben mit *did* umschrieben werden:

Wie hat alles angefangen? — *How did it all start?*

Achte auf die Verwechslungsgefahr bei wer (= *who*) und wo (= *where*)!

2 Wie hat alles angefangen? — Unit 1 Step A

Maike hat vor, für ihre Schülerzeitung einen Bericht über die Entstehung des Notting Hill Carnival zu schreiben. Sie hat sich einige Fragen notiert, die sie ihren englischen Freunden stellen will. Hilf ihr beim Übersetzen.

Wann hat alles angefangen?
Wer hatte die Idee mit dem Festival?
Warum hat Mrs Laslett-O'Brien das Festival veranstaltet?
Welche Probleme gab es am Anfang?
Wie viele Gruppen haben am ersten Umzug teilgenommen?
Welche Nationalität hatten die Gruppen?
Wo hat der Umzug angefangen?
Sind in den sechziger Jahren viele Touristen gekommen?
Warum hat man daraus ein alljährlich wiederkehrendes Ereignis gemacht?

T Beim Ausdruck von Handlungen und Ereignissen der Vergangenheit musst du im Englischen genau darauf achten, ob sie abgeschlossen sind, oder ob noch ein Bezug zur Gegenwart besteht. Je nachdem musst du *past tense* oder *present perfect* verwenden.

- *Shakespeare wrote a lot of plays.*
  (Shakespeare hat die Theaterstücke geschrieben, kann aber keine mehr schreiben.)
- *The New Globe Theatre has performed a lot of Shakespeare's plays.*
  (Die Theaterstücke wurden aufgeführt und können weiterhin aufgeführt werden.)

Ist ein genauer Zeitpunkt in der Vergangenheit angegeben, der die Abgeschlossenheit der Handlung nahelegt, dann ist nur *past tense* möglich.

- *In 1998 the New Globe Theatre performed eight different plays.*

Wenn du das deutsche Wort ‚seit' übersetzt, musst du darauf achten, ob damit ein Zeitpunkt oder ein Zeitraum gemeint ist. Je nachdem wird ‚seit' mit *since* (= Zeitpunkt) oder *for* (= Zeitraum) übersetzt.

3 Ein Interview mit einem Filmstar — Unit 2 Step A

Übersetze folgendes Interview mit einem berühmten Filmstar ins Englische und versuche herauszufinden, um wen es sich handelt.

– Wie viele Oscars haben Sie schon bekommen?
– *I've got three Oscars so far.*
– Wann haben Sie Ihren ersten Oscar bekommen?
– *I got my first Oscar in 1960.*
– Wie lautete der Titel des Films?
– *The title of the film was 'Butterfield 8'.*
– Waren Sie schon einmal in Deutschland?
– *Oh, lots of times of course.*
– Haben Sie schon einmal in einem Sciencefiction-film mitgespielt?
– *Actually I've acted in so many films that I can't remember.*
– Was hat Ihnen mehr Spaß gemacht, Kino oder Theater?
– *Well, I enjoyed both of them really.*
– Haben Sie in einem Film von Hitchcock[1] gespielt?
– *No, he always wanted to have blondes in his films.*
– Wann haben Sie zum ersten Mal geheiratet?
– *I got married for the first time in 1953.*
– Wie oft waren sie schon verheiratet?
– *Eight times so far.*
– Seit wie vielen Jahren sind Sie Schauspielerin?
– *Since I was a child.*

[1] Alfred Hitchcock (1899-1980)

T Während im Deutschen der Unterschied zwischen Adjektiv und Adverb in manchen Fällen nicht deutlich wird, musst du im Englischen immer genau unterscheiden: beim Adverb wird in der Regel die Endung *-ly* angehängt.

Adjektiv	Die Landschaft ist schön.	*The countryside is beautiful.*
Adverb	Tessa singt schön.	*Tessa sings beautifully.*

4 Erdkundestunden

Unit 3 Step A

Liz und Liam unterhalten sich angeregt über die Schule, vor allem über die neue Erdkundelehrerin, Ms Henderson. Übersetze ihren Dialog, und achte besonders auf den Unterschied zwischen Adjektiv und Adverb.

Liam: Hast du schon die neue Erdkundelehrerin gesehen?
Liz: Du meinst doch nicht etwa diese fürchterliche Person, Ms Henderson?
Liam: Sie ist nicht fürchterlich, höchstens fürchterlich nett!
Liz: Aha! Deshalb bist du plötzlich an Erdkunde interessiert! „Waren Sie schon mal in Neuseeland, Ms Henderson? Gab es da im letzten Jahr nicht ein Erdbeben?“ Jetzt können wir diesen plötzlichen Wandel leicht erklären!
Liam: Das ist dummes Zeug! Ich finde, sie ist einfach eine gute Lehrerin. Sie kann Sachen so deutlich erklären.
Liz: Ich finde, sie spricht viel zu schnell.
Liam: Und wenn schon! Das liegt möglicherweise daran, dass sie in ihrem Fach so gut ist.
Liz: Jetzt redest du wirklich dumm daher!
Liam: Ja, ja, dein Mr Evans unterrichtet ja viel besser. Er erklärt auch so gut!
Liz: Wie recht du doch hast!
Liam: Ich finde seine Stunden einfach langweilig! Ms Henderson unterrichtet da viel interessanter.
Liz: Du wolltest ja schon immer alles über Tasmanien wissen.
Liam: Das ist typisch! Mädchen müssen immer das letzte Wort haben!

5 Stonehenge wird in die Steinzeit versetzt

Unit 3 Track 2

Stonehenge wird in die Steinzeit versetzt

Stonehenge, das berühmte Monument aus der Steinzeit, übt eine hohe Anziehungskraft auf Touristen aus. Es ist auf zwei Schnellstraßen leicht zugänglich, ein riesiger Parkplatz und ein Besucherzentrum liegen gleich daneben. Seit den 60er Jahren hat Stonehenge aber viel von seiner Magie eingebüßt.

Das soll nun anders werden. Plan des englischen Denkmalschutzvereins ist es, die A303 in einen Tunnel zu verlegen, den bestehenden Parkplatz samt Besucherzentrum zu schließen und in etwa 1,5 km Entfernung viel größer neu entstehen zu lassen. Beabsichtigt ist auch, die unschönen Zäune abzureißen und die Landschaft in ihren ursprünglichen Zustand zurückzuversetzen.

Kritiker[1] sagen, dass aus Stonehenge für £164 Millionen (250 Millionen Euro) ein gigantisches Disneyland wird, wenn sich der Denkmalschutzverein durchsetzt.
Man plant ein Besucherzentrum mit Geschäften und Restaurants, einem Parkplatz für 3000 Autos sowie einer Minibahn zu den geheimnisvollen[2] Monolithen[3].

[1]*critics* [2]*mysterious* [3]*monolith / stone*

T Wie du bereits gelernt hast, verwendet man im Englischen das *present perfect* zum Ausdruck einer Handlung, die in der Vergangenheit begonnen hat, aber noch in die Gegenwart hereinreicht oder deren Ergebnisse in der Gegenwart im Vordergrund stehen.

Tara has started a project about the story of English.
(Tara hat ein Projekt über die Geschichte der englischen Sprache begonnen.)

Ist ein Vorgang noch nicht abgeschlossen und steht die Handlung an sich im Vordergrund, verwendet man das *present perfect progressive*. Der deutsche Sprecher sieht in solchen Fällen weniger, dass die Handlung in der Vergangenheit begonnen hat, sondern vielmehr in der Gegenwart noch andauert und verwendet daher das Präsens.

Tara has been working on her project for two weeks.
(Tara arbeitet an ihrem Projekt seit zwei Wochen.)

6 Unterrichtsprojekte

Unit 4 Step A

Max unterhält sich am Telefon mit Tara Modi. Sie sprechen über ihre Projekte, natürlich auf Englisch ...

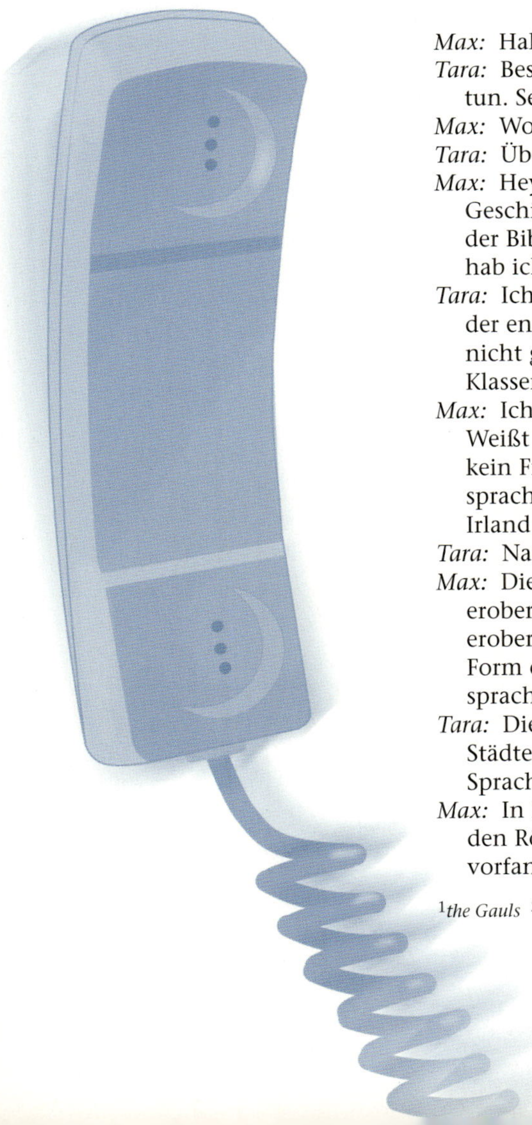

Max: Hallo, Tara. Wie geht's dir?
Tara: Bestens, danke. Aber ich hab momentan wahnsinnig viel zu tun. Seit zwei Wochen arbeite ich schon an meinem Projekt.
Max: Worüber geht es denn?
Tara: Über die Geschichte des Englischen.
Max: Hey, das ist ja interessant! Mein Projekt geht über die Geschichte des Französischen. Ich hab schon eine Menge Zeit in der Bibliothek verbracht, aber die interessantesten Informationen hab ich im Internet gefunden.
Tara: Ich habe schon eine Menge Informationen über die Anfänge der englischen Sprache zusammengetragen, aber ich bin noch nicht ganz fertig. Im Moment arbeite ich an einem Poster für das Klassenzimmer.
Max: Ich arbeite jetzt schon seit drei Wochen an einer Internetseite. Weißt du eigentlich, dass die Gallier[1], die ersten Einwohner, gar kein Französisch gesprochen haben? Die Sprache, die sie sprachen, ähnelt ein wenig der keltischen Sprache, die man in Irland oder Wales hören kann.
Tara: Natürlich, die ersten Briten haben auch Keltisch gesprochen.
Max: Die Römer waren das Volk, welches den größten Teil Galliens[2] eroberte. Natürlich haben sie ein kleines Dorf im Norden nicht erobert! Die Sprache, die mit ihnen nach Gallien kam, war eine Form des Lateinischen, das die ungebildeten Schichten[3] in Rom sprachen. Man nannte diese Sprache „lingua vulgaris".
Tara: Die Römer waren zwar das Volk, das die ersten Straßen und Städte in Großbritannien gebaut hat, aber alles, was sie von ihrer Sprache zurückgelassen haben, sind Ortsnamen.
Max: In Frankreich war das anders. Alle Völker, die Frankreich nach den Römern eroberten, nahmen[4] die Sprache an, die sie dort vorfanden.

[1]*the Gauls* [2]*Gaul* [3]*uneducated classes* [4]*adopt*

7 Ein Interview über die Pilger

Unit 4 Track 2

Stell dir vor, du bewirbst dich für einen Ferienjob als tourist guide *in* Plymouth, Mass., *und bestreitest folgendes Interview.*

Interviewer: Now tell us why you would like to do the work of a tourist guide.
You: Ich interessiere mich sehr für Geschichte, und besonders für die Geschichte der Pilgrims. Ich habe viel darüber in der Schule gelernt und würde mich freuen, wenn ich den Touristen alles darüber erzählen könnte.
Interviewer: Well, let's see ... What do you know about the English and the American Plymouth?
You: Nun, das englische Plymouth ist eine Stadt an der Südküste Englands, und das amerikanische Plymouth liegt an der Ostküste der Vereinigten Staaten von Amerika, im Staat Massachusetts. Viele amerikanische Städte sind nach Orten in Europa benannt, gewöhnlich nach Orten, aus denen die ersten Siedler stammten.
Interviewer: What do you know about the first settlers who landed in Plymouth?
You: Sie waren Puritaner und sie landeten im September 1620. Es handelte sich um eine religiöse Reise, und so nennt man diese Leute auch Pilger. Sie wollten in Amerika, wo sie ihre Religion frei ausüben konnten, ein neues Leben anfangen.
Interviewer: Does the name 'Speedwell' ring a bell with you?
You: Aber natürlich. Die *Speedwell* war eines der beiden Schiffe, die sich auf den Weg gemacht hatten. Sie musste aber umkehren, weil sie ein Leck hatte. Ihre Passagiere schlossen sich denen an, die schon auf der *Mayflower,* dem anderen Schiff, waren. Das Schiff, das man heute in Plymouth besichtigen kann, ist natürlich eine Nachbildung. Wenn die Leute es sehen, können sie es kaum fassen, dass es so klein ist. Sie können sich kaum vorstellen, dass darin ungefähr hundert Menschen über den Atlantik gesegelt sind.
Interviewer: What do you know about Thanksgiving?
You: Naja, als die Pilger im November im heutigen Neuengland landeten, befanden sie sich in völliger Wildnis. Im ersten Winter war das Wetter sehr schlecht und sie hatten nicht genügend Nahrungsmittel. Aber die Ureinwohner wussten, wie man sich in einem solchen Land verhält, halfen ihnen und zeigten ihnen, wie man Nahrungsmittel anbaut. In jenem Jahr fuhren sie eine sehr gute Ernte ein. Und um Gott zu danken, feierten sie ein großes Erntedankfest. Heute ist *Thanksgiving* in den USA ein sehr bedeutender Feiertag. Die Familien treffen sich da zu einem großen Essen mit Truthahn, ...
Interviewer: Thank you, that's all right. When can you start?

T Wenn du im Deutschen über zukünftige Handlungen oder Ereignisse sprichst, verwendest du häufig das Präsens. Im Englischen ist das anders, hier musst du genau darauf achten, ob

• eine spontane Entscheidung,	*Well, I'll take part in the New York Marathon then.*
oder eine Vorhersage,	*It will rain tonight.*
• ein Vorhaben oder	*I'm going to take part in the New York Marathon.*
• eine feste Vereinbarung	*I'm taking part in the New York Marathon.*

ausgedrückt werden soll. Je nachdem musst du entweder *will-future, going to-future* oder *present progressive* verwenden.

8 Pläne für den Schüleraustausch

Unit 5 Step A

Ludwig möchte einen Brief an seinen Austauschpartner schreiben. Er hat ihn zunächst auf Deutsch aufgesetzt, aber wie du weißt, soll man ja nicht Wort für Wort übersetzen, sondern gleich überlegen, wie sich ein(e) englische(r) Sprecher(in) ausdrücken würde.

Lieber Liam,

vielen Dank für deinen Brief mit den netten Fotos von eurem Erdkundeprojekt. Sie sind wirklich interessant, besonders die mit der Lehrerin. Hier nun unser Programm für euren Besuch in Füssen. Am Sonntag Abend geben wir eine Begrüßungsparty in unserer Schule. Am Montag besuchen wir Schloss Neuschwanstein. Am Dienstag machen wir eine Bergwanderung in den Alpen. Wenn das Wetter mitspielt, steigen wir auf den Säuling (2047 m). Am Mittwoch machen wir einen Tagesausflug nach München. Wir hoffen, dass wir Karten für ein Fußballspiel bekommen, aber es ist noch nicht sicher.
Wir wollen euch am Münchner Flughafen abholen, aber ihr habt uns noch nicht genau mitgeteilt, wann ihr ankommt. Wenn ihr euch für bayerische Volksmusik interessiert, dann organisieren wir ein Konzert mit einem Blasorchester[1]. Hast du schon einmal ein Alphorn gehört? Du wirst über den Klang überrascht sein.
Antworte bald!

Alles Gute,
Ludwig

[1]*brass band*

9 ⟨Was würdest du tun, wenn ...⟩

Unit 5 Step B

Ihr unterhaltet euch in der Klasse über Probleme mit Mitschülern. Übersetze für deinen amerikanischen Austauschpartner.

A: Stell dir vor, im Pausenhof würde dich jemand schikanieren. Was würdest du tun?
B: Wenn mich jemand schikanieren würde, würde ich ihm sagen, dass er aufhören soll.
A: Würdest du ihm dein Taschengeld geben, wenn er das verlangen würde?
C: Wenn er dann aufhören würde, mich zu schikanieren, vielleicht.
A: Und wenn er aber nicht aufhören würde, sondern dir einen Schlag in den Magen versetzen würde, was würdest du dann tun?
B: Wenn mich jemand schlagen würde, würde ich zurückschlagen.
A: Wenn er aber größer und stärker wäre als du?
C: Also ich würde nicht zurückschlagen, ich würde es dem Lehrer, der Pausenaufsicht führt, melden.
B: Wenn jetzt aber kein Lehrer da wäre?
C: Wenn ich keine Pausenaufsicht finden würde, würde ich meine Freunde bitten, mir zu helfen.
B: Würdet ihr dann anfangen, ihn zu schikanieren?
C: Vielleicht.
A: Und wenn euch ein Lehrer dabei erwischen würde?
C: Dann würde ich ihm die Wahrheit sagen.
D: Also wenn mich jemand schikanieren würde, würde ich gar nicht darauf reagieren.
B: Das ist leichter gesagt als getan!

10 Die geheimnisvolle Taschenlampe

Unit 6 Step A

Durch geheimnisvolle Taschenlampe gerettet

Gestern abend gegen 22 Uhr kam es zu einer sonderbaren Begegnung. Granville W., 38, traf in seinem Garten einen Mann, der sich als Alfred B. vorstellte. Er trug ein schwarz-weiß kariertes Jacket, einen grauen Pullover und eine schwarze Hose. W. lud den Mann zu einem Getränk in ein anderthalb Kilometer entfernt gelegenes Lokal ein. Sie mussten zu Fuß gehen, da die Fußgängerrollsteige aus Energieersparnisgründen abgeschaltet worden waren. Im Lokal wollte B. W. zu einem Getränk einladen. Sie waren aber nicht in der Lage, ihr Getränk zu sich zu nehmen, weil einer aus einer Gruppe von Jugendlichen an der Bar B. absichtlich anrempelte. Da sie zahlenmäßig hoffnungslos unterlegen waren, verließen die beiden Männer das Lokal. Die Jugendlichen verfolgten sie aber auf Motorrädern und bedrohten sie. Plötzlich nahm B. eine Lampe aus der Tasche und drückte auf den Knopf, als einer von ihnen näher kam. Die Wirkung auf die Motorradfahrer war fatal: Beide konnten nicht mehr weiterfahren. B. sagte: „Sie haben mich angegriffen. Ich musste mich verteidigen." Und er fügte hinzu: „Ich werde das Scheitern meiner Mission melden müssen." W. bat ihn noch, sie nicht völlig abzuschreiben, sondern eines Tages wieder vorbeizukommen. B. schwieg und verschwand so geheimnisvoll wie er gekommen war.

11 Erfahrungen mit einer Gang

Unit 7 Step A

Steve und Robert unterhalten sich über ihren Mitschüler Carlos.

Steve: Stimmt es, dass Carlos Mitglied einer Gang ist?
Robert: Er war es, er hat sie jetzt verlassen.
Steve: Gut, aber warum wurde er Mitglied?
Robert: Sie haben ihm immer das Pausengeld weggenommen und ihn manchmal geschlagen. Sie haben ihm das Leben richtig schwer gemacht. Am Ende war er es Leid, immer geschlagen zu werden, und er hat mitgemacht.
Steve: Ach komm, da muss es doch noch andere Gründe geben.
Robert: Ich weiß nicht, vielleicht haben sie ihm brandneue Designerklamotten verpasst?
Steve: Ich glaube, er hatte Schwierigkeiten mit Zuhause. Stimmt es eigentlich, dass er Drogen und so Zeugs verkauft hat?
Robert: Das glaube ich nicht.
Steve: Wussten eigentlich seine Eltern davon?
Robert: Seine Eltern? Die kümmern sich doch um nichts. Seine Mutter sagt zwar immer zu ihm, er soll sich anstrengen[1], aber er hat seinen Vater seit Jahren nicht mehr gesehen.
Steve: Warum hat er eigentlich die Gang verlassen?
Robert: Weißt du das denn nicht? Er hat eine neue Freundin. Sie wollte, dass er damit aufhört.

[1] *hier:* hart arbeiten

T Die indirekte Rede verwendet man, wenn man Äußerungen einer anderen Person wiedergeben will. Sie wird normalerweise durch ein Verb des Sagens / Fragens eingeleitet.
Wenn diese Wiedergabe in der Gegenwart stattfindet, gibt es zwischen dem Deutschen und dem Englischen kaum Unterschiede. Sehr groß sind diese Unterschiede aber, wenn das Verb des Sagens / Fragens in der Vergangenheit steht.

Direkte Rede	Selima sagte: „Ich **bin** ihre kleine Prinzessin." *Selima said: "I* ***am*** *their little princess."*
Indirekte Rede	Selima sagte, sie **sei** ihre kleine Prinzessin. *Selima said that she* ***was*** *their little princess.*

Im Deutschen wird der Konjunktiv Präsens verwendet, im Englischen findet eine sogenannte Rückverschiebung der Zeiten (= *backshift*) vom *present* zum *past* statt.

12 Zwischen zwei Kulturen

Unit 7 Track 2

In einer deutschen Jugendzeitschrift hast du einen Bericht über ein Interview gelesen, das eine Reporterin mit Aishe, einer türkischen Jugendlichen, die in Deutschland lebt, geführt hat. Du erzählst deinem englischen Austauschgast davon.

Aishe sagte, sie sei in Frankfurt geboren, aber ihre Eltern stammten aus Ankara. Sie hätten vor, eines Tages wieder zurück in die Türkei zu gehen, aber sie fühle sich als Deutsche.
Gefragt, ob sie es schwierig fände, zwischen zwei Kulturen zu leben, antwortete sie, dass ihre Eltern nicht gerade sehr liberal seien. Sie erwarteten von ihr, dass sie sich traditionell kleide. Miniröcke seien beispielsweise tabu. Sie dürfe auch nicht mit Jungs ausgehen oder spät abends weggehen. Sie treffe sich auch nicht heimlich mit Jungs, weil sie ein gutes Verhältnis zu ihren Eltern wolle und sie nicht anlügen könne. Vor einiger Zeit habe sie ein Junge gefragt, ob sie mit ihm ausgehen wolle, sie habe aber nein gesagt. Schule sei ihr wichtiger als abends auszugehen. Überdies erwarteten ihre Eltern von ihr Spitzennoten. Nach dem Willen ihrer Eltern solle sie Ärztin werden und eine Familie mit vielen Kindern haben. Den richtigen Mann für sie würden übrigens ihre Eltern aussuchen. Sie könne aber durchaus ihre eigenen Entscheidungen treffen.

T Das deutsche Wort ‚sich' wird je nach Bedeutung im Englischen unterschiedlich übersetzt.

• Sie fragt sich (selbst) …	*She asks herself … / She wonders …*
Sie fragen sich (selbst) …	*They ask themselves … / They wonder …*
• Sie fragen sich (einander) …	*They ask each other / one another …*
• Sie treffen sich …	*They meet …*

13 Mach es selbst mit EIGENBAU

Unit 8 Step A

Dein Austauschgast ist auf die folgende Werbeanzeige gestoßen. Er bittet dich, für ihn zu übersetzen.

Bauen Sie Ihr Eigenheim selbst!

Es gibt Leute, die legen sich auf die faule Haut[1] und vergnügen sich, es gibt aber auch Leute, die sich ihr Eigenheim selbst bauen. Herr Maurer kann sich noch gut erinnern: Seine Frau und er wollten schon immer ein Haus für sich haben, aber sie konnten es sich nie leisten[2]. Als sie sich letztes Jahr mit alten Freunden trafen, erzählte ihnen einer von seinem Haus, das er sich selbst gebaut hatte. Zuerst konnten sich die Maurers gar nicht vorstellen, wie das funktionieren sollte, aber dann entschlossen sie sich, sich ein EIGENBAU-Haus zu kaufen. Und jetzt fühlen sie sich glücklich in ihrem EIGENBAU-Haus.
Beeilen Sie sich! Sehen Sie sich unsere Musterhäuser[3] an!

[1]*sit back and do nothing* [2]*afford* [3]*show home*

14 Ein ganz normaler Fahrradunfall

Unit 8 Step B

Dein Freund hatte einen Unfall mit dem Fahrrad und schreibt auf seinem Laptop eine E-mail an seinen englischen Austauschpartner. Hilf ihm beim Übersetzen.

Hallo Ronald,
ich schreibe dir, weil ich nicht sicher bin, ob ich in der Lage sein werde, am Austausch mit eurer Schule teilzunehmen. Der Grund: Vor einer Woche hatte ich einen schlimmen Unfall mit dem Fahrrad. Es ist passiert, als ich aus Spaß mit dem Fahrrad meines Freundes gefahren bin. Dummerweise waren meine Beine zu kurz, und als ich einen steilen Berg hinuntergefahren bin, konnte ich plötzlich die Bremsen nicht finden. So bin ich auf den Randstein gefahren und über den Lenker geflogen. Man hat mich gleich ins Krankenhaus gebracht und gründlich untersucht. Erst hat man mir eine Spritze gegen die Schmerzen gegeben, dann hat man mir Fragen zum Unfall gestellt und so blöde Sachen gefragt wie „Welchen Tag haben wir heute?“, um zu prüfen, ob ich eine Gehirnerschütterung hatte. Aber mein Gehirn funktioniert ganz normal, wie du an dieser E-Mail sehen kannst. (Urgh, hihihi, uuaahh!)
Nach ewigem Warten hat man mich in einen anderen Raum gebracht, wo mein Kopf und meine Beine von einer Ärztin geröntgt wurden. Einige Zeit später hat sie mir die Röntgenaufnahmen gezeigt. Mein Gehirn war in Ordnung, nicht aber mein rechter Knöchel, der war gebrochen. Die Ärztin sagte, sie könne nicht verstehen, warum die Leute keine Fahrradhelme beim Radfahren tragen und erklärte, dass jedes Jahr Hunderte von Radfahrern getötet und mehrere Tausend verletzt werden. Ich sagte ihr, dass mein Kopf doch in Ordnung sei und fragte sie, ob sie immer einen Helm trage. Da wurde sie rot und gab keine Antwort.
Man hat mich noch nicht heimgehen lassen, aber es ist ziemlich lustig hier, denn die meisten meiner Freunde sind gekommen und haben mir einen Haufen Geschenke gebracht. Ich werde hier mindestens noch eine Woche bleiben müssen, und ich hoffe, dass ich bis Ende des Monats ohne Krücken[1] laufen kann. So werde ich diesen Sommer wohl nicht nach England kommen können. Sch...pech!!!
Lass bald was von dir hören!

Ulrich :°°-(

[1]*crutches*

Grammar

Es geht weiter mit den grammatischen Regeln, die sich ja in manchen Punkten von der deutschen Grammatik unterscheiden. Die Besonderheiten werden wieder übersichtlich zusammengestellt, erklärt und mit Beispielen erläutert. Diesmal kann bereits auf viel Bekanntes aus dem letzten Jahr zurückgegriffen werden, sodass noch mehr Vernetzung und Wiederholung möglich ist. Schau einfach hier nach, wenn du
- etwas vergessen hast,
- etwas genau wissen willst,
- dich auf einen Test oder eine Klassenarbeit vorbereitest.

Damit dir das Lernen so leicht wie möglich gemacht wird, gibt es Wegweiser, an denen du dich orientieren kannst. Ab und zu ist es hilfreich, Regeln gleich anzuwenden. Deshalb haben wir an einigen Stellen kurze Übungen aufgenommen. Die Lösungen dazu findest du auf Seite 193. Grammatikpunkte mit hochgestelltem $^{+}$ behandeln die neuen Strukturen im *Track* 2. Da alles immer wieder in anderen Zusammenhängen vorkommt, kannst du dich auf die ständige Wiederholung und Absicherung verlassen.

S = Sehen: Die Übersichten zeigen, was zusammengehört.

M = Merken: Die Merkhilfen unterstützen das Gedächtnis.

W = Wissen: Die Zusammenhänge und Hintergründe erleichtern das Verstehen und Behalten.

A = Anwenden: In den Übungen kannst du die Regeln gleich anwenden.

R = Revision: Die Wiederholung hilft beim Einordnen und Vernetzen.

Also dann, viel Spaß weiterhin!

UNIT 1

1 Das Präteritum von *to be* – The simple past of *to be*

S

	I	**am**	at home			I	**was**	at the Carnival.
	you	**are**	early			you	**were**	late.
	he	**is**	happy			he	**was**	unhappy.
Today	she	**is**	at school		yesterday	she	**was**	at home.
At the moment	it	**is**	hot in London	but	last week	it	**was**	not so hot.
	we	**are**	the first			we	**were**	the last.
	you	**are**	nice			you	**were**	not so nice.
	they	**are**	at home			they	**were**	with their friends.

Zum Erzählen von Geschichten und zum Berichten brauchst du das *simple past*. Alle Handlungen, von denen du erzählst, müssen aber eindeutig vergangen und abgeschlossen sein.

I, he, she, it	**was**	(*singular*)
you, we, they	**were**	(*plural*)

Für das *simple past* von *to be* brauchst du zwei Formen.

M to be – **was / wasn't**; **were / weren't**

It **wasn't** hot yesterday.
We **weren't** in Islington a week ago.

Die Verneinung von *was* und *were* bildest du genau wie bei *isn't* und *aren't*: Das verkürzte *not* = *n't* wird direkt angehängt.

Auf Fragen mit *was* und *were* reagierst du höflich und verbindlich mit den Kurzantworten. Du erinnerst dich bestimmt, dass ein einfaches *yes* oder *no* eher unhöflich klingt.

S

Frage	Bestätigung	Verneinung
Was she late?	Yes, she **was.**	No, she **wasn't.**
Were they at the Carnival?	Yes, they **were.**	No, they **weren't.**

W Dass Ereignisse oder Begebenheiten wirklich vergangen und abgeschlossen sind, sagen dir Signalwörter wie: *yesterday, ago, last week/month/year/…, in 1999,* etc.

A Und gleich etwas zum Üben:

1. Jemand will wissen, ob deine Schwester letzte Woche in London war. (a. Frage, b. Verneinung)
2. Du teilst mit, dass deine Freunde vor drei Tagen nicht zu Hause waren.
3. Du sagst aus, dass du letzten Montag nicht in der Schule warst.
4. Du erzählst deinem Freund, dass er nicht zu Hause war, als du gestern angerufen hast. Du willst wissen, wo er war. (a. Feststellung, b. Frage)

2 Das Präteritum (regelmäßige Formen) – The simple past (regular forms)

S

	I	walk**ed**	along the street.
	You	show**ed**	me your photos.
singular	He	laugh**ed**	at me.
	She	cri**ed**	a bit.
	It	rain**ed**	yesterday.
	We	listen**ed**	to some music.
plural	You	talk**ed**	to us.
	They	wait**ed**	for me.

Das *simple past* von regelmäßigen Verben bildest du, indem du die Endung *-ed* an die Stammform des Verbs anhängst: *walk + ed = walked*. Diese Form ist für alle Personen gleich.

Bei der Aussprache und Schreibung der *simple past*-Formen musst du einige Besonderheiten beachten.

Beachte beim Sprechen

show – show**ed** listen – listen**ed** arrive – arriv**ed**	Nach Vokalen und stimmhaften Konsonanten spricht man [d].
walk – walk**ed** watch – watch**ed** pack – pack**ed**	Nach stimmlosen Konsonanten spricht man [t].
wait – wait**ed** want – want**ed**	Nach den Endkonsonanten *-t* und *-d* spricht man [ɪd].

Beachte beim Schreiben

phone – phone**d** live – live**d** like – like**d**	Endet der Infinitiv auf ein stummes *-e*, wird nur ein *-d* angehängt.
stop – sto**pped**	Nach einem kurzen, betonten Vokal wird der Endkonsonant verdoppelt.
cry – cr**ied** try – tr**ied**	Verben, die auf Konsonant + *-y* enden, erhalten die Endung *-ied*. Aber: *play – play**ed**, stay – stay**ed***!

3 Das Präteritum (unregelmäßige Formen) – The simple past (irregular forms)

Du kennst auch im Deutschen regelmäßige und unregelmäßige Präteritumformen: *kommen – kam, singen – sang*. Ähnlich ist es im Englischen.

I **woke** up early	wake – **woke**
She **saw** my shoes.	see – **saw**
They **came** later.	come – **came**

Zur Bildung der unregelmäßigen Formen gibt es keine Regel. Du musst sie einfach auswendig lernen. Eine Liste mit den unregelmäßigen Verben findest du auf den Seiten 228–229.

A Übertrage die folgenden Sätze ins Englische:

1. Wir machten uns früh auf den Weg.
2. Wir trugen alle unsere alten Jeans.
3. Maike vergaß ihr Handy.
4. Kevin kaufte die Fahrkarten.
5. Liz ging hinter ihm.

Am besten kannst du die Verben gruppenweise nach Lautung oder Schreibweise lernen: *bring – brought, think – thought, buy – bought* usw. Genau wie bei den regelmäßigen Verben (vgl. Punkt 2) sind auch bei den unregelmäßigen Verben die Formen für alle Personen gleich (Ausnahme: *to be*).

4 Frage und Verneinung im *simple past* mit *did/didn't* – Questions and negative sentences with *did/didn't*

1

Does she arrive late?	*Kommt sie spät an?*
Did she arrive late?	*Kam sie spät an?*

Do you often go to carnivals?
Did you often go to carnivals when you were young?

Das *simple past* von *do/does* lautet *did*. Die Fragenbildung mit *did* im *simple past* erfolgt genau wie die Fragenbildung mit *do/does* im *simple present*.

S

question words		examples
when?	*wann?*	**When did** they set off?
what?	*was?*	**What did** he have for breakfast?
how?	*wie?*	**How did** you get there?
why?	*warum?*	**Why did** she ask?
where?	*wo?*	**Where did** you stay?
where?	*wohin?*	**Where did** they go?
how much?	*wie viel?*	**How much** money **did** we get?
how many?	*wie viele?*	**How many** tickets **did** he buy?

Bei Fragen mit *did* findest du häufig Fragewörter.

Beachte, dass die Fragewörter immer vor *did* stehen.

2

+	–	examples
was	wasn't	He **wasn't** at home.
were	weren't	They **weren't** happy.

Die Verneinung von *to be* ist dir im *simple past* ja schon geläufig: *was + not = wasn't, were + not = weren't.*

I	**didn't**	see you.
You	**didn't**	phone me.
He	**didn't**	hear her.
She	**didn't**	know about it.
It	**didn't**	happen.
We	**didn't**	start the fire.
You	**didn't**	stay long.
They	**didn't**	ask us.

Zur Verneinung der meisten anderen Verben im *simple past* brauchst du das *simple past* von *do*. Die Kurzform bildest du wie gewohnt: *did + not = didn't.*

Merke dir, dass *did/didn't* grundsätzlich mit der Stammform des Verbs steht und für alle Personen gleich ist. Das gilt sowohl für regelmäßige als auch für unregelmäßige Verben.

S

	Bestätigung	Verneinung
Did I tell you about it?	Yes, you **did**.	No, you **didn't**.
Did you meet them?	Yes, I **did**.	No, I **didn't**.
Did he phone you?	Yes, he **did**.	No, he **didn't**.
Did she know that?	Yes, she **did**.	No, she **didn't**.
Did it happen to them?	Yes, it **did**.	No, it **didn't**.
Did we expect it?	Yes, we **did**.	No, we …

Kurzantworten sind auch bei Fragen im *simple past* mit *did* wieder angebracht. Im Deutschen kannst du eine Entscheidungsfrage einfach mit ‚ja' oder ‚nein' beantworten, im Englischen wird das als etwas unhöflich empfunden.

5 Die Verlaufsform des Präteritums – The past progressive

I tried to phone you yesterday evening.
What **were** you **doing**?

Sorry, I **was listening** to my new CDs.

Wenn du im Englischen einer *simple form* begegnest, kannst du sicher sein, dass es auch eine *progressive form* gibt. Neben dem *simple past* gibt es im Präteritum demnach auch das *past progressive*.

S

past progressive *gerade ablaufende Handlung*	**simple past** *neues Ereignis*
Tessa **was doing** her homework	when the doorbell **rang.**
Jimmy **was washing** his hair	when the lights **went** out.
It **was getting** dark	when they **reached** the house.
While I **was waiting** for the bus,	my mobile phone **began** to ring.
While I **was having** fun in London,	Liam **was sailing** with his friends.

Das *past progressive* wird häufig mit *while* verbunden, das *simple past* dagegen meist mit *when*. Es kommen aber niemals beide Wörter in einem Satz vor. Vorsicht: *When* bedeutet hier ‚als'!

6 +Das Gerundium – The gerund

Sailing is fun.
(Das) Segeln macht Spaß.

Some people don't like **sailing.**
Manche Leute mögen (das) Segeln nicht.

Erinnerst du dich noch daran, dass du die *ing*-Form eines Verbs wie ein Substantiv behandeln kannst? Im ersten Beispielsatz ist *sailing* das Subjekt (wer? / was?) des Satzes, im zweiten das Objekt (wen? / was?).

R

Subjekt		**Objekt**
Going to carnivals	is great fun.	
Sailing	can be dangerous.	
Taking photos	is a good idea.	
	Jimmy enjoys	**sailing.**
	Liz likes	**taking** photos.

M

Das *gerund* kann sowohl Subjekt als auch Objekt eines Satzes sein.

Our dog is crazy about **chasing** cats.
(What is your dog crazy about?)

Einer Reihe von **Adjektiven** sind bestimmte Präpositionen fest zugeordnet: *good at, proud of, interested in, famous for, crazy about* usw. Nach diesen Verbindungen steht immer das *gerund*.

She was thinking of **buying** a new camera.
(What was she thinking of?)

Das gilt auch für **Verben**, die mit bestimmten Präpositionen fest verbunden sind: *to think of, to talk about* usw.

A

Benutze jedes *gerund* zweimal und bilde je zwei Sätze, die inhaltlich zusammenpassen.

Example: I like **reading. Reading** is great.

I like …	sailing	… great.
We love …	cooking	… fun.
She hates …	cycling	… boring.
They enjoy …	riding	… interesting.
He doesn't like …	walking	… keeps you fit.
You …	reading	… terrible.

7 Der Apostroph – The apostrophe

Zur Wiederholung hier noch einmal die Fälle, in denen dir ein Apostroph begegnen kann.

1 Der Apostroph taucht zunächst einmal bei den Kurzformen auf. Der Apostroph zeigt immer an, dass etwas ausgelassen wurde. Leicht zu merken sind die ausgelassenen Vokale. Davon gibt es zum Glück nicht allzu viele. Der Apostroph kann auch für zwei und mehr ausgelassene Buchstaben stehen. Schau dir die Übersicht an:

R

I'm / you're / we're / they're	Der Apostroph steht für das entfallene **a** in *am/are*.
he's / she's / it's / that's	Der Apostroph steht für das entfallene **i** in *is*.
let's	Der Apostroph steht für das entfallene **u** im Wort *us*. (*Let us* ist veraltet.)
isn't / aren't / wasn't / weren't / don't / doesn't / didn't / hasn't / haven't / hadn't / can't / wouldn't / shouldn't / mustn't / needn't	Der Apostroph steht für das entfallene **o** in *not*.
he's got / we've got	Der Apostroph steht für **h** und **a** in *has / have*.
+I'll / you'll / he'll / she'll	+Der Apostroph steht für **w** und **i** im Wort *will*. (Achtung: *will + not = won't*!)
I'd (like to)	Der Apostroph steht für *woul* im Wort *would*.

2

Your **mother's** mother is your grandmother.

Your **parents'** parents are your grandparents.

The **children's** parents are their **grandparents'** children.

This is my **mother's father's** bike.

Sandra likes the **Bradens'** house and Mr **Braden's** hobby.

And Sandra understands **Liz's** problems.

Der zweite Bereich, in dem der Apostroph eine große Rolle spielt, ist der Genitiv. Wenn du sagen willst, dass etwas oder jemand zu einer bestimmten Person gehört, brauchst du den *s-genitive*.

R

the **boy's** books	–	*die Bücher des Jungen*
the **boys'** books	–	*die Bücher der Jungen*
the **women's** bikes	–	*die Räder der Frauen*
the **children's** toys	–	*die Spielsachen der Kinder*
Ms **Mannings'** car Ms **Mannings's** car	–	*Ms Mannings Auto*

Im Singular brauchst du den Apostroph und das *s*.

Bei regelmäßigen Pluralformen mit *-s* im Auslaut, hängst du nur den Apostroph an.

Bei Substantiven mit unregelmäßigem Plural wird der Apostroph und das *s* angehängt: *men, women, children*.

Bei Familiennamen auf *-s* wird meist nur der Apostroph, manchmal auch Apostroph + *s* angehängt: *Mannings, Jones* usw.

M

Beachte bei der Aussprache :
1. Nach stimmlosen Konsonanten, z.B. [p, t, k] sprichst du [s],
2. nach stimmhaften Konsonanten, z.B. [b, d, g, m] sprichst du [z],
3. nach Zischlauten [s, z, ʃ, tʃ, dʒ] sprichst du [ɪz]: Liz's [ˈlɪzɪz] room.

8 Leicht zu verwechselnde Wörter (Teil I) – Easily confused words (Part I)

1 to bring – to take

Beide Verben stehen für das deutsche *bringen*. Im Englischen musst du aber genauer unterscheiden.

Can you **bring** me that blue book over there?

Please **bring** your workbooks every lesson.

My sister **brought** her friend home to listen to some music.

Can you **take** this red book back to the library?

She gave me these books to **take** home.

Did you **take** Aunt Jane to the station?

Bei *bring* ist immer gemeint, etwas zum Standort des Sprechers *her*bringen: *her*ein, *her*auf, *her*unter usw.

Bei *take* ist die Bedeutung entgegengesetzt. Es wird etwas vom Standort des Sprechers weg und zu einem andern Ort *hin*gebracht: *hin*unter, *hin*über.

M

back ⇘ us ⇓ me ⇙ **bring** ⇗ up ⇑ down ⇖ in

Immer im Sinne von *her*bringen!

back ⇖ home ⇑ to … ⇗ **take** ⇙ there ⇓ with … ⇘ over

Immer im Sinne von woanders *hin*bringen!

2 to wear – to carry

Beide Verben bedeuten im Deutschen *tragen*, meinen aber etwas ganz Unterschiedliches.

She **wore** her new trainers.
I can't **wear** my jacket now. It's so hot.
He was **wearing** a new sweatshirt.

She **carried** her old trainers in a box.
Can you **carry** my bag for a while?
He **carried** a box of new sweatshirts to the shelf.

Das Verb *wear* bedeutet, etwas am Körper tragen, d.h. etwas anhaben.

Das Verb *carry* dagegen meint, etwas in den Händen, den Armen, auf den Schultern tragen, d.h. etwas transportieren.

A Übertrage diese Sätze ins Englische:

1. Bringt eure Arbeitsbücher bitte mit.
2. Ich kann das Cello nicht auf dem Rücken tragen.
3. Kannst du das Keyboard ins Wohnzimmer bringen?

UNIT 2

9 Das Perfekt mit *since* und *for* – The present perfect with *since* and *for*

Dass es beim *present perfect* vorwiegend um das Resultat einer Handlung und weniger um die genauen Zeitangaben geht, weißt du bereits aus **Swift 1**.

They **have collected** a lot of information.

Sie haben eine Menge Informationen gesammelt.

Das Ergebnis der Handlung liegt vor.
Es ist unwichtig, wann es erreicht wurde.

In Verbindung mit *since* und *for* werden dagegen die Zeitangaben in den Mittelpunkt gestellt.

I **haven't talked** to her **since** last week.

Seit letzter Woche habe ich nicht (mehr) mit ihr gesprochen.

Bei Ausdrücken mit *since* steht der Zeitpunkt im Vordergrund, von dem aus etwas betrachtet wird.

You **have used** my computer **for** two days.

Du hast meinen Computer (schon) zwei Tage lang benutzt.

Bei Ausdrücken mit *for* steht die Zeitspanne im Mittelpunkt, die eine Handlung gedauert hat. Im Deutschen kann man *for* oft mit ‚lang' wiedergeben.

M

Mit ***since*** stehen Zeitangaben wie

- Uhrzeit (*... since four o'clock.*)
- Datum (*... since 6th April.*)
- Wochentag (*... since Tuesday.*)
- Jahr (*... since 1999.*)

M

Mit ***for*** stehen dagegen

- Zeiträume (*... for two hours, for three days*)
- unbestimmte Ausdrücke (*... for months, for years*)

10 Das Perfekt und das Präteritum – Present perfect and simple past

Das *present perfect* verwendest du, wenn etwas bereits geschehen ist (oder auch nicht) und der genaue Zeitpunkt nicht von Interesse ist. Im Vordergrund der Aussage stehen die Ergebnisse der Handlung.

Das *simple past* benutzt du, wenn die Handlungen und Ereignisse abgeschlossen sind und der genaue Zeitpunkt bekannt ist.

Have you ever **been** to the New Globe Theatre in London?	Yes, we **were** there last February.
And **have** you **seen** the latest film version of Shakespeare's Hamlet yet?	Yes, we **watched** it last Friday.
Look, the workers **have set** up a huge stage.	They **were** very busy and **set** it up yesterday.
And **have** the electricians **installed** all the electric equipment?	Yes, they **did** it early in the morning.
I **haven't had** an ice cream today.	Oh, we **had** one after lunch.
Wow! Robert **has** already **done** his homework.	Yes, he **did** it three hours ago.
I'm looking for John. **Has** he **gone** already?	Yes, he **went** about five minutes ago.

W

Die Signalwörter für das *present perfect* bezeichnen eine Zeitspanne von der Vergangenheit (mit ungenauem Zeitpunkt) bis hin in die Gegenwart: *ever, never, already, yet.*

W

Signalwörter für das *simple past* sind alle Zeitangaben, die einen konkreten Zeitpunkt in der Vergangenheit bezeichnen: *last week (month, Friday, ...), two hours (days, months, ...) ago, after breakfast, ...*

11 Bestätigungsfragen – Question tags

In der gesprochenen englischen Sprache gibt es sogenannte Frageanhängsel (*question tags*), mit denen du Bestätigung oder Zustimmung zu einer Frage einholen kannst. Solche Fragen werden Bestätigungsfragen genannt. Im Deutschen verwendest du: *..., nicht wahr? / ..., oder? / ..., gell?*

S

Aussagesatz: bejaht (+)	**Bestätigungsfrage:** verneint (–)
You are new here,	**aren't you?**
She is with you,	**isn't she?**
You've got time now,	**haven't you?**
We must stop,	**mustn't we?**
He's got your book,	**hasn't he?**
It works,	**doesn't it?**

Aussagesatz verneint (–)	**Bestätigungsfrage** bejaht (+)
You aren't from here,	**are you?**
He wasn't at home,	**was he?**
They haven't finished,	**have they?**
He hasn't got your pen,	**has he?**
They won't come,	**will they?**
It doesn't work,	**does it?**

Die Bestätigungsfrage greift das Hilfsverb und das Subjekt des Aussagesatzes wieder auf, wobei das Subjekt immer als Personalpronomen erscheint.

Steht im Aussagesatz kein Hilfsverb, wird in der Bestätigungsfrage eine Form von *do* verwendet: *do / does / did* bzw. *don't / doesn't / didn't.*

Das gleiche gilt für den verneinten Aussagesatz. Merke dir, dass in Sätzen mit Bestätigungsfragen immer ein bejahter und ein verneinter Satzteil vorhanden sein muss.

Bestätigungsfragen sprichst du mit steigender Satzmelodie (Intonation), wenn du nicht sicher bist, ob deine Aussage richtig oder falsch ist. Bist du deiner Sache sicher und erwartest keine Antwort, gehst du mit der Stimme nach unten.

12 Der *s*-Genitiv und der *of*-Genitiv – The s-genitive and the of-genitive

Lots of people all over the world enjoy **Shakespeare's** plays.

In **Shakespeare's** time boys would play the **women's** parts.

Margaret **Herrick's uncle's** name was Oscar.

Some children enjoy Mr **Bean's** videos and they like his car.

But not everybody knows the titles **of** all his plays.

Unfortunately the music **of** the plays has been lost.

And now it is the nickname **of** the famous statuette for film awards.

And did you know? The name **of** his car is 'Ben Hur'.

Wenn du noch einmal genau nachlesen willst, was es mit dem *s*-Genitiv auf sich hat, blättere zurück zu Punkt 7, Seite 166.

Der *of*-Genitiv gibt nicht den Personen-, sondern den Sachbezug, auch im Sinne von Themen- und Zeitbezug, an.

13 Unregelmäßige Plurale (Zusammenschau) – Irregular plurals

one event	–	two event**s**
a curtain	–	four curtain**s**
an activity	–	some activit**ies**
one day	–	six day**s**
a homepage	–	three homepage**s**
a bus	–	two bus**es**

Die Pluralbildung ist dir seit langem vertraut, auch die Ausspracheregeln (stimmlos / stimmhaft) und die Besonderheiten bei der Schreibung (stummes *-e* am Ende oder das *-y*).

a knife	–	some kni**ves**
a life	–	some li**ves**
one child	–	lots of child**ren**
one man	–	five m**e**n
one woman	–	some wom**e**n
one sheep	–	lots of **sheep**
one mouse	–	two **mice**

Aber es haben sich inzwischen einige weitere unregelmäßige Formen der Pluralbildung hinzugesellt. Du musst sie dir einfach gut merken.

Du weißt auch bereits, dass manche Substantive gar keine Pluralform besitzen. Mit der nachstehenden Tabelle kannst du dir einen Überblick verschaffen. Natürlich kannst du sie jederzeit erweitern.

S

Stoffe / Materialien	Charakteristika / Eigenschaften	Abstrakte Begriffe	Sonstige Begriffe
salt	safety	coolness	volleyball
oil	love	information	footwear
leather	luck	astronomy	money
rubbish	enjoyment	…	homework
…	…		…

There **is** so much **rubbish** in the playground.

Diese Substantive werden als Ganzes betrachtet und deshalb auch nur mit der Singularform des Verbs verbunden.

M

Nicht zählbare englische Substantive können im Deutschen durchaus eine Pluralform haben: *money, homework, information*. Präge dir gut ein, dass sie im Englischen nur im Singular verwendet werden.

Du kennst aber auch Substantive, die im Englischen nur in der Pluralform vorkommen. Das sind z.B. Begriffe, die Einzelteile zusammenfassen. Sie werden immer mit der Pluralform des Verbs verbunden: *trousers, shorts, jeans, sunglasses, scissors*.

Wenn du nur einen Teil von ihnen benennen willst, kannst du dir mit *a pair of* oder *some* helfen.

UNIT 3

14 Adverbien – Adverbs of manner

She is very **nice.**

Wie sind Lebewesen oder Dinge beschaffen? Welche Eigenschaften haben Sie?

Zur Beantwortung dieser Fragen, d.h. zum Beschreiben von Eigenschaften oder Zuständen wählst du immer ein Adjektiv, oft in Verbindung mit einer Form von *to be*.

She said that very **nicely.**

Wie wird etwas getan? Auf welche Weise geschieht etwas?

Zur Beantwortung dieser Fragen, d.h. zur Beschreibung von Aktivitäten, brauchst du stets ein Adverb, das immer mit einem Verb verbunden ist oder sich auf ein Verb bezieht.

1 Abgeleitete Adverbien

S

nice – nice**ly**		sudden – sudden**ly**	
stupid – stupid**ly**		silent – silent**ly**	
clear – clear**ly**		loud – loud**ly**	

Die von Adjektiven abgeleiteten Adverbien stellen die größte Gruppe dar. Die Ableitung erfolgt durch Anhängen der Endung *-ly*.

Bei einigen Ableitungen auf *-ly* musst du Schreibveränderungen beachten:

Verdoppeln des auslautenden *-l*:

careful – careful**ly**
awful – awful**ly**
usual – usual**ly**
real – real**ly**

Verwandlung von *-y* in *-i-*:

easy – eas**ily**
happy – happ**ily**
hungry – hungr**ily**

Entfallen des stummen *-e*:

possible – possi**bly**
terrible – terri**bly**

S

Adjektiv	Beispielsatz	Adverb	Beispielsatz
quick	Harry is a **quick** boy.	quickly	He gives his answers **quickly.**
loud	Your dog is so **loud.**	loudly	Why does he bark so **loudly**?
clear	Our teacher's explanations are always **clear**.	clearly	She always explains things **clearly**.

A

Kannst du die Liste fortsetzen?
Überlege dir weitere Beispiele.

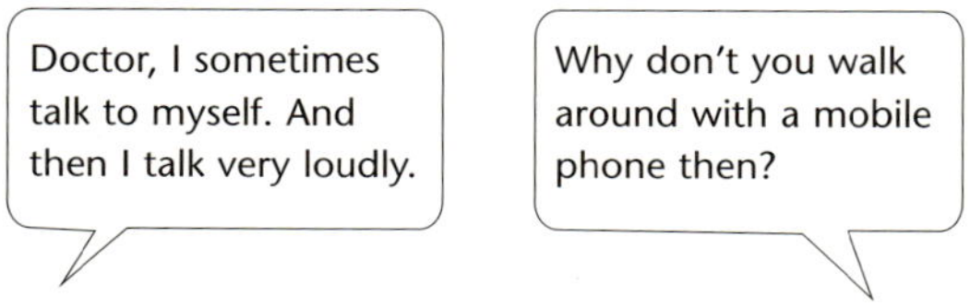

2 Nicht abgeleitete Adverbien

S

good – **well** | fast – **fast**
hard – **hard** | late – **late**

Nicht abgeleitete Adverbien gibt es natürlich auch. Du musst sie dir einfach merken.

Adjektiv	Adverb
That was **hard** work.	Yes, they worked **hard.**
Your dog is **fast!**	Yes, he can run very **fast.**
Oh, am I **late** again?	Yes, you often come **late.**

Bei *hard, fast* und *late* musst du aufpassen, weil diese Formen sowohl als Adjektive als auch als Adverbien gebraucht werden können.

She arrived **early** in the morning.
They explained it to us in a very **friendly** way.

Zu dieser Gruppe gehören auch Wörter, die bereits ein *-ly* am Ende haben: *early*. Hier sorgt die Umschreibung *in a … way* für Klarheit.

3 Steigerung der Adverbien – Comparison of adverbs

You didn't understand that?
OK, then I must explain it **more clearly**.

Jimmy writes **most clearly**.
This story is for my baby sister because she reads **more slowly** than other children.

Genau wie Adjektive, kannst du natürlich auch Adverbien steigern.

Alle abgeleiteten Adverbien werden mit *more* und *most* gesteigert.

early	earl**ier**	earl**iest**
late	late**r**	late**st**
fast	fast**er**	fast**est**

Die Steigerung aller anderen Adverbien erfolgt wie die der einsilbigen Adjektive auf *-er* und *-est*.

well	**better**	**best**
badly	**worse**	**worst**

Die Steigerungsformen zu *well* und *badly* sind mit den Steigerungen der Adjektive *good* und *bad* identisch.

15 Adjektive als Substantive – Adjectives used as nouns

First they cared for the **sick**.
(… kümmerten sich um die (alle) Kranken.)

Then came the **old** and the **young**.
(… die Alten und die Jungen.)

The **poor** were very helpful.
The **good** were all on her side.

We talked to the **rich lady**.
We want to interview the **oldest person**.

Anders als im Deutschen kannst du Adjektive nur dann als Substantive verwenden, wenn du dich ganz allgemein auf die Gesamtheit von Personengruppen beziehst.

Die substantivierten Adjektive werden wie Pluralformen behandelt, haben aber kein Plural-*s*.

Bei Einzelpersonen musst du dem Adjektiv noch ein Substantiv beifügen: *person, man, boy, girl, woman* usw.

16 Der Gebrauch des bestimmten Artikels – The use of the definite article

Der bestimmte Artikel war ursprünglich ein Demonstrativpronomen. Seine Funktion besteht darin, bestimmte Personen oder Dinge aus einer größeren Anzahl herauszuordnen.

She is interested in pop music.

Kein Artikel vor Substantiven, die allgemein gebraucht werden.

She is interested in **the** pop music of the 60s.

Hier steht der bestimmte Artikel, weil eine spezielle Popmusik gemeint ist, nämlich die der 60er Jahre.

Hier eine Übersicht über die wichtigsten Fälle.

- **the** United States, **the** Netherlands
- **the** Thames, **the** Atlantic Ocean
- in **the** west
- **The** dog is a useful animal.

Es steht immer ein bestimmter Artikel bei:

- Ländernamen im Plural,
- Flüssen und Ozeanen,
- Himmelsrichtungen,
- Tieren als Gattungsbezeichnungen.

- England, Denmark
- Oxford Street, Piccadilly Circus
- February is the second month.
  We spent Easter at home. When is lunch?
- Salt is not good for your health.
- Life can be wonderful.
- School is over.
- He's interested in History.
- +They enjoyed singing.

Kein bestimmter Artikel wird verwendet bei:

- Ländernamen im Singular,
- Straßen, Plätzen, Brücken,
- Mahlzeiten, Wochentagen, Monaten und Jahreszeiten, Ferienzeiten (allgemein),
- Substanzen, die allgemein gebraucht werden,
- abstrakten Begriffen,
- Institutionen,
- Schulfächern,
- +Gerundien.

17 Leicht zu verwechselnde Wörter (Teil II) – Easily confused words (Part II)

1 to expect – to wait – to look forward

Diese drei Verben stehen für unterschiedliche Aspekte des Wartens oder Erwartens.

We are **expecting** wonderful sunshine.

Did you **expect** the teacher or the headteacher to come first?

Das Verb *to expect* verwendest du, wenn du erwartest, dass etwas oder jemand in Kürze eintritt bzw. eintrifft.

After the landing we had **to wait for** our baggage.

I'm **waiting for** the bus. It's late.

Bei *to wait (for)* wartest du an einem bestimmten Ort darauf, dass etwas geschieht oder jemand kommt.

We would always **look forward to** our grandparents' visits.

They are **looking forward to** their trip to London.

Bei *to look forward (to)* ist Vorfreude im Spiel. Du freust dich darauf, dass in Kürze etwas geschieht oder jemand kommt.

2 between – among

Die deutsche Bedeutung beider Wörter lautet *zwischen.*

There are some farms **between** the village and the coast.

Do you want to sit **between** Harry and Jenny?

Du verwendest *between* immer dann, wenn du von zwei Dingen, Ereignissen, Personen usw. sprichst.

The reporter moved **among** the people and asked them questions.

They saw Asterix and Obelix **among** the trees.

Wenn von mehr als zwei Lebewesen oder Dingen die Rede ist, brauchst du *among.*

UNIT 4

18 Die Verlaufsform des Perfekts – The present perfect progressive

Wenn du ausdrücken möchtest, dass eine Handlung bis jetzt gedauert hat, aber noch weitergehen wird, benötigst du das *present perfect progressive*.

Mrs Modi **has been working** in the garden since nine o'clock.

Mrs Modi arbeitet (schon) seit neun Uhr im Garten (und wird wohl noch weiterarbeiten).

Die Form wird gebildet aus *have/has + been + VERBing*.

Im Deutschen kannst du das *present perfect progressive* oft mit ‚schon' wiedergeben.

19 Relativsätze – Relative clauses

The Vikings were the people **who** came in long boats.

A telephone is a thing **which** always rings when you are in the bathroom.

Wenn du von Personen sprichst oder dich auf sie beziehst, brauchst du das Relativpronomen *who*.

Bei Gegenständen und Tieren verwendest du dagegen *which*.

Bislang kanntest du *who* und *which* nur als Fragepronomen. Beide Wörter sind im Englischen gleichzeitig auch Relativpronomen. Sie stehen im Singular und Plural. Beachte, dass im Englischen kein Komma vor den Relativpronomen steht.

M

wh**i**ch	wh**o**
th**i**ngs an**i**mals	pers**o**ns pe**o**ple

Relativsätze mit *who* und *which* sind sehr wichtig. Du brauchst sie immer dann, wenn du etwas erklären, beschreiben oder näher definieren möchtest.

What do you call a Viking **that** you see riding a bike?
A biking Viking!

Du kannst *who* und *which* auch durch *that* ersetzen.

W

who — that — which

The software **that** you gave me is wonderful.

The software you gave me is wonderful.

Wenn die erwähnten Personen, Tiere oder Gegenstände im Akkusativ (wen? / was?) stehen, kannst du es dir noch einfacher machen. Das Relativpronomen kann ganz entfallen. Der Relativsatz wird verkürzt und heißt *contact clause*.

Can you hear the dog? It's our neighbours'. = *two sentences*
The dog **that** you can hear is our neighbours'. = *relative clause*
The dog you can hear is our neighbours'. = *contact clause*

20 Relativsätze mit *whose* – Relative clauses with *whose*

I'm interested in people **whose** names come from Celtic words.

Mich interessieren Personen, deren Namen von keltischen Wörtern kommen.

Bei Relativsätzen mit *whose* stehen immer Lebewesen oder Gegenstände im Mittelpunkt, denen etwas zugeordnet wird.
Im Deutschen lautet die Frage *wessen* und das entsprechende Relativpronomen *deren/dessen*.

21 Der Gebrauch des unbestimmten Artikels – The use of the indefinite article

Du weißt ja bereits, dass der unbestimmte Artikel als *a* oder *an* vorkommen kann, abhängig davon, ob du bei dem folgenden Substantiv einen Konsonanten oder einen Vokal im Anlaut hörst: *an hour.*
Beim Gebrauch des unbestimmten Artikels gibt es aber einige Unterschiede zum Deutschen, die du beachten musst.

She works as **a** teacher.
She's **an** actress.
He's **an** Englishman.

Wenn du z.B. über Berufsbezeichnungen oder Nationalitäten sprichst, brauchst du im Englischen immer den unbestimmten Artikel.

It's £8 **a** bottle.
We meet three times **a** week.

Bei Maß- und Zeiteinheiten musst du den unbestimmten Artikels ebenfalls verwenden.

What an excellent meal!
I had **such a** nice evening.

Außerdem gibt es feste Verbindungen mit *a/an*, die du dir gut einprägen solltest: *what a ..., such a ...*

22 Das substantivische Possessivpronomen – Possessive pronouns used as nouns

S

singular			*plural*		
my	–	**mine**	our	–	**ours**
you	–	**yours**	you	–	**yours**
his	–	**his** (!)	their	–	**theirs**
her	–	**hers**			

Das substantivische Possessivpronomen hat (bis auf *his*!) eigene Formen, die du dir gut merken musst.

Eine sächliche Form (für *it*) gibt es nicht.

Is that biro **mine** or **yours**?

Ist der Kuli da deiner oder meiner?

It belongs to my sister. It's **hers**.

Er gehört meiner Schwester. Es ist ihrer.

Das alleinstehende Possessivpronomen bezieht sich immer auf ein vorausgegangenes Substantiv.

My friend is in York. She is staying with **an uncle of hers.**

Meine Freundin ist in York. Sie wohnt bei einem ihrer Onkel.

Das substantivische Possessivpronomen kann auch zusammen mit *of* als Genitiv verwendet werden.
Diese Form (*double genitive*) verwendest du, wenn du z.B. ausdrücken willst, dass deine Freundin mehrere Onkel hat.

23 Leicht zu verwechselnde Wörter (Teil III) – Easily confused words (Part III)

what – which

What language did they speak?

Welche Sprache (von allen Sprachen der Welt) sprechen sie?

Du fragst nach etwas aus einer unbegrenzten oder unbestimmten Menge.

Which one would you like – the green one or the brown one?

Welches (von beiden) hättest du gern – das Grüne oder das Braune?

Du beziehst dich in deiner Frage auf eine zahlenmäßig begrenzte Menge.

24 +Das Reflexivpronomen *-self/-selves* – The reflexive pronoun *-self/-selves*

Du kannst die Verbindungen mit *-self/-selves* einfach als Vokabeln lernen. Schau dir die folgende Übersicht gut an.

S

singular				*plural*			
I	–	**myself**	*(mir/mich) selbst*	we	–	**ourselves**	*(uns) selbst*
you	–	**yourself**	*(dir/dich) selbst*	you	–	**yourselves**	*(euch) selbst*
he	–	**himself**		they	–	**themselves**	*(sich) selbst*
she	–	**herself**	*(sich) selbst*				
it	–	**itself**					

I can do it **myself.**

Ich kann das selbst.

You must help **yourselves.**

Ihr müsst euch selbst helfen.

We bought **ourselves** these CDs.
Wir kauften uns diese CDs (selbst).

Pronomen mit *-self/-selves* verwendest du auch, wenn du sagen willst, dass jemand etwas für sich selbst getan hat.

The headmaster **himself** came to talk to us.
Der Schulleiter kam selbst, um mit uns zu sprechen.

Willst du etwas besonders hervorheben, kannst du ebenfalls die Reflexivpronomen benutzen.

25 +Reflexive Verben – Reflexive verbs

Reflexive Verben kommen im Englischen weniger häufig vor als im Deutschen. Du musst aber beachten, dass es eine Anzahl von Verben gibt, die sowohl transitiv (d.h. mit einem Akkusativobjekt zusammen) als auch reflexiv (d.h. mit einem Reflexivpronomen zusammen) verwendet werden können.

transitiv	*reflexiv*
Did they enjoy **the party**?	Oh, yes. They enjoyed **themselves.**
She respects **her parents.**	But she also respects **herself.**
Poor Jimmy cut **his finger** yesterday.	Oh dear! He cut **himself** last weekend too.

He **remembers** his last birthday party.

Er erinnert sich an sein letztes Geburtstagsfest.

She **moves** very slowly because of her broken leg.

Sie bewegt sich sehr langsam wegen ihres gebrochenen Beines.

Und außerdem gibt es Verben, die im Deutschen reflexiv sind, im Englischen aber nicht. Am häufigsten werden dir in dieser Funktion die Verben *remember, meet* und *move* begegnen.

UNIT 5

26 Formen des Futurs – Future forms

Im letzten Jahr hast du bereits eine Form des Futurs kennen gelernt. Erinnerst du dich an das *going to-future*? Es gibt im Englischen aber noch andere Möglichkeiten, um zukünftige Handlungen auszudrücken. Bei bestimmten Sprechabsichten verwendest du z.B. das *will-future*.

1 S

I / you / he / she / it / we / you / they	**will** **'ll** **won't**	start tomorrow.

Das *will-future* wird aus *will* + Infinitiv gebildet. Das gilt für alle Personen. Häufig wird die Kurzform verwendet: *he will – he'll.* Die Kurzform in der Verneinung (*will not*) lautet *won't.*

2 Du kannst das *will-future* mit unterschiedlichen Absichten benutzen.

His mom **will** always be there for him.

Das *will-future* verwendest du, wenn ein fester Entschluss oder eine feste Verabredung vorliegt.

It **will** rain later in the afternoon.

We hope that the wind **won't** be too strong.

Das *will-future* benutzt du auch, wenn ein Ereignis von äußeren Umständen, z.B. vom Wetter abhängt und nicht unmittelbar beeinflusst werden kann.

I'**ll** go and get your umbrella.

I'**ll** go to Hawaii with someone else.

Wenn du spontan zu etwas bereit bist, ohne es vorher geplant zu haben, benutzt du ebenfalls das *will-future.*

3 Jetzt kennst du schon zwei Varianten zum Ausdruck zukünftiger Handlungen. Es gibt noch weitere Möglichkeiten. Welche Form du wählst, hängt immer von deiner Sprechabsicht ab. Hier alle Futurformen im Überblick:

I'm **going to** take part in the Berlin Marathon.

Mit dem *going to-future* kannst du sagen, was du vorhast oder zu tun beabsichtigst. Meist geht es dabei um ein kurzfristiges Vorhaben, das sich auf die nahe Zukunft bezieht.

Look, there's Harry with his new tennis racket. He's **going to** play tennis again.

Das *going to-future* verwendest du auch, wenn ein Ereignis mit großer Gewissheit zu erwarten ist. Es handelt sich dann um eine logische Schlussfolgerung.

The Marathon **will** start earlier this year.

Will the weather be fine on Sunday?

Das *will-future* verwendest du dagegen, wenn es weniger um deine Absicht geht, als darum, was voraussichtlich passieren wird.

I'**m running** in the Marathon in April.

Du kannst zukünftige Ereignisse auch mit der Verlaufsform des Verbs ausdrücken, wenn du eine Zeitangabe in der Zukunft hinzufügst. Du drückst damit aus, dass du etwas fest vorhast. Du bist gedanklich schon dabei, es zu tun.

Her train **arrives** at half past twelve.

Drama lesson **is** after lunch break.

Wenn etwas genau zeitlich geregelt und festgelegt ist, kannst du Zukünftiges auch mit dem *simple present* ausdrücken. Das gilt insbesondere für Fahrpläne und Stundenpläne.

S

future form	Beispiel	Sprechabsicht
1. going to + verb *(Infinitiv)*	I'**m going** to practise a new dance.	= *Absicht, etwas zu tun*
2. will + verb *(Infinitiv)*	It **will** rain tomorrow.	= *nicht beeinflussbar*
3. ing-Form + *Zeitangabe*	I'**m running** in that race next week.	= *fest eingeplant*
4. simple present	The ferry **leaves** at six o'clock.	= *fest geregelter Ablauf*

27 Bedingungssätze (Typ I) – Conditional clauses (Type I)

Ken practises indoors **when** it rains.

If it rains today, he'**ll** practise indoors.

Du kennst bereits Sätze, die aus einem *when*-Satz und einem Hauptsatz bestehen.

In einem Bedingungssatz drückt der *if-clause* die Bedingung aus und der Hauptsatz sagt, was passiert, falls diese Bedingung erfüllt wird.

S

	***if*-Satz (*simple present*)**		**Hauptsatz (*will-future*)**		
If the weather	**is**	nice tomorrow,	Ken	**will practise**	outdoors.
But **if** it	**rains,**		he	**won't go**	out.
If he	**doesn't use**	an umbrella,	he	**'ll get**	wet.

Im *if-clause* steht immer das *simple present*, während der Hauptsatz mit dem *will-future* gebildet wird. Bedingungssätze können entweder mit dem *if-clause* oder mit dem Hauptsatz beginnen.

If it doesn't rain tomorrow, he'**ll** run a race.

He'**ll** run a race **if** it doesn't rain tomorrow.

M

Zwei wichtige Regeln musst du beachten:

1. Im *if-clause* steht nie ein *will*.
2. Vor *if* steht nie ein Komma.

When Ken is in New York, he runs in Central Park. If it **is** too hot, he **stays** at home.

Wird *if* in der Bedeutung von ‚wenn' gebraucht, kann auch im Hauptsatz das *simple present* stehen.

28 ⟨Bedingungssätze (Typ II) – Conditional clauses (Type II)⟩

If I **lived** in Florida, I **would do** watersports.

Mit Bedingungssätzen vom Typ II drückst du eine Bedingung aus, über die du nachdenkst, die aber ganz offen ist. Sie kann möglicherweise eintreten, vielleicht aber auch nicht.

S

	***if*-Satz (*simple past*)**		**Hauptsatz (*would* + *infinitive*)**		
If I	**saw**	an accident,	I	**would use**	my mobile phone.
If he	**had**	a lot of money,	he	**would live**	in a bungalow.

If you didn't help me, I **would** be in trouble.

I **would** be in trouble **if** you didn't help me.

Der *if-clause* steht immer im Präteritum. Aber gemeint ist damit nicht die tatsächliche Vergangenheit, sondern die gedachte Möglichkeit. Im Hauptsatz steht immer *would* oder *wouldn't*. Wie bei Bedingungssätzen vom Typ I kann entweder der *if-clause* oder der *main clause* am Satzanfang stehen.

29 *When* oder *if*? – *When* or *if*?

When I go shopping tomorrow, I'**ll** get you a comic.

Wenn ich morgen zum Einkaufen gehe, bringe ich dir einen Comic mit.

Wenn du fest vorhast, etwas zu tun, verwendest du *when*.

If I go shopping tomorrow, I'**ll** get you a comic.

Falls ich morgen zum Einkaufen gehe, bringe ich dir einen Comic mit.

Wenn du dir nicht sicher bist, ob du etwas tun wirst, benutzt du *if*.

30 +Das *future perfect* – The future perfect

In the year 2050 NASA **will have built** more space stations.

Im Jahr 2050 wird die NASA weitere Raumstationen gebaut haben.

Das *future perfect* brauchst du, wenn du ausdrücken willst, dass eine Handlung oder ein Ereignis in der Zukunft abgeschlossen sein wird.

Next week they **will have** disappear**ed**.

Nächste Woche werden sie verschwunden sein.

Du bildest das *future perfect* mit *will* + *have* + *past participle*.

I'**ll have finished** all my e-mails **when** you pick me up.

Ich werde alle meine E-Mails fertig haben, wenn du mich abholen kommst.

Für den Zeitpunkt in der Zukunft kannst du entweder eine konkrete Zeit angeben (z.B. *in the year 2050, next month, in December*) oder du leitest den Nebensatz einfach mit *when* ein.

31 +Zeitangaben – Expressions of time

Bei Zeitangaben musst du zwischen den Präpositionen *in*, *at* und *on* unterscheiden.

in the morning / **in** the evening / **in** the afternoon
in February / **in** (the) summer /
in the year 2050

Bei *in* geht es immer um einen Zeitraum.

at quarter to six / **at** nine o'clock / **at** noon /
at Christmas

Bei *at* handelt es sich um einen Zeitpunkt.

on Monday / **on** Friday afternoon

Die Wochentage erfordern die Präposition *on*.

last week / next month

Bei *last* und *next* brauchst du überhaupt keine Präposition.

I can help you **after** dinner.
I must do that **before** seven o'clock.
He waited **until** morning.
We will check in **between** half past nine and ten o'clock.
We watched TV **from** seven **to** nine.
I haven't seen him **since** last year.
She didn't meet him **for** months.

Als weitere Präpositionen in Temporalsätzen können dir begegnen: *after, before, until/till, between, from ... to, since* oder *for* (siehe Punkt 9, Seite 168).

We left **before** the race began.
I visit her **after** school finishes.
They can't leave **until** they have repaired the car.

After, before und *until / till* können auch als Konjunktionen benutzt werden. Hier bezieht sich die Zeitangabe auf den ganzen folgenden Satzteil.

32 Leicht zu verwechselnde Wörter (Teil IV) – Easily confused words (Part IV)

to make – to do

Diese beiden Verben musst du im Englischen genau unterscheiden.

My grandma **makes** the best pancakes.
He **made** a noise.
Did she **make** a phone call?
I hope you've **made** the right decision.
Have you **made** your choice?

Bei *make* musst du daran denken, dass etwas (mit den Händen) hergestellt bzw. gemacht wird.

Das Verb *make* geht außerdem mit bestimmten Substantive eine feste Verbindung ein, z.B. mit Wörtern aus dem Bereich der Kommunikation: *comment, excuse, noise, protest, speech, remark.*

Außerdem steht *make* mit Substantiven, die mit Plänen, Absprachen und Entscheidungen zu tun haben: *plan, appointment, decision, start, choice.*

We **did** a lot of work yesterday.
I can **do** the shopping.
Did you **do** all the cleaning?
They **did** a good job.
You should **do** your homework.

Bei *do* gehst du davon aus, dass eine Handlung oder Aufgabe ausgeführt wird.

Auf *do* folgt oft ein Verb mit *-ing*: *to do the shopping.*

Viele Substantive, an die *do* gebunden ist, haben mit der Arbeitswelt zu tun: *business, cleaning, cooking, duty, exercise, homework, housework, washing, shopping, work, washing-up, job.*

UNIT 6

33 Modale Hilfsverben und ihre Ersatzformen – Modal auxiliaries and defective auxiliaries

1 Modale Hilfsverben – *Modal auxiliaries*

You **must tell** me about it.

He **needn't eat** that.

My dad **can speak** French.

Beachte, dass im Englischen – anders als im Deutschen – die modalen Hilfsverben immer zusammen mit einem Vollverb im Infinitiv stehen. Mit den Hilfsverben kannst du die unterschiedlichsten Sprechabsichten ausdrücken. Hier eine Übersicht:

He **can** play the piano.
We **couldn't** come yesterday.

Mit *can* oder *could* kannst du über ein Können oder eine Fähigkeit sprechen.

May I have a look at your book?
Can I use your pencil?

Wenn du um Erlaubnis bitten willst, brauchst du *may*. Auch *can* wird häufig in der Bedeutung von ‚dürfen' benutzt.

Would you say that again?
Can you give me that CD?
Could you help me?

Wenn du um etwas bittest, verwendest du *will, would, can* oder *could*.

Sue isn't here today. She **might** be ill.

Wenn du über Möglichkeiten sprechen willst, kannst du entweder *may, might* oder *could* benutzen.

You **should** be early next time.
You **shouldn't** say that.

Du brauchst *should*, wenn du jemandem etwas dringend raten oder empfehlen möchtest. Mit *shouldn't* kannst du dein Missfallen ausdrücken.

You **must** tell me that.
You **mustn't** wake them up.

Wenn du jemanden zu etwas auffordern willst, benutzt du *must*. Um etwas zu verbieten, brauchst du *mustn't*.

Shall I open the window?
What **shall** we do?

Mit *shall* kannst du Vorschläge machen oder um Rat bitten.

W

1. Die *modal auxiliaries* haben nur eine oder zwei Zeitformen, meistens *present* und *past tense*.
2. Bei der Verneinung werden in der Regel immer die Kurzformen verwendet (Ausnahme: *may not*).

2 Ersatzformen – *Defective auxiliaries*

Can, may und *must* haben einen kleinen Defekt. Sie heißen deshalb auch *defective auxiliaries*. Ihr Fehler ist, dass sie nicht in allen Zeitformen verwendet werden können. In manchen *tenses* muss man sie mit Ersatzverben umschreiben.

S

	present	*past*	*future*
1. *können*	can am / is / are able to	could was / were able to	– will be able to
2. *nicht können*	can't / cannot am not / isn't / aren't able to	couldn't wasn't / weren't able to	– won't be able to
3. *dürfen*	may can am / is / are allowed to	– could was / were allowed to	– – will be allowed to
4. *nicht dürfen*	may not / mustn't cannot am not / isn't / aren't allowed to	– couldn't wasn't / weren't allowed to	– – won't be allowed to
5. *müssen*	must has / have to	– had to	– will have to
6. *nicht müssen/ nicht brauchen*	needn't doesn't / don't have to	– didn't have to	won't need to won't have to
7. *sollen*	should shall I / we?	should have –	– –

A

Übertrage diese Sätze ins Englische:

1. Peter konnte nicht kommen. (2 Möglichkeiten!)
2. Er wird aber morgen kommen können.
3. Gestern durften wir Lehrer spielen.
4. Die letzte Übung brauchen wir nicht mehr zu machen.
5. Ich muss jetzt nach Hause gehen.
6. Mein Freund kann Französisch (sprechen).
7. Kann ich dein Wörterbuch haben?
8. Oh, das Telefon! Das könnte Mike sein.
9. Du solltest das wirklich nicht tun.

34 Der Infinitiv nach Fragewörtern – The infinitive after question words

They told me where I had to sit down.

They told me **where to sit** down.

Sie sagten mir, wo ich mich hinsetzen sollte.

Nebensätze mit Fragewörtern und mit *can, could, must, have to* usw. wirken oft etwas umständlich und schwerfällig. Deshalb wird häufig eine Verkürzung verwendet, die eleganter klingt: Du verbindest einfach das Fragewort mit dem Infinitiv. Im Deutschen geht das leider nicht.

A

Übertrage diese Sätze in gutes Englisch:

1. Ich wusste nicht, wie man dieses Wort ausspricht.
2. Sage ihr doch bitte, wann sie anrufen soll.
3. Ich hatte keine Idee, was ich sagen sollte.
4. Haben sie dich gefragt, wo sie hingehen müssen?

M

Merke dir:

where to …, what to …,
when to …, how to …

35 Aufforderungssätze – Orders and requests

Aufforderungssätze können beispielsweise eine Bitte, eine Einladung, eine Anweisung oder auch eine Warnung ausdrücken. Sie sind meist knapp gehalten und kommen gleich auf das Wesentliche zu sprechen.

S bejaht	verneint	*let's*
Come quickly, Tom! Telephone for you. **Stop** that noise, children!	**Don't touch** the surface of CDs! **Never drink** when you drive!	**Let's sit** down and **watch** TV together. But **let's not sit** too close to it.

Beim bejahten Imperativ benötigst du den Infinitiv des Verbs. Die Grundform des Verbs ist im Singular und Plural gleich.

Beim verneinten Imperativ benötigst du ebenfalls den Infinitiv. Du musst allerdings *don't* oder *never* ergänzen.

Wenn du dich in die Aufforderung miteinbeziehst, verwendest du *let's* oder *let's not* mit dem Infinitiv. *Let's not* kommt nur selten vor.

36 +Das *past perfect* (einfache Form) – The past perfect (simple form)

Later he found out that his neighbour **had called** the police.

When the ambulance arrived they **had made** all the preparations.

The doctor showed me the photo that he **had taken** the day before.

Wenn du über Ereignisse im Präteritum der Reihe nach berichtest, brauchst du das *past simple*. Blickst du aber von einem bestimmten Ereignis in der Vergangenheit zurück und beschreibst einen Vorgang, der vorher stattgefunden hat, brauchst du das *past perfect*. Diese Zeitform drückt aus, dass das Ereignis in der Vergangenheit, auf das du dich beziehst, bereits damals abgeschlossen war.

Das *past perfect* bildest du aus *had + past participle: had gone, had made, …*

37 +Das *past perfect* (Verlaufsform) – The past perfect (progressive form)

Wenn es eine *simple form* gibt, dann gibt es im Englischen natürlich auch eine *progressive form.*

We **had been trying** to repair it **since** we were in orbit.

They **had been waiting for** two hours when we arrived.

Wenn du im *past perfect* Zeitangaben machst, verwendest du wieder *since* (= Zeitspanne) und *for* (= Zeitpunkt).

Die Verlaufsform wird gebildet aus: *had + been + verb + ing + since/for*

UNIT 7

38 Die indirekte Rede ohne Zeitverschiebung – Reported speech without timeshift

Es gibt Situationen, in denen du weitergeben möchtest, was andere dir mitteilen oder mitgeteilt haben. Dazu brauchst du die indirekte Rede. Deine Aussage besteht in der Regel aus einem Einleitungssatz mit den Verben *say, tell* usw. und einem Folgesatz, der mit *that* eingeleitet werden kann. Die Konjunktion *that* entfällt auch häufig.

Wenn du eine Mitteilung sofort weitergibst, benutzt du im Einleitungssatz das *simple present* und behältst im Folgesatz die Zeitform der direkten Rede bei.

S

direct speech	*reported speech*
"I'm sorry."	He **says** he's sorry.
"I've missed the bus."	He **says** he's missed the bus.
"I'll be there in an hour."	He **says** he'**ll** be here in an hour.

39 Der Infinitiv nach Verben des Wünschens oder Aufforderns – The infinitive after verbs expressing wishes or commands

1 Der Infinitiv steht nach Verben, die einen Wunsch oder eine Absicht ausdrücken.

Her parents **want to go** back to India one day.

Ihre Eltern wollen eines Tages zurück nach Indien gehen.

They **expect her to join** them.

Sie erwarten, dass sie mitkommt.

Nach den Verben *want, wish, would/should like* und *expect* kann entweder der Infinitiv allein oder in Verbindung mit einem Objekt stehen.

Im Deutschen kannst du die Verbindung mit dem Objekt durch einen Nebensatz mit …, *dass* … ausdrücken.

2 Der Infinitiv steht auch nach Verben, die eine Aufforderung, einen Rat oder eine Warnung ausdrücken.

The teacher **told the class to write** a summary.

Die Lehrerin forderte die Klasse auf, eine Nacherzählung zu schreiben.

She **warned the boys not to forget** the last two exercises.

Sie warnte die Jungen, die letzten beiden Aufgaben nicht zu vergessen.

Nach den Verben *tell, ask, warn* usw. steht ebenfalls der Infinitiv in Verbindung mit einem Objekt. Mit dieser Form kannst du in der indirekten Rede Aufforderungssätze wiedergeben.

Im Deutschen bleibt in diesem Fall der Infinitiv erhalten.

40 Adverbien der Zeit und des Ortes – Adverbs of time and place

Du weißt bereits, dass es verschiedene Arten von Adverbien gibt. In Punkt 14, Seite 171 sind dir die *adverbs of manner* begegnet. Jetzt geht es um *adverbs of time* und *adverbs of place*.

1 Bei den *adverbs of time* gibt es zunächst die Adverbien der unbestimmten Zeit und Häufigkeit. Sie stehen in der Regel unmittelbar vor dem Vollverb.

We **often** miss the bus.

Sometimes we miss the bus.

There has **always** been a problem with bullies.

Zu diesen Adverbien gehören z.B. *sometimes, mostly, always, often, never, hardly, ever, soon, usually.*

Einige dieser Adverbien, z.B. *soon* und *sometimes,* können auch am Satzanfang stehen.

In Sätzen mit Hilfsverben oder Modalverben steht das Adverb immer direkt nach dem Hilfsverb bzw. Modalverb.

2 Neben den Adverbien der unbestimmten Zeit und Häufigkeit gibt es bei den *adverbs of time* auch die Adverbien der bestimmten Zeit und Häufigkeit. Die Adverbien der bestimmten Zeit können am Anfang oder Ende des Satzes stehen. Die Adverbien der bestimmten Häufigkeit findest du nur am Ende des Satzes. Beide Formen stehen nie in der Mitte des Satzes.

Yesterday we watched a good film.

They watched that film **twice.**

Last year my brother bought a new computer.

I bought my new computer **a few weeks ago.**

Zu den Adverbien der bestimmten Zeit gehören *today, yesterday, tomorrow* usw.

Adverbien der bestimmten Häufigkeit sind *daily, weekly, once, twice* usw.

Wortgruppen wie *last night, next weekend, a few weeks ago* usw. sind zusammengesetzte adverbiale Bestimmungen, die genau wie einzelne Adverbien behandelt werden. Auch sie stehen entweder am Satzanfang oder am Ende, nie aber in der Mitte.

3 Neben den Zeitadverbien kennst du auch Adverbien des Ortes. Sie stehen meist am Ende des Satzes. Manchmal findest du sie auch am Satzanfang, nie aber in der Mitte.

We heard a loud noise **outside.**

Ann met her dad **at the clothes shop**. He stood at the bus stop **every morning.**

Zu den Ortsadverbien gehören *here, there, upstairs, outside, somewhere, everywhere* usw.

Ortsangaben bestehen oft aus Wortgruppen: *in London, at the clothes shop, back home* usw. Auch sie stehen nie in der Mitte des Satzes. Treten in einem Satz sowohl Ortsadverb als auch Zeitadverb auf, steht die Zeitangabe entweder am Satzanfang oder nach der Ortsangabe.

41 +Die indirekte Rede mit Zeitverschiebung – Reported speech with timeshift

In Punkt 38, Seite 186 hast du die indirekte Rede ohne Zeitverschiebung kennen gelernt. Wenn du eine Mitteilung nicht sofort weitergibst, sondern erst später darüber berichten willst, verwendest du ebenfalls die indirekte Rede. Du musst allerdings zusätzlich die Rückverschiebung der Zeitformen berücksichtigen.

S

direct speech	*reported speech*
"I can't make it."	She said she couldn't make it.
"I may get into trouble."	He told us (that) he might get into trouble.

1 Der Einleitungssatz steht bei einer späteren Berichterstattung immer im Präteritum: *He said … / She told … / They informed …* usw. In dem Folgesatz musst du jetzt die Zeitformen der Verben verändern. Hier tritt eine Rückverschiebung der Zeiten (*backshift of tenses*) auf. Schau dir die folgende Übersicht genau an.

S

present / going to-future	***simple past***
They **make** a lot of money.	He **told** us that they **made** a lot of money.
We'**re going to have** a party on Friday.	She **said** that they **were going to have** a party on Friday.
present perfect	***past perfect***
She **has accepted** their invitation.	She **told** us that she **had accepted** their invitation.
The boy **has checked** the prices.	The boy **mentioned** that he **had checked** the prices.
simple past	***past perfect***
My parents **never went** to London.	She **told** us that her parents **had never gone** to London.
My brother **didn't do** well at school.	He **said** that his brother **had not done** well at school.
⟨***will-future***	***conditional II***⟩
My mum **will make** me a beautiful dress.	She **told** us that her mother **would make** her a beautiful dress.
I **won't follow** fashions blindly.	He **said** that he **wouldn't follow** fashions blindly.

2 Bei der Rückverschiebung der Zeitformen musst du nicht nur auf die Verben, sondern auch auf die Pronomen sowie die Zeit- und Ortsangaben achten.

S

direct speech	*reported speech*
"My mum **didn't give** me enough money **today**."	She **said** her mother **hadn't given** her enough money **that day**.
"I **can't understand** why jeans are so expensive **here**."	He **remarked** that he **couldn't understand** why jeans were so expensive **there**.

M

today	–	that day
yesterday	–	the day before
tomorrow	–	the next / following day
tonight	–	that night
this week	–	that week
last Monday	–	the Monday before
next month	–	the next / following month
here	–	there

Damit du dich in deinen Mitteilungen nicht immer wiederholen musst, solltest du möglichst viele verschiedene Verben zur Einleitung der indirekten Rede parat haben: *say, tell, ask, whisper, inform, remark, mention, fax, shout, answer, order, write down* usw.

42 +Fragen in der indirekten Rede – Questions in reported speech

Bei der Wiedergabe von Fragen in der indirekten Rede musst du berücksichtigen, ob in der direkten Rede ein Fragewort vorhanden ist oder nicht.

S

direct speech	*reported speech*
"**Where** were your grandparents?"	He asked me **where** my grandparents **had been**.
"Did you buy that last week?"	She asked me **whether** I had bought it the week before.

Gibt es ein Fragewort, treten Hilfsverb und Verb an das Satzende. In Entscheidungsfragen, die mit *yes* oder *no* beantwortet werden können und kein Fragewort enthalten, wird der Nebensatz entweder mit *whether* oder mit *if* eingeleitet.

43 +Verben mit zwei Objekten – Verbs with two objects

Es gibt eine Reihe von Verben, die die Beziehung zwischen Menschen und deren gemeinsamem Handeln thematisieren: *give, pay, make, buy, lend, send, show, teach, tell, write* usw.

Diese Verben können zwei Objekte haben, ein direktes Objekt (meist eine Sachbezeichnung) und ein indirektes Objekt (meist eine Personenbezeichnung). Über die Stellung der Objekte im Satz entscheidet deren Länge bzw. die Tatsache, welches der Objekte du besonders hervorheben möchtest. Das Objekt, das hervorgehoben werden soll, steht immer am Satzende.

She showed her parents **the new dress.**	Hier geht es um das Kleid, das gezeigt wird. Es steht als direktes Objekt am Satzende.
She showed the new dress **to her parents.**	Hier geht es darum, dass das Kleid den Eltern (und nicht irgend jemandem) gezeigt wird. Wenn du das indirekte Objekt betonen möchtest, stellst du es mit der Präposition *to* an das Satzende. Das direkte Objekt steht in diesem Fall vor dem indirekten Objekt.

A Wie kannst du diese Sätze ins Englische übertragen?

1. Er hat seiner Großmutter ein Fax geschickt. (keinen Brief)
2. Sie zeigten die Fotos ihren Freunden. (nicht ihren Eltern)
3. Kannst du dieses Buch deiner Schwester geben? (nicht deinem Bruder)
4. Mein Onkel hat mir ein neues Modem geschickt. (keinen Drucker)

UNIT 8

44 Passiv und Aktiv – Passive and active voice

The boy **checks** the batteries.	In diesem Aktivsatz ist der Junge der aktiv Handelnde. Er ist das Subjekt des Satzes, steht im Mittelpunkt der Aussage und deshalb am Satzanfang.
The batteries **are checked** every month.	Hier wird betont, dass die Batterien jeden Monat überprüft werden, egal von wem. Die Batterien stehen im Mittelpunkt des Satzes und rücken als Subjekt an den Satzanfang. Es handelt sich um einen Passivsatz.

Passivsätze werden mit einer Form von *to be* und dem *past participle* gebildet: *are checked.*
Das Objekt des Aktivsatzes (*... the batteries.*) wird zum Subjekt des Passivsatzes (*The batteries are ...*)
Passivsätze können in verschiedenen Zeitformen vorkommen. Hier eine Übersicht:

S

	Präsens	Präteritum	present perfect	past perfect	Futur
be	am / is / are	was / were	has / have been	had been	will be

The passive **is made** with a form of *to be.* The radio **was checked** last week. Oh dear! My bike **has been pushed** over. A lot of work **will be done.**	Passivsätze findet man häufig in Zeitungsberichten, historischen Texten, Polizeiprotokollen oder technischen Beschreibungen. Die Verursacher der Handlungen sind nicht mehr (= historisch) oder noch nicht (= polizeilich) bekannt. Oder sie sind einfach nicht wichtig.

In der *simple form* können alle Zeitformen des Aktivs auch im Passiv gebildet werden:

Hundreds of tornadoes **are counted** every year.	Präsens: *am / is / are*
Hundreds of people **were** badly **injured**.	Präteritum: *was / were*
The bottled water **has** already **been checked**.	*present perfect: has / have been*
+Before the tornado hit, the people **had been warned** by radio.	+*past perfect: had been*
A lot of houses **are going to be damaged**.	*going to-future: am / is / are going to be*
The houses **will be repaired** after the tornado.	*will-future: will be*
+**Will** the damage **have been forgotten** soon?	+*future perfect: will have been*

The damage **can't be repaired** easily.

A lot of work **must be done**.

People **should be warned**.

Nach den Modalverben *can, must, should* usw. werden die Passivformen mit dem Infinitiv von *be + past participle* gebildet.

Lots of dead animals **are being collected** at the moment.

The roads **were being repaired**, so they took a different route.

Die Verlaufsformen des Passivs sind nur im Präsens und Präteritum üblich.

45 Passiv mit *by-agent* – The passive voice with by-agent

Wenn in einem Passivsatz die Nennung des Verursachers einer Handlung erforderlich ist, kannst du ihn mit der Präposition *by* am Satzende anfügen (*by-agent*).

S

active voice			*passive voice*		
Subjekt		**Objekt**	**Subjekt**		***by-agent***
Our dog	bit	the postman.	The postman	was bitten	**by our dog.**

In dem Beispiel ist die Nennung des Verursachers erforderlich, da deutlich gemacht werden muss, dass unser Hund (und nicht irgend ein Hund oder gar eine Schlange) den Briefträger gebissen hat. Du musst folglich immer entscheiden, ob die Nennung des Verursachers in einem Passivsatz erforderlich ist.

Stonehenge was built thousands of years ago.

Die Angabe des *by-agent* ist hier nicht erforderlich. Da wir die Erbauer von Stonehenge nicht kennen, brauchen wir sie auch nicht zu benennen.

In 1996 the American east coast was hit **by hurricane Bertha.**

Die Angabe des *by-agent* ist in diesem Beispiel dagegen erforderlich. Es war ein bestimmter Wirbelsturm, der den Schaden im Jahr 1996 angerichtet hat. Er hat sogar einen eigenen Namen.

46 Das Reflexivpronomen *-self/-selves* und seine Verbindungen – The reflexive pronoun *-self/-selves* and its compounds

Über das Reflexivpronomen *-self/-selves* wurde bereits unter Punkt 24, Seite 177 ausführlich gesprochen. Schau dir die Übersicht dort gut an. Denke daran, dass nicht jedes Verb, das im Deutschen reflexiv ist, auch im Englischen mit einem Reflexivpronomen verbunden werden kann.

Kate and Terry are looking at **themselves.**

Kate und Terry schauen sich (selbst) an.

Kate and Terry are looking at **each other**.

Kate und Terry schauen sich (gegenseitig) an.

Verwechsele *-self/-selves* nicht mit *each other*. Das Reflexivpronomen bezieht sich immer auf das Subjekt zurück, während bei *each other* immer zwei Personen oder Lebewesen etwas gegenseitig tun.

47 +Die Vergangenheit (Zusammenschau) – The past tense

1 *Present perfect*

He **has hurt** himself badly. She's at the hospital with him now.

Wenn du über eine Handlung sprichst, die bereits geschehen ist, deren genauer Zeitpunkt aber nicht von Interesse ist, verwendest du das *present perfect*. Im Mittelpunkt stehen die Ergebnisse der Handlung.

They **haven't received** the results of the blood tests yet.

Das *present perfect* verwendest du auch, wenn du über eine Handlung sprichst, die immer noch andauert.

They**'ve** already **arrived**.

Das *present perfect* brauchst du auch, wenn du über Neuigkeiten berichtest, deren Ergebnis in der Gegenwart zu sehen ist.

Die Signalwörter *ever, never, already* usw. in Verbindung mit dem *present perfect* bezeichnen eine Zeitspanne, die von der Vergangenheit bis in die Gegenwart reicht.

2 *Present perfect progressive*

She **has been working** in the garden **since** lunch time.

Wenn du über eine Handlung berichtest, die bis in die Gegenwart dauert und du die Zeitangabe *since* oder *for* ergänzt, verwendest du das *present perfect progressive.* In diesem Fall ist die Dauer der Handlung wichtiger als das Ergebnis.

3 ***Simple past***

We **went** to the concert last night.

We **left** the theatre and **met** a good friend of ours.

We **looked** for a restaurant to have lunch together.

Das *simple past* brauchst du, wenn du über eine in der Vergangenheit abgeschlossene Handlung berichtest.

Das *simple past* ist die Erzählzeit im Englischen. Wenn du eine zusammenhängende Geschichte erzählen willst, benutzt du diese Zeitform. Oft wird das *simple past* mit dem *past progressive* oder dem *past perfect* zusammen verwendet.

Signalwörter des *simple past* (*last week, two hours ago, after dinner* usw.) sind alle konkreten Zeitangaben.

4 ***Past progressive***

They **were sitting** in the garden when the tornado started.

Das *past progressive* verwendest du, wenn du eine Hintergrundhandlung beschreibst. Das Ereignis, das plötzlich einsetzt, ist wichtiger als die bereits andauernde Handlung.

5 ***Past perfect***

After they **had finished** their homework, they went into the garden.

Mit dem *past perfect* kannst du deutlich machen, welche von mehreren Handlungen zuerst geschah. Beide Handlungen sind in der Vergangenheit bereits beendet.

6 ***Past perfect progressive***

They **had been hiding** in their house **for** two hours when the tornado moved on.

Wenn du den Zeitpunkt betonen willst, bis zu dem eine Handlung in der Vergangenheit gedauert hat, oder die Zeitspanne angeben möchtest, in der ein Ereignis stattgefunden hat, verwendest du das *past perfect progressive*.

Grammar exercises

1 1. Was your sister in London last week? – No, she wasn't. / 2. My friends weren't at home three days ago. / 3. I wasn't at school last Monday. / 4. You weren't at home when I phoned you yesterday. Where were you?

3 1. We left early in the morning. / 2. We all wore our old jeans. / 3. Maike forgot her mobile phone. / 4. Kevin bought the tickets. / 5. Liz walked behind him.

6 Lösungsvorschlag: We love cycling. Cycling keeps you fit. / She hates cooking. Cooking is boring. / They enjoy riding. Riding is fun. / He doesn't like walking. Walking is terrible.

8 1. Bring your workbooks, please. / 2. I can't carry the cello on my back. / 3. Can you take/bring the keyboard into the living-room?

33 1. Peter couldn't come. Peter wasn't able to come. / 2. But he'll be able to come tomorrow. / 3. Yesterday we were allowed to play teacher. / 4. We needn't do the last exercise. /5. I must go home now. / 6. My friend can speak French. / 7. Can I have your dictionary? / 8. Oh, the phone! It might be Mike. / 9. You really shouldn't do that.

34 1. I didn't know how to pronounce this word. / 2. Please tell her when to phone. / 3. I had no idea what to say. / 4. Did they ask you where to go?

43 1. He sent his grandmother a fax. / 2. They showed the photos to their friends. / 3. Can you give this book to your sister? / 4. My uncle has sent me a new modem.

Grammar list

German / Latin	English	Example	Number
Adjektive als Substantive	adjectives as nouns	The **poor** were very helpful.	15
Adverbien	adverbs of manner	She said that very **nicely**.	14
– abgeleitete Adverbien	– *-ly* adverbs	He gives his answers **quickly.**	
– nicht abgeleitete Adverbien	– adverbs same as adjectives	Your dog can run very **fast.**	
– Steigerung der Adverbien	– comparison of adverbs	You must explain it **more** clearly.	
– der Zeit und des Ortes	– adverbs of time and place	We **often** miss the bus.	40
Apostroph	apostrophe	I'**m** / I'**d** / the boys'	7
Artikel	article		
– Gebrauch des bestimmten Artikels	– use of the definite article	**the** United States, **the** west	16
– Gebrauch des unbestimmten Artikels	– use of the indefinite article	She works as **a** teacher. We meet three times **a** week.	21
Aufforderungssätze	commands and requests	**Come** quickly! **Let's** go!	35
Bedingungssätze	conditional sentences		
– Typ I	– type I	**If** it rains, he'**ll** practise indoors.	27
– ⟨Typ II⟩	– type II	**If** I lived in Florida, I **would** do watersports.	28
Bestätigungsfragen	question tags	She is with you, **isn't she?** He isn't at home, **is he?**	11
Formen des Futurs	forms of the future		26
– *will*-Futur	– will-future	It **will** rain later in the afternoon.	
– *going to*-Futur	– going to-future	He's **going to** take part in the race.	
– Verlaufsform im Präsens	– present progressive	She's **running** in the Marathon in May.	
– Präsens (einfache Form)	– simple present	The train **arrives** at half past twelve.	
+*Future perfect*	+future perfect	Next week they **will have gone**.	30
+Gerundium	+gerund	**Sailing** is fun.	6
Indirekte Rede	reported speech		
– ohne Zeitverschiebung	– without timeshift	He **says** he's missed the bus.	38
– +mit Zeitverschiebung	– +with timeshift	She **said** she couldn't make it.	41
– +Fragen in der indirekten Rede	– +questions in reported speech	He **asked** me **where** we had been.	42
Infinitiv	infinitive		
– nach Fragewörtern *where to / what to / how to / when to*	– after question words *where to / what to / how to / when to*	They told me **where to** sit down. I don't know **what to** do.	36
– nach Verben des Wünschens oder Aufforderns	– after verbs expressing wishes and commands	They **expect her to** join them. She **warned them not to** forget the last exercise.	39
Leicht zu verwechselnde Wörter	Easily confused words		
– Teil I: *bring – take / wear – carry*	– Part I: *bring – take / wear – carry*	Did you **take** her to the station? She **wore** her new trainers.	8
– Teil II: *expect – wait (for) – look forward (to) / between – among*	– Part II: *expect – wait (for) – look forward (to) / between – among*	Have you been **waiting for** me? We are **looking forward to** your visit. Do you want to sit **between** them?	17
– Teil III: *what – which*	– Part III: *what – which*	**What** language did they speak?	23
– Teil IV: *make – do*	– Part IV: *make – do*	Have you **made** your choice?	32

German / Latin	English	Example	Number
Modale Hilfsverben – Ersatzformen *be able to / be allowed to / have to*	modal auxiliaries – substitutes *be able to / be allowed to / have to*	He wasn't **allowed to** come. They **have to** go now.	33
of-Genitiv und *s*-Genitiv	*of*-genitive and *s*-genitive	The music **of** the plays has been lost. We love Shakespeare**'s** plays.	12
Passiv und Aktiv – mit *by-agent*	passive and active voice – passive voice with by-agent	The batteries **are checked** every week. The postman was bitten **by** our dog.	44 45
+*Past perfect* – einfache Form – Verlaufsform	+past perfect – simple form – progressive form	He showed me the photo he **had taken** the day before. / They **had been waiting** for two hours.	36 37
Perfekt – mit *since* und *for* – und *simple past*	present perfect – and simple past – with *since* and *for*	**Have you** ever **seen** that film? Yes, we **saw** it last week. I haven't talked to her **since** last week.	10 9
Präteritum (einfache Form) – von *to be* – regelmäßige Formen – unregelmäßige Formen – Frage und Verneinung im *simple past* mit *did/didn't* – und *present perfect*	simple past – of *to be* – regular forms – irregular forms – questions and negative sentences with *did/didn't* – and present perfect	Yesterday it **was** really cold. We **listened** to some music. I **woke** up early this morning. **Did** you often go to carnivals? No, we **didn't**. I **haven't had** an ice cream today. Oh, we **had** one after lunch.	1 2 3 4 10
Reflexive Verben	reflexive verbs	I **remember** his last birthday party.	25
Reflexivpronomen *-self / -selves*	reflexive pronouns *-self / -selves*	He cut **himself.** You must help **yourselves.**	24, 46
Relativsätze – mit *whose*	relative clauses – with *whose*	The Vikings were the people **who** came in long boats.	19 20
s-Genitiv und *of*-Genitiv	*s*-genitive and *of*-genitive	We enjoyed Shakespeare**'s** plays.	12
Substantivisches Possessivpronomen	possessive pronouns used as nouns	That book belongs to Ann. It's **hers**. She's **a friend of ours**.	22
Unregelmäßige Plurale der Substantive (Zusammenschau)	irregular plurals of nouns	activit**ies** / kni**ves** / child**ren** / **sheep**	13
+Verben mit zwei Objekten	+verbs with two objects	She showed **her friend the new CD**.	43
+Vergangenheit (Zusammenschau)	past tenses	He **has hurt** himself badly. We **went** to the concert last night.	47
Verlaufsform des Perfekts	present perfect progressive	She **has been working** in the garden since nine o'clock.	18
Verlaufsform des Präteritums	past progressive	What **were** you **doing**?	5
When oder *if*?	*when* or *if*?	**If** I go shopping, I'll buy a comic. **When** I go shopping, I'll buy a comic.	29
+Zeitangaben	+expressions of time	He waited **until** his mother came.	31

Homeless by Paul Simon and Ladysmith Black Mambazo *(page 57)*

Emaweni
Webaba silale maweni *(repeated)*

Homeless, homeless,
Moonlight sleeping on a midnight lake
Homeless, homeless,
Moonlight sleeping on a midnight lake
We are homeless, we are homeless,
The moonlight sleeping on a midnight lake
And we are homeless, homeless, homeless,
The moonlight sleeping on a midnight lake

Zio Yami, zio yami, nhlizio yami
Nhlizio yami amakhaza asengi bulele
Nhlizio yami, nhlizio yami
Nhlizio yami, angibulele amakhaza
Nhlizio yami, nhlizio yami
Nhlizio yami somandla angibulele mama
Zio yami, nhlizio yami
Nhlizio yami, nhlizio yami

Too loo loo, too loo loo *(repeated)*

Strong wind, destroy our home,
Many dead, tonight it could be you
Strong wind, destroy our home,
Many dead, tonight it could be you
And we are homeless, homeless, homeless ...
(etc.)

Somebody say ih hih ih hih ih
Somebody sing hello, hello, hello
Somebody say ih hih ih hih ih
Somebody cry why, why, why?
(repeated)

Yitho omanqoba (ih hih ih hih ih)
Yitho omanqoba
Esanquoba lonke ilizwe (ih hih ih hih ih)
Yitho omanqoba (ih hih ih hih ih)
Esanquoba phakathi e England
Yitho omanqoba
Esanquoba phakathi e London
Yitho omanqoba
Esanquoba phakathi e England

Somebody say ... *(etc.)*

Kuluman,
Kulumani, kulumani sizwe
Singenze njani
Baya jabula absai thando yo
Ho

Dictionary

In dieser alphabetischen Liste ist das gesamte Vokabular von **Swift 1** und **2** enthalten.
Namen werden in gesonderten Listen am Ende dieses *Dictionary* aufgeführt.
Mit ° versehene Wörter sind rezeptiv, Einträge in ⟨ ⟩ fakultativ.
Ein + vor dem Eintrag bedeutet, dass das Wort zum Wortschatz in *Track* 2 gehört.
Die Belegstelle nach den Einträgen bezieht sich auf das erstmalige Vorkommen der Wörter:

accent ['æksnt] Akzent **II 4**, 63 = **Swift 2**, *Unit* 4, Seite 63

A

a, an [ə, ən] ein/eine **I**
a bit [ə 'bɪt] ein wenig, ein bisschen **I**
a couple *(of)* ['kʌpl‿əv] ein paar **II 5**, 72
(*a*) few [fju:] wenige, ein paar **I**
a lot [ə 'lɒt] viel, eine Menge **I**
+**ability** [ə'bɪləti] Fähigkeit **II 6**, 100
to be **able to** ['eɪbl tə] fähig sein, in der Lage sein **II 6**, 92
Australian **aborigine** [ɒs'treɪliən ˌæbə'rɪdʒni] australische(r) Ureinwohner(in) **II 4**, 59
about [ə'baʊt] über (etw), von (etw) **I**; ungefähr, etwa **I**
to be about [ə'baʊt] sich handeln um **II 3**, 41
to talk *(about)* ['tɔ:k‿əˌbaʊt] sprechen, reden (über) **I**
What about ...? [ˌwɒt‿ə'baʊt] Was ist mit ...? **I**
absolute [ˌæbsə'lu:t] völlig, absolut **II 7**, 112
academy [ə'kædəmi] Akademie **II 2**, 29
accent ['æksnt] Akzent **II 4**, 63
to **accept** [ək'sept] annehmen, akzeptieren **II 5**, 80
accident ['æksɪdnt] Unfall **I**
accommodation [əˌkɒmə'deɪʃn] Unterkunft, Hotelzimmer, Übernachtung **I**
accordion [ə'kɔ:diən] Akkordeon **II 2**, 24
stomach **ache** ['stʌmək‿eɪk] Magenschmerzen **II 8**, 130
achievement [ə'tʃi:vmənt] Leistung, Errungenschaft **II 2**, 29
across [ə'krɒs] über, durch, darüber **I**
°**acrostic** [ə'krɒstɪk] Akrostichon (nacheinander zu lesende Buchstaben, die ein Wort ergeben) **I**
act [ækt] Akt, Aufzug **I**
to **act** [ækt] darstellen, vorführen **I**
action ['ækʃn] Aktion, Handlung **I**
activity [æk'tɪvəti] Aktivität, Tätigkeit **I**
actor ['æktə] Schauspieler **I**
supporting actor [səˌpɔ:tɪŋ‿'æktə] Schauspieler in einer Nebenrolle **II 2**, 30
actress ['æktrəs] Schauspielerin **II 2**, 28
actually ['æktʃuəli] tatsächlich, wirklich **II 3**, 44
AD (= **Anno Domini**) [ˌeɪ'di:] nach Christus **II 3**, 46
to **add** [æd] hinzufügen, addieren **I**
address [ə'dres] Adresse **I**
administrator [əd'mɪnɪstreɪtə] Verwalter(in), Leiter(in) **II 4**, 61
+to **adore** [ə'dɔ:] anbeten, sehr gern haben **I**
adventure [əd'ventʃə] Abenteuer **I**
to **advertise** ['ædvətaɪz] werben, ankündigen **II 3**, 51
ad (**advertisement**) [əd (ə'vɜ:tɪsmənt)] Anzeige **I**
advertising ['ædvətaɪzɪŋ] Werbung, Reklame **II 7**, 110
advice [əd'vaɪs] Rat(schlag), Empfehlung **II 5**, 81
aerobics [eə'rəʊbɪks] Aerobic, rhythmische Gymnastik **II 5**, 72
to be **afraid** [ə'freɪd] sich fürchten, Angst haben **I**
African ['æfrɪkən] afrikanisch, Afrikanisch **II 4**, 57
after ['ɑ:ftə] nach **I**
after all [ˌɑ:ftə‿'ɔ:l] schließlich, letztendlich **I**
to look after [ˌlʊk‿'ɑ:ftə] schauen nach, sorgen für **I**
afternoon [ˌɑ:ftə'nu:n] Nachmittag **I**
again [ə'gen] wieder **I**
against [ə'genst] gegen **I**
age [eɪdʒ] Alter **I**
iron age ['aɪən‿ˌeɪdʒ] Eisenzeit **II 3**, 43
agency ['eɪdʒntsi] Geschäftsstelle, Büro, Agentur **II 7**, 107
travel **agent** ['trævl ˌeɪdʒnt] Reisebüroangestellte(r) **II 4**, 60
aggressive [ə'gresɪv] aggressiv, feindselig **II 6**, 90
ago [ə'gəʊ] vor *(zeitlich)* **II 2**, 26
how long ago? [ˌhaʊ lɒŋ‿ə'gəʊ] wie lange her? **II 3**, 45
to **agree** [ə'gri:] zustimmen **I**
ahead [ə'hed] voran, voraus **II 5**, 79
ahead of time [əˌhed‿əv 'taɪm] im Voraus **II 8**, 124
first **aid** [ˌfɜ:st‿'eɪd] Erste Hilfe **II 2**, 27
air [eə] Luft **II 1**, 14
airmail ['eəmeɪl] Luftpost **II 3**, 45
airport ['eəpɔ:t] Flughafen **I**
⟨**album**⟩ ['ælbəm] Album **II 2**, 32
alcohol ['ælkəhɒl] Alkohol **I**
+**alien** ['eɪliən] Ausländer(in), Fremde(r) **I**
all [ɔ:l] alle(s) **I**
after all [ˌɑ:ftə‿'ɔ:l] schließlich, letztendlich **I**
(*not*) after all [ˌɑ:ftə‿'ɔ:l] doch (nicht) **I**
all over ['ɔ:l‿əʊvə] überall (in) **II 1**, 16
all right [ɔ:l 'raɪt] in Ordnung **I**
all-round fitness [ˌɔ:lraʊnd 'fɪtnəs] Rundum-Fitness **II 5**, 72
all the time [ˌɔ:l ðə 'taɪm] die ganze Zeit **II 1**, 12
all the year round [raʊnd] das ganze Jahr über **II 1**, 8
not ... at all [ˌnɒt‿ə'tɔ:l] überhaupt nicht **I**
+**alleged** [ə'ledʒd] angeblich **II 6**, 100
alligator ['ælɪgeɪtə] Alligator **II 8**, 125
to be **allowed to** [ə'laʊd tʊ] dürfen **II 5**, 78
almost ['ɔ:lməʊst] fast, beinahe **II 2**, 26
along [ə'lɒŋ] entlang, längs **I**
Come along! ['kʌm‿əˌlɒŋ] Komm schon! **II 1**, 14
aloud [ə'laʊd] laut **I**
alphabet ['ælfəbet] Alphabet **I**
already [ɔ:l'redi] schon, bereits **I**
also ['ɔ:lsəʊ] auch, ebenfalls **I**
+**although** [ɔ:l'ðəʊ] obwohl, obgleich **II 5**, 84
always ['ɔ:lweɪz] immer **I**
am [æm] bin **I**
I'm (*I am*) [aɪm] ich bin **I**

amazement [ə'meɪzmənt] Erstaunen, Verblüffung **II 6**, 95
ambitious [æm'bɪʃəs] ehrgeizig **II 5**, 73
⟨**ambulance**⟩ ['æmbjələns] Krankenwagen **II 5**, 77
+**American** [ə'merɪkən] amerikanisch, Amerikaner(in) **I**
Native **American** [ˌneɪtɪv‿ə'merɪkən] amerikanische(r) Ureinwohner(in) **II 4**, 59
among [ə'mʌŋ] zwischen, unter **I**
°**amplifier** ['æmplɪfaɪə] Verstärker **I**
amputation [ˌæmpjə'teɪʃn] Amputation **II 8**, 122
anaesthetic [ˌænəs'θetɪk] Betäubungsmittel, Narkose **II 8**, 122
and [ænd/ənd] und **I**
Angles ['æŋglz] (die) Angeln **II 4**, 58
angry ['æŋgri] wütend, ärgerlich **I**
animal ['ænɪml] Tier **I**
ankle ['æŋkl] Knöchel, Fußgelenk **II 8**, 128
AD (= **Anno Domini**) [ˌeɪ'di:] nach Christus **II 3**, 46
announcement [ə'naʊnsmənt] Ankündigung, Ansage **II 5**, 79
annual ['ænjuəl] jährlich, Jahres- **I**
anorexic [ˌænər'eksɪk] magersüchtig **II 7**, 107
another [ə'nʌðə] ein(e) andere(r/s) **I**; +ein(e) weitere(r/s) **I**
answer ['ɑ:nsə] Antwort **I**
to **answer** ['ɑnsə] antworten **I**
antibiotic [ˌæntɪbaɪ'ɒtɪk] Antibiotikum **II 8**, 122
antique [æn'ti:k] Antik-, Antiquitäten **I**
°**antonym** ['æntənɪm] Antonym **II 8**, 133
any ['eni] irgendeine(r/s), etwas **I**
any time [ˌeni 'taɪm] jederzeit **I**
not ... any more [ˌnɒt ... ˌeni 'mɔ:] (überhaupt) nicht mehr, keine ... mehr **II 1**, 16
anybody ['enibɒdi] irgendjemand **I**
anyone ['eniwʌn] irgendjemand **I**
anything ['eniθɪŋ] etwas **I**
anyway ['eniweɪ] ohnehin, sowieso **I**
anywhere ['eniweə] irgendwohin **I**
to **appear** [ə'pɪə] erscheinen, auftauchen **II 7**, 114
appearance [ə'pɪərnts] Erscheinen, Auftauchen **II 6**, 90
apple ['æpl] Apfel **II 5**, 76
application [ˌæplɪ'keɪʃn] Bewerbungsschreiben **II 3**, 45
to **apply** (*to*) [ə'plaɪ] (sich) wenden (an) **I**
to **approach** [ə'prəʊtʃ] sich (an)nähern (an) **II 3**, 44
April ['eɪprl] April **I**
aquarium [ə'kweəriəm] Aquarium **I**
are [ɑ:] sind **I**
aren't (*are not*) [ɑ:nt] sind nicht **I**
area ['eəriə] Gebiet, Region, Areal **I**
argument ['ɑ:gjəmənt] Argument; Streit, Auseinandersetzung **II 3**, 49
arm [ɑ:m] Arm **I**
army ['ɑ:mi] Armee, Heer **II 4**, 59
around [ə'raʊnd] um ... herum; umher **I**
to **arrest** [ə'rest] festnehmen, verhaften **II 8**, 133
+to get **arrested** [ˌget‿ə'restɪd] festgenommen werden, verhaftet werden **II 3**, 50
arrival [ə'raɪvl] Ankunft **I**
to **arrive** [ə'raɪv] ankommen **II 1**, 15
art [ɑ:t] Kunst **II 2**, 29
°Art [ɑ:t] Kunst (*Fach*) **I**
article ['ɑ:tɪkl] (Zeitungs-)Artikel **I**
+**artist** ['ɑ:tɪst] Künstler(in) **I**
as [æz/əz] wie **II 1**, 11; als, während **II 6**, 95
as ... as [æz/əz] (eben)so ... wie **I**
as well as [əz 'wel‿əz] sowie, sowohl als auch **II 3**, 46
such as ['sʌtʃ‿əz] wie zum Beispiel **II 8**, 124
to **ask** [ɑ:sk] fragen **I**
to ask so. to do sth. [ɑ:sk] jmdn. bitten, etw. zu tun **II 3**, 43
to be **asleep** [ə'sli:p] schlafen **II 3**, 45
to fall asleep [ˌfɔ:l‿ə'sli:p] einschlafen **II 4**, 62
aspect ['æspekt] Gesichtspunkt, Aspekt **II 7**, 107
assembly [ə'sembli] (Schul-)Versammlung **I**
assembly hall [ə'sembli ˌhɔ:l] Aula, Versammlungssaal **I**
+**assistant** [ə'sɪstnt] Assistent(in), Mitarbeiter(in) **II 7**, 115
astronaut ['æstrənɔ:t] Astronaut(in) **II 6**, 92
astronomer [ə'strɒnəmə] Astronom(in) **II 6**, 92
astronomy [ə'strɒnəmi] Astronomie **I**
at [æt/ət] an/am, in/im, bei **I**
at home [ət‿'həʊm] zu Hause, daheim **I**
+at last [ət 'lɑ:st] endlich **II 6**, 100
at least [ət 'li:st] zumindest **II 7**, 110
at the moment ['məʊmənt] im Moment, zur Zeit **I**
to go at so. ['gəʊ ˌət] auf jmdn losgehen **II 1**, 15
athlete ['æθli:t] Leichtathlet(in), Sportler(in) **II 5**, 78
athletics [æθ'letɪks] Leichtathletik **II 5**, 78
atmosphere ['ætməsfɪə] Atmosphäre **I**
attack [ə'tæk] Angriff **II 4**, 58
heart attack ['hɑ:t‿əˌtæk] Herzinfarkt **I**
to **attack** [ə'tæk] angreifen **II 6**, 96
to **attend** [ə'tend] beiwohnen, besuchen **II 2**, 29
+to pay **attention** [ˌpeɪ‿ə'tentʃn] aufmerksam sein, achtsam sein **I**
to draw* attention to [ˌdrɔ: ə'tentʃn] Aufmerksamkeit ziehen auf **II 6**, 95
+**attic** ['ætɪk] Dachboden **I**
to **attract** [ə'trækt] anziehen, anlocken **II 4**, 59
attraction [ə'trækʃn] Besonderheit, Attraktion **I**
audience ['ɔ:diəns] Publikum, Zuhörer **II 2**, 26
August ['ɔ:gəst] August **I**
aunt [ɑ:nt] Tante **I**
Australian aborigine [ɒs'treɪliən ˌæbə'rɪdʒni] australische(r) Ureinwohner(in) **II 4**, 59
author ['ɔ:θə] Autor(in) **II 1**, 15
authority [ɔ:'θɒrəti] Amt, Behörde **II 2**, 27
+**autumn** (*BE*) ['ɔ:təm] Herbst **I**
+**avenue** ['ævənju:] Allee, (breite) Straße **I**
average ['ævrɪdʒ] Durchschnitt **I**
to **awaken** [ə'weɪkn] aufwecken, aufwachen **II 6**, 96
award [ə'wɔ:d] Preis, Auszeichnung **II 2**, 24
away [ə'weɪ] weg, fort **I**
right away [ˌraɪt‿ə'weɪ] sofort **II 8**, 124
to run away [ˌrʌn ə'weɪ] weglaufen **II 1**, 15
to throw* (*away*) [θrəʊ] (weg)werfen **I**
awful ['ɔ:fl] scheußlich, fürchterlich **I**

B

baby ['beɪbi] Baby **I**
baby sister [ˌbeɪbi 'sɪstə] (ganz) kleine Schwester **I**
back [bæk] Rücken **II 1**, 10
at the back [bæk] hinten **II 4**, 57
back [bæk] zurück, Hinter- **I**
to drop back [drɒp 'bæk] zurückfallen **II 5**, 79

to get back [get 'bæk] zurückkommen, ankommen **II 4**, 62
to report back [rɪˌpɔ:t 'bæk] sich zurückmelden **II 6**, 96
backgammon ['bækgæmn] *Name eines Brettspiels* **I**
bacon ['beɪkn] Speck **I**
bad [bæd] böse, schlecht **I**
in a bad way [ˌbæd 'weɪ] in einem schlechten Zustand **II 6**, 96
bag [bæg] Tüte, Tasche **I**
sleeping bag ['sli:pɪŋ ˌbæg] Schlafsack **I**
baggage ['bægɪdʒ] Gepäck **I**
bagpipes ['bægpaɪps] Dudelsack **II 2**, 24
bakery ['beɪkri] Bäckerei **II 4**, 61
bald [bɔ:ld] kahl, glatzköpfig **II 6**, 91
ball [bɔ:l] Ball **I**
banana [bə'nɑ:nə] Banane **I**
band [bænd] Musikgruppe, Band **I**
marching band ['mɑ:tʃɪŋ ˌbænd] Marschkapelle **II 1**, 12
bandleader ['bændˌli:də] Leiter(in) einer Musikgruppe **I**
banjo ['bændʒəʊ] Banjo **II 2**, 25
bank [bæŋk] Bank, Geldinstitut **I**
bank robber ['bæŋk ˌrɒbə] Bankräuber(in) **I**
bottle bank ['bɒtl ˌbæŋk] Altglascontainer **II 2**, 27
bank holiday [ˌbæŋk 'hɒlədeɪ] Feiertag (im Mai und August) **II 1**, 13
bar [bɑ:] Bar, Kneipe **II 6**, 95
coffee bar ['kɒfi ˌbɑ:] (kleines) Café **I**
+**barbecue** ['bɑ:bɪkju:] Grill *(im Freien)* **II 1**, 18
bare [beə] nackt, bloß **II 5**, 73
+**bargain** ['bɑ:gɪn] günstiges Angebot, Gelegenheitskauf **I**
to **bark** [bɑ:k] bellen **I**
barrack ['bærək] Kaserne, Baracke **II 4**, 61
barrier ['bæriə] Schranke, Sperre, Barriere **II 8**, 127
baseball ['beɪsbɔ:l] Baseball **I**
basic ['beɪsɪk] grundlegend, Grund-, Basis- **II 5**, 73
basket ['bɑ:skɪt] Korb **I**
basketball ['bɑ:skɪtbɔ:l] Basketball **I**
°**bass** [beɪs] Bass **I**
+**bat** [bæt] Schlagholz **II 5**, 84
bathroom ['bɑ:θrʊm] Bad, Badezimmer **I**
+**batter** ['bætə] Schlagmann **II 5**, 84
+spare **battery** [ˌspeə 'bætri] Ersatzbatterie **I**
battery-powered ['bætriˌpaʊəd] batteriebetrieben **II 8**, 124
bay [beɪ] Bucht, Bai **I**
BC (= **before Christ**) [ˌbi:'si:] vor Christus **II 3**, 43
to **be*** [bi:] sein **I**
beach [bi:tʃ] Strand **I**
beachgoer ['bi:tʃˌgəʊə] Strandurlauber(in) **I**
beachwatch ['bi:tʃwɒtʃ] Strandaufsicht, Strandwärter(in) **I**
laser **beam** ['leɪzə ˌbi:m] Laserstrahl **II 6**, 91
teddy **bear** ['tedi ˌbeə] Teddybär **I**
to **bear*** [beə] ertragen, aushalten **II 3**, 45
to **beat*** [bi:t] schlagen, besiegen **II 5**, 73
beautiful ['bju:tɪfl] schön **I**
because [bɪ'kɒz] weil, da **I**
because of [bɪ'kɒz‿əv] wegen **II 1**, 11
to **become*** [bɪ'kʌm] werden **II 1**, 19
bed [bed] Bett **I**
bed and breakfast *(B&B)* [ˌbed‿n‿'brekfəst] Frühstückspension **I**
bedroom ['bedrʊm] Schlafzimmer **I**
beep [bi:p] Piepsen **II 4**, 61
before [bɪ'fɔ:] vor **I**
BC (= *before Christ*) [ˌbi:'si:] vor Christus **II 3**, 43
beggar ['begə] Bettler(in) **II 4**, 61
to **begin*** [bɪ'gɪn] beginnen, anfangen **II 1**, 15
+**beginner** [bɪ'gɪnə] Anfänger(in) **I**
beginning [bɪ'gɪnɪŋ] Anfang, Beginn **II 1**, 16
behind [bɪ'haɪnd] hinter **I**
being ['bi:ɪŋ] (Lebe-)Wesen, Geschöpf **II 6**, 91
to **believe** [bɪ'li:v] glauben **I**
bell [bel] Glocke **I**
to **belong to** [bɪ'lɒŋ tʊ] gehören (zu) **II 4**, 63
below [bɪ'ləʊ] unterhalb, unten **I**
bend [bend] Biegung, Kurve **II 5**, 79
to **bend*** [bend] biegen, beugen, knicken **II 3**, 44
bending ['bendɪŋ] Beugen **II 5**, 73
benefit ['benɪfɪt] Vorteil, Nutzen **II 8**, 123
beside [bɪ'saɪd] neben **II 3**, 44
besides [bɪ'saɪdz] außerdem **II 7**, 110
best [best] beste(r/s), der/die Beste **I**
bet [bet] Wette **II 4**, 61
to **bet*** [bet] wetten **I**
better ['betə] besser **I**
better to be safe than sorry lieber auf Nummer sicher gehen **II 1**, 11
between [bɪ'twi:n] zwischen **I**
bhangra ['bæŋgrə] *Musikrichtung aus Indien* **I**
bicycle ['baɪsɪkl] Fahrrad **II 4**, 61
big [bɪg] groß **I**
bike [baɪk] (Fahr-)Rad **I**
exercise bike ['eksəsaɪz ˌbaɪk] Hometrainer **II 5**, 75
mountain bike ['maʊntɪn ˌbaɪk] Geländefahrrad, Mountainbike **I**
bill [bɪl] Rechnung **I**
billion ['bɪliən] Billion, Milliarde *(AE)* **II 2**, 29
Biology [baɪ'ɒlədʒi] Biologie **I**
bird [bɜ:d] Vogel **I**
+to **birdwatch** ['bɜ:dwɒtʃ] Vögel beobachten **I**
birdwatching ['bɜ:dˌwɒtʃɪŋ] Vögel beobachten **II 3**, 46
biro ['baɪərəʊ] Kuli, Kugelschreiber **I**
birthday ['bɜ:θdeɪ] Geburtstag **I**
bit [bɪt] Stück(chen), Teil **I**
a bit [ə 'bɪt] ein wenig, ein bisschen **I**
to **bite*** [baɪt] beißen **II 1**, 14
black [blæk] schwarz **I**
blackboard ['blækbɔ:d] Tafel **I**
blackout ['blækaʊt] Verdunkelung, Stromausfall **II 7**, 111
blanket ['blæŋkɪt] (Woll-)Decke **II 8**, 124
blind ['blaɪnd] blind **II 7**, 109
+colour-blind ['kʌləblaɪnd] farbenblind **I**
blinding ['blaɪndɪŋ] blendend **II 6**, 90
bloke *(coll.)* [bləʊk] Kerl, Typ **II 5**, 78
⟨**blood**⟩ [blʌd] Blut **II 5**, 77
to **blow* up** [ˌbləʊ‿'ʌp] aufblasen, aufpumpen **II 8**, 127
blue [blu:] blau **I**
blues [blu:z] Blues *(Musikrichtung)* **II 2**, 25
board [bɔ:d] Brett, Tafel **I**
notice board ['nəʊtɪs ˌbɔ:d] schwarzes Brett, Anschlagtafel **I**
on board [ɒn 'bɔ:d] an Bord **II 6**, 93
+to **board up** [ˌbɔ:d‿'ʌp] verschalen, mit Brettern vernageln **I**

boat [bəʊt] Boot **I**
body ['bɒdi] Körper **II 5**, 73
bodyguard ['bɒdigɑ:d] Leibwache **II 2**, 24
bone [bəʊn] Knochen **II 8**, 125
to **boo** [bu:] auspfeifen, ausbuhen **II 2**, 26
book [bʊk] Buch **I**
exercise book ['eksəsaɪz ˌbʊk] Übungsheft, Heft **I**
guide book ['gaɪd bʊk] Reiseführer *(Buch)* **I**
bookie ['bʊki] Buchmacher(in) **II 4**, 61
bookshop ['bʊkʃɒp] Buchhandlung **I**
boot [bu:t] Stiefel **I**
border ['bɔ:də] Grenze **II 3**, 41
to get **bored** [bɔ:d] sich langweilen **II 2**, 26
boring ['bɔ:rɪŋ] langweilig **I**
to be **born** [bɔ:n] geboren sein **II 7**, 112
to **borrow** ['bɒrəʊ] (aus)leihen **I**
+**boss** [bɒs] Chef, Boss **II 7**, 115
both [bəʊθ] beide **I**
to **bother** ['bɒðə] belästigen, plagen **I**
to bother about ['bɒðə‿əˌbaʊt] sich kümmern um **II 8**, 128
bottle ['bɒtl] Flasche **I**
bottle bank ['bɒtl ˌbæŋk] Altglascontainer **II 2**, 27
bottled ['bɒtld] in Flaschen (abgefüllt) **II 8**, 124
bottom ['bɒtəm] unteres Ende, Fuß **I**; Po **II 5**, 72
bouncy castle [ˌbaʊntsi 'kɑ:sl] (aufblasbare) Hüpfburg **I**
+**bowler** ['bəʊlə] *(Kricket)* Werfer(in) **II 5**, 84
box [bɒks] Kiste, Schachtel **I**
boxers *(pl.)* ['bɒksəz] Boxershorts **II 7**, 111
boy [bɔɪ] Junge **I**
boyfriend ['bɔɪfrend] Freund **I**
bps (= **bits per second**) ['bi:'pi:'es] *Übertragungsgeschwindigkeit eines Modems* **I**
brain [breɪn] Gehirn **II 8**, 128
brake [breɪk] Bremse **II 8**, 127
brave [breɪv] tapfer, mutig **II 3**, 43
bread [bred] Brot **I**
break [breɪk] Pause **I**
to **break*** [breɪk] (zer)brechen, knacken **II 4**, 61
breakfast ['brekfəst] Frühstück **I**
bed and breakfast *(B&B)* [ˌbed‿n‿'brekfəst] Frühstückspension **I**
Breton ['bretn] bretonisch; Bretone **II 3**, 43
bridge [brɪdʒ] Brücke **I**
watching **brief** ['wɒtʃɪŋ ˌbri:f] Beobachtungsauftrag **II 6**, 95
+**bright** [braɪt] hell, leuchtend **I**
brightly ['braɪtli] hell, leuchtend **II 1**, 13
to **bring*** [brɪŋ] bringen **I**
British ['brɪtɪʃ] britisch **I**
Briton ['brɪtn] Brite/Britin **II 3**, 43
brochure ['brəʊʃə] Broschüre, Prospekt **I**
brother ['brʌðə] Bruder **I**
brown [braʊn] braun **I**
speech **bubble** ['spi:tʃ ˌbʌbl] Sprechblase **II 5**, 79
buck *(AE)* *(coll.)* [bʌk] Dollar **II 7**, 110
to **build*** [bɪld] (er)bauen **II 3**, 43
+**builder** ['bɪldə] Erbauer(in), Begründer(in) **II 3**, 50
building ['bɪldɪŋ] Gebäude **I**
bully, *(pl.)* -ies ['bʊli] Schlägertyp, Angeber(in) **I**
bungalow ['bʌŋgləʊ] Bungalow **II 4**, 59
to **burn* up** [ˌbɜ:n‿'ʌp] verbrennen, verbrauchen **II 5**, 73
bus [bʌs] Bus **I**
bus stop ['bʌs stɒp] Bushaltestelle **I**
double decker bus [ˌdʌbl dekə 'bʌs] Doppeldeckerbus **I**
bush [bʊʃ] Busch **II 3**, 44
business ['bɪznɪs] Geschäft **II 2**, 28; Angelegenheit, Sache **II 8**, 123
businesslike ['bɪznɪslaɪk] geschäftstüchtig, nüchtern **II 4**, 62
businessman ['bɪznɪsmæn] Geschäftsmann **II 4**, 51
to be **busy** ['bɪzi] besetzt sein *(Telefon)* **II 4**, 58; beschäftigt sein **I**
but [bʌt] aber **I**
butter ['bʌtə] Butter **II 4**, 63
button ['bʌtn] Knopf, Schalter **II 6**, 93
to **buy*** [baɪ] kaufen **I**
buzz-game ['bʌzˌgeɪm] *Name eines Spiels* **I**
⟨to get a **buzz** out of sth.⟩ [bʌz] Spaß haben bei etw **II 1**, 18
⟨to **buzz**⟩ [bʌz] surren, schwirren **II 3**, 45
by [baɪ] an, neben, bis **I**
by [baɪ] von, durch **II 8**, 124
to learn by heart [ˌlɜ:n baɪ 'hɑ:t] auswendig lernen **II 1**, 11

C

+tossing the **caber** [ˌtɒsɪŋ ðə 'keɪbə] Baumstammwerfen *(schottische Sportart)* **II 5**, 84
café ['kæfeɪ] Café **I**
motorway café ['məʊtəweɪ ˌkæfeɪ] Cafeteria auf der Autobahn **I**
cafeteria [ˌkæfə'tɪəriə] Cafeteria **I**
+**cage** [keɪdʒ] Käfig **I**
cake [keɪk] Kuchen **II 3**, 51
calendar ['kæləndə] Kalender **I**
(phone) **call** [('fəʊn) kɔ:l] Anruf **I**
to **call** [kɔ:l] nennen, (an)rufen **I**
to be called [kɔ:ld] genannt werden; heißen **II 2**, 29
calorie ['kælri] Kalorie **II 5**, 73
camera ['kæmrə] Kamera, Fotoapparat **I**
cameraman ['kæmrəmæn] Kameramann **II 2**, 30
camp [kæmp] (Ferien-)Lager **I**
to **camp** [kæmp] zelten **I**
campervan ['kæmpəˌvæn] Wohnwagen **I**
camping ['kæmpɪŋ] Zelten **I**
campsite ['kæmpsaɪt] Campingplatz **I**
can opener ['kæn ˌəʊpnə] Dosenöffner **II 8**, 124
can [kæn] kann **I**
canal [kə'næl] Kanal **I**
canvas ['kænvəs] Segeltuch **II 4**, 62
cap [kæp] Kappe, (Schirm-)Mütze **I**
capital ['kæpɪtl] Hauptstadt **I**
capital letter [ˌkæpɪtl 'letə] Großbuchstabe **I**
captain ['kæptɪn] Kapitän **I**
car [kɑ:] Auto **I**
car park ['kɑ: pɑ:k] Parkplatz **I**
car rental ['kɑ: ˌrentl] Autovermietung **I**
flash **card** ['flæʃ ˌkɑ:d] Illustrationstafel, Flashcard **II 5**, 81
credit card ['kredɪt ˌkɑ:d] Kreditkarte **II 3**, 45
to **care** *(about)* [keə] sich Sorgen machen (um) **II 1**, 14
she didn't care [keə] es war ihr egal **II 1**, 14
would you care to? [ˌwʊd ju: 'keə] hätten Sie Lust (zu)? **II 6**, 95
careful ['keəfʊl] vorsichtig **I**
Caribbean [ˌkærɪ'bi:ən] karibisch; Karibik **II 1**, 8

carnival ['kɑ:nɪvl] Karneval **II 1**, 8
carrot juice ['kærət ˌdʒu:s] Karottensaft **II 5**, 74
to **carry** ['kæri] tragen **I**
cartoon [kɑ:'tu:n] Witzzeichnung **I**
cartoonist [kɑ:'tu:nɪst] Karikaturenzeichner(in) **II 6**, 90
case [keɪs] Fall, Sache **II 7**, 110
in case [keɪs] falls **II 8**, 124
pencil case ['pensl ˌkeɪs] Federmäppchen **I**
extra **cash** [ˌekstrə 'kæʃ] Zuschlag, Sonderzahlung **II 7**, 110
cassette [kə'set] Kassette **I**
cast [kɑ:st] (Rollen-)Besetzung, Ensemble **II 7**, 110
castle ['kɑ:sl] Burg, Schloss **I**
bouncy castle [ˌbaʊntsi 'kɑ:sl] (aufblasbare) Hüpfburg **I**
cat [kæt] Katze **I**
to rain cats and dogs ['reɪn ˌkæts‿n‿'dɒgz] heftig regnen, schütten, gießen **I**
catastrophic [ˌkætə'strɒfɪk] katastrophal **II 6**, 95
to **catch*** [kætʃ] fangen; (einen Bus) erreichen **II 1**, 17
category ['kætəgri] Kategorie, Klasse **II 2**, 29
to **cause** [kɔ:z] verursachen, hervorrufen, anrichten **I**
cave [keɪv] Höhle **I**
CD [ˌsi:'di:] CD *(Compact Disc)* **I**
celebrity [sə'lebrəti] Berühmtheit **II 5**, 76
+**cellar** ['selə] Keller **I**
cello ['tʃeləʊ] Cello **I**
+**Celsius** ['selsiəs] Celsius **I**
Celt [kelt] Kelte/Keltin **II 3**, 42
Celtic ['keltɪk] keltisch, Keltisch **II 3**, 41
centre ['sentə] Zentrum **I**
sports centre ['spɔ:ts ˌsentə] Sportzentrum, -anlage **I**
ceremony ['serɪməni] Zeremonie, Feierlichkeit **II 2**, 29
certain ['sɜ:tn] bestimmt, gewiss **II 3**, 48
certainly ['sɜ:tnli] gewiss, sicherlich **II 1**, 12
chair ['tʃeə] Stuhl **I**
chalk [tʃɔ:k] Kreide **I**
chance [tʃɑ:ns] Gelegenheit, Chance **II 1**, 15
change ['tʃeɪndʒ] Wandel, Wechsel, Umschwung **II 3**, 42
to **change** [tʃeɪndʒ] ändern; umsteigen **I**
character ['kærəktə] Charakter **I**
characteristic [ˌkærəktə'rɪstɪk] charakteristisch, kennzeichnend **II 1**, 16
to be in **charge of sth.** [ɪn 'tʃɑ:dʒ‿əv] die Aufsicht haben über etw **II 5**, 78
charity ['tʃærɪti] Wohltätigkeit **I**
charm [tʃɑ:m] Charme **I**
to **chase** [tʃeɪs] (herum)jagen **I**
cheap [tʃi:p] billig **I**
check [tʃek] **I**
check-in ['tʃekɪn] Abfertigungsschalter (am Flughafen), Einchecken **I**
check-out ['tʃekaʊt] Abschlusskontrolle, Auschecken **I**
sound check ['saʊn(d) tʃek] Klang-, Tonkontrolle **I**
to **check** [tʃek] kontrollieren, überprüfen **I**
checklist ['tʃeklɪst] Kontrollliste, Checkliste **II 8**, 124
cheek [tʃi:k] Wange, Backe **II 5**, 79
cheer [tʃɪə] Jubel, Beifall **I**
to **cheer** [tʃɪə] jubeln, Beifall klatschen **II 5**, 79
chemical ['kemɪkl] Chemikalie **I**
chemist's ['kemɪsts] Apotheke, Drogerie **I**
cheque [tʃek] Scheck **II 3**, 44
chest [tʃest] Brust **II 6**, 96
chewing gum ['tʃu:ɪŋ ˌgʌm] Kaugummi **II 4**, 61
chicken ['tʃɪkɪn] Huhn, Hähnchen **II 4**, 60
chieftain ['tʃi:ftn] Häuptling, Anführer(in) **II 3**, 43
child, children *(pl.)* [tʃaɪld/'tʃɪldrn] Kind(er) **I**
an only child [ˌəʊnlɪ 'tʃaɪld] Einzelkind **II 1**, 14
+**Chinese** [tʃaɪ'ni:z] chinesisch, Chinesisch **I**
chips *(pl.)* [tʃɪps] Pommes frites **I**
chocolate ['tʃɒklət] Schokolade **I**
junior **choir** [ˌdʒu:niə 'kwaɪə] Chor der unteren Klassenstufen **I**
to **choose*** [tʃu:z] wählen, aussuchen **I**
chorus ['kɔ:rəs] Refrain, Chor **II 4**, 57
Christmas ['krɪstməs] Weihnachten **I**
church [tʃɜ:tʃ] Kirche **I**
+to **churn** [tʃɜ:n] sich heftig bewegen, aufwühlen **I**
cigarette [ˌsɪgr'et] Zigarette **I**
cinema ['sɪnəmə] Kino **I**
circle ['sɜ:kl] Kreis **II 2**, 26
city ['sɪti] Großstadt, Innenstadt **I**
city shuttle ['sɪti ˌʃʌtl] Pendelverkehr zur Innenstadt **I**
civilization [ˌsɪvlaɪ'zeɪʃn] Zivilisation **II 6**, 90
civilized ['sɪvlaɪzd] zivilisiert **II 3**, 43
to **clap** [klæp] klatschen, applaudieren **I**
clapping ['klæpɪŋ] Klatschen, Applaus **I**
class [klɑ:s] Klasse **I**
classical music ['klæsɪkl 'mju:zɪk] klassische Musik **I**
classroom ['klɑ:srʊm] Klassenzimmer **I**
to **clean** [kli:n] reinigen, putzen **I**
clean [kli:n] sauber **I**
cleaning lady ['kli:nɪŋ ˌleɪdi] Zugehfrau, Putzfrau **I**
clear [klɪə] klar, hell, einleuchtend **I**
clever ['klevə] schlau, klug **I**
cliff [klɪf] Klippe **I**
cliff-side ['klɪfsaɪd] Klippe(n) **I**
climb [klaɪm] Steigung, Aufstieg **II 3**, 44
to **climb** [klaɪm] (hoch)klettern **I**
mountain **climber** ['maʊntɪn ˌklaɪmə] Bergsteiger(in) **II 8**, 123
mountain **climbing** ['maʊntɪn ˌklaɪmɪŋ] Bergsteigen **II 8**, 123
video **clip** ['vɪdiəʊ ˌklɪp] Videoclip **II 2**, 35
cloak [kləʊk] Umhang, (weiter) Mantel **II 3**, 43
clock [klɒk] Uhr **I**
close [kləʊs] Straße, Hof **II 8**, 127
to **close** [kləʊz] schließen **I**
close *(to)* [kləʊs] nah, dicht (bei) **I**; genau **II 3**, 48
⟨**closing price**⟩ ['kləʊzɪŋ ˌpraɪs] Schlusskurs **II 4**, 61
clothes ['kləʊðz] Kleidung, Kleider **I**
cloud [klaʊd] Wolke **II 2**, 33
+**cloudy** ['klaʊdi] wolkig **I**
club [klʌb] Klub, Verein **I**
night club ['naɪt klʌb] Nachtclub **I**
clue [klu:] Anhaltspunkt, Hinweis **II 4**, 57
to **clutch** [klʌtʃ] greifen, packen, festhalten **II 8**, 127
coach [kəʊtʃ] (Eisenbahn-)Wagen **II 3**, 44
coast [kəʊst] Küste **I**
coastal ['kəʊstl] Küsten- **I**
coastguard ['kəʊstgɑ:d] Küstenwache **I**
coat [kəʊt] Mantel **I**
code [kəʊd] Kode **I**
coffee ['kɒfi] Kaffee **I**
coffee bar ['kɒfi ˌbɑ:] (kleines) Café **I**
coin [kɔɪn] Münze **II 8**, 129
cold [kəʊld] Erkältung, Schnupfen **II 5**, 81
cold [kəʊld] kalt **I**

collar ['kɒlə] Hundehalsband **I**
+**colleague** ['kɒliːg] Kollege/Kollegin **II 6**, 100
to **collect** [kə'lekt] sammeln **I**
collection ['kəlekʃn] Sammlung, Kollektion **II 7**, 109
+**colony** ['kɒləni] Kolonie **II 4**, 65
colour ['kʌlə] Farbe **I**
+colour-blind ['kʌləblaɪnd] farbenblind **I**
colourful ['kʌləfl] farbenprächtig, farbenfroh **II 1**, 8
to **come*** [kʌm] kommen **I**
Come along! ['kʌm‿ə'lɒŋ] Komm schon! **II 1**, 14
to come round [ˌkʌm 'raʊnd] vorbeikommen, herüberkommen **I**
comedy ['kɒmədi] Komödie **II 2**, 25
comfort ['kʌmfət] Bequemlichkeit, Komfort **II 1**, 10
comfortable ['kʌmftəbl] bequem, komfortabel **I**
comfy *(coll.)* ['kʌmpfi] komfortabel, bequem **II 5**, 73
comic ['kɒmɪk] Comic(heft) **I**
command [kə'mɑːnd] Befehl, Kommando **II 6**, 94
commander [kə'mɑːndə] Befehlshaber(in), Kommandant(in) **II 6**, 93
commercial traveller [kəˌmɜːʃl 'trævlə] Handelsreisende(r) **II 6**, 95
common ['kɒmən] allgemein **II 7**, 110
in common [ɪn 'kɒmən] gemeinsam **I**
communication [kəˌmjuːnɪ'keɪʃn] Übertragung, Kommunikation **II 4**, 61
community [kə'mjuːnəti] Gemeinschaft, Gemeinde **II 1**, 12
companion [kəm'pænjən] Begleiter(in), Kamerad(in) **II 6**, 95
company ['kʌmpəni] Gesellschaft, Firma **II 2**, 26
to **compare** [kəm'peə] vergleichen **I**
comparison [kəm'pærɪsn] Vergleich **I**
competition [ˌkɒmpə'tɪʃn] Wettbewerb, Wettkampf **I**
competitive [kəm'petɪtɪv] konkurrierend, Wettkampf- **II 5**, 73
competitor [kəm'petɪtə] Wettkämpfer(in), Mitbewerber(in) **II 5**, 79
to **complete** [kəm'pliːt] vervollständigen **I**
complete [kəm'pliːt] vollständig, komplett **II 3**, 48
listening **comprehension** ['lɪsnɪŋ ˌkɒmprɪ'henʃn] Hörverstehen **I**
computer [kəm'pjuːtə] Computer, Rechner **I**
drum computer ['drʌm kəmˌpjuːtə] Rhythmusgerät **I**
the pros and **cons** [ˌprəʊz‿n‿'kɒnz] das Für und Wider, Pro und Contra **I**
to **concentrate** ['kɒntsntreɪt] (sich) konzentrieren **II 8**, 126
concert ['kɒnsət] Konzert **I**
concussion [kən'kʌʃn] Gehirnerschütterung **II 8**, 128
condition [kən'dɪʃn] Bedingung, Kondition **II 7**, 110
+to **confuse** [kən'fjuːz] verwirren, irritieren **I**
congratulations [kənˌgrætʃʊ'leɪʃnz] Gratulation, Glückwunsch **II 5**, 74
+to **connect** [kə'nekt] verbinden, zusammenfügen **I**
contact ['kɒntækt] Kontakt, Verbindung **I**
to **contact** ['kɒntækt] Kontakt aufnehmen (mit) **I**
+**contactee** [kɒntæk'tiː] jmd, der mit einem UFO Kontakt hatte **II 6**, 100
container [kən'teɪnə] Behälter, Container **II 2**, 27
content ['kɒntent] Inhalt **II 3**, 45
wax content ['wæks ˌkɒntent] Wachsgehalt **I**
context ['kɒntekst] Textzusammenhang, Kontext **I**
continent ['kɒntɪnənt] Festland, Kontinent **II 3**, 43
to **continue** [kən'tɪnjuː] fortfahren, weitermachen; fortsetzen **II 3**, 45
+**control** [kən'trəʊl] Kontrolle **II 6**, 100
to **control** [kən'trəʊl] beherrschen, überwachen **II 3**, 43
+**controversy** [kən'trɒvəsi] Streitfrage, Kontroverse **II 3**, 50
conversation [ˌkɒnvə'seɪʃn] Gespräch, Konversation **II 7**, 113
cook [kʊk] Koch/Köchin **I**
to **cook** [kʊk] kochen **I**
cooking ['kʊkɪŋ] +Kochen, Essen **I**; Küche, Kochkünste **II 1**, 16
cool [kuːl] kühl; locker, lässig **II 1**, 11
coolness ['kuːlnəs] Lässigkeit **II 1**, 10
to **cooperate** [kəʊ'ɒpreɪt] kooperieren **II 6**, 96
cooperation [kəʊˌɒpə'reɪʃn] Zusammenarbeit, Kooperation **II 6**, 96
coordination [kəʊˌɔːdɪ'neɪʃn] Koordination **II 5**, 73
copy ['kɒpi] Kopie **I**
to **copy** ['kɒpi] kopieren, abschreiben **II 5**, 72
+**copycat** ['kɒpikæt] Nachahmer(in) **II 7**, 115
+**corn** [kɔːn] Getreide, Korn **II 4**, 65
corner ['kɔːnə] Ecke **I**
cornflakes ['kɔːnfleɪks] Cornflakes **II 1**, 13
Cornish ['kɔːnɪʃ] kornisch, aus Cornwall **I**
to **correct** [kə'rekt] korrigieren, verbessern **I**
correct [kə'rekt] richtig, korrekt **I**
to **cost*** [kɒst] kosten **II 7**, 107
costume ['kɒstjuːm] Kostüm **I**
cottage ['kɒtɪdʒ] Cottage, Häuschen **I**
cotton ['kɒtn] Baumwolle **II 4**, 61
couch potato ['kaʊtʃ pəˌteɪtəʊ] jmd, der ständig vor dem Fernseher sitzt **II 5**, 74
could [kʊd] konnte(n), könnte(n) **I**
to **count** [kaʊnt] zählen **II 1**, 14
+**countdown** ['kaʊntdaʊn] Countdown **II 6**, 100
counter ['kaʊntə] Theke **II 6**, 95
country ['kʌntri] Land **I**
in the country ['kʌntri] auf dem Lande **II 2**, 33
countryside ['kʌntrɪˌsaɪd] Land, Landschaft **I**
a **couple** *(of)* ['kʌpl‿əv] ein paar **II 5**, 72
course [kɔːs] Kurs(us), Lehrgang **II 3**, 46
of course [əv 'kɔːs] natürlich, selbstverständlich **I**
court [kɔːt] (Tennis-)Platz, Spielfeld **II 5**, 73
cousin ['kʌzn] Cousin(e) **I**
cover ['kʌvə] (Buch-)Umschlag **II 1**, 15
to **cover** ['kʌvə] zudecken, abdecken **II 6**, 97
crack [kræk] Krach, Knall, Schlag **II 8**, 127
to **crack** [kræk] knacken, aufbrechen **I**
crash [kræʃ] Krachen, Krach **II 6**, 96
crash helmet ['kræʃ ˌhelmət] Sturzhelm **II 6**, 95
to **crash** [kræʃ] zusammenbrechen, (zusammen)krachen **II 8**, 127
crater ['kreɪtə] Krater **II 6**, 92
crayon ['kreɪɒn] Farbstift **II 1**, 14
crazy ['kreɪzi] verrückt **I**
ice **cream** [aɪs 'kriːm] Eiskrem, (Speise-)Eis **I**
ice cream maker [aɪs 'kriːm ˌmeɪkə] Eismaschine **I**
credit card ['kredɪt ˌkɑːd] Kreditkarte **II 3**, 45
+**crew** [kruː] Besatzung **II 6**, 100
+**cricket** ['krɪkɪt] Kricket *(Ballspiel mit Schläger und hartem Ball aus Kork)* **II 5**, 84
crisp [krɪsp] Kartoffelchip **II 5**, 78
crisp [krɪsp] knusprig **II 4**, 63

crocodile ['krɒkədaɪl] Krokodil, Menschenschlange **II 1**, 14
to **cross** [krɒs] überqueren, kreuzen **II 3**, 44
crowd [kraʊd] (Menschen-)Menge **II 1**, 8
to **crowd** [kraʊd] (sich) drängen **II 6**, 95
crown jewels [ˌkraʊn 'dʒu:əlz] Kronjuwelen **I**
to **cry** [kraɪ] rufen, schreien; weinen **I**
cuisine [kwɪz'ɪ:n] Küche **I**
culture ['kʌltʃə] Kultur **II 3**, 46
cupboard ['kʌbəd] Schrank **I**
curry ['kʌri] Curry(gericht) **I**
curtain ['kɜ:tn] Vorhang **II 1**, 13
customer ['kʌstəmə] Kunde/Kundin **II 4**, 61
customs ['kʌstəmz] Zoll *(Verwaltung)* **I**
to **cut*** [kʌt] schneiden **II 1**, 15
⟨**cyberspace**⟩ ['saɪbəˌspeɪs] Cyberspace **II 3**, 45
to **cycle** ['saɪkl] Rad fahren, radeln **I**
cyclist ['saɪklɪst] Fahrradfahrer(in) **II 8**, 128

D

dad [dæd] Papa, Vati **I**
+**damage** ['dæmɪdʒ] Schaden **I**
to **damage** ['dæmɪdʒ] beschädigen **I**
dance [dɑ:ns] Tanz **II 4**, 58
dancing ['dɑ:nsɪŋ] Tanzen **II 1**, 12
danger ['deɪndʒə] Gefahr **I**
dangerous ['deɪndʒrəs] gefährlich **I**
dark [dɑ:k] dunkel **I**
up to **date** [ˌʌp tə 'deɪt] modern, aktuell **I**
dawn [dɔ:n] Dämmerung, Tagesanbruch **II 3**, 44
day [deɪ] Tag **I**
One Day Travelcard ['trævlkɑ:d] Tageskarte, Netzkarte *(London)* **II 1**, 10
daydream ['deɪdri:m] Tagtraum **II 5**, 79
daylight ['deɪlaɪt] Tageslicht **I**
dead [ded] tot, verstorben **I**
deaf [def] taub **I**
Oh, **dear!** [əʊ 'dɪə] Oh je! **I**
death [deθ] Tod **II 8**, 123
December [dɪ'sembə] Dezember **I**
to **decide** [dɪ'saɪd] entscheiden **I**
decimal point [ˌdesɪml 'pɔɪnt] Komma(stelle) **II 4**, 61
declaration [ˌdeklə'reɪʃn] Erklärung **II 3**, 45
to **declare** [dɪ'kleə] angeben, deklarieren **I**
to **decline** [dɪ'klaɪn] ablehnen, ausschlagen **II 5**, 80
to **decorate** ['dekəreɪt] dekorieren, verzieren **II 3**, 43
deep [di:p] tief **II 3**, 46
to **defeat** [dɪ'fi:t] besiegen, schlagen **II 4**, 59
to **defend** [dɪ'fend] verteidigen **II 6**, 96
to **define** [dɪ'faɪn] näher bestimmen, definieren **II 4**, 58
+**degree** [dɪ'gri:] Grad **I**
+**delicatessen**, deli [ˌdelikə'tesn, 'deli] Delikatessengeschäft, -lokal **I**
to **demand** [dɪ'mɑ:nd] fordern, verlangen **II 6**, 95
demo tape ['deməʊ ˌteɪp] Demo(nstrations)band **I**
deodorant [di'əʊdrnt] Deodorant **II 1**, 10
department [dɪ'pɑ:tmənt] Abteilung **I**
department store [dɪ'pɑ:tmənt ˌstɔ:] Kaufhaus **I**
departure [dɪ'pɑ:tʃə] Abflug, Abfahrt **I**
to **depend** (*on*) [dɪ'pend] abhängen (von) **II 1**, 15
to **descend** [dɪ'send] absteigen, hinunterfahren **II 3**, 44
to **describe** [dɪ'skraɪb] beschreiben **I**
to be described [dɪ'skraɪbd] beschrieben werden **II 6**, 91
description [dɪ'skrɪpʃn] Beschreibung **I**
design [dɪ'zaɪn] Design **I**
°Design and Technology [dɪ'zaɪn‿ən‿tek'nɒlədʒi] Gestalten und Technik **I**
to **design** [dɪ'zaɪn] entwerfen, konstruieren **II 8**, 123
designer [dɪ'zaɪnə] Designer(in) **II 7**, 107
desk [desk] Schreibtisch **I**
to **destroy** [dɪ'strɔɪ] zerstören **I**
detail ['di:teɪl] Detail, Einzelheit **I**
detective [dɪ'tektɪv] Detektiv(in) **I**
smoke **detector** ['sməʊk dɪˌtektə] Rauchmelder **II 8**, 124
diagnosis [ˌdaɪəg'nəʊsɪs] Diagnose **II 8**, 122
to **dial** ['daɪəl] wählen **I**
dialogue ['daɪəlɒg] Dialog, Gespräch **I**
diary ['daɪəri] Tagebuch **I**
dictionary ['dɪkʃənəri] Wörterbuch **I**
didgeridoo [ˌdɪdʒri'du:] Didgeridoo *(australisches Blasinstrument)* **II 2**, 24
to **die** [daɪ] sterben **I**
diesel ['di:zl] Dieselöl, -motor **II 3**, 45
diet ['daɪət] Diät **II 5**, 74
difference ['dɪfrnts] Unterschied, Differenz **I**
different ['dɪfrnt] verschieden, anders(artig) **I**
difficult ['dɪfɪklt] schwierig **I**
+**dining room** ['daɪnɪŋ ˌrʊm] Esszimmer **I**
dinner ['dɪnə] Abendessen **I**
dinnertime ['dɪnəˌtaɪm] Essenszeit **II 5**, 78
dinosaur ['daɪnəsɔ:] Dinosaurier **II 3**, 49
direct [dɪ'rekt] direkt **I**
+**direction** [dɪ'rekʃn] Richtung **I**
director [dɪ'rektə] Regisseur(in) **II 2**, 29
dirtiest ['dɜ:tiɪst] schmutzigste(r/s) **I**
dirty ['dɜ:ti] schmutzig **I**
to **disagree** [ˌdɪsə'gri:] ablehnen **I**
+to **disappear** [ˌdɪsə'pɪə] verschwinden **II 6**, 100
to be **disappointed** [ˌdɪsə'pɔɪntɪd] enttäuscht sein **II 4**, 62
disaster [dɪ'zɑ:stə] Katastrophe, Unglück **I**
disco ['dɪskəʊ] Disko(thek) **I**
to **discover** [dɪ'skʌvə] entdecken **II 3**, 40
discovery [dɪ'skʌvri] Entdeckung **II 4**, 62
to **discuss** [dɪ'skʌs] diskutieren, besprechen **I**
disease [dɪ'zi:z] Krankheit **II 8**, 122
to **disintegrate** [dɪ'sɪntɪgreɪt] (sich) auflösen, zersetzen **II 6**, 96
to **dispose of** [dɪ'spəʊz‿ɒv] beseitigen, loswerden **I**
+**district** ['dɪstrɪkt] Bezirk, (Stadt-)Viertel **I**
to **divide** [dɪ'vaɪd] aufteilen, dividieren **I**
to **do*** [du:] tun, machen **I**
to do well [du: 'wel] erfolgreich sein **II 4**, 67
How d'you do? [ˌhaʊ djʊ 'du:] Guten Tag! Sehr erfreut! **II 7**, 113
+to **dock** [dɒk] anlegen, andocken **II 6**, 100
doctor ['dɒktə] Arzt/Ärztin, Doktor **II 4**, 61
documentary [ˌdɒkjə'mentri] Dokumentarfilm **II 2**, 29
dog [dɒg] Hund **I**
+guide dog ['gaɪd dɒg] Blindenhund **I**
hot dog ['hɒt dɒg] Hotdog *(langes weiches Brötchen mit Würstchen)* **I**
to rain cats and dogs ['reɪn ˌkæts‿n‿'dɒgz] heftig regnen, schütten, gießen **I**
dollar ['dɒlə] *amerikanische Währung* **I**
door [dɔ:] Tür **I**
next door [ˌnekst 'dɔ:] nebenan **II 3**, 44

double ['dʌbl] doppelt(e/r) **I**
double decker bus [ˌdʌbl dekə 'bʌs] Doppeldeckerbus **I**
to **double** ['dʌbl] (sich) verdoppeln **II 2**, 29
down [daʊn] herunter, nieder **I**; nach unten **II 1**, 10
to note *(down)* [ˌnəʊt 'daʊn] notieren, (auf)schreiben **I**
to sit down [sɪt 'daʊn] sich setzen **II 1**, 13
to turn down [ˌtɜ:n 'daʊn] herunterdrehen, leiser stellen **I**
to write* *(down)* [ˌraɪt 'daʊn] (auf)schreiben **I**
to **download** [ˌdaʊn'ləʊd] herunterladen, downloaden **I**
downstairs [ˌdaʊn'steəz] unten; Erdgeschoss **I**
+**downstream** [ˌdaʊn'stri:m] stromabwärts **I**
+**downtown** *(AE)* [ˌdaʊn'taʊn] *südlicher Teil der Insel Manhattan in New York; sonst:* Stadtzentrum **I**
dozen ['dʌzn] Dutzend **II 2**, 29
draft [drɑ:ft] Entwurf, Skizze **II 8**, 129
to **drain** [dreɪn] leeren **II 6**, 95
drama ['drɑ:mə] Drama **II 2**, 30
Drama ['drɑ:mə] °Theaterspielen *(Fach)* **I**
to **draw*** [drɔ:] zeichnen **I**
to draw* attention to [ˌdrɔ: ə'tentʃn] Aufmerksamkeit ziehen auf **II 6**, 95
+**dreadful** ['dredfl] furchtbar, schrecklich **I**
dream [dri:m] Traum **II 3**, 45
to **dream** [dri:m] träumen **II 3**, 45
dress [dres] Kleid **I**
dressing gown ['dresɪŋ ˌgaʊn] Morgenrock **II 6**, 96
to **drift** [drɪft] (ab)treiben, (ab)driften **I**
drink [drɪŋk] Getränk **II 1**, 10
to **drink*** [drɪŋk] trinken **I**
to **drive*** [draɪv] fahren **I**
to drive off [draɪv‿'ɒf] vertreiben **II 4**, 67
to drive so. out [ˌdraɪv‿'aʊt] jmdn verjagen, hinausjagen **II 4**, 59
driver ['draɪvə] Fahrer(in) **II 3**, 46
long-distance truck driver [ˌlɒŋ'dɪstns 'trʌk ˌdraɪvə] Fernfahrer(in) **II 4**, 60
to **drop** [drɒp] fallen lassen, abwerfen **I**
to drop back [drɒp 'bæk] zurückfallen **II 5**, 79
to drop in [drɒp‿'ɪn] vorbeischauen **II 4**, 61
drowning ['draʊnɪŋ] Ertrinken **II 8**, 128
drowsy ['draʊzi] schläfrig **II 8**, 128
drug [drʌg] Droge **I**
Druid ['dru:ɪd] Druide **II 3**, 43
drum [drʌm] Trommel **I**
drum computer ['drʌm kəmˌpju:tə] Rhythmusgerät **I**
°drum kit ['drʌm kɪt] Schlagzeugausrüstung **I**
+**due** *(to)* [dju:] zurückzuführen (auf) **I**
to **dump** [dʌmp] auskippen, hinwerfen **I**
during ['djʊərɪŋ] während **II 7**, 112
dust [dʌst] Staub **II 6**, 96
Dutch [dʌtʃ] holländisch, niederländisch **II 4**, 67
duty ['dju:ti] Zoll *(Gebühr)* **I**
to be on duty ['dju:ti] im Dienst sein, Aufsicht haben **II 5**, 78

E

each [i:tʃ] jede(r/s) Einzelne **I**
each other [ˌi:tʃ‿'ʌðə] einander **II 1**, 13
ear [ɪə] Ohr **II 2**, 32
early ['ɜ:li] früh **I**
+to **earn** [ɜ:n] verdienen **II 7**, 116
earth [ɜ:θ] Erde **II 6**, 90
earthquake ['ɜ:θkweɪk] Erdbeben **II 8**, 124
+**east** [i:st] östlich, Osten **I**
easy ['i:zi] leicht, einfach **I**
to **eat*** [i:t] essen **I**
edge [edʒ] Ufer, Rand (eines Sees) **I**
visual **effects** [ˌvɪʒuəl ɪ'fekts] (optische) Tricks **II 2**, 29
egg [eg] Ei **I**
scrambled eggs [ˌskræmbld‿'egz] Rührei **II 4**, 63
either ... or ['aɪðə ... 'ɔ:] entweder ... oder **II 5**, 79
elbow ['elbəʊ] Ellbogen **II 6**, 95
+**elderly** ['eldəli] älter(e/r/s) **I**
electric [ɪ'lektrɪk] elektrisch **I**
electrician [ˌelɪk'trɪʃn] Elektriker(in) **II 2**, 27
electricity [ˌelɪk'trɪsəti] Elektrizität, Strom **I**
electronic [ˌelek'trɒnɪk] elektronisch **II 4**, 61
+**elevator** *(AE)* ['elɪveɪtə] Aufzug, Fahrstuhl **I**
else [els] (sonst) noch, außerdem **I**
e-mail ['i:meɪl] elektronische Post, E-Mail **I**
emergency [ɪ'mɜ:dʒnsi] Notfall **II 8**, 122
emotion [ɪ'məʊʃn] Gefühl, Emotion **II 2**, 24
emperor ['emprə] Kaiser **II 3**, 46
employee [ɪm'plɔɪi:] Arbeitsnehmer(in), Angestellte(r) **II 7**, 111
empty ['emti] leer **II 2**, 33
+**encyclopedia** [ɪnˌsaɪklə'pi:diə] Nachschlagewerk, Enzyklopädie **II 3**, 50
end [end] Ende, Schluss **I**
to put an end to sth. [ˌpʌt‿ən‿'end] einer Sache ein Ende setzen **II 1**, 19
to **end** [end] (be)enden **I**
energy ['enədʒi] Energie **II 5**, 77
engine ['endʒɪn] Motor **II 6**, 95
fire engine ['faɪə‿ˌendʒɪn] Feuerwehrauto **II 2**, 27
English ['ɪŋglɪʃ] englisch, Englisch *(Fach)* **I**
to **enjoy** [ɪn'dʒɔɪ] genießen, mögen **II 2**, 27
enjoyment [ɪn'dʒɔɪmənt] Freude, Spaß **II 1**, 15
enough [ɪ'nʌf] genug, ausreichend **I**
to **enter** ['entə] melden, sich beteiligen an **II 5**, 73; einschreiben, auf die Liste setzen **II 5**, 79
entertainer [ˌentə'teɪnə] Unterhaltungskünstler(in) **II 2**, 26
entertainment [ˌentə'teɪnmənt] Unterhaltung, Animation **I**
entry ['entri] Eintrag **II 8**, 128
envelope ['envələʊp] (Brief-)Umschlag **II 2**, 29
environment [ɪn'vaɪərnmənt] Umwelt **I**
⟨**equinox**⟩ ['i:kwɪnɒks] Tagundnachtgleiche **II 3**, 50
equipment [ɪ'kwɪpmənt] Ausrüstung, Ausstattung **II 2**, 27
+to **erase** [ɪ'reɪz] entfernen, löschen **II 6**, 100
escape [ɪ'skeɪp] Flucht **II 8**, 124
to **escape** [ɪ'skeɪp] entkommen, entfliehen **II 6**, 95
especially [ɪ'speʃli] besonders, vor allem **II 3**, 46
+**euro** ['jʊərəʊ] Euro *(europäische Währung)* **II 7**, 115
European [ˌjʊərə'pi:ən] europäisch **II 2**, 28
+**evacuation** [ɪˌvækju'eɪʃn] Evakuierung, Räumung **I**
even ['i:vn] sogar **I**
evening ['i:vnɪŋ] Abend **I**
event [ɪ'vent] Ereignis **II 1**, 8
ever ['evə] je(mals), immer **I**
every ['evri] jede(r/s) **I**
everybody ['evriˌbɒdi] jeder, alle (zusammen) **I**
everyone ['evriwʌn] jeder **I**
everything ['evriθɪŋ] alles **I**

everywhere ['evriweə] überall **I**
exact [ɪg'zækt] exakt, genau **I**
to **examine** [ɪg'zæmɪn] untersuchen **II 8**, 128
example [ɪg'zɑ:mpl] Beispiel **I**
excellent ['ekslnt] ausgezeichnet, exzellent **I**
except [ɪk'sept] außer **II 1**, 15
exchange [ɪks'tʃeɪndʒ] Austausch **II 7**, 113
to be **excited** [ɪk'saɪtɪd] aufgeregt sein **II 1**, 11
excitement [ɪk'saɪtmənt] Aufregung **II 4**, 61
exciting [ɪk'saɪtɪŋ] aufregend, spannend **I**
excuse [ɪk'skju:s] Entschuldigung **II 5**, 80
excuse me [ɪk'skju:z mi:] entschuldigen Sie **I**
exercise bike ['eksəsaɪz ˌbaɪk] Hometrainer **II 5**, 75
exercise book ['eksəsaɪz ˌbʊk] Übungsheft, Heft **I**
to **exercise** ['eksəsaɪz] üben, trainieren **II 5**, 72
exhibition [ˌeksɪ'bɪʃn] Ausstellung **I**
to **exit** ['eksɪt] hinausgehen, von der Bühne abgehen **II 7**, 111
to **expect** [ɪk'spekt] erwarten **II 1**, 12
expectation [ˌekspek'teɪʃn] Erwartung, Aussicht **II 5**, 75
expensive [ɪk'spensɪv] teuer **I**
experience [ɪk'spɪəriənts] Erfahrung **I**
experiment [ɪk'sperɪmənt] Versuch, Experiment **I**
expert ['ekspɜ:t] Experte/Expertin **II 2**, 26
to **explain** [ɪk'spleɪn] erklären **I**
expression [ɪk'spreʃn] Ausdruck **II 7**, 108
extra ['ekstrə] zusätzlich, extra **I**
extra cash [ˌekstrə 'kæʃ] Zuschlag, Sonderzahlung **II 7**, 110
extraterrestrial [ˌekstrətə'restriəl] außerirdisch, Außerirdische(r) **II 6**, 90
eye [aɪ] Auge **II 2**, 32

F

fabled ['feɪbld] sagenhaft, fabelhaft **II 7**, 111
face [feɪs] Gesicht **I**
to make a face [feɪs] ein Gesicht ziehen **II 1**, 14
fact [fækt] Tatsache, Fakt **I**
in fact [ɪn 'fækt] eigentlich **I**; tatsächlich **II 4**, 57
factory ['fæktri] Fabrik, Werk **II 7**, 110
failure ['feɪljə] Misserfolg, Scheitern **II 6**, 96
faint [feɪnt] schwach, matt **II 8**, 127
fair [feə] Fest, Jahrmarkt **II 1**, 12
Yours **faithfully**, ['feɪθfli] mit freundlichen Grüßen, hochachtungsvoll (*Briefschluss*) **I**
+**fall** (*AE*) [fɔ:l] Herbst **I**
to **fall*** [fɔ:l] fallen, stürzen **I**
to fall asleep [ˌfɔ:l‿ə'sli:p] einschlafen **II 4**, 62
false [fɔ:ls] falsch **II 8**, 126
family, (*pl.*) -ies ['fæməlɪ] Familie **I**
famous ['feɪməs] berühmt **I**
fan [fæn] Anhänger(in), Fan **II 5**, 76
fancy ['fæntsi] ausgefallen **II 5**, 73; +Stell' dir vor! **I**
Do you fancy ...? [dju: 'fæntsi] Hättest du Lust ...? **II 5**, 80
fantastic [fæn'tæstɪk] fantastisch **I**
fantasy ['fæntəsi] Fantasie **I**
far [fɑ:] weit **I**
farm [fɑ:m] Bauernhaus, Farm **I**
farmer ['fɑ:mə] Landwirt(in), Bauer/Bäuerin **II 2**, 33
fashion ['fæʃn] Mode **I**
fashionable ['fæʃnəbl] modisch, schick **II 7**, 107
fast [fɑ:st] schnell, rasch **I**
to **fasten** ['fɑ:sn] befestigen, anschnallen **II 6**, 93
fat [fæt] fett, dick **II 5**, 76
father ['fɑ:ðə] Vater **I**
fault [fɔ:lt] Fehler, Schuld **II 7**, 110
favorite (*AE*) ['feɪvrɪt] bevorzugt, Lieblings- **I**
favourite ['feɪvrɪt] bevorzugt, Lieblings- **I**
+**fax** [fæks] (Tele-)Fax **II 7**, 115
+**feast** [fi:st] Festmahl, Bankett **II 4**, 65
feather ['feðə] Feder, Gefieder **I**
February ['februri] Februar **I**
to **feed*** [fi:d] füttern **I**
to **feel*** [fi:l] fühlen **II 1**, 15
to feel sorry for [fi:l 'sɒri] bemitleiden **II 7**, 111
feeling ['fi:lɪŋ] Gefühl **II 1**, 17
feet (*pl.*) [fi:t] Füße **I**
+**female** ['fi:meɪl] weiblich **II 6**, 100
fence [fens] Zaun **II 6**, 95
ferry ['feri] Fähre **II 3**, 41
festival ['festɪvl] Festival **I**
to **fetch** [fetʃ] (ab)holen **I**
(a) **few** [fju:] wenige, ein paar **I**
science **fiction** [ˌsaɪənts 'fɪkʃn] Sciencefiction **II 6**, 90
field [fi:ld] Feld **I**
to **fight*** [faɪt] streiten, kämpfen **I**
figure ['fɪgə] Figur, Gestalt **II 3**, 43
to **fill** [fɪl] einfügen, auffüllen **I**
film [fɪlm] Film **I**
film-maker ['fɪlm ˌmeɪkə] Filmemacher(in) **II 2**, 25
final ['faɪnl] (aller)letzte/r/s **II 7**, 110
finally ['faɪnli] schließlich, endlich **II 3**, 48
financial [faɪ'nænʃl] finanziell, Finanz- **II 3**, 45
to **find*** [faɪnd] finden **I**
fine [faɪn] gut, prima **I**
finger ['fɪŋgə] Finger **I**
to **finish** ['fɪnɪʃ] beenden **I**
fire ['faɪə] Feuer **I**
fire engine ['faɪə‿endʒɪn] Feuerwehrauto **II 2**, 27
fireman ['faɪəmən] Feuerwehrmann **II 2**, 27
fireplace ['faɪəpleɪs] (offener) Kamin **I**
first ['fɜ:st] erste(r/s), der/die Erste **I**; zuerst **II 1**, 11
at first [ət 'fɜ:st] zunächst **II 1**, 11
first aid [ˌfɜ:st‿'eɪd] Erste Hilfe **II 2**, 27
fish [fɪʃ] Fisch **I**
⟨snapper fish⟩ ['snæpə ˌfɪʃ] Schnapper (*tropische Fischart*) **II 1**, 18
to **fish** [fɪʃ] angeln **I**
fishing line ['fɪʃɪŋ ˌlaɪn] Angelschnur **I**
to **fit** [fɪt] passen **I**
fit [fɪt] gesund, in Form **I**
to get fit [ˌget 'fɪt] fit werden **II 5**, 72
all-round **fitness** [ˌɔ:lraʊnd 'fɪtnəs] Rundum-Fitness **II 5**, 72
to **fix** [fɪks] befestigen, reparieren **I**
flash card ['flæʃ ˌkɑ:d] Illustrationstafel, Flashcard **II 5**, 81
in a flash [flæʃ] blitzschnell **I**
to **flash** [flæʃ] aufblitzen, aufleuchten **II 6**, 95
flashlight (*AE*) ['flæʃlaɪt] Taschenlampe **II 8**, 124
flat [flæt] (Etagen-)Wohnung **I**
flat tyre [ˌflæt 'taɪə] platter Reifen, Plattfuß **I**
flight [flaɪt] Flug **I**
to **fling* on** [ˌflɪŋ‿'ɒn] (*Kleidung*) schnell überwerfen, anziehen **II 6**, 96
float [fləʊt] Festzugswagen, Umzugswagen **II 1**, 8

flood [flʌd] Hochwasser, Überschwemmung **II 8**, 124
+to **flood** [flʌd] überfluten, überschwemmen **I**
floor [flɔː] +Fußboden **I**; +Stockwerk, Etage **I**
+**flow** [fləʊ] Strömung, Fließen **I**
flower ['flaʊə] Blume **I**
flu [fluː] Grippe **II 8**, 130
to **fly*** [flaɪ] fliegen **I**
+**focus group** ['fəʊkəs ˌgruːp] Gruppengespräch, Gesprächsgruppe **II 7**, 115
fog [fɒg] Nebel **I**
+**foggy** ['fɒgi] neb(e)lig **I**
folder ['fəʊldə] Mappe, Ordner **I**
folk [fəʊk] Volksmusik, Folk(-) **I**
  Irish folk [ˌaɪərɪʃ 'fəʊk] *Musikrichtung aus Irland* **I**
to **follow** ['fɒləʊ] folgen **I**
food [fuːd] Essen, Nahrung **I**
to **fool** [fuːl] zum Narren halten, hereinlegen **II 4**, 62
foot [fʊt] Fuß **I**; Fuß *(engl. Längenmaß, ca. 30 cm)* **II 7**, 113
  +on foot [ɒn 'fʊt] zu Fuß **II 3**, 50
  to step on so.'s foot [step] jmdm auf den Fuß treten **II 1**, 15
football ['fʊtbɔːl] Fußball **I**
footpath ['fʊtpɑːθ] Fußweg, Pfad **I**
footprint ['fʊtprɪnt] Fußstapfen **I**
footwear ['fʊtweə] Schuhe **I**
for [fɔː] für **I**; seit **II 2**, 26; … lang **II 4**, 62
  to look for ['lʊk fɔː] suchen **II 3**, 44
forever [fə'revə] für immer **I**
to **forget*** [fə'get] vergessen **I**
form [fɔːm] Form, Art **I**
formal ['fɔːml] förmlich, formell, offiziell **I**
+**forward** ['fɔːwəd] vorwärts **I**
  to look forward *(to)* [ˌlʊk 'fɔːwəd] sich freuen (auf) **I**
found [faʊnd] gefunden **I**
⟨**four-forty**⟩ [ˌfɔː 'fɔːti] eine Viertelmeile *(440 yards)* **II 5**, 79
frail [freɪl] zart, zerbrechlich **II 6**, 95
frame [freɪm] (Bilder-)Rahmen **I**
freak [friːk] Fan, Anhänger(in) **I**
free-climbing ['friːˌklaɪmɪŋ] Klettern ohne Ausrüstung **II 8**, 123
free [friː] frei, kostenlos **I**
freedom ['friːdəm] Freiheit **I**
°**French** ['frentʃ] französisch, Französisch **I**
frequent ['friːkwənt] häufig **II 3**, 48
fresh [freʃ] frisch **II 5**, 73
Friday ['fraɪdeɪ] Freitag **I**
fridge [frɪdʒ] Kühlschrank **I**
friend [frend] Freund(in) **I**
friendly ['frendli] freundlich, angenehm **I**
  friendly match [ˌfrendli 'mætʃ] Freundschaftsspiel **I**
+**friendship** ['fren(d)ʃɪp] Freundschaft **I**
to **frighten** ['fraɪtn] erschrecken, Angst machen **II 8**, 128
fringe [frɪndʒ] Franse, Rand- **II 3**, 41
from [frɒm] von **I**
  from … on [frəm ... 'ɒn] ab *(zeitl.)* **II 2**, 29
in **front** *(of)* [ɪn 'frʌnt] davor, vor **I**
front [frʌnt] Vor-, Vorder- **I**
  (at) the front [frʌnt] vorne **II 1**, 15
fruit [fruːt] Obst, Früchte **II 5**, 82
to **fry** [fraɪ] frittieren, braten **I**
full [fʊl] voll **I**
fun [fʌn] Spaß **I**
function ['fʌŋkʃn] Funktion, Aufgabe **II 4**, 59
to **function** ['fʌŋkʃn] arbeiten, funktionieren **II 8**, 128
funny ['fʌni] komisch, witzig, spaßig **I**
further ['fɜːðə] weiter **I**
future ['fjuːtʃə] Zukunft **II 5**, 74
+**fuzzy** ['fʌzi] unscharf, verschwommen **II 6**, 100

G

Gaelic ['geɪlɪk] gälisch, Gälisch **II 3**, 42
+**gallery** ['gæləri] Galerie **I**
to **gamble** ['gæmbl] (um Geld) spielen **II 4**, 61
gambling ['gæmblɪŋ] (Glücks-)Spiel **II 4**, 61
game [geɪm] Spiel **I**
°**Games** [geɪmz] Sport *(Fach)* **I**
gammon ['gæmən] geräucherter Schinken **II 5**, 78
+**gang** [gæŋ] Gang, Bande **II 7**, 116
gap [gæp] Lücke, Abstand **I**
garage ['gærɑːʒ] Garage **I**
garden ['gɑːdn] Garten **I**
gas *(AE)* [gæs] Benzin **II 6**, 92
  gas station *(AE)* ['gæs ˌsteɪʃn] Tankstelle **II 6**, 92
gate [geɪt] Tor **II 1**, 14
gear [gɪə] Ausrüstung **I**
geek [giːk] Langweiler(in), Spießer(in) **II 1**, 10
general ['dʒenrl] allgemein, generell **II 3**, 46
generation [ˌdʒenə'reɪʃn] Generation **II 4**, 62
+ladies and **gentlemen** ['leɪdiz‿ən 'dʒentlmən] (meine) Damen und Herren **I**
gently ['dʒentli] sanft, mild **II 3**, 44
geography [dʒi'ɒgrəfi] Erdkunde, Geografie **II 3**, 46
  Geography [dʒi'ɒgrəfi] °Erdkunde, Geografie *(Fach)* **I**
German ['dʒɜːmən] deutsch, Deutsch *(Fach)* **I**
to **get*** [get] bekommen; werden **I**; etw holen **II 5**, 74
  to get back [get 'bæk] zurückkommen, ankommen **II 4**, 62
  to get behind [get bɪ'haɪnd] in Rückstand geraten **II 5**, 78
  to get bored [bɔːd] sich langweilen **II 2**, 26
  to get into *(sth.)* [ˌget‿'ɪntə] einsteigen (in …) **I**
  to get into trouble ['trʌbl] in Schwierigkeiten geraten **II 8**, 79
  to get off [ˌget‿'ɒf] aussteigen, absteigen *(Zug, Bus, Fahrrad)* **I**
  to get on *(well with so.)* [ˌget‿ɒn 'wel] (gut mit jmdm) zurechtkommen **I**
  to get talking [get 'tɔːkiŋ] ins Gespräch kommen **II 5**, 78
  +to get through ['get θruː] verschleißen **II 5**, 83
  to get out [ˌget‿'aʊt] aussteigen *(Auto, Wagen, Waggon)* **I**
  to get up [get‿'ʌp] aufstehen *(vom Bett)* **II 1**, 13
ghost [gəʊst] Geist, Gespenst **I**
+**giant** ['dʒaɪənt] Riese, Gigant **I**
+**gift** [gɪft] Geschenk **II 4**, 65
gigantic [dʒaɪ'gæntɪk] gigantisch, riesig **II 6**, 90
girl [gɜːl] Mädchen **I**
girlfriend ['gɜːlfrend] Freundin **I**
gist [dʒɪst] Kernpunkt, (das) Wesentliche **II 4**, 57
to **give*** [gɪv] geben **I**
  to give a talk ['tɔːk] ein (Kurz-)Referat halten **I**
  to give up [gɪv‿'ʌp] aufgeben **II 5**, 78
glass [glɑːs] Glas **I**
glen [glen] (enges) Tal **II 3**, 44
glove [glʌv] Handschuh **I**
glow [gləʊ] Glut, grelles Licht **II 6**, 90
to **go*** [gəʊ] gehen **I**

to go at so. ['gəʊ ət] auf jmdn losgehen **II 1**, 15
to go for sth. ['gəʊ fɔ:] etw. anpacken, ausprobieren **II 5**, 72
to go in for [gəʊ‿'ɪn fɔ:] sich beteiligen an *(Wettbewerb)* **II 5**, 79
to go on [ˌgəʊ‿'ɒn] weitermachen, fortsetzen **I**; vorgehen **II 2**, 26
to go with ['gəʊ wɪð] passen zu **II 4**, 62
+**goal** [gəʊl] Tor **II 5**, 84
+**God** [gɒd] Gott **II 4**, 65
goddess ['gɒdes] Göttin **II 3**, 46
goggles ['gɒglz] Schutzbrille **II 5**, 72
gold [gəʊld] Gold **II 3**, 43
golden ['gəʊldn] golden **I**
golf [gɒlf] Golf **I**
gone [gɒn] ausgegangen, zu Ende gegangen **I**
good [gʊd] gut **I**
goodbye, bye [(ˌgʊd)'baɪ] (auf) Wiedersehen, tschüs, servus *(regional)* **I**
goodie-goodie ['gʊdiˌgʊdi] Streber(in), Brave(r) **II 1**, 15
+**gorgeous** ['gɔ:dʒəs] prächtig, prachtvoll **I**
+**gorilla** [gə'rɪlə] Gorilla **I**
gossip ['gosɪp] Klatsch, Tratsch **II 3**, 45
to have* **got** [ˌhæv 'got] haben **I**
government ['gʌvnmənt] Regierung **II 6**, 95
dressing **gown** ['dresɪŋ ˌgaʊn] Morgenrock **II 6**, 96
to **grab** [græb] packen, schnappen **II 6**, 95
graffiti [grə'fi:ti] Graffiti **I**
grandfather ['grænˌfɑ:ðə] Großvater **II 1**, 16
grandma ['grænmɑ:] Großmutter, Oma **I**
grandmother ['grænˌmʌðə] Großmutter **II 1**, 16
grandparent ['grænˌpeərnt] Großelternteil **II 1**, 16
grass [grɑ:s] Gras **II 3**, 44
⟨marram grass⟩ ['mærəm ˌgrɑ:s] Marramgras **II 3**, 47
to be **grateful** ['greɪtfl] dankbar sein **I**
graze [greɪz] Schürfwunde **II 8**, 128
great-grandmother [ˌgreɪt'grænˌmʌðə] Urgroßmutter **II 1**, 16
great [greɪt] großartig, spitze **I**
greedy ['gri:di] gierig, gefräßig **II 6**, 90
green [gri:n] grün **I**
greeting [gri:tɪŋ] Begrüßung, Gruß **II 7**, 113
grey [greɪ] grau **I**
grid [grɪd] Netz, Gitter **II 5**, 72
to **grin** [grɪn] grinsen **II 1**, 15
group [gru:p] Gruppe **I**
+focus group ['fəʊkəs ˌgru:p] Gruppengespräch, Gesprächsgruppe **II 7**, 115
vocal group ['vəʊkl ˌgru:p] Musikgruppe mit Gesang **II 4**, 57
to **grow*** [grəʊ] wachsen **I**; +anbauen **II 4**, 65
to grow up [grəʊ‿'ʌp] aufwachsen **II 1**, 16
grown-up ['grəʊnˌʌp] Erwachsene(r) **I**
to **guess** [ges] raten, vermuten **I**
guest [gest] Gast **I**
guide [gaɪd] Fremdenführer(in) **II 3**, 46
guide book ['gaɪd bʊk] Reiseführer *(Buch)* **I**
+guide dog ['gaɪd dɒg] Blindenhund **I**
guitar [gɪ'tɑ:] Gitarre **I**
chewing **gum** ['tʃu:ɪŋ ˌgʌm] Kaugummi **II 4**, 61
guy [gaɪ] +Freund, Kumpel **I**; Junge, Kerl **II 4**, 58
gym*(nasium)* [dʒɪm('neɪziəm)] Sporthalle **I**
gymnast ['dʒɪmnæst] Turner(in) **II 5**, 73
gymnastics [dʒɪm'næstɪks] Turnen **II 5**, 73

H

hair [heə] Haar **I**
half [hɑ:f] Hälfte **II 3**, 51
half [hɑ:f] halb **I**
hall [hɔ:l] Diele, (Eingangs-) Halle **I**
assembly hall [ə'sembli ˌhɔ:l] Aula, Versammlungssaal **I**
village hall [ˌvɪlɪdʒ 'hɔ:l] Gemeindehaus **I**
hand [hænd] Hand **I**
handbag ['hændbæg] Handtasche **I**
handlebar ['hændlbɑ:] Lenkstange, Lenker **II 6**, 95
handstand ['hændstænd] Handstand **II 5**, 75
to **hang* out** [ˌhæŋ‿'aʊt] herumlungern **II 4**, 61
hangout ['hæŋaʊt] Stammplatz, Stammlokal **II 4**, 61
to **happen** ['hæpn] geschehen, passieren **I**
happy ['hæpi] froh, glücklich **I**
+**harbor** *(AE)* ['hɑ:bə] Hafen **I**
harbour ['hɑ:bə] Hafen **I**
hard [hɑ:d] hart **I**
hardly ['hɑ:dli] kaum **II 7**, 109
to mean so. **harm** [ˌmi:n 'hɑ:m] jmdm. weh tun wollen **II 6**, 95
harmless ['hɑ:mləs] ungefährlich, harmlos **II 6**, 95
harmonica [hɑ:'mɒnɪkə] Mundharmonika **II 2**, 24
+leather **harness** [ˌleðə 'hɑ:nɪs] Ledergeschirr, -gurtwerk **I**
+**harvest** ['hɑ:vɪst] Ernte **II 4**, 65
hat [hæt] Hut **I**
to **hate** [heɪt] nicht mögen, hassen **I**
to **have*** [hæv] haben **I**
to have a look *(at)* [ˌhæv‿ə 'lʊk] (an)schauen, (an)gucken **II 8**, 130
to have got [ˌhæv 'got] haben **I**
to have to do sth. [ˌhæv tə 'du:] etw tun müssen **II 4**, 61
to have to do with [ˌhæv tə 'du:] mit etw zu tun haben **II 1**, 13
he [hi:] er **I**
head [hed] Kopf **I**
to **head for** ['hed fɔ:] zugehen auf **II 5**, 79
headache ['hedeɪk] Kopfschmerz, Kopfweh **II 8**, 128
heading ['hedɪŋ] Überschrift **I**
headline ['hedlaɪn] Schlagzeile **II 8**, 125
headphones ['hedfəʊnz] Kopfhörer **II 4**, 61
+**headstone** ['hedstəʊn] Grabstein **II 2**, 34
headteacher [ˌhed'ti:tʃə] Schulleiter(in) **I**
health [helθ] Gesundheit **II 7**, 107
Health [helθ] °Gesundheitslehre *(Fach)* **I**
healthy ['helθi] gesund **I**
to **hear*** [hɪə] hören **I**
heart [hɑ:t] Herz **II 3**, 45
heart attack ['hɑ:t‿əˌtæk] Herzinfarkt **I**
to learn by heart [ˌlɜ:n baɪ 'hɑ:t] auswendig lernen **II 1**, 11
heated ['hi:tɪd] geheizt **I**
heating ['hi:tɪŋ] Heizung **I**
heavy ['hevi] schwer **I**
hell [hel] Hölle **II 8**, 127
hello [hə'ləʊ] hallo **I**
crash **helmet** ['kræʃ ˌhelmət] Sturzhelm **II 6**, 95
help [help] Hilfe **I**
to **help** [help] helfen **I**
helpless ['helpləs] hilflos **I**
her [hɜ:] ihr/ihre **I**; sie *(Akk.)*; ihr *(Dat.)* **I**
here ['hɪə] hier **I**
+**heritage** ['herɪtɪdʒ] Erbe **II 3**, 50

+**hero** ['hɪərəʊ] Held **I**
hers [hɜ:z] ihre(r/s), der/die/das ihre **II 4**, 58
hey! [heɪ] He! **I**
hi [haɪ] hallo **I**
to be **hidden** ['hɪdn] versteckt sein **I**
to **hide*** [haɪd] (sich) verstecken, verbergen **I**
high-jump ['haɪˌdʒʌmp] Hochsprung **II 5**, 79
high [haɪ] hoch **I**
hill [hɪl] Hügel **I**
him [hɪm] ihn, ihm **I**
himself [hɪm'self] sich (selbst) **I**
hint [hɪnt] Hinweis, Andeutung **II 3**, 48
+to **hint** [hɪnt] andeuten, anspielen (auf) **II 2**, 34
hip hop ['hɪpˌhɒp] Hip-Hop *(Musikrichtung)* **II 2**, 25
his [hɪz] sein/seine **I**
to **hiss** [hɪs] zischen, fauchen **II 1**, 14
history ['hɪstri] Geschichte **II 3**, 42
°History ['hɪstri] Geschichte *(Fach)* **I**
hit [hɪt] Hit, Schlager **II 2**, 24
to **hit*** [hɪt] schlagen, stoßen **II 5**, 78; +(auf)treffen (auf), erreichen **I**
+**hitchhiker** ['hɪtʃhaɪkə] Anhalter(in), Tramper(in) **II 2**, 34
hobby, *(pl.)* -ies ['hɒbi] Hobby **I**
hockey ['hɒki] Hockey **I**
to **hold*** [həʊld] halten **II 3**, 43
+**holder** ['həʊldə] Inhaber(in), Pächter(in), Halter(in) **II 1**, 18
record-holder ['rekɔ:d ˌhəʊldə] Rekordhalter(in) **II 2**, 29
hole [həʊl] Loch **I**
holiday ['hɒlədeɪ] +Feiertag **II 4**, 65; Ferien, Urlaub **I**
bank holiday [ˌbæŋk 'hɒlədeɪ] Feiertag (im Mai und August) **II 1**, 13
holidaymaker ['hɒlədiˌmeɪkə] Urlauber(in) **I**
hols (= **holidays**) [hɒlz] Ferien **I**
home [həʊm] Heimat, Zuhause **II 3**, 47
at home [ət‿'həʊm] zu Hause, daheim **I**
+mobile home [ˌməʊbaɪl 'həʊm] Wohnmobil **I**
homeless ['həʊmləs] heimatlos **II 4**, 57
homepage ['həʊmpeɪdʒ] Homepage **I**
homework *(sing.)* ['həʊmwɜ:k] Hausaufgaben **I**
hope [həʊp] Hoffnung **II 6**, 96
to **hope** [həʊp] hoffen **I**
horrible ['hɒrəbl] schrecklich, entsetzlich **II 6**, 94
horror ['hɒrə] Entsetzen, Horror **II 2**, 32
horse [hɔ:s] Pferd **I**
horse-riding ['hɔ:sˌraɪdɪŋ] Reiten **II 5**, 73
hospital ['hɒspɪtl] Krankenhaus, Klinik **II 8**, 122
host [həʊst] Gastgeber(in) **II 7**, 113
hostel ['hɒstl] Herberge **I**
youth hostel ['ju:θ ˌhɒstl] Jugendherberge **I**
youth **hostelling** ['ju:θ ˌhɒstlɪŋ] in Jugendherbergen übernachten **I**
hot [hɒt] heiß; scharf (gewürzt) **I**
hot dog ['hɒt dɒg] Hotdog *(langes weiches Brötchen mit Würstchen)* **I**
hotel [həʊ'tel] Hotel **I**
hour ['aʊə] Stunde **I**
house [haʊs] Haus **I**
to **hover** ['hɒvə] schweben **II 6**, 90
how [haʊ] wie **I**
How are you? [ˌhaʊ‿'ɑ: ju:] Wie geht's (dir/euch/Ihnen)? **I**
How d'you do? [ˌhaʊ djʊ 'du:] Guten Tag! Sehr erfreut! **II 7**, 113
how long ago? [ˌhaʊ lɒŋ‿ə'gəʊ] wie lange her? **II 3**, 45
how many? ['haʊ ˌmeni] wie viele? **I**
how much? ['haʊ ˌmʌtʃ] wie viel? **I**
huge [hju:dʒ] riesig, gewaltig **II 7**, 110
humour ['hju:mə] Humor **II 2**, 35
hungry ['hʌŋgri] hungrig **I**
hurricane ['hʌrɪkən] Wirbelsturm, Orkan **II 8**, 124
in a **hurry** ['hʌri] in Eile, eilig **I**
to **hurry** *(up)* [ˌhʌri‿'ʌp] (sich) beeilen **I**
to **hurt*** [hɜ:t] wehtun, schmerzen **I**
hygiene ['haɪdʒi:n] Gesundheitspflege, Hygiene **II 8**, 122
+**hypnosis** [hɪp'nəʊsɪs] Hypnose **II 6**, 100

I

I [aɪ] ich **I**
I'd (= *I would*) like [aɪd‿'laɪk] ich hätte gerne **I**
I'm (*I am*) [aɪm] ich bin **I**
ice [aɪs] Eis **I**
ice cream [aɪs 'kri:m] Eiskrem, (Speise-)Eis **I**
ice cream maker [aɪs 'kri:m ˌmeɪkə] Eismaschine **I**
ice skate ['aɪs ˌskeɪt] Schlittschuh **II 7**, 108
ice-skating ['aɪsˌskeɪtɪŋ] Schlittschuhlaufen **II 7**, 108
+**icy** ['aɪsi] eisig **I**
idea [aɪ'dɪə] Idee, Einfall **I**; Eindruck, Vorstellung **II 2**, 26
ideal [aɪ'dɪəl] ideal, hervorragend **I**
idiot ['ɪdiət] Idiot **I**
if [ɪf] wenn, falls **I**; +ob **II 4**, 65
to **ignore** [ɪg'nɔ:] hinwegsehen, ignorieren **II 5**, 79
ill [ɪl] krank **II 8**, 133
illegal [ɪ'li:gl] ungesetzlich, illegal **I**
illness ['ɪlnəs] Krankheit **II 8**, 122
+**image** ['ɪmɪdʒ] Bild, Image **II 7**, 115
to **imagine** [ɪ'mædʒɪn] sich vorstellen, annehmen **I**
immigrant ['ɪmɪgrənt] Einwanderer / Einwanderin **II 1**, 16
important [ɪm'pɔ:tnt] wichtig **II 1**, 10
+**impossible** [ɪm'pɒsəbl] unmöglich **II 5**, 83
to **improve** [ɪm'pru:v] verbessern **II 5**, 72
to **improvise** ['ɪmprəvaɪz] improvisieren **II 4**, 57
in [ɪn] in/im **I**
in a flash [flæʃ] blitzschnell **I**
in a hurry ['hʌri] in Eile, eilig **I**
in case [keɪs] falls **II 8**, 124
in common [ɪn 'kɒmən] gemeinsam **I**
in fact [ɪn 'fækt] eigentlich **I**
in front [ɪn 'frʌnt] vorne **I**
in public ['pʌblɪk] in der Öffentlichkeit **II 5**, 72
+in return [ɪn rɪ'tɜ:n] dafür **I**
in total [ɪn 'təʊtl] insgesamt, total **II 7**, 110
to **include** [ɪn'klu:d] einschließen, einbeziehen **II 1**, 12
to **increase** [ɪn'kri:s] (an)steigen, zunehmen **II 2**, 29
independent [ˌɪndɪ'pendənt] unabhängig **I**
Indian ['ɪndiən] Inder(in) **I**; +Indianer(in) **II 4**, 65
+Seminole Indian ['semɪnəʊl ˌɪndiən] *Angehörige(r) eines indianischen Stamms* **I**
+**individualist** [ˌɪndɪ'vɪdʒuəlɪst] Individualist(in) **II 7**, 115
indoor [ˌɪn'dɔ:] Innen-, Hallen- **I**
indoors [ɪn'dɔ:z] drinnen, zu Hause **II 8**, 127
industry ['ɪndəstri] Industrie **II 2**, 29
influence ['ɪnfluəns] Einfluss **II 7**, 107
to **inform** [ɪn'fɔ:m] informieren, benachrichtigen **II 2**, 27
information [ˌɪnfə'meɪʃn] Information **I**

to **inject** [ɪn'dʒekt] (ein)spritzen **II 8**, 123
injection [ɪn'dʒekʃn] Spritze, Injektion **II 8**, 128
to **injure** ['ɪndʒə] verletzen **II 8**, 124
inside [ˌɪn'saɪd] im Innern (von) **I**
insider [ˌɪn'saɪdə] Eingeweihte(r), Insider(in) **II 7**, 106
inspiration [ˌɪntspr'eɪʃn] Eingebung, Inspiration **II 6**, 90
to **install** [ɪn'stɔ:l] installieren, einbauen **II 2**, 27
instead of [ɪn'sted‿əv] anstelle von, statt **II 5**, 82
institution [ˌɪnstɪ'tju:ʃn] Institution, Einrichtung **II 3**, 46
+to **instruct** [ɪn'strʌkt] anweisen, instruieren **II 6**, 100
instruction [ɪn'strʌkʃn] Anweisung, Anleitung **II 8**, 128
+**instructions** [ɪn'strʌkʃnz] Anweisungen, Instruktionen **I**
instrument ['ɪnstrəmənt] Instrument **I**
insurance [ɪn'ʃʊərns] Versicherung **II 8**, 122
intelligence [ɪn'telɪdʒnts] Intelligenz **II 6**, 98
intelligent [ɪn'telɪdʒnt] intelligent **II 6**, 99
intention [ɪn'tenʃn] Absicht, Intention **I**
interest ['ɪntrəst] Interesse **II 7**, 113
to be **interested** *(in)* ['ɪntrəstɪd‿ɪn] interessiert sein (an) **II 3**, 42
interesting ['ɪntrəstɪŋ] interessant **I**
international [ˌɪntə'næʃnl] international **I**
Internet ['ɪntənet] Internet **I**
interview ['ɪntəvju:] Interview **I**
to **interview** ['ɪntəvju:] interviewen, befragen **I**
interviewer ['ɪntəvju:ə] Interviewer(in) **II 3**, 46
into ['ɪntə] in ... hinein **I**
  I'm into ... ['ɪntə] ich stehe auf .../ ich bin begeistert von ... **I**
  to get* into *(sth.)* [ˌget‿'ɪntə] einsteigen (in ...) **I**
  to turn into ['tɜ:n‿ɪntʊ] (sich)verwandeln in **II 7**, 111
to **introduce** [ˌɪntrə'dju:s] vorstellen, bekannt machen **II 6**, 95
to **invade** [ɪn'veɪd] einmarschieren **II 4**, 58
to **invent** [ɪn'vent] erfinden **II 8**, 126
invention [ɪn'venʃn] Erfindung **II 4**, 61
inventor [ɪn'ventə] Erfinder(in) **II 4**, 61
invitation [ˌɪnvɪ'teɪʃn] Einladung **II 3**, 45
to **invite** [ɪn'vaɪt] einladen **I**
to **involve** [ɪn'vɒlv] einbeziehen, verwickeln **II 8**, 128
Irish ['aɪərɪʃ] irisch, Irisch **II 3**, 51
  Irish folk [ˌaɪərɪʃ 'fəʊk] *Musikrichtung aus Irland* **I**
iron age ['aɪən‿ˌeɪdʒ] Eisenzeit **II 3**, 43
irregular [ɪ'regjələ] unregelmäßig **II 3**, 42
is [ɪz] ist **I**
  's *(is)* [ɪz] ist **I**
  isn't *(is not)* ['ɪznt] ist nicht **I**
island ['aɪlənd] Insel **II 3**, 48
°**IT** *(Information Technology)* [ˌaɪ'ti: (ˌɪnfə'meɪʃn tek'nɒlədʒi)] Informatik **I**
it [ɪt] es **I**
+**Italian** [ɪ'tæliən] italienisch, Italienisch **I**
+**item** ['aɪtəm] Gegenstand, Artikel **I**
itself [ɪt'self] (es) selbst, sich **II 2**, 24

J

jacket ['dʒækɪt] Jacke, Jackett **I**
traffic **jam** ['træfɪk ˌdʒæm] Verkehrsstau **II 3**, 48
January ['dʒænjuri] Januar **I**
jazz [dʒæz] Jazz *(Musikrichtung)* **I**
+**jeans** [dʒi:nz] Jeans **I**
crown **jewels** [ˌkraʊn 'dʒu:əlz] Kronjuwelen **I**
jewellery ['dʒu:əlri] Juwelen, Schmuck **II 3**, 43
+**jewelry** *(AE)* ['dʒu:əlri] Schmuck **I**
+**Jewish** ['dʒu:ɪʃ] jüdisch **I**
job [dʒɒb] Job, Arbeit, Stelle **I**
to **jog** [dʒɒg] anstoßen, antippen **II 6**, 95
to **join** [dʒɔɪn] beitreten, Mitglied werden **II 5**, 72
  to join in *(with)* [ˌdʒɔɪn‿'ɪn] teilnehmen (an) **II 1**, 12
  +to join so. [dʒɔɪn] sich jmdm anschließen **II 4**, 65
journey ['dʒɜ:ni] Reise **II 3**, 41
joy [dʒɔɪ] Freude, Vergnügen **II 3**, 45
jug [dʒʌg] Krug, Kanne **II 3**, 44
to **juggle** ['dʒʌgl] jonglieren **I**
carrot **juice** ['kærət ˌdʒu:s] Karottensaft **II 5**, 74
  orange juice ['ɒrɪndʒ ˌdʒu:s] Orangensaft **II 5**, 76
July [dʒʊ'laɪ] Juli **I**
to **jump** [dʒʌmp] springen **I**
jumper ['dʒʌmpə] Strickjacke **I**
June [dʒu:n] Juni **I**
junior choir [ˌdʒu:niə 'kwaɪə] Chor der unteren Klassenstufen **I**
just [dʒʌst] gerade, eben **I**; nur, bloß **II 3**, 49; +genau **II 4**, 65

K

to **keep*** [ki:p] (be)halten **I**
  to keep doing sth [ˌki:p 'du:ɪŋ] etw immer wieder, ununterbrochen tun **II 5**, 79
  to keep sth up [ˌki:p‿'ʌp] etw (durch)halten **II 5**, 79
  to keep *(warm)* [ki:p] (warm) bleiben **II 8**, 124
  to keep up *(with so.)* [ˌki:p‿'ʌp] Schritt halten (mit jmdm) **II 1**, 15
kerb [kɜ:b] Bordsteinkante **II 8**, 127
key [ki:] Schlüssel(-) **II 5**, 79
  key word ['ki: wɜ:d] Schlüsselbegriff **I**
keyboard ['ki:bɔ:d] elektronische Orgel, Keyboard **I**
keyboarder ['ki:bɔ:də] Keyboardspieler(in) **I**
kick [kɪk] (Fuß-)Tritt, Stoß **II 1**, 15
to **kick** [kɪk] treten, (mit dem Fuß) stoßen **II 1**, 15
kid [kɪd] Kind **I**
to **kill** [kɪl] töten, umbringen **II 6**, 96
kilometre [kɪ'lɒmɪtə] Kilometer **I**
kind [kaɪnd] Art, Sorte **I**
  What kind *(of)* ...? [kaɪnd] Was für eine/welche Art ...? **I**
king [kɪŋ] König **I**
⟨to **kiss**⟩ [kɪs] küssen **II 5**, 77
kit [kɪt] Ausrüstung **II 8**, 124
  °drum kit ['drʌm kɪt] Schlagzeugausrüstung **I**
kitchen ['kɪtʃɪn] Küche **I**
knee-bend ['ni:bend] Kniebeuge **II 5**, 75
knife, *(pl.)* -ves [naɪf] Messer **I**
knight [naɪt] Ritter **I**
knob [nɒb] Knopf, Knauf **II 4**, 61
knock [nɒk] Klopfen, Pochen **II 3**, 45
°to **knock** [kɒk] klopfen **I**
  to knock so. out [nɒk‿'aʊt] jmdn bewusstlos schlagen/werden lassen **II 8**, 128
to be **knocked down** [bi: ˌnɒkt 'daʊn] umgefahren werden **II 6**, 95
to **know*** [nəʊ] wissen, kennen **I**
knowledge ['nɒlɪdʒ] Wissen, Kenntnis **II 7**, 110
kung fu film [ˌkʊŋ 'fu: fɪlm] Kung-Fu-Film **I**

L

label ['leɪbl] Etikett, Label **II 7**, 111
labour ['leɪbə] Arbeit, Arbeitskräfte **II 7**, 110
ladder ['lædə] Leiter **II 8**, 131
lady ['leɪdi] Dame, Frau **I**
cleaning lady ['kli:nɪŋ ˌleɪdi] Zugehfrau, Putzfrau **I**
+ladies and gentlemen ['leɪdiz‿ən 'dʒentlmən] (meine) Damen und Herren **I**
lake [leɪk] See **II 3**, 51
lamb [læm] Lamm(fleisch) **II 4**, 60
land [lænd] Land **I**
+to **land** [lænd] landen **I**
lander ['lændə] Landeeinheit **II 6**, 92
landing ['lændɪŋ] Landung **II 6**, 91
landscape ['lændskeɪp] Landschaft **I**
lane [leɪn] Gasse, Sträßchen **II 6**, 95
language ['læŋgwɪdʒ] Sprache **II 3**, 41
large [lɑ:dʒ] groß, weitläufig **II 2**, 26
laser beam ['leɪzə ˌbi:m] Laserstrahl **II 6**, 91
+to **last** [lɑ:st] andauern, anhalten **II 8**, 132
last [lɑ:st] letzte(r/s), der/die Letzte **I**
+at last [ət 'lɑ:st] endlich **II 6**, 100
late [leɪt] spät **I**
to be late (for) [leɪt] zu spät kommen (für), spät dran sein **II 1**, 17
later ['leɪtə] später **I**
latest ['leɪtɪst] neueste(r/s), zuletzt erschienene(r/s) **I**
Latin ['lætɪn] lateinisch, Latein **I**
to **laugh** [lɑ:f] lachen **I**
laughter ['lɑ:ftə] Gelächter, Lachen **II 1**, 12
+**launch** [lɔ:ntʃ] Abschuss **II 6**, 100
+to **launch** [lɔ:ntʃ] abschießen **II 6**, 100
law [lɔ:] Gesetz **II 7**, 110
+**lawn** [lɔ:n] Rasen **I**
layout ['leɪaʊt] Gestaltung, Layout **I**
lazy ['leɪzi] faul **II 5**, 78
lead singer [ˌli:d 'sɪŋə] Leadsänger(in) **II 4**, 57
leader ['li:də] Anführer(in) **II 3**, 43
to **learn*** [lɜ:n] lernen **I**
to learn by heart [ˌlɜ:n baɪ 'hɑ:t] auswendig lernen **II 1**, 11
learning tip ['lɜ:nɪŋ ˌtɪp] Lerntipp **I**
at **least** [ət 'li:st] zumindest **II 7**, 110
least said soonest mended [ˌli:st 'sed ˌsu:nəst 'mendɪd] je weniger geredet wird, desto schneller wird es wieder gut **II 6**, 95
leather ['leðə] Leder **I**
+leather harness [ˌleðə 'hɑ:nɪs] Ledergeschirr, -gurtwerk **I**
to **leave*** [li:v] weggehen, verlassen **I**
to leave behind [ˌli:v bɪ'haɪnd] zurück-, hinterlassen **II 2**, 33
left [left] links **I**
leg [leg] Bein **II 4**, 59
legal ['li:gl] gesetzlich, legal **II 4**, 61
legend ['ledʒənd] Legende **I**
to **lend*** [lend] (ver)leihen **I**
leotard ['li:ətɑ:d] Trikot, Gymnastikanzug **II 5**, 73
less [les] weniger **I**
lesson ['lesn] Unterrichtsstunde **I**
+to **let*** [let] lassen **II 3**, 50
let's (*let us*) [lets] lass(t) uns **I**
letter ['letə] Buchstabe; Brief **I**
capital letter [ˌkæpɪtl 'letə] Großbuchstabe **I**
level ['levl] Ebene, Niveau **II 5**, 73
liar ['laɪə] Lügner(in) **II 4**, 62
librarian [laɪ'breəriən] Bibliothekar(in) **II 2**, 29
library ['laɪbri] Bibliothek, Bücherei **I**
⟨**lie**⟩ [laɪ] Lüge **II 5**, 77
+to **lie** [laɪ] lügen **II 7**, 116
to **lie*** [laɪ] liegen **I**
life, (*pl.*) -ves [laɪf] Leben **I**
lifebelt ['laɪfbelt] Rettungsgurt, Rettungsring **I**
lifeboat ['laɪfbəʊt] Rettungsboot **I**
lifeguard ['laɪfgɑ:d] Rettungsschwimmer(in) **I**
lifejacket ['laɪfˌdʒækɪt] Schwimmweste **I**
lifeline ['laɪflaɪn] Rettungsleine **I**
lifetime ['laɪftaɪm] Lebenszeit, Leben **I**
light [laɪt] Licht **I**
traffic light ['træfɪk ˌlaɪt] Ampel **I**
lighthouse ['laɪthaʊs] Leuchtturm **I**
to **like** [laɪk] mögen, gerne haben **I**
I'd (= *I would*) like [aɪd‿'laɪk] ich hätte gerne **I**
would you like to? [ˌwʊd ˌju: 'laɪk tə] möchtest du?/möchtet ihr/möchten Sie? **I**
like [laɪk] (ebenso) wie **I**
to be (sound/look) like [laɪk] sein (sich anhören/aussehen) wie **II 3**, 47
likely ['laɪkli] wahrscheinlich **II 6**, 99
line [laɪn] Linie **I**; ⟨Zitat⟩ **II 1**, 18; Zeile **II 4**, 57
fishing line ['fɪʃɪŋ ˌlaɪn] Angelschnur **I**
+supply line [sə'plaɪ ˌlaɪn] Versorgungsleitung **I**
to **line up** [ˌlaɪn‿'ʌp] (sich) aufstellen **II 1**, 14
+**lipstick** ['lɪpstɪk] Lippenstift **II 6**, 100
list [lɪst] Liste **I**
to **listen** ['lɪsn] zuhören **I**
listening comprehension ['lɪsnɪŋ ˌkɒmprɪ'henʃn] Hörverstehen **I**
to **litter** ['lɪtə] verstreuen, übersäen **II 6**, 95
little ['lɪtl] klein **I**; wenig **II 5**, 73
to **live** [lɪv] wohnen, leben **I**
live [laɪv] lebendig, direkt, live **I**
to **liven up** [ˌlaɪvn‿'ʌp] beleben, aufmuntern **II 1**, 12
living room ['lɪvɪŋ ˌrʊm] Wohnzimmer **I**
ll. (= **lines**) [laɪnz] Zeilen **I**
local ['ləʊkl] lokal, örtlich, Orts- **I**
location [ləʊ'keɪʃn] Standort, (Dreh-)Ort **II 2**, 29
loch [lɒk/lɒx] See *(schottisch)* **II 3**, 44
logo ['ləʊgəʊ] Logo, Emblem **I**
Londoner ['lʌndənə] Londoner(in) **II 3**, 42
to **long** (*for*) ['lɒŋ ˌfɔ:] sich sehnen (nach) **II 3**, 45
long [lɒŋ] lang **I**
how long ago? [ˌhaʊ lɒŋ‿ə'gəʊ] wie lange her? **II 3**, 45
long-distance truck driver [ˌlɒŋ'dɪstns 'trʌk ˌdraɪvə] Fernfahrer(in) **II 4**, 60
long-jump ['lɒŋˌdʒʌmp] Weitsprung **II 5**, 79
look [lʊk] Blick, Anblick **II 5**, 79
to have a look *(at)* [ˌhæv‿ə 'lʊk] (an)schauen, (an)gucken **II 8**, 130
to **look** [lʊk] schauen, betrachten **I**; aussehen **II 4**, 62
to look after [ˌlʊk‿'ɑ:ftə] schauen nach, sorgen für **I**
to look for ['lʊk fɔ:] suchen **II 3**, 44
to look forward (*to*) [ˌlʊk 'fɔ:wəd] sich freuen (auf) **I**
to look like [laɪk] aussehen wie **II 3**, 47
to look sth. up [ˌlʊk‿'ʌp] etw nachschlagen **I**
loose [lu:s] lose, locker **II 3**, 43
to **lose*** [lu:s] verlieren **I**
loser ['lu:zə] Verlierer(in) **II 5**, 78

lost [lɒst] verloren **I**
to be lost [lɒst] sich verlaufen haben **I**
a **lot** [ə 'lɒt] viel, eine Menge **I**
lots of ['lɒts‿əv] viele (von) **I**
loud [laʊd] laut **I**
out loud [ˌaʊt 'laʊd] laut (vorlesen, sprechen) **II 3**, 45
love [lʌv] (in) Liebe; herzlichst **I**
to **love** [lʌv] lieben, gern haben, mögen **I**
lovely ['lʌvli] hübsch, schön **I**
lover ['lʌvə] Liebhaber(in), Geliebte(r) **II 3**, 45
low [ləʊ] niedrig **I**
luck [lʌk] Glück **I**
to be **lucky** ['lʌki] Glück haben **II 1**, 19
lunch [lʌntʃ] Mittagessen **I**
lung [lʌŋ] Lunge **II 5**, 72
⟨**lyrics** (*pl.*)⟩ ['lɪrɪks] (Lied-)Text **II 2**, 32

M

machine [mə'ʃi:n] Apparat, Maschine **II 6**, 93
mad [mæd] verrückt, wahnsinnig **I**
madam ['mædəm] gnädige Frau (*Anrede*) **I**
magazine [ˌmægə'zi:n] Zeitschrift **I**
magic ['mædʒɪk] magisch, zauberhaft **II 4**, 67
mail [meɪl] Post **II 3**, 44
main [meɪn] Haupt- **II 3**, 41
major ['meɪdʒə] größter, Haupt- **I**
make-up ['meɪkʌp] Makeup, Maske **II 2**, 29
to **make*** [meɪk] machen **I**
to make a face [feɪs] ein Gesicht ziehen **II 1**, 14
to make so. do sth. ['meɪk ˌsʌmwʌn 'du: ˌsʌmθɪŋ] jmdn veranlassen etw zu tun **I**
to make sure [ˌmeɪk 'ʃʊə] sicherstellen **I**
to make the most of sth. [məʊst] das Beste aus etw machen **I**
to make up [ˌmeɪk‿'ʌp] (sich) ausdenken, erfinden **I**
make yourself at home [ˌmeɪk‿jɔ:ˌself‿ət 'həʊm] machen Sie es sich gemütlich **II 8**, 126
ice cream **maker** [aɪs 'kri:m ˌmeɪkə] Eismaschine **I**
shopping **mall** (*AE*) ['ʃɒpɪŋ ˌmɑ:l] Einkaufszentrum **I**
man, (*pl.*) men [mæn/men] Mann / Männer **I**
to **manage** ['mænɪdʒ] bewältigen, schaffen **II 3**, 46
⁺**manager** ['mænɪdʒə] Manager(in) **II 7**, 115
manned [mænd] bemannt **II 6**, 92
⁺**manufacturer** [ˌmænjə'fæktʃərə] Hersteller(in), Produzent(in)(in), Fabrikant **II 7**, 116
how **many?** ['haʊ ˌmeni] wie viele? **I**
map [mæp] Stadtplan, Landkarte **I**
mind map ['maɪnd mæp] *etwa:* Gedankennetz **I**
Marathon ['mærəθn] Marathon **I**
March [mɑ:tʃ] März **I**
marching band ['mɑ:tʃɪŋ ˌbænd] Marschkapelle **II 1**, 12
to **mark** [mɑ:k] markieren **I**
marked [mɑ:kt] markiert **I**
market ['mɑ:kɪt] Markt **I**
⁺**marketing** ['mɑ:kɪtɪŋ] Vertrieb, Absatz, Marketing **II 7**, 115
⟨**marram grass**⟩ ['mærəm ˌgrɑ:s] Marramgras **II 3**, 47
to **marry** ['mæri] heiraten **II 5**, 80
to be married ['mærid] verheiratet sein **II 5**, 76
to get married [ˌget 'mærɪd] heiraten **II 5**, 74
marsh [mɑ:ʃ] Marschland, Sumpf **I**
mass [mæs] Menge, Masse **II 6**, 95
match [mætʃ] Streichholz; Spiel (*Sport*) **I**
friendly match [ˌfrendli 'mætʃ] Freundschaftsspiel **I**
to **match** [mætʃ] zuordnen **I**
mate [meɪt] Freund(in), Kumpel **II 8**, 127
°**Maths** [mæθs] Mathe(matik) **I**
matter ['mætə] Sache, Angelegenheit **II 5**, 74
May [meɪ] Mai **I**
may [meɪ] dürfen, können **I**
maybe ['meɪbi] vielleicht **I**
mayor [meə] Bürgermeister(in) **II 1**, 19
me [mi:] mich **I**
meal [mi:l] Mahlzeit, Essen **I**
to **mean*** [mi:n] bedeuten; meinen **I**
to mean so. harm [ˌmi:n 'hɑ:m] jmdm weh tun wollen **II 6**, 95
meaning ['mi:nɪŋ] Bedeutung, Sinn **II 3**, 51
meaningless ['mi:nɪŋləs] sinnlos, bedeutungslos **II 2**, 29
means [mi:nz] Mittel **II 3**, 46
mechanic [mɪ'kænɪk] Mechaniker(in) **II 4**, 61
media ['mi:diə] Medien **II 2**, 27
medicine ['medsn] Medizin **II 8**, 122
to **meet*** [mi:t] treffen, begegnen **I**
Pleased to meet you. [pli:zd] Angenehm. Sehr erfreut. **II 7**, 113
meeting ['mi:tɪŋ] Treffen, Begegnung **I**
member ['membə] Mitglied **I**
memory ['memri] Erinnerung **I**; Gedächtnis **I**
to **mend** [mend] ausbessern, reparieren **I**
least said soonest mended [ˌli:st 'sed ˌsu:nəst 'mendɪd] je weniger geredet wird, desto schneller wird es wieder gut **II 6**, 95
to **mention** ['mentʃn] erwähnen **II 6**, 99
merit ['merɪt] Verdienst, Leistung **II 2**, 29
mess [mes] Unordnung, Durcheinander **II 8**, 126
⁺**message** ['mesɪdʒ] Nachricht, Mitteilung **I**
metal ['metl] Metall **II 3**, 43
to **miaow** [ˌmi:'aʊ] miauen **II 1**, 14
mice (*pl.*) [maɪs] Mäuse **II 1**, 19
°**microphone** ['maɪkrəfəʊn] Mikrofon **I**
microwave oven [ˌmaɪkrəʊweɪv‿'ʌvn] Mikrowellenherd **II 6**, 92
⁺**mid-town** ['mɪdtaʊn] *mittlerer Teil der Insel Manhattan in New York* **I**
⁺**middle** ['mɪdl] Mitte **I**
midnight ['mɪdnaɪt] Mitternacht **II 4**, 57
might [maɪt] könnte(n), dürfte(n) **II 5**, 73
mile [maɪl] Meile *(Längenmaß = 1,61 km)* **I**
military ['mɪlɪtri] militärisch, Militär- **II 4**, 62
million ['mɪljən] Million **I**
mind map ['maɪnd mæp] *etwa:* Gedankennetz **I**
to **mind** [maɪnd] etw dagegen haben **II 5**, 72
minibus ['mɪnɪbʌs] Kleinbus **I**
minimal ['mɪnɪml] gering, minimal **II 8**, 123
minimum ['mɪnɪməm] Minimum **II 7**, 110
Prime **Minister** [ˌpraɪm 'mɪnɪstə] Premierminister(in) **II 8**, 128
⁺**minus** ['maɪnəs] minus **I**
minute ['mɪnɪt] Minute **I**
miserable ['mɪzrəbl] unglücklich, miserabel **II 5**, 78
misery ['mɪzri] Qual, Misere **II 5**, 78
Miss [mɪs] Fräulein (*Anrede*) **I**
to **miss** [mɪs] nicht treffen, verfehlen **II 1**, 15; verpassen, versäumen **I**
to be **missing** ['mɪsɪŋ] fehlen **II 7**, 112

mission ['mɪʃn] Auftrag, Mission **II 6**, 92
mistake [mɪ'steɪk] Fehler **I**
+**mobile home** [ˌməʊbaɪl 'həʊm] Wohnmobil **I**
mobile phone [ˌməʊbaɪl 'fəʊn] Mobiltelefon, Handy **I**
model ['mɒdl] Modell **I**
modem ['məʊdem] Modem **I**
modern ['mɒdn] modern, zeitgemäß **II 7**, 108
mom (*AE*) [mɒm] Mama, Mutti **II 5**, 74
at the **moment** ['məʊmənt] im Moment, zur Zeit **I**
Monday ['mʌndeɪ] Montag **I**
money ['mʌni] Geld **I**
pocket money ['pɒkɪt ˌmʌni] Taschengeld **I**
+**monorail** ['mɒnəreɪl] Einschienenbahn **II 3**, 50
+**monotone** ['mɒnətəʊn] monotoner Klang **II 6**, 100
monster ['mɒnstə] Ungeheuer, Monster **II 3**, 45
month [mʌntθ] Monat **II 2**, 28
+**monument** ['mɒnjəmənt] Baudenkmal, Monument **II 3**, 50
+**moon** [mu:n] Mond **I**
moonlight ['mu:nlaɪt] Mondlicht **II 4**, 57
+**moped** ['məʊped] Moped, Kleinkraftrad **I**
more [mɔ:] mehr **I**
not ... any more [ˌnɒt ... ˌeni 'mɔ:] (überhaupt) nicht mehr, keine ... mehr **II 1**, 16
morning ['mɔ:nɪŋ] Morgen, Vormittag **I**
most (*of*) ['məʊst‿əv] meiste(r/s) **I**
to make the most of sth. [məʊst] das Beste aus etw machen **I**
mostly ['məʊstli] meistens, hauptsächlich **II 1**, 19
mother ['mʌðə] Mutter **I**
motion picture ['məʊʃn ˌpɪktʃə] Film (*wörtl.:* Bewegungsbild) **II 2**, 29
motorbike ['məʊtəˌbaɪk] Motorrad **I**
motorcycle ['məʊtəˌsaɪkl] Motorrad **II 6**, 95
motorcyclist ['məʊtəˌsaɪklɪst] Motorradfahrer(in) **II 8**, 128
motorhome ['məʊtəˌhəʊm] Wohnmobil **I**
motorway café ['məʊtəweɪ 'kæfeɪ] Cafeteria auf der Autobahn **I**
+**motto** ['mɒtəʊ] Motto, Leitsatz **I**
mountain ['maʊntɪn] Berg **II 8**, 123
mountain bike ['maʊntɪn ˌbaɪk] Geländefahrrad, Mountainbike **I**
mountain climber ['maʊntɪn ˌklaɪmə] Bergsteiger(in) **II 8**, 123
mountain climbing ['maʊntɪn ˌklaɪmɪŋ] Bergsteigen **II 8**, 123
mouse [maʊs] Maus **I**
°**mouth** [maʊθ] Mund **I**
to **move** [mu:v] (sich) bewegen; umziehen **I**
+**movement** ['mu:vmənt] Bewegung **II 3**, 50
movie (*AE*) ['mu:vi] Film **I**
moving ['mu:vɪŋ] beweglich **II 6**, 95
Mr ['mɪstə] Herr (*Anrede*) **I**
Mrs ['mɪsɪz] Frau (*Anrede für verheiratete Frauen*) **I**
Ms [mɪz/məz] Frau (*Anrede*) **I**
much [mʌtʃ] viel **I**
how much? ['haʊ ˌmʌtʃ] wie viel? **I**
mud [mʌd] Schlamm, Matsch **II 8**, 129
muddy ['mʌdi] schmutzig, schlammig **II 5**, 72
muesli ['mju:zli] Müsli **II 5**, 74
muffin ['mʌfɪn] weiches Brötchen, kleiner Kuchen **II 4**, 63
mum [mʌm] Mama, Mutti **I**
mummy ['mʌmi] Mami, Mutti **II 5**, 74
murmur ['mɜ:mə] Gemurmel **II 7**, 110
muscle ['mʌsl] Muskel **II 5**, 73
museum [mju:'zi:əm] Museum **I**
music ['mju:zɪk] Musik **I**
classical music ['klæsɪkl 'mju:zɪk] klassische Musik **I**
pop music ['pɒp ˌmju:zɪk] Popmusik **I**
rock music ['rɒk ˌmju:zɪk] Rockmusik **I**
musical ['mju:zɪkl] Musical **I**
musician [mju:'zɪʃn] Musiker(in) **I**
Muslim ['mʊzlɪm] moslemisch, mohammedanisch **II 7**, 108
must [mʌst] müssen **I**
to **mutter** ['mʌtə] murmeln **II 8**, 127
my [maɪ] mein/meine **I**
mysteriously [mɪ'stɪəriəsli] geheimnisvoll, mysteriös **II 6**, 96
mystery ['mɪstri] Geheimnis, Mysterium **I**
myth [mɪθ] Mythos **II 6**, 99

N

nail [neɪl] Nagel **I**
name [neɪm] Name **I**
to **name** [neɪm] nennen **II 3**, 51
narrator [nə'reɪtə] Erzähler(in) **II 5**, 78
narrow ['nærəʊ] eng, schmal **II 4**, 61
nasty ['nɑ:sti] scheußlich, abscheulich **II 8**, 128
nation ['neɪʃn] Nation, Volk **II 3**, 45
national ['næʃnl] staatlich, national **II 3**, 46
national park [ˌnæʃnl 'pɑ:k] Nationalpark **II 3**, 46
nationality [ˌnæʃn'æləti] Nationalität **I**
+**native** ['neɪtɪv] Eingeborene(r), Ureinwohner(in) **I**
⟨**native**⟩ ['neɪtɪv] einheimisch, Heimat-, Mutter- **II 3**, 47
Native American [ˌneɪtɪv‿ə'merɪkən] amerikanische(r) Ureinwohner(in) **II 4**, 59
natural ['nætʃrl] natürlich **I**
nature ['neɪtʃə] Natur **II 3**, 46
navigation [ˌnævɪ'geɪʃn] Navigation, Schiffsverkehr **I**
near [nɪə] in der Nähe, nah **I**
+**nearer** ['nɪərə] näher **I**
nearly ['nɪəli] fast, beinahe **I**
necessary ['nesəsri] nötig, notwendig **I**
neck [nek] Hals, Genick **II 5**, 78
to **need** [ni:d] brauchen **I**
needn't ['ni:dnt] nicht brauchen **I**
to need to [ni:d] müsen **II 4**, 60
negative ['negətɪv] negativ, verneinend **I**
neighbour ['neɪbə] Nachbar(in) **II 6**, 95
neighbourhood ['neɪbəhʊd] Nachbarschaft **II 4**, 61
neither ['naɪðə] keine(r) (von beiden); auch nicht **I**
neither ... nor ['naɪðə...'nɔ:] weder ... noch **I**
net [net] Netz **I**
never ['nevə] nie(mals) **I**
new [nju:] neu **I**
news (*sing.*) [nju:z] Nachrichten, Neuigkeit(en) **I**
newspaper ['nju:speɪpə] Zeitung **I**
next [nekst] nächste(r/s), der/die Nächste **I**
+next to ['nekst tu:] neben, in der Nähe von **I**
next door [ˌnekst 'dɔ:] nebenan **II 3**, 44
nice [naɪs] hübsch, nett **I**
nickname ['nɪkneɪm] Spitzname **II 2**, 29
night [naɪt] Nacht **I**
night club ['naɪt klʌb] Nachtclub **I**

no [nəʊ] nein; kein/keine **I**
no one ['nəʊwʌn] niemand **I**
no way (*coll.*) [ˌnəʊ 'weɪ] auf keinen Fall, keineswegs **I**
nobody ['nəʊbədi] niemand **I**
to **nod** [nɒd] nicken **II 6**, 96
noise [nɔɪz] Geräusch, Lärm **II 1**, 15
noisy [nɔɪzi] laut, geräuschvoll **I**
nomad ['nəʊmæd] Nomade/Nomadin **II 4**, 67
to **nominate** ['nɒmɪneɪt] ernennen, nominieren **II 2**, 24
nomination [ˌnɒmɪ'neɪʃn] Nominierung, Ernennung **II 2**, 30
non-stop [ˌnɒn'stɒp] pausenlos, ununterbrochen **I**
none [nʌn] keine(r/s) **II 3**, 45
nonsense ['nɒnsəns] Unsinn, Quatsch **II 3**, 42
noon [nu:n] Mittag **II 1**, 8
nor [nɔ:] noch, (und) auch nicht **I**
neither ... nor ['naɪðə...'nɔ:] weder ... noch **I**
normal ['nɔ:ml] normal **I**
Norman ['nɔ:mən] Normanne/Normannin **II 4**, 59
north [nɔ:θ] Norden, nördlich **I**
nose [nəʊz] Nase **I**
not [nɒt] nicht **I**
(*not*) after all [ˌɑ:ftə‿'ɑ:l] doch (nicht) **I**
not ... any more [ˌnɒt ... ˌeni 'mɔ:] (überhaupt) nicht mehr, keine ... mehr **II 1**, 16
not ... at all [ˌnɒt‿ə'tɔ:l] überhaupt nicht **I**
not ... yet [jet] noch nicht **I**
note [nəʊt] Banknote **II 4**, 61; Notiz, (kurzer) Brief, Mitteilung **II 3**, 45
to **note** (*down*) [ˌnəʊt 'daʊn] notieren, (auf)schreiben **I**
vocabulary **notebook** [vəʊˌkæbjəlri 'nəʊtbʊk] Vokabelheft **I**
nothing ['nʌθɪŋ] nichts **I**
notice board ['nəʊtɪs ˌbɔ:d] Schwarzes Brett, Anschlagtafel **I**
to take notice (*of*) [ˌteɪk 'nəʊtɪs] beachten, Notiz nehmen (von) **I**
to **notice** ['nəʊtɪs] bemerken, wahrnehmen **II 2**, 29
November [nəʊ'vembə] November **I**
now [naʊ] nun, jetzt **I**
now and then [ˌnaʊ‿n‿'ðen] ab und zu **I**
nowhere ['nəʊweə] nirgends, nirgendwo **I**
numb [nʌm] taub, gefühllos **II 8**, 128
number (*no.*) ['nʌmbə] Zahl, Nummer (Nr.) **I**
nurse [nɜ:s] Krankenschwester, -pfleger **II 8**, 122

O

10 **o'clock** [ə'klɒk] 10 Uhr **I**
⁺to **obey** [ə'beɪ] gehorchen **I**
object ['ɒbdʒɪkt] Gegenstand, Objekt **II 6**, 91
observer [əb'zɜ:və] Beobachter(in) **II 6**, 95
to be **obsessed** (*by*) [əb'sest] besessen sein (von) **II 7**, 110
⁺**ocean** ['əʊʃn] Ozean, Meer **II 4**, 66
October [ɒk'təʊbə] Oktober **I**
odd one out [ˌɒd wʌn‿'aʊt] das Nichtdazupassende scheidet aus **I**
of [ɒv/əv] von/vom **I**
of course [əv 'kɔ:s] natürlich, selbstverständlich **I**
off [ɒf] weg, fort **I**
to drive off [draɪv‿'ɒf] vertreiben **II 4**, 67
to get* off [ˌget‿'ɒf] aussteigen, absteigen *(Zug, Bus, Fahrrad)* **I**
to set* off [ˌset‿'ɒf] losziehen, (eine Reise) antreten **II 1**, 10
to show off [ˌʃəʊ‿'ɒf] angeben **I**
⁺to step off [step‿'ɒf] aussteigen **II 4**, 67
to take* off [ˌteɪk‿'ɒf] starten, abheben **I**
to tear* off [ˌteər‿'ɒf] abreißen **II 7**, 110
to write sth. off [ˌraɪt‿'ɒf] abschreiben **II 6**, 96
offer ['ɒfə] Angebot **II 7**, 108
to **offer** (to do sth.) ['ɒfə] anbieten (etw. zu tun) **II 5**, 76
office ['ɒfɪs] Arbeitszimmer, Büro **I**
post office ['pəʊst‿ˌɒfɪs] Postamt **II 3**, 44
⟨**officer**⟩ ['ɒfɪsə] (Polizei-)Beamter/-beamtin **II 5**, 77
official [ə'fɪʃl] offiziell **I**
often ['ɒfn] oft, öfters **I**
Oh, dear! [əʊ 'dɪə] Oh je! **I**
oil [ɔɪl] Öl **I**
oil slick ['ɔɪl slɪk] Ölteppich **I**
OK [əʊ'keɪ] in Ordnung, okay **I**
old [əʊld] alt **I**
on [ɒn] auf, an/am **I**
on board [ɒn 'bɔ:d] an Bord **II 6**, 93
on purpose ['pɜ:pəs] absichtlich **II 8**, 127
on time [ɒn 'taɪm] pünktlich **II 3**, 44
to fling* on [ˌflɪŋ‿'ɒn] *(Kleidung)* schnell überwerfen, anziehen **II 6**, 96
to go* on [ˌgəʊ‿'ɒn] weitermachen, fortsetzen **I**; vorgehen **II 2**, 26
to put* on [ˌpʊt‿'ɒn] herausbringen, auf die Bühne bringen **I**
to switch on [ˌswɪtʃ‿'ɒn] einschalten **II 1**, 13
once [wʌns] einmal **II 4**, 62
one [wʌn] eins **I**
the only ones [wʌnz] die Einzigen **I**
One Day Travelcard ['trævlkɑ:d] Tageskarte, Netzkarte *(London)* **II 1**, 10
only ['əʊnli] nur **I**
an only child [ˌəʊnli 'tʃaɪld] Einzelkind **II 1**, 14
to **open** ['əʊpn] öffnen, aufmachen **I**
open ['əʊpn] offen **I**
open-air [ˌəʊpn'eə] im Freien, Freiluft- **II 2**, 26
can **opener** ['kæn ˌəʊpnə] Dosenöffner **II 8**, 124
opening ['əʊpnɪŋ] Eröffnung, Beginn **I**
⟨**opening price**⟩ ['əʊpnɪŋ ˌpraɪs] Eröffnungskurs **II 4**, 61
operating theatre ['ɒpəreɪtɪŋ ˌθɪətə] Operationssaal **II 8**, 122
operation [ˌɒpr'eɪʃn] Operation **II 8**, 122
opinion [ə'pɪnjən] Meinung, Ansicht **II 7**, 111
⁺**opponent** [ə'pəʊnənt] Gegenspieler(in), Gegner(in) **II 5**, 84
opposite ['ɒpəzɪt] Gegenteil; gegenüber **I**
optimistic [ˌɒptɪ'mɪstɪk] optimistisch **II 4**, 62
or [ɔ:] oder **I**
either ... or ['aɪðə ... 'ɔ:] entweder ... oder **II 5**, 79
orange juice ['ɒrɪndʒ ˌdʒu:s] Orangensaft **II 5**, 76
⁺**orbit** ['ɔ:bɪt] Erdumlaufbahn **II 6**, 100
senior **orchestra** [ˌsi:niə‿'ɔ:kɪstrə] Orchester der oberen Klassenstufen **I**
order ['ɔ:də] Reihenfolge **II 7**, 109
postal order ['pəʊstl‿ˌɔ:də] Postanweisung **II 3**, 44
organization [ˌɔ:gnaɪ'zeɪʃn] Organisation, Veranstalter **I**
to **organize** ['ɔ:gnaɪz] organisieren, durchführen **I**
organizer ['ɔ:gənaɪzə] Organisator(in) **II 1**, 12
original [ə'rɪdʒnl] original, ursprünglich **II 2**, 26
originally [ə'rɪdʒnli] ursprünglich, anfänglich **II 3**, 44

other ['ʌðə] andere(r/s) **I**
each other [ˌi:tʃ‿'ʌðə] einander **II 1**, 13
otherwise ['ʌðəwaɪz] sonst, ansonsten **II 8**, 124
ouch! [aʊtʃ] au!, autsch! **I**
our ['aʊə] unser **I**
ours ['aʊəz] der/die/das Unsere **I**
+**ourselves** [ˌaʊə'selvz] wir (selbst) **II 3**, 50
out (*of*) [aʊt] hinaus, heraus **I**
out of shape [ˌaʊt‿əv 'ʃeɪp] außer Form **II 5**, 74
out loud [ˌaʊt 'laʊd] laut (vorlesen, sprechen) **II 3**, 45
to drive* so. out [ˌdraɪv‿'aʊt] jmdn verjagen, hinausjagen **II 4**, 59
to get* out [ˌget‿'aʊt] aussteigen *(Auto, Wagen, Waggon)* **I**
to hang* out [ˌhæŋ‿'aʊt] herumlungern **II 4**, 61
to set* out to do sth. [ˌset‿'aʊt] etw fest vorhaben **II 1**, 12
to stick out ['stɪk‿aʊt] herausstrecken **II 8**, 130
to work out [wɜ:k‿'aʊt] ausarbeiten, herausfinden **II 7**, 109
+**outdoors** [ˌaʊt'dɔ:z] im Freien, draußen **II 5**, 73
outer space [ˌaʊtə 'speɪs] der äußere Weltraum **II 6**, 99
outfit ['aʊtfɪt] Kleidung, Ausstattung **II 7**, 109
outnumbered [ˌaʊt'nʌmbəd] zahlenmäßig unterlegen **II 6**, 95
outside [aʊt'saɪd] draußen **I**
outsider [ˌaʊt'saɪdə] Außenseiter(in) **II 7**, 106
outstanding [ˌaʊt'stændɪŋ] hervorragend, überragend **II 2**, 29
+**oval** ['əʊvl] oval **II 5**, 84
microwave **oven** [ˌmaɪkrəʊweɪv‿'ʌvn] Mikrowellenherd **II 6**, 92
over ['əʊvə] hinüber **I**
all over ['ɔ:l‿əʊvə] überall (in) **II 1**, 16
over there [ˌəʊvə 'ðeə] da drüben **I**
to push so. over [ˌpʊʃ‿'əʊvə] jmdn umstoßen **I**
overall [ˌəʊvr'ɔ:l] insgesamt, allgemein **II 7**, 107
overboard ['əʊvəbɔ:d] über Bord **I**
to **overlook** [ˌəʊvə'lʊk] überschauen; mit Blick über/auf **I**
overseas [ˌəʊvə'si:z] in/im Übersee **II 3**, 45
overtime ['əʊvətaɪm] Überstunden **II 7**, 110
+to **own** [əʊn] besitzen **II 7**, 111
own [əʊn] eigene(r/s) **I**
on one's own [ˌɒn wʌnz‿'əʊn] allein, ohne Hilfe **II 3**, 48
owner ['əʊnə] Eigentümer(in), Besitzer(in) **I**

P

p (*pence, pl. of penny*) [pens] *britische Währung (100 pence = £1)* **I**
to **pack** [pæk] packen **I**
page [peɪdʒ] Seite **I**
pain [peɪn] Schmerz, Leid(en) **II 8**, 122
paint [peɪnt] Farbe **I**
to **paint** [peɪnt] anmalen, streichen **I**
painter ['peɪntə] (Kunst-)Maler(in) **II 6**, 90
+**painting** ['peɪntɪŋ] Gemälde, Bild **I**
pair [peə] Paar **I**
palace ['pælɪs] Palast **II 4**, 67
pale [peɪl] bleich, blass **II 3**, 44
pancake ['pænkeɪk] Pfannkuchen **II 5**, 74
to **panic** ['pænɪk] in Panik geraten **II 3**, 48
pants (*AE*) [pænts] Hose **II 7**, 110
paper ['peɪpə] Papier **II 3**, 45; Zeitung **II 4**, 61
parade [pə'reɪd] Parade, Aufmarsch **II 1**, 8
paramedic [ˌpærə'medɪk] Sanitäter(in) **II 8**, 122
parcel ['pɑ:sl] Paket, Päckchen **II 2**, 33
parents ['peərnts] Eltern **I**
park ['θi:m ˌpɑ:k] Park **I**
car park ['kɑ: ˌpɑ:k] Parkplatz **I**
national park [ˌnæʃnl 'pɑ:k] Nationalpark **II 3**, 46
theme park ['θi:m ˌpɑ:k] Erlebnispark **I**
part [pɑ:t] Teil **I**; Rolle **II 2**, 26
to take part (*in*) [ˌteɪk 'pɑ:t] teilnehmen (an) **I**
to **part** [pɑ:t] sich trennen, auseinandergehen **II 6**, 95
partly ['pɑ:tli] teilweise, zum Teil **II 4**, 57
partner ['pɑ:tnə] Partner(in) **I**
parts (*pl.*) [pɑ:ts] Gegend, Region **II 6**, 95
party ['pɑ:ti] Party, Fest **I**
to **pass** [pɑ:s] vorbeifahren, vorbeikommen **II 3**, 44; +(einen Ball) passen **II 5**, 84
passenger ['pæsndʒə] Reisende(r), Fahrgast, Passagier **II 1**, 19
past [pɑ:st] nach **I**; vorbei (an) **II 3**, 44
pasta ['pæstə] Teigwaren, Nudeln **II 5**, 77
+**pastrami** [pæs'trɑ:mi] geräuchertes Rindfleisch **I**
pasty ['pæsti] (Fleisch-)Pastete **II 5**, 78
path [pɑ:θ] Weg, Pfad **I**
patient ['peɪʃnt] Patient(in) **II 2**, 30
pavement ['peɪvmənt] Bürgersteig, Gehweg **II 4**, 61
paw [pɔ:] Pfote **II 3**, 44
pay [peɪ] Bezahlung, Vergütung **II 7**, 110
to **pay*** [peɪ] (be)zahlen **I**
+to pay attention [ˌpeɪ‿ə'tenʃn] aufmerksam sein, achtsam sein **I**
payment ['peɪmənt] Zahlung **II 8**, 131
°**PE** (*Physical Education*) [ˌpi:'i: ('fɪzɪkl ˌedʒʊ'keɪʃn)] Sport, Turnen **I**
peace [pi:s] Frieden **II 3**, 48
peaceful ['pi:sfl] friedlich **II 3**, 43
pedestrian [pɪ'destriən] Fußgänger(in) **II 6**, 95
pen [pen] Füller, Füllfederhalter **I**
pencil ['pensl] Bleistift **I**
pencil case ['pensl ˌkeɪs] Federmäppchen **I**
pencil sharpener ['pensl ˌʃɑ:pnə] Bleistiftspitzer **I**
penfriend ['penfrend] Brieffreund(in) **I**
people ['pi:pl] Leute, Menschen **I**
percent [pə'sent] Prozent **I**
perfect ['pɜ:fɪkt] perfekt, vollkommen **I**
to **perform** [pə'fɔ:m] aufführen, vorführen **II 2**, 26; durchführen **II 8**, 126
perhaps [pə'hæps] vielleicht **I**
person ['pɜ:sn] Person **I**
+**personal** ['pɜ:snl] persönlich **I**
pet [pet] Haustier, Liebling **II 1**, 15
petrol station ['petrl ˌsteɪʃn] Tankstelle **I**
phew! [fju:] puh! **I**
phone [fəʊn] Telefon **I**
(*phone*) call [('fəʊn) kɔ:l] Anruf **I**
mobile phone [ˌməʊbaɪl 'fəʊn] Mobiltelefon, Handy **I**
to **phone** [fəʊn] telefonieren, anrufen **I**
photo ['fəʊtəʊ] Foto **I**
to take a photo [ˌteɪk‿ə 'fəʊtəʊ] ein Foto machen **II 1**, 12
phrase [freɪz] Phrase, kurzer Satz **I**
piano [pi'ænəʊ] Klavier, Piano **II 2**, 24
piccolo ['pɪkələʊ] Piccolo(-flöte) **I**
to **pick** (*out*) [ˌpɪk‿'aʊt] (heraus)picken, (heraus)suchen **I**

⁺to pick up [pɪk‿'ʌp] aufheben, -lesen **II 1**, 18; abholen **II 4**, 61
picnic ['pɪknɪk] Picknick **I**
picture ['pɪktʃə] Bild **I**
motion picture ['məʊʃn ˌpɪktʃə] Film (*wörtl.:* Bewegungsbild) **II 2**, 29
piece [pi:s] Stück, Teil **I**
pile [paɪl] Haufen, Stapel **II 6**, 96
pilot ['paɪlət] Pilot(in) **I**
pin [pɪn] Nadel **II 8**, 128
pink [pɪŋk] pink **I**
pioneer [ˌpaɪə'nɪə] Pionier **I**
pirate ['paɪərət] Pirat(in) **I**
pitch [pɪtʃ] (Fußball-)Feld, (Sport-)Platz **II 5**, 72
place [pleɪs] Ort, Platz **I**
to take place [ˌteɪk 'pleɪs] stattfinden **II 2**, 29
to **place** [pleɪs] setzen, platzieren **II 4**, 61
plain [pleɪn] schlicht, einfach **I**
plan [plæn] Plan **I**
to **plan** [plæn] planen, vorhaben **I**
plane [pleɪn] Flugzeug **I**
planet ['plænɪt] Planet **II 6**, 90
plastic ['plæstɪk] Plastik **I**
plate [pleɪt] Teller **I**
play [pleɪ] Theaterstück **I**
role play ['rəʊl pleɪ] Rollenspiel **I**
to **play** [pleɪ] spielen **I**
player ['pleɪə] Spieler(in) **I**
record player ['rekɔ:d ˌpleɪə] (Schall-)Plattenspieler **II 2**, 27
playground ['pleɪgraʊnd] (Schul-)Hof **II 1**, 14
playtime ['pleɪtaɪm] *(Schule)* Pause **II 5**, 78
please [pli:z] bitte **I**
as you please [ˌaz ju: 'pli:z] wie es dir/euch/Ihnen beliebt **I**
Pleased to meet you. [pli:zd] Angenehm. Sehr erfreut. **II 7**, 113
plenty ['plenti] reichlich, im Überfluss **II 5**, 73
plus [plʌs] plus, extra **II 5**, 73
pm [ˌpi:'em] nachmittags *(12-24 Uhr)* **I**
pocket ['pɒkət] (Hosen-/Jacken-)Tasche **I**
pocket money ['pɒkɪt ˌmʌni] Taschengeld **I**
poem ['pəʊɪm] Gedicht **I**
poet ['pəʊɪt] Dichter(in), Poet(in) **II 3**, 44
point [pɔɪnt] Punkt **I**
decimal point [ˌdesɪml 'pɔɪnt] Komma(stelle) **II 4**, 61
to get so.'s point (*coll.*) [pɔɪnt] jmdn verstehen **II 7**, 111
to see no point in sth. [ˌsi: nəʊ 'pɔɪnt‿ɪn] etw für sinnlos halten **II 5**, 79
poisonous ['pɔɪznəs] giftig **II 8**, 124
police [pə'li:s] Polizei **I**
policeman [pə'li:smən] Polizist **II 4**, 61
polite [pə'laɪt] höflich **I**
polo shirt ['pəʊləʊ ˌʃɜ:t] Polohemd **I**
swimming **pool** ['swɪmɪŋ ˌpu:l] Swimmingpool **I**
poor [pɔ:] arm **II 3**, 41
pop music ['pɒp ˌmju:zɪk] Popmusik **I**
popular ['pɒpjələ] beliebt, populär **I**
popularity [ˌpɒpjə'lærəti] Beliebtheit, Popularität **II 4**, 59
position [pə'zɪʃn] Position **I**
to **position** [pə'zɪʃn] aufstellen, in Position bringen **II 2**, 27
positive ['pɒzətɪv] positiv, bejahend **I**
possibility [ˌpɒsə'bɪləti] Gelegenheit, Möglichkeit **II 6**, 90
possible ['pɒsəbl] möglich **I**
post [pəʊst] Post **II 3**, 44
post office ['pəʊst‿ˌɒfɪs] Postamt **II 3**, 44
to **post** [pəʊst] abschicken, zur Post geben **II 4**, 60
postal order ['pəʊstl‿ˌɔ:də] Postanweisung **II 3**, 44
postcard ['pəʊstkɑ:d] Postkarte **I**
poster ['pəʊstə] Poster, Plakat **I**
postman ['pəʊstmən] Briefträger(in), Postbote/-botin **II 2**, 33
posture ['pɒstʃə] (Körper-)Haltung **II 5**, 73
potato, *pl.* -oes [pə'teɪtəʊ] Kartoffel **II 5**, 82
couch potato ['kaʊtʃ pəˌteɪtəʊ] jmd, der ständig vor dem Fernseher sitzt **II 5**, 74
£ **(pound sterling)** [paʊnd] Pfund *(britische Währung)* **I**
poverty ['pɒvəti] Armut **II 7**, 107
power ['paʊə] Kraft, Stärke, Macht **II 3**, 43
practical ['præktɪkl] praktisch **I**
to **practise** ['præktɪs] üben, proben **I**; ⁺ausüben, praktizieren **II 4**, 65
⁺to **pray** [preɪ] beten **II 3**, 50
⁺to **predict** [prɪ'dɪkt] vorhersagen, prophezeien **II 6**, 93
prehistoric [ˌpri:hɪ'stɒrɪk] vorgeschichtlich, prähistorisch **II 6**, 92
to **prepare** [prɪ'peə] vorbereiten **II 1**, 9
to be **prepared** [prɪ'peəd] vorbereitet sein **II 8**, 124
prescription [prɪ'skrɪpʃn] Verordnung, Rezept **II 8**, 130
present ['preznt] ⁺gegenwärtig, momentan **II 3**, 50
present ['preznt] Geschenk **I**
press-up ['presʌp] Liegestütz **II 5**, 75
to **press** [pres] drücken **II 6**, 93
to **pretend** (*to*) [prɪ'tend] vorgeben (zu), vortäuschen **I**
pretty ['prɪti] hübsch, nett **II 8**, 128
to **prevent** [prɪ'vent] verhindern, vermeiden **II 8**, 123
price [praɪs] Preis **I**
⟨closing price⟩ ['kləʊzɪŋ ˌpraɪs] Schlusskurs **II 4**, 61
⟨opening price⟩ ['əʊpnɪŋ ˌpraɪs] Eröffnungskurs **II 4**, 61
⁺price shopper ['praɪs ˌʃɒpə] Schnäppchenjäger(in) **II 7**, 115
Prime Minister [ˌpraɪm 'mɪnɪstə] Premierminister(in) **II 8**, 128
to **print** (*out*) [prɪnt] (aus)drucken **I**
printer ['prɪntə] Drucker **I**
prize [praɪz] Preis, Gewinn **I**
the **pros and cons** [ˌprəʊz‿n‿'kɒnz] das Für und Wider, Pro und Contra **I**
probably ['prɒbəbli] wahrscheinlich **II 3**, 48
problem ['prɒbləm] Problem **I**
to **produce** [prə'dju:s] produzieren, herstellen **I**
producer [prə'dju:sə] Produzent(in), Hersteller(in) **II 6**, 90
production [prə'dʌkʃn] Herstellung, Produktion **II 7**, 110
profit ['prɒfɪt] Gewinn, Profit **II 7**, 110
⁺**program** ['prəʊgræm] (Computer-) Programm **I**
programme ['prəʊgræm] Sendung **II 1**, 13
project ['prɒdʒekt] Projekt **I**
promise ['prɒmɪs] Versprechen, Zusicherung **II 5**, 75
to **promise** ['prɒmɪs] versprechen **II 6**, 96
promotion [prə'məʊʃn] Förderung, Unterstützung **II 7**, 110
proper ['prɒpə] passend, geeignet **II 5**, 72
properly ['prɒpli] ordentlich, pünktlich **II 4**, 58
to **protect** [prə'tekt] (be)schützen **II 4**, 62
proud (*of*) [praʊd] stolz (auf) **II 3**, 43
⁺**psychic** ['saɪkɪk] telepathisch **II 6**, 100

pub [pʌb] Kneipe, Pub, Lokal **I**
in **public** ['pʌblɪk] in der Öffentlichkeit **II 5**, 72
public ['pʌblɪk] öffentlich **II 4**, 61
to **pull** [pʊl] ziehen **I**
punctuation [ˌpʌŋktʃu'eɪʃn] Zeichensetzung, Interpunktion **I**
pupil ['pju:pl] Schüler(in) **I**
puppet ['pʌpɪt] (Hand-)Puppe, Marionette **II 2**, 29
purse [pɜ:s] Portmonee, Geldbörse **I**
to **push** [pʊʃ] stoßen, schieben **II 6**, 96
to push so. over [ˌpʊʃ‿'əʊvə] jmdn umstoßen **I**
to **put*** [pʊt] setzen, stellen, legen **I**
to put an end to sth. [ˌpʊt‿ən‿'end] einer Sache ein Ende setzen **II 1**, 19
to put on [ˌpʊt‿'ɒn] herausbringen, auf die Bühne bringen **I**
to put up [ˌpʊt‿'ʌp] aufgeben, aufhängen **I**

Q

quality ['kwɒləti] Qualität **II 7**, 110
quarter *(to/past)* ['kwɔ:tə] Viertel (vor/nach) **I**
queen [kwi:n] Königin **I**
question ['kwestʃən] Frage **I**
queue [kju:] (Menschen)Schlange **II 3**, 51
quick [kwɪk] schnell, rasch **I**
quiet ['kwaɪət] Stille, Ruhe **II 3**, 48
quiet ['kwaɪət] ruhig **I**
quite [kwaɪt] ziemlich **I**
quiz [kwɪz] Fragespiel, Quiz **I**

R

race [reɪs] (Wett-)Rennen **II 5**, 74
to **race** [reɪs] um die Wette rennen, rasen **II 6**, 91
racket ['rækɪt] (Tennis-)Schläger **II 5**, 73
radio ['reɪdiəʊ] Radio **I**
+whitewater **rafting** [ˌwaɪtwɔ:tə 'rɑ:ftɪŋ] Wildwasserfahren **I**
railway ['reɪlweɪ] Eisenbahn **I**
rain [reɪn] Regen **II 1**, 10
to **rain** ['reɪn] regnen **I**
to rain cats and dogs ['reɪn ˌkæts‿n‿'dɒgz] heftig regnen, schütten, gießen **I**
rainy ['reɪni] regnerisch **II 4**, 67
rap [ræp] Rap *(Musikrichtung)* **II 3**, 44
+**rapids** ['ræpɪdz] Stromschnellen **I**
rat [ræt] Ratte **II 1**, 19
rat-bag ['rætbæg] Miststück **II 1**, 14
rather ['rɑ:ðə] eher, lieber, ziemlich **II 5**, 80
to X-**ray** ['eksreɪ] durchleuchten, röntgen **II 8**, 128
to **reach** [ri:tʃ] erreichen, gelangen **I**
to **react** [ri'ækt] reagieren **I**
to **read*** [ri:d] lesen **I**
ready ['redi] fertig, bereit (sein) **I**
real [rɪəl] echt, wirklich **I**
reality [ri'æləti] Wirklichkeit, Realität **II 3**, 51
+virtual reality [ˌvɜ:tʃuəl ri'æləti] virtuelle Realität **II 3**, 50
to **realize** ['rɪəlaɪz] bemerken, erkennen, realisieren **II 6**, 95
really ['rɪəli] wirklich **I**; in Wirklichkeit, eigentlich **II 4**, 59
reason ['ri:zn] Grund, Ursache **II 3**, 45
to **receive** [rɪ'si:v] erhalten, empfangen **II 2**, 29
+**recent** ['ri:snt] kürzlich **II 8**, 132
+**recipe** ['resɪpi] (Koch-)Rezept **II 5**, 83
reconstruction [ˌri:kən'strʌkʃn] Wiederherstellung, Rekonstruktion **II 2**, 26
record ['rekɔ:d] Rekord **II 5**, 78; Schallplatte **I**
record player ['rekɔ:d ˌpleɪə] (Schall-)Plattenspieler **II 2**, 27
record-holder ['rekɔ:d ˌhəʊldə] Rekordhalter(in) **II 2**, 29
to **record** [rɪ'kɔ:d] aufzeichnen, aufnehmen **I**
recorder [rɪ'kɔ:də] (Video-/Kassetten-) Rekorder **I**
recording [rɪ'kɔ:dɪŋ] Aufzeichnung, (Ton-) Aufnahme **I**
recovery [rɪ'kʌvri] Genesung, Erholung **II 8**, 129
red [red] rot **I**
to **reduce** [rɪ'dju:s] verringern, reduzieren **II 8**, 123
to **refuse** [rɪ'fju:z] ablehnen, verweigern **II 7**, 108
regard [rɪ'gɑ:d] (Hoch-)Achtung, Wertschätzung **II 2**, 29
to **register** ['redʒɪstə] sich eintragen, sich einschreiben **II 5**, 74
regular ['regjələ] regelmäßig **II 4**, 61
to **rehearse** [rɪ'hɜ:s] proben, üben **I**
to be **related** *(to)* [rɪ'leɪtɪd] mit etw zusammenhängen, mit jmdm verwandt sein **II 3**, 51
relation [rɪ'leɪʃn] Verwandte(r) **II 3**, 45
relationship [ˌrɪ'leɪʃnʃɪp] Beziehung, Verhältnis **II 7**, 108
relative ['relətɪv] Verwandte(r) **I**
to **relax** [rɪ'læks] ausruhen, sich erholen **I**
religion [rɪ'lɪdʒn] Religion **II 7**, 107
+**religious** [rɪ'lɪdʒəs] religiös **II 4**, 65
to **remain** [rɪ'meɪn] zurückbleiben **II 6**, 96
to **remember** [rɪ'membə] sich erinnern (an), denken (an) **I**
rent [rent] Miete **II 7**, 112
rental ['rentl] Miet- **I**
car rental ['kɑ: ˌrentl] Autovermietung **I**
to **repair** [rɪ'peə] reparieren **II 4**, 61
to **repeat** [rɪ'pi:t] wiederholen **I**
repetition [ˌrepɪ'tɪʃn] Wiederholung **II 3**, 45
to **replace** [rɪ'pleɪs] ersetzen, austauschen **II 8**, 125
replica ['replɪkə] Nachbildung **II 3**, 51
report [rɪ'pɔ:t] Bericht **I**; (Schul)Zeugnis **II 5**, 78
to **report** [rɪ'pɔ:t] berichten **I**
to report back [rɪˌpɔ:t 'bæk] sich zurückmelden **II 6**, 96
reporter [rɪ'pɔ:tə] Reporter(in), Journalist(in) **I**
rescue ['reskju:] Rettung **I**
to **rescue** ['reskju:] retten **I**
+**research** [rɪ'sɜ:tʃ] Forschung **II 6**, 100
+**reservation** [ˌrezə'veɪʃn] Reservat **I**
+**resident** ['rezɪdnt] Bewohner(in), Einwohner(in) **I**
responsibility [rɪˌspɒnsə'bɪləti] Verantwortung **II 7**, 111
to be **responsible** [rɪ'spɒnsəbl] verantwortlich sein **I**
rest [rest] Rast, Pause **I**; Rest **II 3**, 48
restaurant ['restrɔ:ŋ] Restaurant **I**
to **restore** [rɪ'stɔ:] wiederherstellen, restaurieren **II 3**, 51
result [rɪ'zʌlt] Ergebnis **I**
+in **return** [ɪn rɪ'tɜ:n] dafür **I**
to **return** [rɪ'tɜ:n] zurückkehren **II 1**, 12
to **revise** [rɪ'vaɪz] wiederholen **II 5**, 81
to **reward** [rɪ'wɔ:d] belohnen, auszeichnen **II 2**, 29
to **rewrite*** [ˌri:'raɪt] neu schreiben **II 6**, 101
rhyme [raɪm] Reim **II 3**, 45
+to **rhyme** [raɪm] (sich) reimen **II 2**, 34
rhythm ['rɪðm] Rhythmus **II 3**, 45
rice [raɪs] Reis **II 5**, 82

rich [rɪtʃ] reich **II 2**, 26
+to thumb a **ride** [ˌθʌm‿ə ˈraɪd] per Anhalter fahren, trampen **II 2**, 34
to **ride*** [raɪd] fahren, reiten **I**
rider [ˈraɪdə] Fahrer(in) **II 6**, 95
+**rigging** [ˈrɪgɪŋ] Tauwerk, Takelage **II 4**, 66
right [raɪt] rechts; richtig **I**
all right [ɔ:l ˈraɪt] in Ordnung **I**
right away [ˌraɪt‿əˈweɪ] sofort **II 8**, 124
ring [rɪŋ] Ring **I**
to **ring* so. up** [ˌrɪŋ‿ˈʌp] jmdn anrufen **I**
rip-off [ˈrɪpɒf] Wucher, Nepp **II 7**, 107
risk [rɪsk] Gefahr, Risiko **II 8**, 123
risky [ˈrɪski] gefährlich, riskant **II 8**, 123
river [ˈrɪvə] Fluss **I**
road [rəʊd] Straße **I**
bank **robber** [ˈbæŋk ˌrɒbə] Bankräuber(in) **I**
robot [ˈrəʊbɒt] Roboter **II 6**, 94
rock [rɒk] Fels **I**
rock music [ˈrɒk ˌmju:zɪk] Rockmusik **I**
soft rock [ˈsɒft ˌrɒk] Softrock *(Musikrichtung)* **II 2**, 25
rock'n'roll [ˌrɒknˈrəʊl] Rock'n'Roll *(Musikrichtung)* **II 2**, 25
rocky [ˈrɒki] felsig, steinig **I**
role [rəʊl] Rolle **I**
role play [ˈrəʊl pleɪ] Rollenspiel **I**
Roman [ˈrəʊmən] Römer(in) **II 3**, 43
roof [ru:f] Dach **I**
room [rʊm] Zimmer **I**
+dining room [ˈdaɪnɪŋ ˌrʊm] Esszimmer **I**
living room [ˈlɪvɪŋ ˌrʊm] Wohnzimmer **I**
rope [rəʊp] Seil, Tau **I**
to **rot** [rɒt] verrotten, (ver)faulen **I**
round [raʊnd] rund **II 3**, 43
round [raʊnd] um … herum **I**
all-round fitness [ˌɔ:lraʊnd ˈfɪtnəs] Rundum-Fitness **II 5**, 72
all the year round [raʊnd] das ganze Jahr über **II 1**, 8
to come* round [ˌkʌm ˈraʊnd] vorbeikommen, herüberkommen **I**
⟨to round up the usual suspects⟩ [ˈraʊnd‿ʌp ðə ˈju:ʒl ˈsʌspekts] die gewöhnlichen Verdächtigen festnehmen **II 1**, 18
rounders [ˈraʊndəz] Schlagball **II 1**, 14
route [ru:t] Route, Strecke **I**
rover [ˈrəʊvə] Vagabund; Erkundungsfahrzeug **II 6**, 92
row [rəʊ] Reihe **I**
to **rub** [rʌb] reiben **I**
rubber [ˈrʌbə] Radiergummi **I**
rubbish [ˈrʌbɪʃ] Abfall, Müll **I**
+**rugby** [ˈrʌgbi] Rugby *(Ballspiel mit eiförmigem Ball aus Leder)* **II 5**, 84
rule [ru:l] Herrschaft **II 4**, 62; Regel **I**
ruler [ˈru:lə] Herrscher(in) **II 3**, 43; Lineal **I**
to **run*** [rʌn] rennen, laufen **I**; führen, leiten **II 4**, 61
to run away [ˌrʌn əˈweɪ] weglaufen **II 1**, 15
running-track [ˈrʌnɪŋˌtræk] Aschenbahn **II 5**, 78
rupee [ru:ˈpi:] *indische Währung* **II 4**, 61
Russian [ˈrʌʃn] russisch, Russisch **II 4**, 61

S

to **sack** *(coll.)* [sæk] entlassen **II 7**, 111
sad [sæd] traurig **I**
safe [seɪf] sicher **I**
better to be safe than sorry lieber auf Nummer sicher gehen **II 1**, 11
safety [ˈseɪfti] Sicherheit **I**
to **sail** [seɪl] segeln **I**
+**sailing trip** [ˈseɪlɪŋ ˌtrɪp] Segeltörn **I**
sailor [ˈseɪlə] Matrose, Seemann **II 4**, 60
sale [seɪl] +Ausverkauf, Schlussverkauf **II 7**, 115; Verkauf **I**
salt [sɔ:lt] Salz **I**
same [seɪm] gleich, dasselbe **I**
sand [sænd] Sand **I**
+**sandwich** [ˈsænwɪdʒ] Sandwich, belegtes Brot **I**
sandy [ˈsændi] rötlich, rotblond *(Haarfarbe)* **II 1**, 14
sarcastic [sɑ:ˈkæstɪk] sarkastisch **II 7**, 111
satellite [ˈsætlaɪt] Satellit **I**
Saturday [ˈsætədeɪ] Samstag **I**
sausage [ˈsɒsɪdʒ] Würstchen **I**
to **save** [seɪv] sichern, abspeichern **I**; retten **II 8**, 122
saw [sɔ:] Säge **II 8**, 122
Saxons [ˈsæksnz] (die) Sachsen **II 4**, 58
saxophone [ˈsæksəfəʊn] Saxophon **I**
to **say*** [seɪ] sagen, reden **I**
scalpel [ˈskælpl] Skalpell **II 8**, 122
to be **scared** [ˈskeəd] Angst haben, verschreckt sein **II 4**, 62
scarf, *(pl.)* -ves [skɑ:f] Schal, Halstuch **I**
scene [si:n] Szene **I**
scenery [ˈsi:nəri] Bühnenbild, Kulisse **I**
school [sku:l] Schule **I**
⟨**schoolbag**⟩ [ˈsku:lbæg] Schultasche, -ranzen **II 5**, 77
schoolboy [ˈsku:lbɔɪ] Schuljunge **II 4**, 61
schoolfriend [ˈsku:lfrend] Schulfreund(in) **I**
schoolwatch [ˈsku:lwɒtʃ] Schulaufsicht, Schulwärter(in) **I**
science [ˈsaɪənts] (Natur-)Wissenschaften *(Fach)* **I**; Wissenschaft **II 2**, 29
science fiction [ˌsaɪənts ˈfɪkʃn] Sciencefiction **II 6**, 90
scientist [ˈsaɪəntɪst] Wissenschaftler(in) **I**
scissors [ˈsɪzəz] Schere **I**
+**score** [skɔ:] Punkte, Spielstand **II 4**, 66
+to **score** [skɔ:] Punkte erzielen **II 5**, 84
Scottish [ˈskɒtɪʃ] schottisch **I**
scrambled eggs [ˌskræmbld‿ˈegz] Rührei **II 4**, 63
scrapbook [ˈskræpbʊk] Sammelalbum **I**
scratch [skrætʃ] Kratzer **II 8**, 127
scream [skri:m] Schrei, Heulen **II 6**, 96
screen [skri:n] Leinwand **II 2**, 24
script [skrɪpt] Drehbuch, Textbuch **I**
sculpture [ˈskʌlptʃə] Skulptur **II 6**, 99
sea [si:] Meer, (die) See **I**
seabird [ˈsi:bɜ:d] Seevogel **I**
season [ˈsi:zn] Jahreszeit **I**
seat [si:t] Sitz(platz) **II 2**, 26
seatbelt [ˈsi:tbelt] Sicherheitsgurt **II 6**, 93
second [ˈseknd] Sekunde; zweite(r/s) **II 6**, 95
+**second-hand** [ˈsekndˌhænd] gebraucht, aus zweiter Hand **I**
+**secret** [ˈsi:krət] Geheimnis **II 5**, 83
secret [ˈsi:krət] geheim, verborgen **I**
section [ˈsekʃn] Absatz, Abschnitt **II 3**, 45
to **see*** [si:] sehen, erblicken **I**
to see no point in sth. [ˌsi: nəʊ ˈpɔɪnt‿ɪn] etw für sinnlos halten **II 5**, 79
to **seem** [si:m] (er)scheinen **I**

self-catering [ˌselfˈkeɪtrɪŋ] Selbstversorgung **I**
sell-out [ˈselaʊt] Ausverkauf **II 1**, 12
to **sell*** [sel] verkaufen **I**
+**Seminole Indian** [ˈsemɪnəʊl ˌɪndiən] *Angehörige(r) eines indianischen Stamms* **I**
to **send*** [send] schicken, senden **I**
sender [ˈsendə] Absender(in) **II 3**, 44
senior orchestra [ˌsi:niə‿ˈɔ:kɪstrə] Orchester der oberen Klassenstufen **I**
sense [sens] Sinn **II 6**, 97
sensible [ˈsensɪbl] vernünftig **II 5**, 73
sentence [ˈsentns] Satz **I**
separate [ˈseprət] getrennt, separat **I**
September [sepˈtembə] September **I**
serious [ˈsɪəriəs] ernsthaft, seriös **II 4**, 61
servant [ˈsɜ:vnt] Diener(in) **I**
service [ˈsɜ:rvɪs] Dienst(leistung), Service **I**
+**session** [ˈseʃn] Sitzung, Treffen **II 6**, 100
set [set] Satz, Garnitur **II 4**, 61
to **set*** (*up*) [ˌset‿ˈʌp] (auf)stellen, (auf)bauen **I**
  to be set in [ˈset‿ɪn] in … spielen **II 2**, 25
  to set* off [ˌset‿ˈɒf] losziehen, (eine Reise) antreten **II 1**, 10
  to set* out to do sth. [ˌset‿ˈaʊt] etw fest vorhaben **II 1**, 12
setting [ˈsetɪŋ] Schauplatz, Umgebung **II 2**, 25
to **settle** [ˈsetl] (be)siedeln **II 4**, 58
+**settler** [ˈsetlə] Siedler(in) **II 4**, 65
several [ˈsevrl] einige, mehrere **II 5**, 72
sewage [ˈsu:ɪdʒ] Abwasser **I**
shadow [ˈʃædəʊ] Schatten **II 2**, 29
to **shake*** [ʃeɪk] schütteln **II 3**, 44
shall (*old*) [ʃæl] werde(n) **II 3**, 45
shape [ʃeɪp] Gestalt, (äußere) Form **I**
  out of shape [ˌaʊt‿əv ˈʃeɪp] außer Form **II 5**, 74
sharp [ʃɑ:p] scharf, hart **II 1**, 15
pencil **sharpener** [ˈpensl ˌʃɑ:pnə] Bleistiftspitzer **I**
she [ʃi:] sie (*sing.*) **I**
sheep, (*pl.*) sheep [ʃi:p] Schaf(e) **I**
sheepdog [ˈʃi:pdɒg] Schäferhund, Hirtenhund **I**
+**shelf**, (*pl.*) -ves [ʃelf] Regal(brett) **I**
+**shepherd** [ˈʃepəd] Schäferhund; Schäfer **I**
to work **shift** [ˌwɜ:k ˈʃɪft] Schicht arbeiten, Schichtdienst machen **I**
to **shine*** [ʃaɪn] scheinen **II 1**, 13
ship [ʃɪp] Schiff **I**
polo **shirt** [ˈpəʊləʊ ˌʃɜ:t] Polohemd **I**
to feel **shivery** [ˈʃɪvri] frösteln **II 8**, 130
shock [ʃɒk] Schreck, Schock **I**
shoe [ʃu:] Schuh **I**
shop [ʃɒp] Geschäft, Laden **I**
  video shop [ˈvɪdiəʊ ˌʃɒp] Videothek, Videoladen **I**
+**shoplifter** [ˈʃɒpˌlɪftə] Ladendieb(in) **I**
+price **shopper** [ˈpraɪs ˌʃɒpə] Schnäppchenjäger(in) **II 7**, 115
shopping [ˈʃɒpɪŋ] Einkaufen **I**
  shopping mall (*AE*) [ˈʃɒpɪŋ ˌmɑ:l] Einkaufszentrum **I**
  to go shopping [ˌgəʊ ˈʃɒpɪŋ] Einkaufen gehen **I**
short-cut [ˈʃɔ:tkʌt] Abkürzung **I**
short [ʃɔ:t] kurz **I**
shorts [ʃɔ:ts] kurze Hose, Shorts **I**
should [ʃʊd/ʃəd] sollen **I**
shoulder [ˈʃəʊldə] Schulter **I**
to **shout** [ʃaʊt] rufen **I**
to **shovel** [ˈʃʌvl] schaufeln, schippen **II 3**, 44
show [ʃəʊ] Show **I**
  talk show [ˈtɔ:k ˌʃəʊ] Talkshow, Gesprächsrunde **II 2**, 30
to **show*** [ʃəʊ] zeigen **I**
  to show off [ˌʃəʊ‿ˈɒf] angeben **I**
to **shut*** [ʃʌt] schließen **I**
  to shut up [ˌʃʌt‿ˈʌp] den Mund halten **II 8**, 127
+**shuttle** [ˈʃʌtl] Transporter **II 6**, 100
  city shuttle [ˈsɪti ˌʃʌtl] Pendelverkehr zur Innenstadt **I**
shy [ʃaɪ] schüchtern **II 5**, 72
sick [sɪk] krank, übel **I**
side [saɪd] Seite **I**
sight [saɪt] Sehenswürdigkeit **I**; ⟨Anblick⟩ **II 5**, 77
sightseeing [ˈsaɪtˌsi:ɪŋ] Besichtigung von Sehenswürdigkeiten **I**
sign [saɪn] Schild, Zeichen **II 2**, 27
to **sign** [saɪn] unterzeichnen, unterschreiben **I**
signal [ˈsɪgnl] Signal **I**
signpost [ˈsaɪnpəʊst] Wegweiser **I**
silent [ˈsaɪlənt] still, stumm **II 2**, 24
silly [ˈsɪli] dumm, kindisch **I**
silly [ˈsɪli] Dumme(r), Dummkopf **I**
silver [ˈsɪlvə] Silber **I**
similar [ˈsɪmɪlə] ähnlich, gleichartig **II 7**, 107
simple [ˈsɪmpl] einfach, gewöhnlich **I**
since [sɪns] seit **I**
Yours **sincerely**, [ˌjɔ:z sɪnˈsɪəli] Mit freundlichen Grüßen (*Briefschluss*) **II 2**, 33
to **sing** [sɪŋ] singen **I**
singer [ˈsɪŋə] Sänger(in) **I**
  lead singer [ˌli:d ˈsɪŋə] Leadsänger(in) **II 4**, 57
singing [ˈsɪŋɪŋ] Singen **II 1**, 12
to **sink*** [sɪŋk] sinken, (ab)fallen **II 4**, 62
sir [sɜ:] mein Herr (*Anrede*) **I**
siren [ˈsaɪərən] Sirene **II 8**, 127
sister [ˈsɪstə] Schwester **I**
  baby sister [ˌbeɪbi ˈsɪstə] (ganz) kleine Schwester **I**
sit-up [ˈsɪtʌp] Klappmesser **II 5**, 75
to **sit*** [sɪt] sitzen **I**
  to sit down [sɪt ˈdaʊn] sich setzen **II 1**, 13
site [saɪt] Gelände, Platz **II 3**, 51
situation [ˌsɪtjuˈeɪʃn] Situation, Arbeitsstelle **II 3**, 45
size [saɪz] Größe **I**
skate [skeɪt] Rollschuh, Schlittschuh **II 7**, 111
  ice skate [ˈaɪs ˌskeɪt] Schlittschuh **II 7**, 108
skateboard [ˈskeɪtbɔ:d] Skateboard **II 6**, 92
+**skating** [ˈskeɪtɪŋ] Schlittschuhlaufen, Rollschuhlaufen **II 5**, 73
  ice-skating [ˈaɪsˌskeɪtɪŋ] Schlittschuhlaufen **II 7**, 108
sketch [sketʃ] Sketch, Szene **II 4**, 62
ski-jumping [ˈski:ˌdʒʌmpɪŋ] Skispringen **II 8**, 123
skill [skɪl] Fähigkeit, Fertigkeit **II 7**, 113
to **skim** [skɪm] flüchtig lesen, überfliegen **II 3**, 48
skinny [ˈskɪni] mager, dürr **II 7**, 107
skirt [skɜ:t] Rock **I**
skull [skʌl] Schädel **II 8**, 128
sky [skaɪ] Himmel **II 3**, 44
  sky-diving [ˈskaɪˌdaɪvɪŋ] Fallschirmspringen **II 8**, 123
+**skyline** [ˈskaɪlaɪn] (Stadt-) Silhouette, Skyline **I**
slave [sleɪv] Sklave/Sklavin **II 7**, 107
sleep [sli:p] Schlaf **II 5**, 82
to **sleep*** [sli:p] schlafen **I**
sleeping bag [ˈsli:pɪŋ ˌbæg] Schlafsack **I**

oil **slick** ['ɔɪl slɪk] Ölteppich **I**
slide [slaɪd] Dia(positiv) **I**
to **slip** [slɪp] (aus)rutschen, (aus)gleiten **II 8**, 123
°**slogan** ['sləʊgən] Slogan, Wahl-/Werbespruch **I**
slow [sləʊ] langsam **II 3**, 41
to **slumber** ['slʌmbə] schlummern, schlafen **II 3**, 44
small [smɔ:l] klein **I**
to **smash** [smæʃ] zerschlagen, zerschmettern **II 4**, 62
smell [smel] Geruch, Duft **II 1**, 10
to **smell** [smel] riechen **II 3**, 47
smile [smaɪl] Lächeln **I**
to **smile** [smaɪl] lächeln **I**
smoke detector ['sməʊk dɪˌtektə] Rauchmelder **II 8**, 124
to **smoke** [sməʊk] rauchen **I**
smoking ['sməʊkɪŋ] (das) Rauchen **I**
to **smuggle** ['smʌgl] schmuggeln **I**
smuggler ['smʌglə] Schmuggler(in) **I**
snack [snæk] Imbiss **I**
+**snail-mail** ['sneɪlmeɪl] Schneckenpost **II 4**, 66
⟨**snake**⟩ [sneɪk] Schlange **II 5**, 77
⟨**snapper fish**⟩ ['snæpə ˌfɪʃ] Schnapper *(tropische Fischart)* **II 1**, 18
to **snort** [snɔ:t] schnauben **II 3**, 44
snow [snəʊ] Schnee **I**
to **snow** [snəʊ] schneien **I**
so [səʊ] so (sehr); so, also **I**
sock [sɒk] Socke **I**
sofa ['səʊfə] Sofa, Couch **I**
soft rock ['sɒft ˌrɒk] Softrock *(Musikrichtung)* **II 2**, 25
software ['sɒftweə] Software **I**
soldier ['səʊldʒə] Soldat(in) **II 4**, 61
⟨**solstice**⟩ ['sɒlstɪs] Sonnenwende **II 3**, 50
some [sʌm] einige **I**
somebody ['sʌmbədi] jemand **I**
somehow ['sʌmhaʊ] irgend wie **II 7**, 110
someone ['sʌmwʌn] jemand **I**
+**something** ['sʌmθɪŋ] etwas **I**
sometimes ['sʌmtaɪmz] manchmal **I**
somewhere ['sʌmweə] irgendwo **I**
soon [su:n] bald, rasch **I**
least said soonest mended [ˌli:st 'sed ˌsu:nəst 'mendɪd] je weniger geredet wird, desto schneller wird es wieder gut **II 6**, 95
sore throat [ˌsɔ: 'θrəʊt] Halsschmerzen, Halsweh **II 8**, 130
sorry ['sɒri] (es) tut mir Leid **I**
better to be safe than sorry lieber auf Nummer sicher gehen **II 1**, 11
to feel sorry for [fi:l 'sɒri] bemitleiden **II 7**, 111
sort [sɔ:t] Sorte, Art **II 4**, 61
sound [saʊnd] Klang, Ton **I**
sound check ['saʊn(d) tʃek] Klang-, Tonkontrolle **I**
to **sound** [saʊnd] klingen **I**
to sound like [laɪk] sich anhören wie **II 3**, 47
source [sɔ:s] Quelle, Ursprung **II 6**, 90
south [saʊθ] südlich, Süden **I**
southern ['sʌðən] südlich, Süd- **II 7**, 110
+**southernmost** ['sʌðənməʊst] südlichste(r/s) **I**
souvenir [ˌsu:vn'ɪə] Souvenir, Andenken **I**
+**Soviet** ['səʊviət] sowjetisch **II 6**, 100
space [speɪs] Raum **II 2**, 29
outer space [ˌaʊtə 'speɪs] der äußere Weltraum **II 6**, 99
space travel ['speɪs ˌtrævl] Raumfahrt **II 6**, 91
+**spacecraft** ['speɪskrɑ:ft] Raumfahrzeug **II 6**, 100
spaceship ['speɪsʃɪp] Raumschiff **II 6**, 90
spacious ['speɪʃəs] geräumig, weitläufig **II 4**, 61
+**spare battery** [ˌspeə 'bætri] Ersatzbatterie **I**
to **speak*** [spi:k] sprechen **I**
is spoken ['spəʊkn] wird gesprochen **II 4**, 57
speaker ['spi:kə] °Lautsprecher **I**; Sprecher(in) **II 1**, 9
special ['speʃl] besondere(r/s) **I**
speech bubble ['spi:tʃ ˌbʌbl] Sprechblase **II 5**, 79
+**speed** [spi:d] Geschwindigkeit **I**
to **spell*** [spel] buchstabieren **I**
spelling ['spelɪŋ] Rechtschreibung **II 1**, 15
to **spend*** [spend] verbrauchen, ausgeben; verbringen **I**
spider ['spaɪdə] Spinne **II 8**, 124
to **spill*** [spɪl] auslaufen, verschütten **I**
to **splash** [splæʃ] plantschen, spritzen **II 5**, 72
to **split* up** [ˌsplɪt‿'ʌp] sich (voneinander) trennen **I**
sponge [spʌndʒ] Schwamm **I**
sponsor ['spɒntsə] Sponsor(in) **II 5**, 75
sport [spɔ:t] Sport **I**
sports centre ['spɔ:ts ˌsentə] Sportzentrum, Sportanlage **I**
sportsfield ['spɔ:tsfi:ld] Sportplatz **I**
sporty ['spɔ:ti] sportlich **II 5**, 72
⟨**spot**⟩ [spɒt] Fleck, Pickel **II 5**, 77
to **spot** [spɒt] entdecken **I**
to **spread*** *(over)* [spred] sich ausdehnen, sich verbreiten (über) **II 3**, 43
spring [sprɪŋ] Frühling **I**
to **spurt** [spɜ:t] sprinten, spurten **II 5**, 79
°**spy**, *(pl.)* spies [spaɪ] Spion(in), Spitzel **I**
square [skweə] Platz **II 4**, 61
staffroom ['stɑ:frʊm] Lehrerzimmer **I**
stage [steɪdʒ] Bühne **I**
+**stairs** *(pl.)* [steəz] Treppe **I**
stall [stɔ:l] (Verkauf-)Stand **I**
stamina ['stæmɪnə] Durchhaltevermögen, Ausdauer **II 5**, 72
stamp [stæmp] Briefmarke **II 8**, 131
to **stand*** [stænd] stehen **I**
I can't stand *(it)* [ˌkɑ:nt 'stænd] ich halte (es) nicht aus, ich ertrage (es) nicht **II 1**, 14
to stand up [stænd‿'ʌp] aufstehen *(vom Stuhl)* **II 1**, 13
star [stɑ:] Stern **I**; Star **II 2**, 26
⟨**to star**⟩ [stɑ:] die Hauptrolle spielen **II 5**, 85
to **stare** [steə] starren **II 3**, 44
to **start** [stɑ:t] anfangen, beginnen **I**
to **startle** ['stɑ:tl] erschrecken, aufschrecken **II 6**, 90
state [steɪt] Staat **I**; Zustand, Status **II 4**, 58
statement ['steɪtmənt] Feststellung, Behauptung, Aussage **II 7**, 109
station ['steɪʃn] Haltestelle, Station **I**
gas station *(AE)* ['gæs ˌsteɪʃn] Tankstelle **II 6**, 92
petrol station ['petrl ˌsteɪʃn] Tankstelle **I**
statue ['stætju:] Statue, Standbild **II 4**, 59
statuette [ˌstætju'et] Statuette **II 2**, 29
to **stay** [steɪ] bleiben **I**
steady ['stedi] ständig, ununterbrochen **II 3**, 44
to **steal*** [sti:l] stehlen **II 1**, 15
steam [sti:m] Dampf **II 3**, 44
steep [sti:p] steil **II 8**, 127
step [step] Schritt, Stufe, Abschnitt **I**
+to step off [step‿'ɒf] aussteigen **II 4**, 67
to **step on so.'s foot** [step] jmdm auf den Fuß treten **II 1**, 15
stepfather ['stepfɑ:ðə] Stiefvater **I**
stick [stɪk] Stock **I**

walking stick ['wɔ:kɪŋ ˌstɪk] Gehstock, Spazierstock **II 4**, 62
to **stick*** [stɪk] kleben **I**
to stick out ['stɪk‿aʊt] herausstrecken **II 8**, 130
+to stick to sth. ['stɪk] etw treu bleiben, bleiben (bei) **II 7**, 115
sticker ['stɪkə] Sticker, Aufkleber **I**
still [stɪl] noch **I**
stomach ['stʌmək] Magen, Bauch **II 5**, 72
stomach ache ['stʌmək‿eɪk] Magenschmerzen **II 8**, 130
stone [stəʊn] Stein **I**
stop [stɒp] Halt, Stopp **I**
bus stop ['bʌs stɒp] Bushaltestelle **I**
to **stop** [stɒp] anhalten, stoppen **I**
store ['stɔ:] (großes) Geschäft, Laden **I**
department store [dɪ'pɑ:tmənt ˌstɔ:] Kaufhaus **I**
storm [stɔ:m] Sturm **I**
+**stormy** ['stɔ:mi] stürmisch **I**
story ['stɔ:ri] Geschichte **I**
storyteller ['stɔ:riˌtelə] Geschichtenerzähler(in) **II 3**, 49
straight ['streɪt] geradeaus **I**
strange [streɪndʒ] merkwürdig, sonderbar **I**
straw [strɔ:] Stroh **I**
to **stray** [streɪ] herumschweifen, herumstreunen **I**
street [stri:t] Straße **I**
stress [stres] Betonung **I**; +Stress, Anspannung **II 1**, 18
to **stress** [stres] betonen **I**
stressful ['stresfʊl] stressig **II 5**, 82
stretching ['stretʃɪŋ] Strecken, Dehnen **II 5**, 73
string [strɪŋ] Faden; Saite **I**
strip [strɪp] Streifen **I**
to **stroke** [strəʊk] streicheln **II 1**, 14
strong [strɒŋ] stark **II 3**, 42; +streng, rau **I**
structure ['strʌktʃə] Struktur, Aufbau **II 5**, 75
student ['stju:dnt] Student(in) **II 3**, 46
studio ['stju:diəʊ] Studio **II 4**, 57
to **study** ['stʌdi] studieren **II 1**, 16
stuff [stʌf] Zeug, Sachen **II 7**, 110
to **stuff** [stʌf] füllen, stopfen **II 4**, 62
stunt [stʌnt] Kunststück **II 2**, 30
stuntman ['stʌntmən] Stuntman, Double **II 2**, 30
stupid ['stju:pɪd] Dummkopf, Blödmann **II 2**, 32
stupid ['stju:pɪd] dumm, dämlich **I**
style [staɪl] Stil **I**
subject ['sʌbdʒɪkt] (Unterrichts-)Fach; Thema **I**
+**subway** (*AE*) ['sʌbweɪ] U-Bahn **I**
+**success** [sək'ses] Erfolg **II 5**, 83
successful [sək'sesfl] erfolgreich **II 1**, 12
such [sʌtʃ] solch(e/r/s) **I**
such as ['sʌtʃ‿əz] wie zum Beispiel **II 8**, 124
sucker ['sʌkə] Idiot(in) **II 7**, 110
sudden ['sʌdn] plötzlich, unerwartet **II 3**, 42
suddenly ['sʌdnli] plötzlich **I**
⟨**sugar**⟩ ['ʃʊgə] Zucker **II 5**, 77
suggestion [sə'dʒestʃn] Vorschlag **I**
suitcase ['su:tkeɪs] Koffer **I**
suit [su:t] Anzug **II 6**, 100
summary ['sʌmri] Zusammenfassung **II 5**, 79
summer ['sʌmə] Sommer **I**
sun [sʌn] Sonne **II 1**, 10
Sunday ['sʌndeɪ] Sonntag **I**
sunglasses ['sʌnglɑ:sɪz] Sonnenbrille **II 1**, 10
sunny ['sʌni] sonnig **I**
sunshine ['sʌnʃaɪn] Sonnenschein **II 1**, 14
super ['su:pə] super, spitze **I**
⟨**supermodel**⟩ ['su:pəˌmɒdl] Mannequin, Topmodel **II 5**, 77
suppleness ['sʌplnəs] Elastizität, Flexibilität **II 5**, 73
+**supply line** [sə'plaɪ ˌlaɪn] Versorgungsleitung **I**
+**support** [sə'pɔ:t] Unterstützung **II 3**, 50
to **support** [sə'pɔ:t] unterstützen **II 5**, 72
supporting actor [səˌpɔ:tɪŋ‿'æktə] Schauspieler in einer Nebenrolle **II 2**, 30
to **suppose** [sə'pəʊz] denken, meinen, annehmen, vermuten **II 6**, 95
sure [ʃʊə] sicher, klar **I**
to make sure [ˌmeɪk 'ʃʊə] sicherstellen **I**
surface ['sɜ:fɪs] Oberfläche **II 6**, 92
surfing ['sɜ:fɪŋ] Surfen **I**
surgeon ['sɜ:dʒn] Chirurg **II 8**, 122
surprise [sə'praɪz] Überraschung **II 7**, 112
to be **surprised** (*at*) [sə'praɪzd] überrascht sein (über) **II 1**, 15
+**survey** ['sɜ:veɪ] Umfrage, Untersuchung **II 7**, 115
surveyor [sə'veɪə] Gutachter(in) **II 6**, 95
to **survive** [sə'vaɪv] überleben **II 6**, 92
⟨to round up the usual **suspects**⟩ ['raʊnd‿ʌp ðə 'ju:ʒl 'sʌspekts] die gewöhnlichen Verdächtigen festnehmen **II 1**, 18
to **swear*** [sweə] fluchen **II 8**, 127
sweater ['swetə] Pullover **II 6**, 95
sweatshirt ['swetʃɜ:t] Sweatshirt **I**
sweatshop ['swetʃɒp] Ausbeuterbetrieb **II 7**, 110
⟨**sweeper**⟩ ['swi:pə] Straßenkehrer(in) **II 1**, 18
sweet [swi:t] Bonbon, (*pl.*) Süßigkeiten **I**
sweet [swi:t] süß, niedlich **I**
to **swim*** [swɪm] schwimmen **I**
swimming ['swɪmɪŋ] Schwimmen **II 5**, 72
swimming pool ['swɪmɪŋ ˌpu:l] Swimmingpool **I**
swimsuit ['swɪmsu:t] Badeanzug **II 5**, 72
to **switch on** [ˌswɪtʃ‿'ɒn] einschalten **II 1**, 13
sword [sɔ:d] Schwert **II 2**, 32
syllable ['sɪləbl] Silbe **I**
symptom ['sɪmptəm] Anzeichen, Symptom **II 8**, 130
°**synonym** ['sɪnənɪm] Synonym **II 8**, 133
system ['sɪstəm] System **II 4**, 61

T

tabby ['tæbi] getigert; getigerte Katze **II 1**, 14
table [teɪbl] Tisch **I**
to **take*** [teɪk] nehmen, (hin)bringen **I**
to take a photo [ˌteɪk‿ə 'fəʊtəʊ] ein Foto machen **II 1**, 12
to take notice (*of*) [ˌteɪk 'nəʊtɪs] beachten, Notiz nehmen (von) **I**
to take off [ˌteɪk‿'ɒf] starten, abheben **I**
to take part (*in*) [ˌteɪk 'pɑ:t] teilnehmen (an) **I**
to take place [ˌteɪk 'pleɪs] stattfinden **II 2**, 29
to take turns [tɜ:n] (sich) miteinander abwechseln **I**
takings (*pl.*) ['teɪkɪŋz] Einnahmen **II 2**, 29
talented ['tæləntɪd] begabt, talentiert **II 2**, 29
to tell **tales** [ˌtel 'teɪlz] petzen, klatschen **II 1**, 14
talk [tɔ:k] Gespräch **I**
talk show ['tɔ:k ˌʃəʊ] Talkshow, Gesprächsrunde **II 2**, 30
to give a talk [ˌgɪv‿ə 'tɔ:k] ein (Kurz-) Referat halten **I**
to **talk** (*about*) ['tɔ:k‿əˌbaʊt] sprechen, reden (über) **I**
tall [tɔ:l] hoch, groß, lang **II 6**, 97; +hohe(r/s) **I**
tangled ['tæŋgld] verheddert **II 6**, 95

tank [tæŋk] Tank **I**
tanker ['tæŋkə] Tanker, Tankschiff **I**
+**tape** [teɪp] (Ton-)Band **II 6**, 100
demo tape ['deməʊ ˌteɪp] Demo(nstrations)band **I**
⟨to **taste**⟩ [teɪst] schmecken **II 3**, 47
taxi ['tæksi] Taxi **I**
tea [ti:] Tee **I**
to **teach*** [ti:tʃ] richten, lehren **II 3**, 42
teacher ['ti:tʃə] Lehrer(in) **I**
team [ti:m] Mannschaft, Team **II 5**, 72
teapot ['ti:pɒt] Teekanne **I**
tear [tɪə] Träne **II 5**, 79
to **tear*** *(off)* [teər] (ab)reißen **II 7**, 110
to **tease** [ti:z] auf den Arm nehmen, necken **II 5**, 78
technical ['teknɪkl] technisch **II 2**, 30
techno ['teknəʊ] Techno *(Musikrichtung)* **II 2**, 25
technology [tek'nɒlədʒi] Technologie, Technik **II 6**, 91
°Design and Technology [dɪ'zaɪn‿ən‿tek'nɒlədʒi] Gestalten und Technik **I**
teddy bear ['tedi ˌbeə] Teddybär **I**
teenager ['ti:neɪdʒə] Teenager, Jugendliche(r) **II 7**, 107
telephone ['telɪfəʊn] Telefon **I**
telescope ['telɪskəʊp] Teleskop, Fernrohr **II 6**, 92
television ['telɪvɪʒn] Fernsehen **II 2**, 29
to **tell*** [tel] erzählen **I**
to tell so. to do sth [tel] jmdm sagen, dass er/sie etw tun soll **II 5**, 79
to tell tales [ˌtel 'teɪlz] petzen, klatschen **II 1**, 14
telly ['teli] Fernseher **I**
temperature ['temprətʃə] Temperatur, Fieber **II 8**, 130
temple ['templ] Tempel **II 4**, 67
(ten) times [ˌten 'taɪmz] (zehn)mal **II 4**, 62
+**tennis** ['tenɪs] Tennis **I**
tent [tent] Zelt **I**
term [tɜ:m] (Schul-) Trimester, Semester **I**; Ausdruck, Terminus **II 3**, 46
terminal ['tɜ:mɪnl] Terminal **I**
terrible ['terəbl] schrecklich, furchtbar **I**
terrifying ['terəfaɪɪŋ] erschreckend, grauenvoll **II 3**, 45
test [test] Test **I**
to **test** [test] prüfen, testen **II 5**, 81
tetanus ['tetnəs] Wundstarrkrampf, Tetanus **II 8**, 128
+**text** [tekst] Text **I**
than [ðæn/ðən] als **I**
°to **thank** [θæŋk] danken **I**
thank you ['θæŋk‿jʊ] danke **I**
thanks [θæŋks] danke **I**
that [ðæt] das; dass **I**
the [ðə/ði] der/die/das **I**
the 60s ['sɪkstiz] die Sechziger (Jahre) **II 2**, 27
the … the [ðə ... ðə] je … desto **II 5**, 73
operating **theatre** ['ɒpəreɪtɪŋ ˌθɪətə] Operationssaal **II 8**, 122
theatreland ['θɪətəˌlænd] Theaterviertel **I**
their [ðeə] ihr/ihre *(pl.)* **I**
theirs [ðeəz] ihre(r/s), der/die/das ihre **II 4**, 59
them [ðem] sie *(Akk.)*; ihnen *(Dat.)* **I**
theme [θi:m] Thema **I**
theme park ['θi:m ˌpɑ:k] Erlebnispark **I**
themselves [ðəm'selvz] sich, (sie) selbst **II 2**, 26
then [ðen] dann, danach **I**
now and then [ˌnaʊ‿n‿'ðen] ab und zu **I**
theory ['θɪəri] Theorie **II 6**, 99
there is / are [ðeə(r)‿'ɪz / 'ɑ:] es gibt, da ist/sind **I**
thermometer [θə'mɒmɪtə] Thermometer **II 8**, 128
these [ði:z] dies (sind), das (sind); diese(r/s) *(pl.)* **I**
they [ðeɪ] sie *(pl.)* **I**
thick [θɪk] dick, dicht **I**
thigh [θaɪ] Oberschenkel **II 5**, 73
thin [θɪn] dünn **I**
thing [θɪŋ] Sache, Ding **I**
to **think*** [θɪŋk] denken, glauben. meinen **I**
to be **thirsty** ['θɜ:sti] Durst haben **II 2**, 33
this [ðɪs] dies (ist), das (ist); diese(r/s) *(sing.)* **I**
those [ðəʊz] jene, diese *(pl.)* **I**
though [ðəʊ] obwohl, obgleich **II 2**, 29
thousand ['θaʊznd] tausend **I**
to **threaten** ['θretn] drohen, bedrohen **II 6**, 91
thriller ['θrɪlə] Thriller, spannender Film **II 2**, 25
sore **throat** [ˌsɔ: 'θrəʊt] Halsschmerzen, Halsweh **II 8**, 130
through [θru:] durch, über **I**
throughout [θru'aʊt] überall (in) **II 6**, 90
to **throw*** *(away)* [θrəʊ] (weg)werfen **I**
to throw up *(coll.)* [θrəʊ‿'ʌp] kotzen **II 8**, 128
+**thrower** ['θrəʊə] Werfer(in) **II 5**, 84
+**thumb** [θʌm] Daumen **II 8**, 132
+to **thumb a ride** [ˌθʌm‿ə 'raɪd] per Anhalter fahren, trampen **II 2**, 34
thunderstorm ['θʌndəˌstɔ:m] Gewitter **II 2**, 33
Thursday ['θɜ:zdeɪ] Donnerstag **I**
ticket ['tɪkət] Flugschein, Fahrkarte **I**
tie [taɪ] Krawatte **I**
tights [taɪts] Strumpfhose **I**
time [taɪm] (Uhr-)Zeit **I**
ahead of time [əˌhed‿əv 'taɪm] im Voraus **II 8**, 124
all the time [ˌɔ:l ðə 'taɪm] die ganze Zeit **II 1**, 12
on time [ɒn 'taɪm] pünktlich **II 3**, 44
time out [taɪm‿'aʊt] Auszeit; Zeitbedarf **II 5**, 72
(ten) **times** [ˌten 'taɪmz] (zehn)mal **II 4**, 62
timetable ['taɪmˌteɪbl] Stundenplan **I**
tip [tɪp] Hinweis, Tipp **II 5**, 73
learning tip ['lɜ:nɪŋ ˌtɪp] Lerntipp **I**
to be **tired** ['taɪəd] müde (sein) **I**
title ['taɪtl] Titel, Überschrift **I**
to [tʊ/tu] in/im, zu **I**
toast [təʊst] Toast(brot) **II 4**, 63
today [tə'deɪ] heute **I**
toe [təʊ] (Fuß-)Zehe **II 5**, 73
together [tə'geðə] zusammen **I**
toilet ['tɔɪlɪt] Toilette **I**
tomato, *(pl.)* -oes [tə'mɑ:təʊ] Tomate **I**
tomorrow [tə'mɒrəʊ] morgen **I**
to **tone up** [ˌtəʊn‿'ʌp] stärken, festigen **II 5**, 72
tongue [tʌŋ] Zunge **II 8**, 130
tonight [tə'naɪt] heute Abend, heute Nacht **I**
too [tu:] auch, ebenfalls **I**; zu (sehr, viel) **I**
tooth, *pl.* teeth [tu:θ, ti:θ] Zahn, Zähne **II 2**, 32
top [tɒp] Top, ärmelloses T-Shirt **I**
top [tɒp] oben **I**; +obere(r/s) **II 4**, 65
topic ['tɒpɪk] Thema **I**
torch [tɔ:tʃ] Taschenlampe **II 6**, 95
tornado, *pl.* -o(e)s [tɔ:'neɪdəʊ] Wirbelsturm, Tornado **II 8**, 124
to **toss** [tɒs] werfen **II 1**, 14
+**tossing the caber** [ˌtɒsɪŋ ðə 'keɪbə] Baumstammwerfen *(schottische Sportart)* **II 5**, 84
in **total** [ɪn 'təʊtl] insgesamt, total **II 7**, 110

to **touch** [tʌtʃ] berühren, anfassen **II 4**, 61
touchscreen [ˈtʌtʃˌskriːn] Kontaktbildschirm, Tastenbildschirm **II 6**, 93
tour [tʊə] Reise, Tour **II 3**, 46
to **tour** [tʊə] reisen, besichtigen **I**
tourism [ˈtʊərɪzm] Tourismus **I**
tourist [ˈtʊərɪst] Tourist(in) **I**
toward(*s*) [təˈwɔːd(z)] auf … zu, in Richtung auf, (ent)gegen **I**
towel [ˈtaʊəl] Handtuch **II 5**, 72
tower [ˈtaʊə] Turm **I**
town [taʊn] (Klein-)Stadt **I**
trace [treɪs] Spur **II 6**, 92
track [træk] Spur, Weg, Pfad **I**
tracksuit [ˈtræksuːt] Jogginganzug **II 5**, 78
trader [ˈtreɪdə] Händler(in) **II 4**, 61
traditional [trəˈdɪʃnl] traditionell **I**
traffic [ˈtræfɪk] Verkehr **I**
traffic jam [ˈtræfɪk ˌdʒæm] Verkehrsstau **II 3**, 48
traffic light [ˈtræfɪk ˌlaɪt] Ampel **I**
tragedy [ˈtrædʒədi] Tragödie **I**
train [treɪn] (U-Bahn-) Zug **I**
to **train** [treɪn] trainieren **II 5**, 72
trainer [ˈtreɪnə] Trainer(in) **II 5**, 77; Turnschuh **I**
training [ˈtreɪnɪŋ] Training **I**
to **translate** [trænsˈleɪt] übersetzen **I**
⟨**translation**⟩ [trænzˈleɪʃn] Übersetzung **II 3**, 47
transplant [ˈtrænsplɑːnt] Transplantation **II 8**, 126
transport [ˈtrænspɔːt] Transport, Beförderung **I**
travel [ˈtrævl] Reise- **I**
space travel [ˈspeɪs ˌtrævl] Raumfahrt **II 6**, 91
travel agent [ˈtrævl ˌeɪdʒnt] Reisebüroangestellte(r) **II 4**, 60
to **travel** [ˈtrævl] reisen **I**
One Day **Travelcard** [ˈtrævlkɑːd] Tageskarte, Netzkarte *(London)* **II 1**, 10
commercial **traveller** [kəˌmɜːʃl ˈtrævlə] Handelsreisende(r) **II 6**, 95
treasure [ˈtreʒə] Schatz **II 4**, 59
to **treat** [triːt] behandeln, umgehen (mit) **II 8**, 128
tree [triː] Baum **I**
tribe [traɪb] Stamm **II 3**, 43
⟨**tricky**⟩ [ˈtrɪki] kompliziert, schwierig **II 8**, 133
trip [trɪp] Kurzreise, Trip **I**
⁺sailing trip [ˈseɪlɪŋ ˌtrɪp] Segeltörn **I**
trouble [ˈtrʌbl] Ärger, Schwierigkeiten **II 1**, 15
to get into trouble [ˈtrʌbl] in Schwierigkeiten geraten **II 8**, 79
trousers [ˈtraʊzəz] Hose(n) **I**
long-distance **truck driver** [ˌlɒŋˈdɪstns ˈtrʌk ˌdraɪvə] Fernfahrer(in) **II 4**, 60
true [truː] wahr **I**
trumpet [ˈtrʌmpɪt] Trompete **II 2**, 24
trunks [trʌŋks] Badehose(n) **II 5**, 72
to **try** [traɪ] versuchen, probieren **I**
T-shirt [ˈtiːʃɜːt] T-Shirt **I**
tube [tjuːb] *Name der Londoner U-Bahn* (*wörtlich:* Röhre) **I**
Tuesday [ˈtjuːzdeɪ] Dienstag **I**
tunnel [ˈtʌnl] Tunnel **I**
⁺**turkey** [ˈtɜːki] Truthahn **II 4**, 65
Turkish [ˈtɜːkɪʃ] türkisch, Türkisch **I**
to take **turns** [tɜːn] (sich) miteinander abwechseln **I**
it's his/her turn [tɜːn] er/sie ist an der Reihe **I**
to **turn** [tɜːn] (um)drehen, wenden **I**
to turn down [ˌtɜːn ˈdaʊn] herunterdrehen, leiser stellen **I**
to turn into [ˈtɜːn‿ɪntʊ] (sich) verwandeln in **II 7**, 111
TV [ˌtiːˈviː] Fernseher **I**
twice [twaɪs] zweimal **I**
two [tuː] zwei **I**
⁺**type** [taɪp] Typ, Art **II 7**, 115
to **type** [taɪp] tippen, mit der Maschine schreiben **II 3**, 45
typical [ˈtɪpɪkl] typisch **I**
flat **tyre** [ˌflæt ˈtaɪə] platter Reifen, Plattfuß **I**

U

UFO (*Unidentified Flying Object*) [ˌjuːefˈəʊ] UFO (unbekanntes Flugobjekt) **II 6**, 90
ugly [ˈʌgli] hässlich **I**
umbrella [ʌmˈbrelə] (Regen-)Schirm **II 5**, 74
uncle [ˈʌŋkl] Onkel **I**
under [ˈʌndə] unter **I**
Underground [ˈʌndəgraʊnd] U-Bahn **I**
to **underline** [ˌʌndəˈlaɪn] unterstreichen **I**
underpants (*pl.*) [ˈʌndəpænts] Unterhose **II 8**, 128
to **understand*** [ˌʌndəˈstænd] verstehen **I**
unfortunately [ʌnˈfɔːtʃnətli] unglücklicherweise, leider **II 2**, 26
unidentified [ˌʌnaɪˈdentɪfaɪd] unbekannt, nicht identifiziert **II 6**, 91
uniform [ˈjuːnɪfɔːm] Uniform **I**
unit [ˈjuːnɪt] Lektion, Einheit **I**
unknown [ʌnˈnəʊn] unbekannt **II 6**, 91
to be **unlucky** [ʌnˈlʌki] Pech haben **II 4**, 62
unmanned [ʌnˈmænd] unbemannt **II 6**, 92
⁺**unnatural** [ʌnˈnætʃrl] unnatürlich **II 6**, 100
until [ənˈtɪl] bis **I**
unused [ˌʌnˈjuːzd] unbenutzt, nicht mehr benutzt **I**
⁺**unusual** [ʌnˈjuːʒl] ungewöhnlich **II 2**, 34
up [ʌp] oben (auf); hinauf **I**
to get up [get‿ˈʌp] aufstehen *(vom Bett)* **II 1**, 13
to give up [gɪv‿ˈʌp] aufgeben **II 5**, 78
to grow up [grəʊ‿ˈʌp] aufwachsen **II 1**, 16
it's up to you [ˌʌp tə ˈjuː] es liegt an dir/Ihnen **II 5**, 72
to blow* up [ˌbləʊ‿ˈʌp] aufblasen, aufpumpen **II 8**, 127
⁺to board up [ˌbɔːd‿ˈʌp] verschalen, mit Brettern vernageln **I**
to burn* up [ˌbɜːn‿ˈʌp] verbrennen, verbrauchen **II 5**, 73
to hurry (*up*) [ˌhʌri‿ˈʌp] (sich) beeilen **I**
to keep* up (*with so.*) [ˌkiːp‿ˈʌp] Schritt halten (mit jmdm) **II 1**, 15
to line up [ˌlaɪn‿ˈʌp] (sich) aufstellen **II 1**, 14
to liven up [ˌlaɪvn‿ˈʌp] beleben, aufmuntern **II 1**, 12
to look sth. up [ˌlʊk‿ˈʌp] etw nachschlagen **I**
to make* up [ˌmeɪk‿ˈʌp] (sich) ausdenken, erfinden **I**
⁺to pick up [pɪk‿ˈʌp] aufheben, -lesen **II 1**, 18; abholen **II 4**, 61
to put* up [ˌpʊt‿ˈʌp] aufgeben, aufhängen **I**
to ring* so. up [ˌrɪŋ‿ˈʌp] jmdn anrufen **I**
to set* (*up*) [ˌset‿ˈʌp] (auf)stellen, (auf)bauen **I**
to shut* up [ˌʃʌt‿ˈʌp] den Mund halten **II 8**, 127
to split* up [ˌsplɪt‿ˈʌp] sich (voneinander) trennen **I**
to stand up [stænd‿ˈʌp] aufstehen *(vom Stuhl)* **II 1**, 13

to throw up *(coll.)* [θrəʊ‿'ʌp] kotzen **II 8**, 128
to tone up [ˌtəʊn‿'ʌp] stärken, festigen **II 5**, 72
to wake* *(up)* [ˌweɪk‿'ʌp] (auf)wachen **I**
to warm up [ˌwɔ:m‿'ʌp] aufwärmen **II 5**, 73
⟨to wire up⟩ [ˌwaɪə‿'ʌp] eine Leitung (ver)legen **II 1**, 18
up to date [ˌʌp tə 'deɪt] modern, aktuell **I**
+to **uproot** [ʌp'ru:t] entwurzeln, herausreißen **I**
+**upstairs** [ˌʌp'steəz] oben; Obergeschoss **I**
+to **upturn** [ʌp'tɜ:n] umdrehen, umwerfen **I**
+**urban** ['ɜ:bn] städtisch **II 2**, 34
us [ʌs] uns **I**
to **use** [ju:z] benutzen, gebrauchen **I**
used to do sth. [ˌju:st tə 'du:] pflegte zu tun, machte früher **II 5**, 78
useful ['ju:sfl] nützlich, brauchbar **I**
usual ['ju:ʒl] gewöhnlich, üblich **II 3**, 42
⟨to round up the usual suspects⟩ ['raʊnd‿ʌp ðə 'ju:ʒl 'sʌspekts] die gewöhnlichen Verdächtigen festnehmen **II 1**, 18
usually ['ju:ʒli] gewöhnlich, normalerweise **I**
utterance ['ʌtrns] Äußerung **II 6**, 101

V

vacation *(AE)* [və'keɪʃn] Urlaub, Ferien **I**
vaccination [ˌvæksɪ'neɪʃn] Impfung **II 8**, 122
van [væn] Kleinlaster, Lieferwagen **I**
vanilla [və'nɪlə] Vanille **I**
varied ['veərɪd] verschieden(artig), unterschiedlich **II 2**, 29
various ['veəriəs] verschiedene **I**
vegetable ['vedʒətəbl] Gemüse **II 4**, 60
verandah [və'rændə] Veranda **II 4**, 59
verse [vɜ:s] Strophe, Vers **II 4**, 57
version ['vɜ:ʃn] Version **II 2**, 25
very ['veri] sehr **I**
vet *(veterinarian)* [vet (ˌvetrɪ'neəriən)] Tierarzt/-ärztin **I**
via [vaɪə] über **II 1**, 12
vibes *(vibrations)* [vaɪbz (vaɪ'breɪʃnz)] Vibrationen, Schwingungen **I**
video ['vɪdiəʊ] Video **I**
video clip ['vɪdiəʊ ˌklɪp] Videoclip **II 2**, 35
video shop ['vɪdiəʊ ˌʃɒp] Videothek, Videoladen **I**
view [vju:] Aussicht, Blick, Ansicht **I**
Viking ['vaɪkɪŋ] Wikinger(in) **II 4**, 58
village ['vɪlɪdʒ] Dorf, Ortschaft **I**
village hall [ˌvɪlɪdʒ 'hɔ:l] Gemeindehaus **I**
vinegar ['vɪnɪgə] Essig **I**
violet ['vaɪələt] violett **II 3**, 45
violin [ˌvaɪə'lɪn] Geige, Violine **II 2**, 25
+**virtual reality** [ˌvɜ:tʃuəl ri'æləti] virtuelle Realität **II 3**, 50
virtual ['vɜ:tʃuəl] virtuell **II 3**, 51
to **visit** ['vɪzɪt] besuchen **I**
visitor ['vɪzɪtə] Besucher(in) **II 3**, 46
visual effects [ˌvɪʒuəl ɪ'fekts] (optische) Tricks **II 2**, 29
vocabulary notebook [vəʊˌkæbjəlri 'nəʊtbʊk] Vokabelheft **I**
vocal group ['vəʊkl ˌgru:p] Musikgruppe mit Gesang **II 4**, 57
vocals ['vəʊklz] Gesang **II 3**, 47
voice [vɔɪs] Stimme **I**
volleyball ['vɒlibɔ:l] Volleyball **I**
volunteer [ˌvɒlən'tɪə] Freiwillige(r) **I**
to **vote** [vəʊt] wählen **II 2**, 29

W

wage [weɪdʒ] (Arbeits-)Lohn **II 7**, 107
to **wait** ['weɪt fɔ:] warten auf **I**
to wait for [weɪt] warten auf **II 6**, 93
waiter ['weɪtə] Kellner **II 4**, 60
to **wake*** *(up)* [ˌweɪk‿'ʌp] (auf)wachen **I**
walk [wɔ:k] Spaziergang **I**
to **walk** [wɔ:k] spazierengehen **I**
walking stick ['wɔ:kɪŋ ˌstɪk] Gehstock, Spazierstock **II 4**, 62
wall [wɔ:l] Wand **I**
wallet ['wɒlɪt] Brieftasche **II 6**, 95
to **wander** ['wɒndə] herumwandern **II 5**, 78
to **want** [wɒnt] wollen, wünschen **I**
war [wɔ:] Krieg **II 4**, 62
to **warm up** [ˌwɔ:m‿'ʌp] aufwärmen **II 5**, 73
warm [wɑ:m] warm **I**
to **warn** [wɑ:n] warnen **I**
warning ['wɔ:nɪŋ] Warnung **II 5**, 76
to **wash** [wɒʃ] waschen, putzen **I**
waste [weɪst] Abfall, Müll **I**
watch [wɒtʃ] Armbanduhr **I**
to **watch** [wɒtʃ] anschauen, zuschauen **I**
to watch TV [ˌwɒtʃ ti:'vi:] fernsehen **I**
watching brief ['wɒtʃɪŋ ˌbri:f] Beobachtungsauftrag **II 6**, 95
water ['wɔ:tə] Wasser **I**
water-skiing ['wɔ:təski:ɪŋ] Wasserskifahren **I**
wave [weɪv] Welle **I**
wax content ['wæks ˌkɒntent] Wachsgehalt **I**
way [weɪ] Art und Weise; Weg **I**
in a bad way [ˌbæd 'weɪ] in einem schlechten Zustand **II 6**, 96
no way *(coll.)* [ˌnəʊ 'weɪ] auf keinen Fall, keineswegs **I**
we [wi:] wir **I**
weapon ['wepən] Waffe **II 6**, 96
to **wear*** [weə] anhaben, tragen **I**
weather ['weðə] Wetter **I**
Wednesday ['wenzdeɪ] Mittwoch **I**
week [wi:k] Woche **I**
weekday ['wi:kdeɪ] Wochentag, Arbeitstag **II 4**, 61
weekend [ˌwi:k'end] Wochenende **I**
to **weigh** [weɪ] wiegen **II 7**, 112
to **welcome** ['welkəm] begrüßen, willkommen heißen **II 3**, 46
welcome ['welkəm] willkommen **I**
you're welcome [ˌjɔ: 'welkəm] bitte sehr, nichts zu danken **II 4**, 63
well [wel] (Öl-)Quelle, Bohrloch **II 6**, 95
as well as [əz 'wel‿əz] sowie, sowohl als auch **II 3**, 46
to do well [du: 'wel] erfolgreich sein **II 4**, 67
+**well-managed** [ˌwel'mænɪdʒd] gut organisiert, gut geführt **I**
well [wel] gut **II 3**, 42; nun gut, na ja **I**
Welsh [welʃ] walisisch, Walisisch **I**
west [west] westlich, Westen **I**
western ['westən] Western **II 2**, 25
wet [wet] nass **I**

what [wɒt] was? **I**; welche(r/s), was für eine(r/s) **I**
What about ...? [ˌwɒt‿ə'baʊt] Was ist mit ...? **I**
What kind *(of)* ...? [kaɪnd] Was für eine/welche Art ...? **I**
whatever [wɒt'evə] was (auch immer), egal was **II 4**, 63
wheel [wi:l] Rad **I**
wheelchair ['wi:ltʃeə] Rollstuhl **II 1**, 12
when [wen] wenn, wann **I**
where [weə] wo, wohin, woher **I**
where *(from/to)* [weə] woher/wohin **I**
whether ['weðə] ob **I**
which [wɪtʃ] welche(r/s) **I**
while [waɪl] während **II 1**, 11; +(eine) Weile **I**
to **whine** [waɪn] jammern, wimmern **II 1**, 14
whisky ['wɪski] Whisky **II 4**, 59
whistle ['wɪsl] (Triller-)Pfeife **II 1**, 10
white [waɪt] weiß **I**
+the whites [waɪts] die Weißen **I**
white-faced ['waɪtfeɪst] mit weißem Gesicht **II 8**, 127
+**whitewater rafting** [ˌwaɪtwɔ:tə 'rɑ:ftɪŋ] Wildwasserfahren **I**
who [hu:] wer, wem, wen **I**; der/die/das, welche(r/s) **I**
whole [həʊl] ganz, komplett **I**
whom [hu:m] wem, wen **II 5**, 79
whose [hu:z] deren, dessen **II 4**, 59
+**whose** [hu:z] wessen **I**
why [waɪ] warum **I**
+**wicket** ['wɪkɪt] Krickettor **II 5**, 84
wide [waɪd] weit **II 7**, 112
wild [waɪld] wild **I**
wildlife ['waɪldlaɪf] Tierwelt **I**
+**will** [wɪl] werden **I**
to **win*** [wɪn] gewinnen **I**
+**wind** [wɪnd] Wind **I**
window ['wɪndəʊ] Fenster **I**
+**windy** ['wɪndi] windig **I**
wine [waɪn] Wein **I**
⟨**wing**⟩ [wɪŋ] Flügel **II 5**, 84
winner ['wɪnə] Gewinner(in) **II 2**, 29
winter ['wɪntə] Winter **I**
⟨to **wire up**⟩ [ˌwaɪə‿'ʌp] eine Leitung (ver)legen **II 1**, 18
to **wish** [wɪʃ] wünschen **II 4**, 58
witch [wɪtʃ] Hexe **I**
with [wɪð] mit **I**
within [wɪ'ðɪn] in, innerhalb **II 6**, 95
without [wɪ'ðaʊt] ohne **I**
woman, *(pl.)* women ['wʊmən/'wɪmɪn] Frau(en) **I**
to **wonder** ['wʌndə] sich fragen, sich wundern **II 6**, 90
wonderful ['wʌndəfl] wunderbar, wundervoll **II 1**, 17
+**wood** [wʊd] Holz **II 5**, 84
woods [wʊdz] Wald **I**
word [wɜ:d] Wort **I**
key word ['ki: wɜ:d] Schlüsselbegriff **I**
work [wɜ:k] Arbeit **I**
to **work** [wɜ:k] arbeiten **I**
to work out [wɜ:k‿'aʊt] ausarbeiten, herausfinden **II 7**, 109
to work shift [ˌwɜ:k 'ʃɪft] Schicht arbeiten, Schichtdienst machen **I**
worker ['wɜ:kə] Arbeiter(in) **II 2**, 27
workout ['wɜ:kaʊt] Training **II 5**, 72
workshop ['wɜ:kʃɒp] Werkstatt **II 4**, 62
world [wɜ:ld] Welt **I**
to **worry** ['wʌri] sich Sorgen machen **I**
worse [wɜ:s] schlechter **II 1**, 15
worst [wɜ:st] schlechteste(r/s) **I**
would play [ˌwʊd/ˌwəd 'pleɪ] spielte gewöhnlich **II 2**, 24
I'd (= *I would*) like [aɪd‿'laɪk] ich hätte gerne **I**
would you like to? [ˌwʊd ju: 'laɪk tə] möchtest du?/möchtet ihr/möchten Sie? **I**
would you care to [ˌwʊd ju: 'keə] hätten Sie Lust (zu) **II 6**, 95
wow! [waʊ] *Ausruf der Bewunderung* **I**
to **wrap** [ræp] einwickeln, verpacken **II 8**, 127
wrist [rɪst] Handgelenk **II 8**, 128
to **write*** *(down)* [ˌraɪt 'daʊn] (auf)schreiben **I**
to write sth. off [ˌraɪt‿'ɒf] abschreiben **II 6**, 96
writer ['raɪtə] Schriftsteller(in) **II 4**, 61
wrong [rɒŋ] falsch **I**
to go wrong [ˌgəʊ 'rɒŋ] schief gehen **II 1**, 11

X

X-ray ['eksreɪ] Röntgenaufnahme, -strahlen **II 8**, 122
to **X-ray** ['eksreɪ] durchleuchten, röntgen **II 8**, 128

Y

yard [jɑ:d] *englisches Längenmaß (= 0,914 m)* **II 4**, 61
yeah [jeə] ja **I**
year [jɪə] (Schul-) Jahr; Jahrgang, Klasse **I**
all the year round [raʊnd] das ganze Jahr über **II 1**, 8
yellow ['jeləʊ] gelb **I**
yep *(coll.)* [jep] ja **II 7**, 111
yes [jes] ja **I**
+**yesterday** ['jestədeɪ] gestern **I**
not ... **yet** [jet] noch nicht **I**
yo-yo ['jəʊjəʊ] Jojo **II 5**, 72
yoga ['jəʊgə] Joga **I**
you [ju:] du, ihr, Sie **I**
it's up to you [ˌʌp tə 'ju:] es liegt an dir/Ihnen **II 5**, 72
young [jʌŋ] jung **I**
younger ['jʌŋgə] jünger(e/r/s) **I**
your [jɔ:] dein/deine, euer/eure, Ihr/Ihre **I**
you're welcome [ˌjɔ: 'welkəm] bitte sehr, nichts zu danken **II 4**, 63
+**yours** [jɔ:z] deine(r/s), eure(r/s), Ihre(r/s) **I**
Yours faithfully, ['feɪθfli] mit freundlichen Grüßen, hochachtungsvoll *(Briefschluss)* **I**
Yours sincerely, [jɔ:z sɪn'sɪəli] Mit freundlichen Grüßen *(Briefschluss)* **II 2**, 33
yourself [jɔ:'self] dich (selbst) **I**
+**yourselves** [jɔ:'selvz] euch (selbst) **II 4**, 66
youth [ju:θ] Jugendliche(r) **II 6**, 95
youth hostel ['ju:θ ˌhɒstl] Jugendherberge **I**
youth hostelling ['ju:θ ˌhɒstlɪŋ] in Jugendherbergen übernachten **I**

Z

zero ['zɪərəʊ] null **I**
Zulu ['zu:lu] *afrikanische Sprache* **II 4**, 57

Boys' names

Alfie ['ælfi]
Alfred ['ælfrɪd]
Andrew ['ændru:]
Archie ['ɑ:tʃi]
Arthur ['ɑ:θə]
Ben [ben]
Bernie ['bɜ:ni]
B.J. ['bi: 'dʒeɪ]
Bruce [bru:s]
Carlos ['kɑ:lɒs]
Dick [dɪk]
Dinsy ['dɪnzi]
Eddie ['edi]
Farrukh ['færuk]
Gary ['gæri]
George [dʒɔ:dʒ]
Glen [glen]
+**Greg** [greg]
Hassan [hə'sɑ:n]
Henry ['henri]
Imran ['ɪmrən]
Jake [dʒeɪk]
James [dʒeɪmz]
Jasmit ['dʒæzmɪt]
+**Jason** ['dʒeɪsn]
Jimmy ['dʒɪmi]
John [dʒɒn]
Jonathan ['dʒɒnəθn]
Julian ['dʒu:liən]
Kevin ['kevɪn]
Lance [lɑ:ns]
+**Lee** [li:]
Liam ['lɪəm]
Marc [mɑ:k]
Mark [mɑ:k]
Mike [maɪk]
Nathan ['neɪθən]
Nick [nɪk]
Paul [pɔ:l]
Pete [pi:t]
Peter ['pi:tə]
Phil [fɪl]
Rizwan ['rɪzwən]
Ron ['rɒn]
Sam [sæm]
Sanjay ['sændʒeɪ]
Stan ['stæn]
Steve [sti:v]
Terry ['teri]
Tim [tɪm]
Timmy ['tɪmi]
Timothy ['tɪməθi]
Tony ['təʊni]
Trevor ['trevə]
Wayne [weɪn]
William ['wɪljəm]

Girls' names

Abby ['æbi]
Angela ['ændʒlə]
Ann(*e*) [æn]
+**Ashley** ['æʃli]
Brenda ['brendə]
Denise [də'ni:z]
Diana [daɪ'ænə]
Elizabeth [ɪ'lɪzəbəθ]
Emily ['emɪli]
Faith ['feɪθ]
Fanny ['fæni]
Georgina [dʒɔ:'dʒi:nə]
Gina ['dʒi:nə]
Hamida [hæ'mɪdə]
Hilary ['hɪlri]
Jean [dʒi:n]
Jessica ['dʒesɪkə]
Joanna [dʒəʊ'ænə]
Julia ['dʒu:liə]
Karen ['kærən]
Kate [keɪt]
Lauren ['lɔ:rən]
Linda ['lɪndə]
Liz [lɪz]
Lynn [lɪn]
Maggie ['mægi]
Margaret ['mɑ:grət]
Mary ['meəri]
Mary Ann [ˌmeəri‿'æn]
Maureen ['mɔ:ri:n]
Molly ['mɒli]
Nicola ['nɪkələ]
Nora ['nɔ:rə]
Pamela ['pæmlə]
Pramila [præ'mɪlə]
Rachel ['reɪtʃl]
Rhaune [rəʊn]
Rukshana ['rʌkʃɑ:nə]
Samantha [sə'mæntθə]
Selima [sə'li:mə]
Shamira [ʃə'mi:rə]
+**Shannon** ['ʃænən]
Sharon ['ʃærən]
Stella ['stelə]
Stephanie ['stefəni]
Sue [su:]
Susan ['su:zn]
Susie ['su:zi]
Tara ['tɑ:rə]
Tessa ['tesə]
+**Wendy** ['wendi]

Surnames

Aziz [ə'zi:z]
Barling ['bɑ:lɪŋ]
Bell ['bel]
Blake [bleɪk]
Block [blɒk]
Boocock ['bu:kɒk]
Braden ['breɪdn]
Browne ['braʊn]
Burns [bɜ:nz]
Clifford ['klɪfəd]
Clifton ['klɪftən]
+**Cooper** ['ku:pə]
Cummings ['kʌmɪŋz]
Daly ['deɪli]
Dawson ['dɔ:sn]
Driver ['draɪvə]
Evans ['evnz]
Fitzwarren ['fɪtsˌwɒrən]
Forth [fɔ:θ]
Grimsby ['grɪmzbi]
Harrington ['hærɪŋtən]
Harrison ['hærɪsn]
Henrey ['henri]
Herrick ['herɪk]
+**Hopkins** ['hɒpkɪnz]
Howard ['haʊəd]
James [dʒeɪmz]
Jones [dʒəʊnz]
Kapadia [kə'pædɪə]
Kwang [kwæŋ]
Laslett-O'Brien [ˌlɑ:zlət‿əʊ'braɪən]
Lee [li:]
Lenoir [lə'nwɑ:]
+**Lucid** ['lu:sɪd]
Lynch [lɪntʃ]
Macintosh ['mækɪntɒʃ]
Manning ['mænɪŋ]
+**Maryn** ['mærɪn]
McBride [mək'braɪd]
Melrose ['melrəʊz]
Mills [mɪlz]
Modi ['məʊdi]
Moore ['mɔ:]
Morton ['mɔ:tn]
Norton ['nɔ:tn]
O'Brien [əʊ'braɪən]
O'Hare [əʊ'heə]
Osceola [ˌɒskɪ'əʊlə]
Patel [pə'tel]
Pitman ['pɪtmən]
Pollard ['pɒlɑ:d]
Quentin ['kwentɪn]
+**Reed** ['ri:d]
Smith [smɪθ]
Stewart ['stju:ət]
Storr [stɔ:]
Todd [tɒd]
Trelawne [trɪ'lɔ:n]
Troublemaker ['trʌblˌmeɪkə]
Wilson ['wɪlsn]
Winter ['wɪntə]
Wong [wɒŋ]

Geographical names

Aberdeen [ˌæbə'di:n]
Africa ['æfrɪkə]
Alton Towers [ˌɔ:ltn 'taʊəz]
America [ə'merɪkə]
Asia ['eɪʃə]
+**Atlantic** [ət'læntɪk]
Australia [ɒs'treɪliə]
+the **Bahamas** [bə'hɑ:məz]
Bath [bɑ:θ]

Belfast [belˈfɑːst]
Benidorm [ˈbenɪdɔːm]
Boston [ˈbɒstn]
Bristol [ˈbrɪstl]
Britain [ˈbrɪtn]
the **British Isles** [ˌbrɪtɪʃ‿ˈaɪlz]
California [ˌkælɪˈfɔːniə]
Cambridge [ˈkeɪmbrɪdʒ]
+**Canada** [ˈkænədə]
Cardiff [ˈkɑːdɪf]
+**Chicago** [ʃɪˈkɑːgəʊ]
China [ˈtʃaɪnə]
Clifford [ˈklɪfəd]
+**Colorado** [ˌkɒlrˈɑːdəʊ]
Corbridge [ˈkɔːbrɪdʒ]
Cornwall [ˈkɔːnwɔːl]
Creekville [ˈkriːkvɪl]
Cumbria [ˈkʌmbriə]
Deepdale Lane [ˈdiːpdeɪl ˌleɪn]
Denmark [ˈdenmɑːk]
Dingle Bay [ˌdɪŋgl ˈbeɪ]
Drumnadrochit [ˌdrɒmnəˈdrɒxɪt]
Dublin [ˈdʌblɪn]
Easter Island [ˈiːstə ˌaɪlənd]
Edgecombe [ˈedʒkəm]
Edinburgh [ˈedɪnbrə]
England [ˈɪŋglənd]
Europe [ˈjʊərəp]
European Union [ˌjʊərəˈpiːən ˈjuːnjən]
+**Everglades** [ˈevəgleɪdz]
Falmouth [ˈfælməθ]
+**Florida** [ˈflɒrɪdə]
France [frɑːnts]
Germany [ˈdʒɜːməni]
Glasgow [ˈglɑːzgəʊ]
Grand Canyon [ˌgræn ˈkænjən]
Great Britain [ˌgreɪt ˈbrɪtn]
+**Gulf of Mexico** [ˌgʌlf‿əv ˈmeksɪkəʊ]
Hadrian's Wall [ˌheɪdriənz ˈwɔːl]
Hampstead Heath [ˌhæmstəd ˈhiːθ]
Hawaii [həˈwaɪiː]
Hebrides [ˈhebrɪdiːz]
Helston [ˈhelstən]
Highlands [ˈhaɪləndz]
Hollywood [ˈhɒliwʊd]
India [ˈɪndiə]
Ireland [ˈaɪələnd]
+**Islamorada** [ˌɪzləməˈrɑːdə]
Isle of Skye [ˌaɪl‿əv ˈskaɪ]
Islington [ˈɪzlɪŋtən]
Jamaica [dʒəˈmeɪkə]
Java [ˈdʒɑːvə]
Kansas [ˈkænzəs]
+**Key West** [ˌkiː ˈwest]
+**Keys** [kiːz]
+**Lake Michigan** [ˌleɪk ˈmɪʃɪgən]
Lancashire [ˈlæŋkəʃə]
Land's End [ˌlændz‿ˈend]
Las Vegas [ˌlæs ˈveɪgəs]
Liverpool [ˈlɪvəpuːl]
Llanfair P.G. [ˈhlænfeə ˌpiːˈdʒiː]
Loch Lomond [ˌlɒk ˈləʊmənd]
Loch Ness [ˌlɒk/lɒx ˈnes]
London [ˈlʌndən]
Los Angeles [lɒs‿ˈændʒɪliːz]
Lowlands [ˈləʊləndz]
Machynlleth [məˈkʌnhleθ]
+**Maine** [meɪn]
+**Massachusetts** [ˌmæsəˈtʃuːsɪts]
+**Miami Beach** [maɪˌæmiˈbiːtʃ]
Munich [ˈmjuːnɪk]
+**New England** [ˌnjuː ˈɪŋglənd]
+**New Jersey** [ˌnjuːˈdʒɜːzi]
New Orleans [ˌnjuː ˈɔːliənz]
New York [ˌnjuː ˈjɔːk]
Newcastle upon Tyne [ˌnjuːkɑːsl‿əpɒn ˈtaɪn]
Norfolk [ˈnɔːfək]
Norfolk Broads [ˌnɔːfək ˈbrɔːdz]
+**North Carolina** [ˌnɔːθ kærəˈlaɪnə]
Notting Hill [ˌnɒtɪŋˈhɪl]
Ontario [ɒnˈteəriəʊ]
+**Overseas Highway** [ˌəʊvəsiːz ˈhaɪweɪ]
Paris [ˈpærɪs]
Penzance [penˈzænts]
Plymouth [ˈplɪməθ]
the Republic of Ireland [rɪˌpʌblɪk‿əv‿ˈaɪəlnd]
Riviera [ˌrɪviˈeərə]
Rome [rəʊm]
Scilly Isles [ˈsɪli‿aɪlz]
Scotland [ˈskɒtlənd]
Sennen Cove [ˌsenən ˈkəʊv]
Snowdonia [snəʊˈdəʊniə]
Spain [speɪn]
St Columba [ˌsnt kəˈlʌmbə]
St Ives [snt‿ˈaɪvz]
Stonehenge [ˌstəʊnˈhendʒ]
Swansea [ˈswɒnzi]
+**the Netherlands** [ˈneðələndz]
the West Indies [ˌwest ˈɪndiz]
Tokyo [ˈtəʊkiəʊ]
Toronto [təˈrɒntəʊ]
Trinidad [ˈtrɪnɪdæd]
Turkey [ˈtɜːki]
the United Kingdom [juːˌnaɪtɪd ˈkɪŋdəm]
the United States (*US*) [juːˌnaɪtɪd ˈsteɪts]
Wales [weɪlz]
Washington DC [ˌwɒʃɪŋtən ˌdiːˈsiː]
Westbury [ˈwestbri]
Yorkshire [jɔːkʃə]
Yorkshire Dales [ˌjɔːkʃə ˈdeɪlz]

Other names

+**American Airlines** [əˈmerɪkən‿ˈeəˌlaɪnz]
Angel [ˈeɪndʒl]
+**Barnes and Noble** [ˈbɑːnz‿ən ˈnəʊbl]
Bayeux Tapestry [baɪˌjɜː ˈtæpɪstri]
Beano [ˈbiːnəʊ]
Big Ben [bɪg ˈben]
+**Blacky** [ˈblæki]
Boudicca [ˈbuːdɪkə]
Britrail Pass [ˈbrɪtreɪl ˌpɑːs]
Brixton [ˈbrɪkstn]
+**Calvin Klein** [ˌkælvɪn ˈklaɪn]
Camden Lock [ˌkæmdən ˈlɒk]
Camden Passage [ˌkæmdən ˈpæsɪdʒ]
Celtica [ˈkeltɪkə]
Central Park [ˈsentrl ˌpɑːk]
Chicago Cub [ʃɪˈkɑːgəʊ ˈkʌb]
+**Chinatown** [ˈtʃaɪnətaʊn]
Chris de Burgh [ˌkrɪs də ˈbɜːg]
Christian Barnard [ˌkrɪstʃən bɑːˈnɑːd]
Circle Line [ˈsɜːklˌlaɪn]
CNN [ˌsiːenˈen]
Covent Garden [ˌkɒvnt ˈgɑːdn]
Red Cross [ˌred ˈkrɒs]
Daniel Boone [ˌdænjəl ˈbuːn]
Dick Whittington [ˌdɪk ˈwɪtɪŋtn]
Disney World [ˈdɪzni ˌwɜːld]
Doc Martens [ˌdɒk ˈmɑːtɪnz]
+**Empire State Building** [ˌempaɪə ˈsteɪt ˌbɪldɪŋ]
Enid Blyton [ˌiːnɪd ˈblaɪtn]
Friends of the Earth [ˈfrendz‿əv ði‿ˈɜːθ]
Gagarin [gəˈgɑːrɪn]
Galahad [ˈgæləhæd]
+**George Mikes** [ˌdʒɔːdʒ ˈmiːkeʃ]
Giovanni Schiaparelli [ˌdʒi əʊˈvɑːni ˌskæpəˈreli]
Girlzone [ˈgɜːlzəʊn]
Gosforth & Sons [ˈgɒsfɔːθ‿ən ˌsʌnz]
⟨**Grammy**⟩ [ˈgræmi]
Hadrian [ˈheɪdriən]
Harold [ˈhærəld]
Harrods [ˈhærədz]
Heathrow [ˌhiːθˈrəʊ]
High Street [ˈhaɪ striːt]
Hubble [ˈhʌbl]
Islington Green [ˌɪslɪŋtən ˈgriːn]
Jack the Ripper [ˌdʒæk ðə ˈrɪpə]
James Cook [ˌdʒeɪmz ˈkʊk]
Jennifer Kolby [ˌdʒenɪfə ˈkɒlbi]
Joseph Shabalala [ˌdʒəʊzɪf ˈʃɑːbəlɑːlə]
Kennedy Movie Theater [ˌkenədi ˈmuːvi ˌθɪətə]
King Arthur [ˌkɪŋ ˈɑːθə]
King Kong [ˌkɪŋ ˈkɒŋ]
Kirrin Cottage [ˌkɪrɪn ˈkɒtɪdʒ]
Ladysmith Black Mambazo [ˈleɪdismɪθ ˌblæk mæmˈbɑːzəʊ]
Lancelot [ˈlɑːntsəlɒt]
Leonardo di Caprio [ˌliːəˈrɑːdəʊ‿dɪ‿ˈkæpriəʊ]
+**Little Italy** [ˌlɪtl ˈɪtli]
London Dungeon [ˌlʌndən ˈdʌndʒn]
Lord Kitchener [ˌlɔːd ˈkɪtʃɪnə]
+**Lower East Side** [ˌləʊə‿ˈiːst saɪd]
+**Macy's** [ˈmeɪsiz]
Madonna [məˈdɒnə]
Mariner [ˈmærɪnə]

Mars [mɑ:z]
+**Mayflower** ['meɪflaʊə]
Megan ['megən]
Mercury ['mɜ:kjri]
Merlin the Magician [ˌmɜ:lɪn ðə məˈdʒɪʃn]
Metropolitan [ˌmetrəˈpɒlɪtn]
Michael Jackson [ˌmaɪkl ˈdʒæksn]
Midas ['maɪdəs]
Milly ['mɪli]
+**Mir crew** ['mɪə ˌkru:]
the **Monument** ['mɒnjəmənt]
Monty ['mɒnti]
Moon and Stars [ˌmu:n‿ən ˈstɑ:z]
Morgan le Fay [ˌmɔ:gn lə ˈfeɪ]
Mumbles View [ˌmʌmblz ˈvju:]
NASA ['næsə]
Nessie ['nesi]
New Globe Theatre [ˌnju: ˈgləʊb ˈθɪətə]
New Zealand [ˌnju:ˈzi:lənd]
North Sea [ˌnɔ:θ ˈsi:]
+**O'Hare** [əʊˈheə]
Orbiter ['ɔ:bɪtə]
+**Orchard Street** ['ɔ:tʃəd ˌstri:t]
Orion [əˈraɪən]
Oscar ['ɒskə]
Oxford Street ['ɒksfəd ˌstri:t]
Pathfinder ['pɑ:θˌfaɪndə]
Paul Simon [ˌpɔ:l ˈsaɪmən]
Penryn College [penˌrɪn ˈkɒlɪdʒ]
Percival Lowell [ˌpɜ:sɪvl ˈləʊəl]
Petticoat Lane [ˌpetɪkəʊt ˈleɪn]
+**Pilgrim** ['pɪlgrɪm]
the **Plush** [plʌʃ]
Princess Elaine [prɪnˈses ɪˈleɪn]
+**Puritan** ['pjʊərɪtn]
Queensway ['kwi:nzweɪ]
Red Cross [ˌred ˈkrɒs]
Red Nose Day [ˌred ˈnəʊz ˌdeɪ]
Rolling Stones [ˌrəʊlɪŋ ˈstəʊnz]
⟨**Runrig**⟩ ['rʌnrɪg]
+**Saks Fifth Avenue** ['sæks ˌfɪfθ ˈævənju:]
+**Sears Tower** [ˌsɪəz ˈtaʊə]
Sloane Square [ˌsləʊn ˈskweə]
+**SoHo** ['səʊhəʊ]
Sojourner [sɒˈdʒɜ:nə]
+**Speedwell** ['spi:dwel]
Sputnik ['spʌtnɪk]
St. Anthony [snt‿ˈæntəni]
Starlight Express [ˌstɑ:laɪt‿ɪkˈspres]
Stuart Lodge [ˌstjʊət ˈlɒdʒ]
Superman ['su:pəmæn]
Temple ['templ]
Thanksgiving [ˌθæŋksˈgɪvɪŋ]
The Windrush ['wɪndrʌʃ]
Third World [ˌθɜ:d ˈwɜ:ld]
+**Tiffany's** ['tɪfniz]
Top Girls ['tɒp ˌgɜ:lz]
Tottenham Court Road [ˌtɒtnəm kɔ:t ˈrəʊd]
Tower Hill station ['taʊə ˌhɪl ˈsteɪʃn]
Tower of London [ˌtaʊə‿əv ˈlʌndən]
Trafalgar Square [trəˌfælgə ˈskweə]
Victoria Line [vɪkˈtɔ:riəˌlaɪn]
the **West End** [ˌwest‿ˈend]
Westminster Bridge [ˌwestmɪnstə ˈbrɪdʒ]
Whitney Houston [ˌwɪtni ˈhju:stn]
Wild West [ˌwaɪld ˈwest]
William Shakespeare [ˌwɪljəm ˈʃeɪkspɪə]
William the Conqueror [ˌwɪljəm ðə ˈkɒŋkrə]
Wonky Towers [ˌwɒŋki ˈtaʊəz]
YHA (*Youth Hostelling Association*) [ˌju:θ ˌhɒstlɪŋ əˌsəʊʃiˈeɪʃn]

Irregular verbs

infinitive	simple past	past participle	German
be [bi:]	was, were [wɒz, wɜ:]	been [bi:n]	sein
bear [beə]	bore [bɔ:]	borne [bɔ:rn]	aushalten
beat [bi:t]	beat [bi:t]	beaten ['bi:tn]	schlagen, besiegen
become [bɪ'kʌm]	became [bɪ'keɪm]	become [bɪ'kʌm]	werden
begin [bə'gɪn]	began [bə'gæn]	begun [bə'gʌn]	beginnen
bend [bend]	bent [bent]	bent [bent]	beugen, biegen
bet [bet]	bet [bet]	bet [bet]	wetten
bite [baɪt]	bit [bɪt]	bitten ['bɪtn]	beißen
blow [bləʊ]	blew [blu:]	blown [bləʊn]	blasen
break [breɪk]	broke [brəʊk]	broken ['brəʊkn]	brechen
bring [brɪŋ]	brought [brɔ:t]	brought [brɔ:t]	bringen
build [bɪld]	built [bɪlt]	built [bɪlt]	bauen
burn [bɜ:n]	burnt [bɜ:nt]	burnt [bɜ:nt]	brennen
buy [baɪ]	bought [bɔ:t]	bought [bɔ:t]	kaufen
catch [kætʃ]	caught [kɔ:t]	caught [kɔ:t]	fangen
choose [tʃu:z]	chose [tʃəʊz]	chosen ['tʃəʊzn]	(aus)wählen
come [kʌm]	came [keɪm]	come [kʌm]	kommen
cost [kɒst]	cost [kɒst]	cost [kɒst]	kosten
cut [kʌt]	cut [kʌt]	cut [kʌt]	schneiden
do [du:]	did [dɪd]	done [dʌn]	machen, tun
draw [drɔ:]	drew [dru:]	drawn [drɔ:n]	zeichnen
drink [drɪŋk]	drank [dræŋk]	drunk [drʌŋk]	trinken
drive [draɪv]	drove [drəʊv]	driven ['drɪvn]	fahren
eat [i:t]	ate [et]	eaten ['i:tn]	essen
fall [fɔ:l]	fell [fel]	fallen ['fɔ:ln]	fallen
feed [fi:d]	fed [fed]	fed [fed]	füttern
feel [fi:l]	felt [felt]	felt [felt]	(sich) fühlen
fight [faɪt]	fought [fɔ:t]	fought [fɔ:t]	kämpfen
find [faɪnd]	found [faʊnd]	found [faʊnd]	finden
fling [flɪŋ]	flung [flʌŋ]	flung [flʌŋ]	werfen, schleudern
fly [flaɪ]	flew [flu:]	flown [fləʊn]	fliegen
forget [fə'get]	forgot [fə'gɒt]	forgotten [fə'gɒtn]	vergessen
get [get]	got [gɒt]	got [gɒt]	holen, bekommen
give [gɪv]	gave [geɪv]	given ['gɪvn]	geben
go [gəʊ]	went [went]	gone [gɒn]	gehen
grow [grəʊ]	grew [gru:]	grown [grəʊn]	wachsen, (an)bauen
hang [hæŋ]	hung [hʌŋ], hanged [hæŋgd]	hung [hʌŋ], hanged [hæŋgd]	hängen
have [hæv]	had [hæd]	had [hæd]	haben
hear [hɪə]	heard [hɜ:d]	heard [hɜ:d]	hören
hide [haɪd]	hid [hɪd]	hidden ['hɪdn]	(sich) verstecken
hit [hɪt]	hit [hɪt]	hit [hɪt]	schlagen
hold [həʊld]	held [held]	held [held]	halten
hurt [hɜ:t]	hurt [hɜ:t]	hurt [hɜ:t]	verletzen, wehtun
keep [ki:p]	kept [kept]	kept [kept]	(be)halten
know [nəʊ]	knew [nju:]	known [nəʊn]	wissen, kennen
learn [lɜ:n]	learned [lɜ:nt], learnt [lɜ:nt]	learned [lɜ:nt], learnt [lɜ:nt]	lernen
leave [li:v]	left [left]	left [left]	(ver)lassen
lend [lend]	lent [lent]	lent [lent]	(ver)leihen

infinitive	simple past	past participle	German
let [let]	let [let]	let [let]	lassen
lie [laɪ]	lay [leɪ]	lain [leɪn]	liegen
lose [lu:z]	lost [lɒst]	lost [lɒst]	verlieren
make [meɪk]	made [meɪd]	made [meɪd]	machen
mean [mi:n]	meant [ment]	meant [ment]	bedeuten; meinen
meet [mi:t]	met [met]	met [met]	treffen, begegnen
pay [peɪ]	paid [peɪd]	paid [peɪd]	zahlen, bezahlen
put [pʊt]	put [pʊt]	put [pʊt]	setzen, stellen, legen
read [ri:d]	read [red]	read [red]	lesen
rid [rɪd]	rid [rɪd]	rid [rɪd]	befreien (von)
ride [raɪd]	rode [rəʊd]	ridden ['rɪdn]	reiten, fahren
ring [rɪŋ]	rang [ræŋ]	rung [rʌŋ]	klingeln, anrufen
run [rʌn]	ran [ræn]	run [rʌn]	laufen, rennen
say [seɪ]	said [sed]	said [sed]	sagen
see [si:]	saw [sɔ:]	seen [si:n]	sehen
sell [sel]	sold [səʊld]	sold [səʊld]	verkaufen
send [send]	sent [sent]	sent [sent]	schicken, senden
set [set]	set [set]	set [set]	setzen, stellen, legen
shake [ʃeɪk]	shook [ʃʊk]	shaken ['ʃeɪkn]	schütteln
shine [ʃaɪn]	shone [ʃɒn]	shone [ʃɒn]	scheinen
show [ʃəʊ]	showed [ʃəʊd]	shown [ʃəʊn]	zeigen
shoot [ʃu:t]	shot [ʃɒt]	shot [ʃɒt]	schießen
shut [ʃʌt]	shut [ʃʌt]	shut [ʃʌt]	schließen
sing [sɪŋ]	sang [sæŋ]	sung [sʌŋ]	singen
sink [sɪŋk]	sank [sæŋk]	sunk [sʌŋk]	sinken
sit [sɪt]	sat [sæt]	sat [sæt]	sitzen
sleep [sli:p]	slept [slept]	slept [slept]	schlafen
speak [spi:k]	spoke [spəʊk]	spoken ['spəʊkn]	sprechen
spell [spel]	spelled [spelt], spelt [spelt]	spelled [spelt], spelt [spelt]	buchstabieren
spend [spend]	spent [spent]	spent [spent]	ausgeben (*Geld*), verbringen (*Zeit*)
spill [spɪl]	spilled [spɪlt], spilt [spɪlt]	spilled [spɪlt], spilt [spɪlt]	ausschütten, vergießen
split [splɪt]	split [splɪt]	split [splɪt]	aufsplitten, trennen
spread [spred]	spread [spred]	spread [spred]	(sich) ausbreiten
stand [stænd]	stood [stʊd]	stood [stʊd]	stehen
steal [sti:l]	stole [stəʊl]	stolen ['stəʊln]	stehlen
stick [stɪk]	stuck [stʌk]	stuck [stʌk]	kleben, stecken
swear [sweə]	swore [swɔ:]	sworn [swɔ:n]	schwören; fluchen
swim [swɪm]	swam [swæm]	swum [swʌm]	schwimmen
take [teɪk]	took [tʊk]	taken ['teɪkn]	nehmen, (hin)bringen
teach [ti:tʃ]	taught [tɔ:t]	taught [tɔ:t]	lehren
tear [teə]	tore [tɔ:]	torn [tɔ:n]	zerreißen
tell [tel]	told [təʊld]	told [təʊld]	erzählen, sagen
think [θɪŋk]	thought [θɔ:t]	thought [θɔ:t]	denken
throw [θrəʊ]	threw [θru:]	thrown [θrəʊn]	werfen
understand [ˌʌndə'stænd]	understood [ˌʌndə'stʊd]	understood [ˌʌndə'stʊd]	verstehen
wake [weɪk]	woke [wəʊk]	woken ['wəʊkn]	wecken, aufwachen
wear [weə]	wore [wɔ:]	worn [wɔ:n]	tragen (*Kleidung*)
win [wɪn]	won [wʌn]	won [wʌn]	gewinnen
write [raɪt]	wrote [rəʊt]	written ['rɪtn]	schreiben

Classroom phrases

What you can say to your friends or to your teacher:

I'm / We're against it. That's not the same at all. How do you know? I don't agree with you.	**Ablehnen**	Ich bin / Wir sind dagegen. Das ist überhaupt nicht dasselbe. Woher willst du/wollt ihr das wissen? Ich stimme nicht zu. / Da bin ich anderer Meinung.
Can I get the OHP ready? Can I get the cassette recorder/ CD player / video / ...? Can I play / rewind / ... the tape? Can I operate the video recorder?	**Arbeitsmittel**	Kann ich den OHP fertig machen? Kann ich den Rekorder / ... / holen? Kann ich das Band / ... / abspielen / zurückspulen ...? Kann ich den Videorekorder bedienen?
Can we ... do this / that? Let's read / sing / act / ... Can we play / clap / ...? Can I start / go on / ...? Can we do that in pairs / in groups / together / ...?	**Arbeits-vorschläge**	Können wir das / dieses hier machen? Lass(t) uns lesen / singen / spielen / ... Können wir spielen / klatschen / ...? Kann ich anfangen / weitermachen / ...? Können wir das zu zweit / in Gruppen / zusammen / ... machen?
Hi (there)! Hello everybody/you two / ... Good morning.	**Begrüßen**	Hallo, ihr da (alle)! Guten Morgen.
Can I open the window? Can I go out for a moment? Can we act this story? Can't we do something else?	**Bitten**	Darf ich das Fenster öffnen? Kann ich mal kurz hinausgehen? Können wir diese Geschichte spielen? Können wir nicht etwas anderes machen?
Thank you (very much). Thanks. Thanks a lot.	**Danken**	Danke schön / sehr. Vielen Dank.
I'm sorry! / Sorry! I'm so / very sorry. I'm sorry I'm late.	**Entschuldigen**	Entschuldigung. Es tut mir (sehr) Leid. Tut mir Leid, dass ich zu spät komme.
What's the matter with you? Are you feeling ill? What's wrong with you? Are you better now?	**Erkundigen**	Was ist mit dir? Fühlst du dich krank? Stimmt etwas nicht? Geht es dir jetzt besser?
That's wrong, I'm afraid. Sorry, that's not right. I think you're wrong there. I think he / she's got it all wrong.	**Falsch**	Das ist leider falsch. Tut mir Leid, aber das ist nicht richtig. Ich glaube, da irrst du. Ich glaube, er / sie hat das alles nicht richtig mitgekriegt.
Finished! / I've finished. I've done it already.	**Fertig**	Fertig! / Ich bin fertig. Ich habe das schon gemacht.

What's that in English / German? What does that mean? Can I ask a question, please? What's next? Who's next?	**Fragen**	Wie heißt das auf Englisch / Deutsch? Was heißt / bedeutet das? Kann ich bitte etwas fragen? Was ist als Nächstes dran? Wer kommt als Nächste(r)?
What must we do for homework? What's for homework? Have you done your homework?	**Hausaufgaben**	Was sollen wir zu Hause machen? Was sind die Hausaufgaben? Hast du/Habt ihr deine / eure Hausaufgaben gemacht?
Can / Could you help me, please? Can I have your ...? How do you do this exercise? How do you pronounce this word? Could you spell that? Could you write it down for me?	**Hilfe**	Kannst du / Könnten Sie mir bitte helfen? Kann ich dein(e) / euer(e)/ Ihr(e) ... haben? Wie geht diese Übung? Wie spricht man dieses Wort aus? Könntest du / Könnten Sie das buchstabieren? Könntest du / Könnten Sie das für mich aufschreiben?
Sorry, I can't hear/see that! It's so / too loud in here. Sorry, that's too fast. That's very / too difficult.	**Klagen**	Tut mir Leid. Ich kann das nicht hören / sehen. Es ist so laut hier drinnen. Tut mir Leid, das ist zu schnell. Das ist sehr / zu schwierig.
Could you repeat that, please? I'm sorry, I don't understand this! Pardon! Could you explain that again?	**Nicht verstanden**	Könntest du / Könnten Sie das bitte wiederholen? Tut mir Leid, das verstehe ich nicht. Wie bitte? Könntest du / Könnten Sie das noch einmal erklären?
(Very) Good! / That's good! Well done! Fantastic! Correct! / That's right. / You're right.	**Richtig**	(Sehr) Gut! / Das ist gut! Gut gemacht! Fantastisch! Korrekt. / Das ist richtig. / Du hast Recht.
Quiet, please. / Silence, please. Be quiet.	**Ruhe**	Ruhig, bitte! / Ruhe, bitte! Sei(d) ruhig!
Where's my ... I can't find my ... Has anyone seen / taken my ...? I must look for my ...	**Suchen**	Wo ist mein(e) ...? Ich kann mein(e) ... nicht finden. Hat jemand mein(e) ... gesehen / genommen? Ich muss mein(e) ... suchen.
I'm not feeling well. I've got a headache. Can I go to the toilet, please.	**Unwohl**	Ich fühle mich nicht gut. Ich habe Kopfschmerzen. Kann ich mal zur Toilette gehen?
Bye. Goodbye. See you.	**Verabschieden**	Tschüs. Auf Wiedersehen. Bis bald.
Sorry, I've forgotten it. I'm afraid I've forgotten my ... Sorry, I can't / don't remember it. Sorry, I don't know. Sorry, no idea.	**Vergessen**	Tut mir Leid, ich hab's vergessen. Ich fürchte, ich hab mein(e) ... vergessen. Tut mir Leid, es fällt mir nicht ein. Das weiß ich leider nicht. Tut mir Leid. Keine Ahnung.

Quellenverzeichnis

Bildquellen

S. 8 o.li./o.re.: Richard Greenhill; u.li.: Topham Picturepoint (Stefan Rousseau); u.re./S. 9 u.li.: Topham Picturepoint (Michael Stephens); S. 9 u.re.: Topham Picturepoint (Tony Harris); S.16: Punch; S. 19: Topham Picturepoint (Tony Mwai); S. 24 re.: pwe Kinoarchiv Hamburg (8x); o.li.: Mauritius (SDP); u.li.: Mauritius (Matassa); o.mi.: Mauritius (Fichtl), o.re.: Mauritius (Hubatka); u.re.: Mauritius (Grafica); S. 25 o.: Cinetext GmbH, Frankfurt; mi./u.li.: pwe Kinoarchiv Hamburg; u.re.: Archiv für Kunst und Geschichte, Berlin; S. 26/29: dpa; S. 32: pwe Kinoarchiv Hamburg; S. 40: © British Tourist Authority; S. 41 o.re.: © British Railways Board; u.li./u.mi.: © The English Heritage; u.re.: © Bath City Council (David Sellman/Stephen Bird); S. 43 o.re.: © Photodisc; S. 44/45: Robert Harding (Roy Rainford); S. 47: © Runrig, Searchlight 1989; S. 49: Punch; S. 50 (Fond): Robert Harding (Nigel Francis); li.: Richard Greenhill; re./mi.: J. Allan Cash Ltd.; S. 51: © Celtica Guidebook; S. 56 u.li.: Harding (K. Gillnam); o.li./o.re./mi.: J. Allan Cash Ltd.; u.re.: © Photodisc; S. 57: Redfern (David Redfern); S. 58 o.li.: J. Allan Cash Ltd.; u.li.: © Carlsen Verlag GmbH, Hamburg 1989; mi.: © EHAPA-Verlag, Stuttgart 1971; re.: www.kingfeatures.com © by Chris Browne; S. 59: © Roland Lefranc, Edition Ville de Bayeux; S. 60: Greenhill; S.: 63: A: Dilip Mehta/Contact Press Images/PNI; B: Jaques M. Chenet/ Corbis/Picture Press, Hamburg; C: Dean Conger/Corbis/Picture Press, Hamburg; D: Mauritius (Hubatka); E: Charles O'Rear/Corbis/Picture Press, Hamburg; F: Michael S. Vamashita/Corbis/Picture Press, Hamburg; S. 64: © *The New Yorker Album 1925-1950*, Harper & Brothers, NY; S. 65 o.: Harding (David Lomax); mi.: J. Allan Cash Ltd.; u.: © The Bettmann Archive, Inc.; S. 72 o.: J. Allan Cash Ltd.; li./re.: © Photodisc; u.re: © *The Spectator*; S. 73: o./u.li.: © Photodisc; u.re.: J. Allan Cash Ltd.; S. 80 li.: Harding; 2.v.li.: J. Allan Cash Ltd.; 3.v.re./3.v.li.: © Photodisc; o.re.: pwe Kinoarchiv Hamburg; u.re.: © Corbis (Nevada Wier); S. 81 o.2.v.li./o.re./u.re./u.2.v.re.: J. Allan Cash Ltd.; o.mi./u.li./u.2.v.li.: Mel Smith, Nottingham/Klett-Archiv; S. 84 li.: © Corbis (Paul A. Sonders); 2.v.li.: Greenhill; 2.v.re.: © Corbis (Kevin R. Morris); re.: Mauritius (ACE); S. 92 mi.: Image Bank (Antonio Rosario); u.: Christian Gutendorf, Stuttgart; S. 93 o.: © J. Eshuys and V. Guest; S. 94 o.: © Disney J6DM3603; u.: © Nigel Calder, 1970; S. 97 o.: Christian Gutendorf, Stuttgart; u.: Redferns (Patrick Ford); S. 99 o.: J. Allan Cash Ltd.; mi.: © Corbis (Wolfgang Kaehler); S. 106: o.li.: Bilderberg (Andrej Reiser); o.re.: Bilderberg (Hans-Jürgen Burkard); mi.re.: Greenhill; u.li./u.re.: Das Fotoarchiv (Martin Sasse); S. 109: © *The Spectator*; S. 122 o.re.: © National Health Service; o.li./u.: Bavaria; mi.: Mauritius; S. 123 li.: Chris Simpson/Corbis/Picture Press, Hamburg; mi.: Karl Weatherly/Corbis/Picture Press, Hamburg; re.: Gahn Rowell/Corbis/ Picture Press, Hamburg; S. 140: dpa (Terzy Dabrowski); S. 142: o.re./u.mi.: J. Allan Cash Ltd.; o.mi.: Mary Evans Picture Library; 2.v.o.mi.: Preußischer Kulturbesitz, Berlin; u.li.: Peter Newark's Historical Pictures; u.re.: Archiv für Kunst und Geschichte, Berlin; S. 147: dpa (Scheidemann)

Textquellen

S. 10/12/18: *Touch Magazine 1998*, © Jamie de Cruz; S. 14/15: © Ruth Thomas; S. 17: © Mike and Trevor Phillips; S. 29: © *The Guardian Education*; S. 32: © NICK-O-VAL Music Co., Inc., Text/Melodie N. Ashford/V: Simpson; S. 34: © Universal Publishing Consultants; S. 44/45: © W.H. Auden, Faber & Faber Ltd.; S. 47: © EMI Music Publishing GmbH, Hamburg; S. 49: Loch Ness & Nairn Tourist Board; S. 61/62: © Farrukh Dhondy; S. 63: From *Far Eastern Economic Review*, © Dow Jones & Co., Inc.; S. 72/73: © *Bliss*; S. 78/79: © George Layton; S. 82: © National Health Service; S. 90: © Deborah Stone, London; S. 92 o.: Repr. with permission from *The World Almanac for Kids*, © World Almanac Education Group. All rights reserved; S. 95/96: © Granville Wilson; S. 97: © EMI Music Publishing GmbH, Hamburg; S. 100 (Text/Photo): © Hilary Evans; S. 107: © *This week's letter*, www.the-times.co.uk; S. 110/111: © Blair Francey, www.web.net/˜msn/ 3nikeply.htm, 04.05.2000; S. 112: © Carolyn Graham; S. 121: © Ernst Klett Verlag, Stuttgart; S. 123: © National Health Service; S. 124: Courtesy of the American Red Cross. All Rights Reserved in all Countries; S. 127/128: © Aidan MacFarlane & Ann McPherson; S. 129: © *The Daily Telegraph*; S. 138: © Ethnic Media Group; S. 139: © Roger McGough; S. 140: © Plexus Publishing Ltd., London; S. 141: © Adrian Mitchell; S. 144: © Annette Kosseris-Haynes; S. 145: © *The Guardian Education*; S. 146: © Onward Music, Essex Musikvertrieb GmbH, Hamburg; S. 147: *The Sunday Times*; S. 148: © *Bliss;* S. 149: © Nicholas Evans; S. 196: Copyright © 1968 Paul Simon. Used by permission of the Publisher: Paul Simon Music.

THE UNITED STATES OF AMERICA

CT = Connecticut
DE = Delaware
MA = Massachusetts
MD = Maryland
NH = New Hampshire
NJ = New Jersey
RI = Rhode Island
VT = Vermont
NE = New England

Alaska (U.S.)
Aleutian Is. (U.S.)
CANADA
UNITED STATES OF AMERICA
UNITED KINGDOM
IRELAND
Channel Is. (U.K.)
Gibraltar (U.K.)
MALT
Bermuda (U.K.)
Hawaiian Islands (U.S.)
BAHAMAS
Turks and Caicos Is. (U.K.)
Virgin Is. (U.K./ U.S.)
Cayman Is. (U.K.)
Anguilla (U.K.)
ANTIGUA AND BARBUDA
BELIZE
JAMAICA
Puerto Rico (U.S.)
DOMINICA
ST. CHRISTOPHER AND NEVIS
ST. LUCIA
Montserrat (U.K.)
BARBADOS
GRENADA
ST. VINCENT AND GRENADINES
TRINIDAD AND TOBAGO
GUYANA
GAMBIA
NIGERIA
SIERRA LEONE
LIBERIA
GHANA
CAMEROO
Palmyra Is. (U.S.)
Howland Is. (U.S.)
Jarvis Is. (U.S.)
KIRIBATI
Tokelau Is. (N.Z.)
WESTERN SAMOA
American Samoa (U.S.)
Cook Is. (N.Z.)
Pitcairn Is. (U.K.)
Ascension (U.K.)
Saint Helena (U.K.)
NAMIB
Tristan da Cunha (U.K.)
Gough Is. (U.K.)
Falkland Is./ Islas Malvinas
Countries in which English is the / an official language
NAME Independent states